W9-BFG-089

The Ultimate Batch File Book!

Ronny Richardson

Warranty and information for the included CD-ROM are contained on the last page of this book.

McGraw-Hill, Inc.

New York San Francisco Washington, D.C. Auckland Bogotá
Caracas Lisbon London Madrid Mexico City Milan
Montreal New Delhi San Juan Singapore
Sydney Tokyo Toronto

Product or brand names used in this book may be trade names or trademarks. Where we believe that there may be proprietary claims to such trade names or trademarks, the name has been used with an initial capital or it has been capitalized in the style used by the name claimant. Regardless of the capitalization used, all such names have been used in an editorial manner without any intent to convey endorsement of or other affiliation with the name claimant. Neither the author nor the publisher intends to express any judgment as to the validity or legal status of any such proprietary claims.

Library of Congress Cataloging-in-Publication Data

Richardson, Ronny.
    The ultimate batch file book! / Ronny Richardson.
        p. cm.
    Includes index.
    ISBN 0-07-912051-2 (p) ISBN 0-07-912050-4 (h)
    1. Electronic data processing—Batch processing. I. Title.
QA76.9.B38R538 1995
005.5'465—dc20   94-39036
                                                            CIP

Copyright © 1995 by McGraw-Hill, Inc. Printed in the United States of America. Except as permitted under the United States Copyright Act of 1976, no part of this publication may be reproduced or distributed in any form or by any means, or stored in a data base or retrieval system, without the prior written permission of the publisher.

 2 3 4 5 6 7 8 9 DOC / DOC 9 8 7 6 5

The Acquiring Editor for this book was Brad Schepp, the Book Editor was Kellie Hagan, the Executive Editor was Robert E. Ostrander, and the production supervisor was Katherine G. Brown. This book was set in ITC Century Light. It was composed by TAB Books.

Printed and bound by R.R. Donnelley & Sons Company, Crawfordsville, Indiana.

Information contained in this work has been obtained by McGraw-Hill, Inc. from sources believed to be reliable. However, neither McGraw-Hill nor its authors guarantee the accuracy or completeness of any information published herein and neither McGraw-Hill nor its authors shall be responsible for any errors, omissions, or damages arising out of use of this information. This work is published with the understanding that McGraw-Hill and its authors are supplying information but are not attempting to render engineering or other professional services. If such services are required, the assistance of an appropriate professional should be sought.

About the enclosed CD-ROM . . .

Refer to Appendix B for both instructions on using and a list of files on the CD-ROM. The CD-ROM is attached to the front inside cover of this book.

Important

Opening the CD-ROM package constitutes acceptance of the Disk Warranty terms (see other side of this page) and renders the entire book/CD-ROM package unreturnable except for replacement in kind due to material defect.

CD-ROM WARRANTY

This software is protected by both United States copyright law and international copyright treaty provision. You must treat this software just like a book. By saying "just like a book," McGraw-Hill means, for example, that this software may be used by any number of people and may be freely moved from one computer location to another, so long as there is no possibility of its being used at one location or on one computer while it also is being used at another. Just as a book cannot be read by two different people in two different places at the same time, neither can the software be used by two different people in two different places at the same time (unless, of course, McGraw-Hill's copyright is being violated).

LIMITED WARRANTY

McGraw-Hill takes great care to provide you with top-quality software, thoroughly checked to prevent virus infections. McGraw-Hill warrants the physical diskette(s) contained herein to be free of defects in materials and workmanship for a period of sixty days from the purchase date. If McGraw-Hill receives written notification within the warranty period of defects in materials or workmanship, and such notification is determined by McGraw-Hill to be correct, McGraw-Hill will replace the defective diskette(s). Send requests to:

McGraw-Hill, Inc.
Customer Services
P.O. Box 545
Blacklick, OH 43004-0545

The entire and exclusive liability and remedy for breach of this Limited Warranty shall be limited to replacement of defective diskette(s) and shall not include or extend to any claim for or right to cover any other damages, including but not limited to, loss of profit, data, or use of the software, or special, incidental, or consequential damages or other similar claims, even if McGraw-Hill has been specifically advised of the possibility of such damages. In no event will McGraw-Hill's liability for any damages to you or any other person ever exceed the lower of suggested list price or actual price paid for the license to use the software, regardless of any form of the claim.

McGRAW-HILL, INC. SPECIFICALLY DISCLAIMS ALL OTHER WARRANTIES, EXPRESS OR IMPLIED, INCLUDING, BUT NOT LIMITED TO, ANY IMPLIED WARRANTY OF MERCHANTABILITY OR FITNESS FOR A PARTICULAR PURPOSE.

Specifically, McGraw-Hill makes no representation or warranty that the software is fit for any particular purpose and any implied warranty of merchantability is limited to the sixty-day duration of the Limited Warranty covering the physical CD-ROM only (and not the software) and is otherwise expressly and specifically disclaimed.

This limited warranty gives you specific legal rights; you may have others which may vary from state to state. Some states do not allow the exclusion of incidental or consequential damages, or the limitation on how long an implied warranty lasts, so some of the above may not apply to you.

Contents

Trademarks

A Batch View	Robin R. Latham
AMenu	René Bollinger
AskIt	David MacLean
BatKit	Ken Hipple
BatUtil and StacKey	CTRLALT Associates
Builder and Builder Lite	hyperkinetix
CAPSTAT	Gary Tessler
CEnvi	Nombas
CFG	Mark Treadwell
CFGCntrl	Gary Tessler
ChkParm	Gary Tessler
Choose	HFK Software
Cleave	Samuel Kaplin
ClockIt	David Smith
Complete Martial Artist	David Smith
ControlP	Gary Tessler
Copy It Over Here	David Smith
CronTab	Thomas Harold
Crush	Pocketware
DaysLeft	Bob Lafleur
DelEx	Samuel Kaplin
Digger	David Smith
Dir2Bat	Gary Tessler
Do-For	Glenn Snow
Do-Once	Glenn Snow
DOS Tool Box	Solid Oak Software
Driv_Man	MicroMetric
DrMenu (freeware)	T. D. Roper
DSpace	Bob Lafleur
Envi_Man	MicroMetric
EnviMenu	Nombas

Everyday	David Smith
EXE Master	David Smith
FDate	Stephen Ferg
ForAge	Pinnacle Software
FreeFile	Mark Treadwell
Get	Bob Stephan
GetColor	Richard B. Simpson
Getkey	Matthew G. Moody
GetKey	Pinnacle Software
GetSet	Bob Lafleur
Go	Pinnacle Software
HiDir	Samuel Kaplin
Hold	The Unique Solutions Center
HoldOn	Samuel Kaplin
IconEase	Dave Lester of New Freedom Data Center
Interval	Samuel Kaplin
KbStuff	David MacLean
KeyToggle	Samuel Kaplin
MakeName	Pinnacle Software
MasDir	Bob Stephan
Maxi	Herne Data Systems Ltd
Menu_Man	MicroMetric
Multi-Print	Rob W. Smetana of Pro-Formance
OneADay	Gray Software Development
Opal Batch Organizer and Extender	Opal Computing
OpenTrap	Nombas
Parse-O-Matic	Pinnacle Software
Path Master	David Smith
Path_Man	MicroMetric
PB Plus+	Computing Systems Design
PocketD Plus	Pocketware
PowerBatch	Computing Systems Design
Press Any Key	David Smith
Qic-Bat for CMS	Command Line Software
QTOD	Thomas Harold
Quick Permanent File Deleter	David Smith
Ram-Man	Rob W. Smetana of Pro-Formance
Scanlon Enterprises Batch File Utilities	Paul Scanlon
Scan	EZ Software
See	Pinnacle Software
SetEr	Samuel Kaplin
SlowDOS	Nombas
SmilerShell	Bardon Data Systems
Some of the REXX programs	Gary Murphy of Hilbert Computing

Sound Effects for Windows	David Smith
Sound Effects	David Smith
Sparkle & Menu Magic	Rob W. Smetana of Pro-Formance
Sparkle-2	Rob W. Smetana of Pro-Formance
Steenburgh's Stuff	Tay-Jee Software
StripX	Joseph R. Ellis
Summit	Summit Memory Systems
Text Font	Rob W. Smetana of Pro-Formance
TmpSpace	Bob Lafleur
TurboBat and TurboTxt	Foley Hi-Tech
Ultra ToolBox	David Smith
Utility Belt	Herne Data Systems Ltd
VASN	Samuel Kaplin
VB Icon Browser	Valley Programming
VB Icon Extractor	Valley Programming
VGA Clear Screen	David Smith
Video FX	David Smith
WhaTape	Samuel Kaplin
Wpsbkup	Dave Lester of New Freedom Data Center
XSet	Stern Marc
Y_or_N	Joseph R. Ellis

Acknowledgments

The section on Pascal programming in Chapter 34 was written by Namir Shammas and I want to thank him for his help.

This book includes the EnvLib Library, which allows Turbo Pascal programs to read from and write to the master copy of the environment. It was developed by Sunny Hill Software and is currently sold by TurboPower Software as part of their Turbo Professional package. I want to thank both companies for allowing me to use it with this book.

I also want to thank the folks at hyperkinetix. Chris Bascom (the president) agreed to let one of his programmers, Doug Amaral, write BatCmd and BatScreen especially for my batch books. Doug did a wonderful job on those custom programs, and I appreciate all his work. I think you'll find BatCmd and BatScreen to both be wonderful programs. Best of all, you get full-use unrestricted copies of both programs when you buy this book. Another hyperkinetix programmer, William Richardson, wrote the excellent Ultimate CD-ROM Manager program, which you can use to navigate the CD-ROM that comes with this book, as well as the BATEdit batch file editor, also contained on the CD-ROM.

TheWindows help files were produced with Doc-To-Help from WexTech, and Bill Ash of WexTech was very helpful in resolving a number of technical issues that came up during their production.

Personally, I want to thank my wife Cicinda, my son Tevin, and my daughter Dawna for their support and patience. Because I have only a limited pool of time available, some of the time I spent writing this book had to come from the time I would have spent with my family. They were all very understanding and supportive.

Introduction

To paraphrase a country and western song, I was writing about batch files when batch files weren't cool. In fact, I wrote the very first book on batch files ever, *MS-DOS Batch File Programming*. That book was so well received that it's currently in its fourth edition and is a bestseller. Now, if you go into any bookstore you'll see any number of books on writing batch files. It's interesting to note that none of them offers much that you couldn't find in my original book.

MS-DOS Batch File Programming sold so well that my publisher asked me to write more about batch files. My next book was *MS-DOS Batch File Utilities*, which described many of the commercial, shareware, and public-domain utilities you could use to supercharge your batch files. It even came with a floppy disk packed with as many of those utilities I could compress and fit on one disk.

Along the way, I also wrote versions of my batch file programming book especially for DR DOS 6 and OS/2 2.1. These operating systems use batch files that are similar to MS-DOS, but there are enough differences that users could benefit from a separate book.

Recently I was asked to update *MS-DOS Batch File Programming*. I was willing to do that, but felt that I now needed to give readers even more information and value than all those "me-too" batch file programming books cluttering up the shelves. My publisher agreed and asked me what I had in mind.

I started off by suggesting that, in addition to covering MS-DOS, I cover the two other flavors of DOS that are developing a following—PC DOS from IBM and Novell DOS 7. I also planned to include the discontinued DR DOS 6. Then I pointed out that readers are looking beyond DOS, using Windows and OS/2 and thinking about Windows 95. I suggested that I also cover these operating systems in the book. The publisher said no one had ever attempted to cover seven operating systems in one book. I replied that no one had ever written a book about just batch files until I wrote the first one and no one was going to write about seven operating systems in one book until someone wrote the first book. Finally, they agreed.

Then I pointed out that the biggest frustration readers had with *MS-DOS Batch File Utilities* was that I had covered more than 50 shareware and public-domain utilities, but had room for only a few on the single floppy disk included with the book. I suggested they include a CD-ROM containing every program discussed in the book, where I could get the necessary permissions.

You're holding the results of these negotiations in your hand—a book that covers seven operating systems, gives you more depth on batch files than any other book you can purchase, and contains a CD-ROM that's packed with over 200 sample batch files and over 100 batch file utilities.

What more could you ask for? If you can think of anything else, drop me a line and it just might make it into the next edition of this book. After all, I have to come up with something to really impress the publisher next time.

Who This Book Is For

This book will help you learn to use the power of batch files. In writing this book, I'm assuming you have a general understanding of your operating system. You don't have to be a computer whiz, but you should know how to boot the computer, format a disk, erase and rename files, and perform similar tasks. If you have a hard disk, you should know how to make, delete, and change directories. In general, you should feel comfortable performing simple tasks from the command-line prompt. If this isn't the case, start with a general book on your specific operating system.

Even More Help

This is the first batch file book ever that offers you not only printed help and batch file examples, but also electronic help. The CD-ROM that comes with this book contains two Windows help files, BAT-HELP.HLP and UTILITY.HLP. BAT-HELP.HLP will help you write better batch files and UTILITY.HLP will help you find just the batch file utility you're looking for.

Both files have text you can read just like the text in this book. In fact, these files are like electronic books. However, the text is completely searchable and has hypertext links, neither of which are available with a book. This gives you a real choice. You can read the book while you're away from your computer, or find much of the same information quickly and easily electronically with these two help files.

You can use these files like you would any Windows help file. From Windows, press F1 to get to the Program Help Manager, and then use the File menu to load either of the help files. In fact, you can load them from any Windows program that supports help. From there, you can use them like any other Windows help program. I chose Windows because it's widely available and even OS/2 users can read the help files. You'll find the files in the \WINHELP subdirectory on the CD-ROM.

This is my first experiment with electronic publishing and I'd love to hear your comments on what you like and what could be done better. You can reach me at the address listed later in the Introduction.

How This Book Is Structured

When this book addresses batch files, it covers one topic per chapter. Sometimes the topic involves one command, and other times it involves several commands. Most chapters include one or more example batch files. The first time you read the book, you'll get much more from it if you're in front of your computer. As you read about each new topic, enter and run the batch file or run the batch file from the included CD-ROM. This is also an excellent time to experiment; you'll retain the information much longer if you try to modify it to your own needs. As you read about the various batch files, try to think if you could modify them to better suit your needs or perform some similar task that interests you. This is the best way to learn new material.

When this book covers utilities, each chapter covers a similar grouping of utilities. However, just because they're similar doesn't mean you should read about only one of the utilities in each chapter. Since the functionality of the various utilities differs, you might find several different utilities in a chapter that are useful on the same system.

Hardware and Software

This book was written using the following operating systems: MS-DOS 6.2, PC DOS 6.3, DR DOS 6.0, Novell DOS 7, OS/2 2.1, Windows 3.1 and the Windows 95 beta. Most of the MS-DOS batch files will work back to DOS 3.3. There's also a high degree of compatibility between MS-DOS and PC DOS. It would be rare to find an MS-DOS batch file that DR DOS, PC DOS, or Novell DOS couldn't run, but the reverse of that isn't always true. The OS/2 batch files will run under most versions of OS/2, including Warp.

As I'm writing this, Windows 95 (Windows 4.0) is still in beta and no utilities are available for it. However, I'll comment on the usefulness of the DOS and Windows 3.1 utilities of Windows 95 when their performance under Windows 95 differs from that under Windows 3.1. If you have a modem or access to the Internet, you can always get up-to-the-minute information on Windows 95 direct from Microsoft on WinNews:

On CompuServe. GO WINNEWS

On the Internet. ftp://ftp.microsoft.com/PerOpSys/Win_News/Chicago
http://www.microsoft.com

On AOL. keyword WINNEWS

On Prodigy. jumpword WINNEWS

On Genie. WINNEWS file area on Windows RTC

You can also subscribe to Microsoft's WinNews electronic newsletter by sending Internet e-mail to enews@microsoft.nwnet.com and putting the words SUBSCRIBE WINNEWS in the text of the e-mail.

For most of the examples in this book, I assume that the files supporting external commands for the operating system, like FORMAT and BACKUP, are either in the current subdirectory or in the path when an example batch file requires one of the programs. I also assume that the few utility programs included with this book are either in the current subdirectory or in a subdirectory that's in your path.

Writing the Book

I wrote this book using a Gateway 486/66. The word processor I used for everything except the batch files and tables was Microsoft Word for Windows 6.0. I edited batch files and other ASCII files with the extremely nice editor that's built into MS-DOS 6.2. The tabular batch file figures were created using the Tableworks Plus extension to QuarkXPress running on a Macintosh.

I tested most of my DOS batch files on an Apple Macintosh IIcx running SoftPC. SoftPC emulates an 8088 computer on the Macintosh. SoftPC treats each simulated 8088 computer as a single document, much like a word processor treats your letters. I was able to set up multiple 8088 computers on my Macintosh and then install different operating systems on each one. I had ten versions of MS-, DR, PC, and Novell DOS all running on one Macintosh! While each had their own boot drives (C:), I configured them all to attach to the same D drive. By copying my batch files and utilities to this drive, I was then able to easily switch between operating systems to test the batch files and utilities under all versions of DOS. Try this with a PC and you're stuck booting from floppy disks! All the problems I encountered were confirmed as operating system bugs by the DOS vendors; not one was due to running these operating systems on the Macintosh! OS/2, Windows, and Windows 95 batch files were tested on various "real" PCs.

Conventions

You should keep a few important pieces of information in mind when reading this book:

- The numbered function keys on the keyboard are shown as F1 through F12. Most older keyboards have ten function keys on the left side of the keyboard, labeled from F1 to F10. Newer keyboards have twelve function keys, F1 to F12, generally along the top of the keyboard.

- Enter stands for the Enter or Return key, which can also be represented on the keyboard as Rtrn or a bent arrow. Most other named keys, like Del or Tab, are also referred to by their name. The directional keys are simply up, down, right, and left arrow.

- Information you type into the computer and pieces of programs broken out from the regular text are in an alternate typeface. The names of keys you hit, like F6 or Enter, and explanatory text are in regular type.

- The caret symbol, ^ , generally means that you hold down the Control, or Ctrl, key and then tap the following key. So ^Z means hold down the Ctrl key and press the Z key. This type of key combination is also shown as Ctrl–Z.

- Any command inside brackets, [], is optional. Brackets are generally used in the syntax for a command. In the command DIR [/P], for example, the /P switch is optional. It causes the listing to pause each time the screen is full. Pressing any key will restart the listing.

- Information in a command that's lowercase italic is variable. In the command COPY *filename*, for example, *filename* stands for typing in the name of the filename you want to copy.

- Most of the commands in this book are shown in uppercase on a command line. For the most part, the computer doesn't care. Entering DIR, dir, or DiR are all the same to the computer. About the only time it matters is when you're using the equal sign to compare two strings.

Last Notes

While I certainly hope it doesn't happen and I've done everything I know of to keep it from happening, it's possible that you'll get lost at some point while reading this book or you'll fail to understand something. If this happens, please make a note and send it to me. Tell me what you didn't understand and why. If you're too confused to clearly state the problem, then let me know where I started to lose you.

I have a very selfish reason for asking you to do this. I want to keep this book in print as long as there is a market for it. If you help me spot the confusing portions, I can work on them and make the next edition even better. Plus, knowing where I failed to clearly explain something will help me as I write other books. I'd also appreciate a note if this book causes you to develop a nice batch-related hint.

I'll add the usual disclaimer that I can't always respond to individual letters in case I get swamped, but I've managed to answer all the letters I've received so far. The address is:

Ronny Richardson
c/o McGraw-Hill, Inc.
Blue Ridge Summit, PA 17294-0850

If you're active in the online community, you can reach me on CompuServe, at 70322,3100. This is the best way to reach me.

Commands for the Operating System

The basic idea of a batch file is really very ingenious. When you want the computer to perform a given task more than once, why not have it store the steps used to perform that task? A batch file is the way the operating system does that. When you tell the computer to execute a batch file, it reads and follows that batch file the same way an actor reads and follows a script. In fact, the concept of the computer following a script is an excellent mental image of a batch file to use throughout this book.

What Are Batch Files Good for?

Think of this section as a batch file "sales pitch" where I try to convince you that batch files are worth using! As you'll see, batch files have four major functions:

- Keystroke reduction
- New command construction
- Consistency
- Safety

You'll look at each of these in more detail.

Keystrokes Reduction

When I want to start a DOS word processing program from the command line, I have to enter the following commands:

C:. My computer has drives A through F, with most of the data stored on the D drive and most of the programs stored on the C drive. This command accesses the C drive.

CD\WORD. This accesses the subdirectory containing the word processing program.

1

WORD. This starts the program.

Counting the Return needed at the end of each line, I had to type 16 keystrokes to start my word processor. As you'll see, a computerized script (in other words, a batch file) can easily reduce this to as few as two keystrokes. So the first advantage of a batch file is keystroke reduction. Of course, keystroke reduction is rarely a benefit under Windows, Windows 95, or OS/2 since you can assign your word processor to the desktop and start it simply by double-clicking on it.

I'll offer an example of using a batch file for keystroke reduction, which will work with any version of DOS and OS/2. It will also work if the resulting batch file is installed on a Windows, Windows 95, or OS/2 desktop. The command to get a directory from the A drive is:

```
DIR A:*/P
```

but you can shorten this command. Without worrying about what you're doing, type the following at the command line (if you're using OS/2, enter these commands from the command line, only change the .BAT to .CMD):

```
COPY CON A.BAT
```

and hit the Enter key. Then type:

```
DIR A:/P
```

hit the F6 key, then hit the Enter key. You should see the message "1 file(s) copied." Now put a disk in drive A, type A, and hit the Enter key. If everything goes well, you'll now see a directory of the A drive. If you don't want to create this batch file, you'll find a copy in the \BAT-FILE\DOS\A\CHAP-01 subdirectory of the CD-ROM. If you're an OS/2 user, it's in \BAT-FILE\OS2\A\CHAP-01.

You might be thinking to yourself, "So what? I can simply type DIR A:/P when I want a directory." If you have to type a command or series of commands very often, like the ones I'd have to use to start my word processing program, reducing the number to two can be a real time-saver.

New Command Construction

When I first started using computers, I had a great deal of difficulty remembering the command to check a disk. Instead of trying to force myself to remember CHKDSK, I wrote a batch file called CHECK.BAT, containing the single command CHKDSK. Typing CHECK instead of CHKDSK saves one keystroke, but that isn't the primary purpose of CHECK.BAT. Since *check* is a real word, I can remember it much easier than I can remember *chkdsk*.

The term *new command construction* is just a fancy name for making a command accessible under another name, much like calling a garbage collector a sanitation engineer or a salesman a purchase consultant. As you'll see near the end of this book, with batch file utilities or alternative batch languages, you can even use batch files to write truly new commands.

Consistency

Now it's time for a simple one-question test. Put away your DOS manual and don't look at the command on a line by itself after the next paragraph. What's the solution to this problem: You know how important it is to back up your hard disk. You should be making frequent full backups, say weekly or monthly, and daily incremental backups. Write down the proper syntax of an incremental backup using the DOS program BACKUP.COM.

Most of you probably didn't do well on this test. Computer software often uses complex commands on the command line that are difficult to remember. Happily, you don't have to. Figure out the command syntax once and then put it into a batch file and forget it. That way, you'll never have to remember. By the way, in case you still haven't figured it out, the syntax to make an incremental backup with DOS is:

```
BACKUP C:\*.* A: /S /M
```

but you could easily store this in a batch file called I.BAT and just have to remember the letter I, for *incremental*. If you can't remember that, you can pick another name. With batch files, you get to decide.

I can see you mentally waving a flag. You're asking "Hey, isn't this just another example of new command construction?" The answer is both yes and no. True, you've created a new command called I that's easier to remember than the string of switches previously listed, just as CHECK is easier to remember than CHKDSK. That statement can be made about almost every batch file you construct. However, the real purpose of this batch file was to perform the backup consistently—without having to remember the syntax each time.

Most of the batch files you've looked at so far have one thing in common—they each do only one thing. They don't need to be limited to one activity. The operating system keeps track of its location in a batch file even while it's doing something else. Let's do away with that one-command constraint right now. Consider this simple two-line batch file:

```
CHKDSK
DIR
```

First, it runs CHKDSK. While CHKDSK is running, the operating system maintains its place in the batch file. Think of putting your finger in a book so you won't lose your place while answering the phone. After your phone conversation is over, you can pick up reading where you left off.

When CHKDSK finishes, the operating system reads the next command in the batch file and runs DIR. Although CHKDSK takes only a few seconds to run, it could have been a program that takes hours. It doesn't matter. The operating system remembers and picks up the batch file whenever the program finishes.

In the previous example, the batch file established a standard script to be followed each time it's run. While this wasn't important for that example, consider the next one:

```
C:
CD\WORD
```

```
WORD
CD\
MENU
```

This batch file automates loading a DOS-based word processor. The first three lines are similar to the commands I discussed when I manually start Windows. The last two lines reload my menu program once my word processor has finished. This way, the word processor starts and terminates consistently—always starting on the same drive and in the same subdirectory, and always terminating in the root directory of the C drive.

Safety

A final reason for using batch files is safety. Some commands are dangerous. In fact, any operating system is inherently dangerous. Anything that gives you the power to format disks and erase files has the potential for accidents!

Typing FORMAT instead of FORMAT A: can destroy the data on your hard disk. Sure, the operating system has safeguards and built-in unformatting to help you recover from such an accident, but do you really want to even take the chance of a mishap? ERASE *.DOC instead of ERASE *.BAK can erase all your documents, and the operating system has no safeguards against this. You'll need an unerasing program or a utility program and some luck to get your files back. And if you don't notice the mistake right away, your chances of recovery are greatly reduced. Batch files can form a strong line of defense against the indiscriminate use of these powerful commands.

You can prevent accidental formatting of a hard disk by renaming FORMAT.COM to XYZ.COM and then creating FORMAT.BAT, which contains the single command @XYZ A:. I'll explain the @ sign later, but it keeps the XYZ from showing on the screen. If users saw the name, they might be tempted to bypass the batch file and just enter XYZ on the command line. You'll find out later how to construct more complex batch files to help prevent erasing our .DOC files.

When most people think of programming, they think of spending months to learn languages such as Pascal or C. Like programs created with Pascal or C, batch files are programs. Unlike other programming languages, however, batch file commands are made up of operating system commands, most of which you're already familiar with. Therefore, you already know most of the commands you need to write a batch file. If you know how to use your operating system, you know most of what you need to know in order to write effective batch files.

When you learn to program in most computer languages, you must learn a great deal before you're able to write even the simplest program. This isn't true with batch files. As you'll soon see, you can write some very powerful batch files with standard operating system commands and just a few special batch commands.

Although batch files are easy to write, this ease comes at a price: they're limited in what they can do. One of your most common thoughts as you study this book will probably be "If only . . ." You'll see many situations where you could really automate things if only batch files had specific commands. That is the real drawback to batch files: they're easy to learn and easy to write, but they always seem to stop just short of having enough power.

One way to overcome many of the limitations of batch files is with the many batch utilities available as shareware and commercial programs. Many of these are described later and many of them are on the CD-ROM that comes with this book.

Windows

Windows doesn't offer a batch language of its own, but you can install DOS batch files to the desktop like any other program and execute them under Windows by either double-clicking on the installed icon or using the File menu to run them. Chapter 3 discusses this in more detail.

DOS batch files can be extremely useful under Windows. Chapter 41 discusses utilities to enhance DOS batch files running under Windows, and Chapter 42 discusses utilities you can use to write batch files designed specially for Windows.

Windows 95 is Microsoft's code name for the next release of Windows. You can't currently buy Windows 95 in the store, so all of my comments are based on the system's beta version. The final shipping version of Windows 95 could be significantly different from the beta, although it's not likely.

Like Windows, Windows 95 doesn't offer a special batch language to take advantage of its graphical environment. Also like Windows, Windows 95 will allow DOS batch files to run. As mentioned above, Chapters 41 and 42 discuss utilities designed for writing batch files under Windows. Where their use differs between Windows and Windows 95, this will also be discussed.

OS/2

OS/2 batch files are almost identical to DOS batch files, except they need a .CMD extension. While batch files are built into OS/2, they work very much like DOS batch files under Windows or Windows 95 because OS/2 batch files offer no functions or commands to take advantage of the graphical environment of OS/2. Chapter 43 discusses utilities especially designed for OS/2 batch files, and Chapter 32 discusses using the OS/2 REXX language to write your own batch file utilities.

Summary

You can use batch files to:

- Reduce the number of keystrokes needed to execute a command.
- Combine one or more existing commands into your own specialized commands.
- Store the proper syntax of command sequence in a script file so you don't have to remember the information.
- Protect yourself from dangerous commands.

Batch files are the easiest programs to write because they consist of mostly operating system commands with just a few special batch file commands thrown in.

2

Creating Your Own Batch Files

Since a batch file must be an ASCII file, your first consideration is the editor to use in order to create it. Then you must decide on a name.

Operating System Editors

Most operating systems include an editor that works well for batch files:

Windows 95. Windows 95 comes with a small, icon-driven editor called WordPad. It gives you the option of working with unformatted ASCII files or formatted files.

DR DOS. DR DOS includes a WordStar-like editor, called Editor, for editing batch and ASCII files.

MS-DOS. Under MS-DOS, you start the editor using the command Edit. This loads the QBasic editor, only it's configured to edit ASCII files rather than BASIC programs.

Novell DOS. Novell DOS 7 includes a menu-based, mouse-aware editor called Edit for editing batch files and other ASCII files.

OS/2. The OS/2 Enhanced Editor from the Productivity folder does an excellent job of editing batch files.

PC DOS. PC DOS includes the E editor for editing batch and ASCII files. It's a small, function-key-driven editor.

Windows. You can use the Notepad in the Accessories folder to edit batch files. Additionally, since Windows must run on top of DOS or OS/2, the editor for that operating system can also be used to edit batch files.

If you aren't already familiar with the editor that comes with your operating system, please refer to the documentation. If you prefer to use the BatEdit editor that comes with this book or your current word processor, please refer to the help file on the CD-ROM entitled EDITORS.

Picking a Name

The easy part of picking a name is choosing the extension. DOS (and therefore Windows and Windows 95) gives you no choice except for .BAT. OS/2 gives you two choices, .CMD or .BAT. If you select .CMD, then your batch file runs in an OS/2 session; if you pick .BAT, then OS/2 loads a DOS session before running your batch file.

When naming a batch file, you want to choose a name that describes the function of the batch file as well as possible. This is much easier under OS/2 running its high-performance file system (HPFS) or Windows 95, where names can be long and contain spaces. Given the constraints of the eight-character limitation on filenames under DOS, it can be difficult to find a descriptive name.

If you were naming your word-processed documents, eight characters for the name and a three-character extension are probably the only limitations you'd face. However, batch file authors face other limitations. In addition to batch files, the operating systems will accept three kinds of commands: internal, internal CONFIG.SYS, and external. Beginning with MS-DOS 5, DOSKEY macros were added to this list. In choosing names for your batch files, you must avoid naming conflicts with these other commands.

Internal Commands

Internal commands are commands so important that they're built directly into the operating system. Every time the operating system receives a command, it first checks to see if that command is internal, like ERASE. If so, it executes that command.

Internal commands represent a trade-off. Having every possible command built into the operating system would take up so much memory that there would be less left for applications. If no commands were built into the operating system, however, every system would require numerous programs to perform simple tasks, which would waste a lot of space. The trade-off is that the most important commands are built-in, while the remaining commands are external programs that require an .EXE or .COM file to run.

The names for internal commands are part of the operating system, which is why you can't name your batch file the same name as an internal command. If you do, there'd be no way to execute your program. If you created a file called COPY.BAT and tried to run it under MS-DOS, which has an internal COPY command, then MS-DOS would automatically run the built-in COPY command and try to copy nothing to nothing.

The names of internal commands will vary depending on which operating system you have and even which version of that operating system you're using. The documentation for that system will list its internal commands. Review this list and avoid using any of these names for batch files.

Internal CONFIG.SYS commands

Internal CONFIG.SYS commands are also built into the operating system, just like internal commands. However, these commands can be accessed only by the CONFIG.SYS file, which means that most of the names can be used for batch files without conflict. Some of them, like the SET command under MS-DOS 6.x, duplicate internal commands and so can't be used for batch file names. As long as you avoid naming conflicts with internal commands, internal CONFIG.SYS commands should pose no problem.

This isn't the case for OS/2. OS/2 combines the DOS CONFIG.SYS and AUTOEXEC .BAT files into its CONFIG.SYS file. As a result, some internal OS/2 CONFIG.SYS commands can be run from the command line and therefore from a batch file. As a result, under OS/2 you should avoid giving your batch files the name of any internal command that will execute from the command line.

External Commands

If a command isn't an internal command built into the operating system itself, then it's an external command that exists as a .COM or .EXE program. You don't want a situation where a batch file has the same name as one of these programs. Spotting and avoiding the names are easy. Just perform a directory of your system subdirectory and record the names of the programs (files with .EXE and .COM extensions).

While you don't want to use the same name for a batch file that's already in use for a program, external commands aren't nearly as intractable as internal commands. With an internal command, the only way to change the command is to modify the operating system files—a topic too advanced for this book.

However, it's easy to alter external commands. Just rename FORMAT.COM to XYZ.COM, and the name of the command changes. Then if you create a batch file called FORMAT.BAT, there's no conflict. As you'll see later on in this book, there are often very good reasons for doing this.

My point with external commands is to simply avoid any name conflicts. You want to avoid the same conflicts with all your other software as well. If the file that runs your word-processing program is WP.EXE, then you want to avoid creating WP.BAT because you'll end up running WP.EXE under some conditions and WP.BAT under others. While it has been said that a foolish consistency is the hobgoblin of small minds, it seems reasonable to me that you would always want the WP command to do the same thing on your system.

MS-DOS DOSKEY Macros

DOSKEY is a memory-resident program added to MS-DOS that allows you to write macros to shorten commands. For example, the command:

```
DOSKEY A=CD\LOTUS\PROJECTS\MILTON
```

will cause DOS to issue the command CD\LOTUS\PROJECTS\MILTON each time a command line starts with an a or A. It's interesting to note that DOSKEY macros supersede and can therefore "turn off" internal commands. If you issue the command:

```
DOSKEY DIR=ECHO DIR Command Turned Off
```

then the message "DIR Command Turned Off" is displayed each time the user requests a directory.

It's also interesting to note that DOSKEY is more particular about how its commands are entered than DOS is. While DOS treats DIR and DIR preceded by a space, and DIR/P and DIR /P as the same commands, DOSKEY does not. As a result, if you've "turned off" the DIR command with the previous DOSKEY macro, you can still get a directory with DIR preceded by a space or DIR/P. If you have a batch file with the same name as a DOSKEY macro, then either of these tricks with allow you to run the batch file without having to alter its name or the name of the DOSKEY macro.

How the Operating System Decides Which Command to Run

Since the issue has come up, let's look at the process DOS (and OS/2) goes through in deciding what to run when you issue a command. Under MS-DOS, the computer first checks to see if the command is a DOSKEY macro and, if so, runs it. Next, the operating system checks to see if it's an internal command. If it finds the command is an internal command, it runs it. This explains why COPY.BAT (just mentioned) would never run: the operating system always finds COPY in its internal list of commands first.

If the command isn't an internal command, the operating system next checks the current subdirectory for a .COM file by that name, then an .EXE file, and finally a .BAT (.CMD for OS/2) file. If it finds a program with the correct name, it executes that program. If it doesn't find a file with the correct name in the current directory, then it searches the PATH subdirectory by subdirectory, looking for a .COM, .EXE, or .BAT file (in that order) in each subdirectory. If the operating system finds a program in the path with the correct name, it executes that program. Otherwise, it returns the "Bad command or file name" error message.

Look back at the earlier example of WP.EXE and WP.BAT. Assume that WP.EXE is in the C:\WP subdirectory and that WP.BAT is in the C:\BAT subdirectory. If the path is C:\;C:\DOS;C:\BAT;C:\WP, then WP.BAT will usually be run in response to the WP command because its subdirectory comes earlier in the path. However, when the user is in the C:\WP subdirectory, then WP.EXE is run instead of WP.BAT in response to the WP command because the operating system always checks the current subdirectory before searching the path.

This uncertainty about whether WP.EXE or WP.BAT will run is why you should avoid naming conflicts. In general, remember that batch files have the lowest priority of anything on your computer so you have to work especially hard to avoid naming conflicts.

Summary

Batch files shouldn't have the same name as an internal command, and it's generally not a good idea to give batch files the same name as an existing .COM or .EXE program.

When deciding which programs to run, MS-DOS first looks for a DOSKEY macro and next for internal commands. If the command isn't an internal command, then DOS looks for a .COM program, .EXE program, or batch file in the current subdirectory. Then DOS looks for a .COM program, .EXE program, or batch file in each subdirectory on the path, in the order they're listed in the path. When checking for batch files, OS/2 also looks for .CMD files.

Batch File Construction

So far, you've been introduced to some good reasons to use batch files and you've seen how to construct batch files. Now it's time to begin writing your own batch files. But first you'll need to know how to run your batch files.

Executing Your Batch Files

As you might expect, the method of executing a batch file under a graphical operating system is different than that of executing one under a command-line operating system. Since all command-line operating systems work similarly, I'll discuss them together, then discuss each graphical operating system individually.

DOS

You run a batch file by entering its name at the command-line prompt. You can enter the .BAT extension, but you don't have to. For example, to run a batch file named FRED.BAT, enter FRED. Some batch files require additional information, called *replaceable parameters*, which you must enter after the batch file name. The batch file name and each separate piece of information must be separated by either a space or a comma, for example:

```
FRED Yes,1,*.BAK No
```

Methods for using these replaceable parameters in your batch files are discussed in Chapter 10.

If you want to be able to run your batch file from any location on your hard disk, then you need to store your batch files in a subdirectory that's in your path. It's not a good idea to store them in the same subdirectory as the operating system because they could end up being overwritten when you upgrade to a new version. Store all your batch files in one central location. This will make finding one easier and make the help system discussed in Chapter 28 much more useful.

I use a lot of batch files, so I lump them together in the \BAT subdirectory, which I use only for batch files. Of course, I have \BAT in my path. If you use fewer batch files, you might want to store them in the same subdirectory you use for small utility programs. The actual subdirectory you end up using isn't important, as long as it's in your path.

Windows

There are two primary ways to run a batch from Windows and neither of them requires that the batch file be in a specific location or even in your path. Still, it makes a lot of sense to store your batch files in a common subdirectory. If you're running a dual system where some batch files are run from DOS while others are run from Windows, then you might need to have this batch subdirectory in your path. Additionally, having the batch file in your path can save a lot of typing if you run the batch file from the Program Manager.

The first method to run a batch file is to access the File menu of the Program Manager and select the Run option. This will bring up a dialog box where you can enter the command, just as you would from the DOS prompt. This method also allows you to enter replaceable parameters on the command line after the name of the batch file, just as you do from DOS.

There are two main disadvantages. First, you bypass the main benefit of the Windows graphical user interface by having to type commands. Also, it takes a lot of typing. It's not too bad if the batch file is in your path since you have to enter only its name, just as you would on the DOS command line. However, if the batch file isn't stored in a subdirectory in your path, then you must enter the full path to the batch file into the dialog box.

The second method to run a batch file is to install it to the desktop. The steps to do this are as follows:

1. Open the folder to contain the batch file.

2. Select the New option from the File menu in the Program Manager.

3. A dialog box will appear, giving you the choice of Program Group or Program Item, where the latter is the default. Select Program Item.

4. Another dialog box will appear, where you describe the batch file to Windows. The Description is the text that will appear in the folder. The Command Line is the command that Windows needs to issue in order to run the batch file. This will be the same command you'd enter to run the batch file from the Program Manager, and must include the full path to the program if it isn't stored in a subdirectory in your path. The Working Directory is the subdirectory where you want the batch file to start its execution; this isn't generally used with batch files. The Shortcut Key is also generally not used with batch files.

5. Click on the Change Icon button to select a new icon for the batch file. Unlike many programs, batch files don't have built-in icons. Windows will display a warn-

ing box to this effect and give you the opportunity to select from a few extra icons included with Windows. If one of these looks fine, double-click on it to select it. If none of the icons included with Windows looks appropriate for your batch file, don't despair. The CD-ROM that comes with this book contains over 3,400 icons suitable for use with Windows. Each of them is stored in two different formats, individually as .ICO files and grouped together as small .DLL files. These icon files are discussed in more detail in Appendix B. If you know the name of the .ICO file you want to use, enter it into the File Name dialog field. If you prefer to select from a .DLL file containing multiple icons, enter the name of the .DLL file and double-click on the appropriate icon. In either case, you probably want to copy the file you're using off the CD-ROM and onto your hard disk so it will always be available.

6. Click on the OK button and your batch file will be installed to the desktop with its new icon. Now all you have to do to run the batch file is double-click on its icon.

There are two more issues you need to be aware of: replaceable parameters and .PIF files. When you install a batch file to the desktop, you enter a constant command line for Windows to execute each time it runs that batch file. This isn't a problem if your batch file doesn't use replaceable parameters or uses the same replaceable parameters each time. In order to have Windows prompt you for replaceable parameters each time it executes a batch file, you must create a .PIF file for that batch file and enter a question mark in the Optional Parameters field.

Be careful when you write a .PIF file for a batch file. If that batch file is designed to run some other program—as might be the case when a batch file is used to start a word processor—then the .PIF file you create for the batch file must be compatible with the program the batch file is going to execute.

Windows 95

Once the batch file is on your hard disk, the steps to installing it to the desktop are:

1. Open up the Explorer.
2. Find the batch file you want to install.
3. Click on the .BAT file you want to install using the right mouse button and drag it to the desktop.
4. Windows 95 will ask you if you want to Move Here, Copy Here, or Create Shortcut(s) Here. Respond with Copy Here.

At this point, the batch file will be installed on the desktop with a generic icon. To change the icon, the steps are:

1. Right-click on the new icon. This will bring up a pop-up menu.
2. Click on Properties in this pop-up menu, which will bring up a tabbed list of properties. Click on the Program tab.
3. You'll see a Change Icon... button near the bottom. Click on this button. This will bring up a dialog box.

4. Type in the name of the icon or .DLL file name at the top of the box. If the file contains more than one icon, pick the one you want in the display at the bottom.

5. Close the dialog box by clicking on OK and close the Properties dialog box by again clicking on OK.

OS/2

The easiest way to run a batch file is to get to an OS/2 command prompt and just enter name of the batch file on the command line. If the subdirectory containing the batch file is in your path, you can run the batch file from any location on your hard disk. If the batch file requires replaceable parameters, you can enter them on the command line.

OS/2 is a graphical user interface, so it seems backwards to go to a command line to run a batch file. Fortunately, OS/2 makes it easy for you to install a batch file as an icon either on your desktop or in a folder. That way, all you have to do is double-click on the icon to run the batch file. The steps for installing a batch file as a desktop icon are described in the following paragraphs.

The first step is to open the Template folder. OS/2 uses templates to install new items onto the desktop. Then move the mouse cursor over the Program icon and press and hold down the right mouse button. Drag the icon out of the folder and onto the desktop. With templates, this creates a new copy wherever you drag the icon. To position the batch file icon inside a folder, open that folder first and then drag the Program icon to that folder. As soon as you release the right mouse button, OS/2 brings up the first page of a dialog box you fill out on every new program and batch file. On this Program page, enter the path to the batch file and the name of the batch file. You can also enter parameters to pass to the batch file.

The next page is the Sessions page. Here you tell OS/2 what type of session to run and how to handle the window when the program terminates. When installing a .CMD batch file, OS/2 will automatically know it's an OS/2 program and gray out the DOS and Windows options. When installing a .BAT batch file, OS/2 will automatically know it's a DOS program and gray out the OS/2 options.

The next page is the Association page, which is used to link data files to programs. This page isn't generally used for batch files. The next page is the Window page. This is used to control the behavior of the OS/2 window while the program is running. It too isn't generally used for batch files. The final page is the General page. Use this page to enter a title for the desktop and optionally redesign the icon to appear any way you want it to look.

Once you've filled in the necessary information, you can close the dialog box and the batch file icon will be ready to use. To run the batch file, simply double-click on its icon. From that point on, it will run just as it would if you had run it from an OS/2 command line.

Batch File Formatting

A batch file script is a special ASCII file containing one or more commands for the operating system and a few specialized batch commands, with each command on a separate line. That's it—nothing more and nothing less.

Batch files don't need any special formatting. The computer doesn't care either; it will successfully execute any properly written batch file, no matter how it's formatted. The only reason to format batch files in any special way is for readability.

What follows is the scheme I've developed for use with my batch files. It makes the batch files easily readable, while using the limited formatting allowed in ASCII files. If you develop a different system that works better for you, feel free to use it.

Capitalization

I use capitalization in the following fashion:

- I use all capital letters for operating systems commands and program names in the batch files. They're also capitalized in this book.

- I capitalize the first letter of each word in most messages and remarks.

- When a message tells you what to enter on the command line, I capitalize the command line.

- When a message is very important, I capitalize the entire message, for example, "WARNING: THIS TAKES AN HOUR."

Spacing

In a long program, it can be difficult to see the different sections if you enter text on each line. To visually break the program, I leave one or more blank lines between each section. These blank lines don't affect the operation of the batch file because the operating system ignores them, but they make it much easier to read.

While the batch files in this book have blank lines between the sections, I've left them out of the tabular format I use for the longer batch files. I've found that, while blank lines enhance the readability of programs, they don't enhance the tables.

Indenting sections

It can also be useful to indent the lines of a section between the beginning and ending labels. If you do that, a batch file segment might look like this:

```
HELP
    ECHO This Runs Your Backup Program
    ECHO You Must Start It With Either An F or I
    ECHO On The Command Line
    ECHO The F Is For A Full Backup
    ECHO The I Is For An Incremental Backup
GOTO END
```

As you can see, this clarifies which statements belong in this section, something that's especially useful in longer programs.

Message length

You'll notice that most of the messages in my programs have fairly short lines. For longer messages, I use multiple lines. It's been my experience that shorter lines are easier to read on the screen than longer ones. It's a lot like printing your documents in a multicolumn format, except the batch files use only the left column.

Line-length limit

Commands entered from the command line are limited to 127 characters under DOS and 255 characters under OS/2. Batch file lines are limited to this same number. As you'll see later in this book, the operating system treats some lines in your batch file as being longer than their physical length. This can make it difficult to gauge the actual length of the line, and the line must still be below the set limits after the operating system expands it to its final length. Happily, the limits are high enough that you rarely need to be concerned with them.

If a line exceeds the limit, one of two things are likely to happen. Either the computer will lock up or the operating system will truncate the command after the last allowable character. In either case, the batch file won't perform as expected. Try to keep the line-length limit in the back of your mind in case you ever find yourself typing in a very long line.

Writing a Batch File

So far in this book I haven't introduced a single batch file command. I'm not going to introduce any until the next chapter, but you can still write some useful batch files. You've already seen a couple of useful batch files: I.BAT, which performs an incremental backup, and CHECK.BAT, which runs the DOS CHKDSK program. Both of these are included on the CD-ROM that comes with this book. Now, let's look at two more situations where batch files can be useful.

The problem

A number of major software packages like Lotus, Word, and WordPerfect let you shell out to DOS to perform some minor task. The original program stays in memory so only a small amount of free memory is available. Generally, it's difficult to tell you shelled out of a program, so you might be tempted to start another program from this second DOS prompt. However, you either don't have enough memory to load another program or memory is so scarce that the second program runs poorly.

The solution

A few programs will take care of this problem for you. Windows 3.1 won't let you load a second copy or Windows, but it will happily let you run any other program. If you create an environmental variable called WINPMT, then Windows 3.1 will use this as the prompt when you shell out of Windows, so a WINPMT value like "Type EXIT To Return To Windows" will give you a constant reminder that Windows is loaded. A few other programs automatically modify your prompt when you shell out.

However, most programs operate like Lotus and require you to build in whatever protection you want. You want to make it plain that you've shelled out of Lotus to run

DOS, but Lotus won't do that by itself. If you start Lotus with a batch file, however, it's easy to do just that. Create a batch file and have it do the following:

- Change to the drive containing Lotus. This will be a command like C:.
- Change to the subdirectory containing Lotus. This would be a command like CD\123 or CD\LOTUS, depending on how you have your hard disk structured.
- Change the prompt from the usual PG (displays the drive and subdirectory path at the prompt) to a reminder that Lotus is running. This would be a command like PROMPT Type EXIT To Return To Lotus$_$P$G. You can't see this prompt in Lotus, but if you shell out of Lotus it will use the same prompt that was present when Lotus started, so you'll see the reminder.
- Start Lotus. This would be a command like 123.
- Once Lotus terminates and the batch file has taken back over, reset the prompt with a command like PROMPT PG.

None of these steps requires a batch file command, so you already know enough to write this batch file. You might even want to put this book down, fire up an editor, and give it a shot. The resulting batch file requires five lines, one for each of the things I just listed:

```
C:
CD\LOTUS
PROMPT Type EXIT To Return To LOTUS$_$P$G
123
PROMPT $P$G
```

With the Type EXIT To Return To Lotus C:\> prompt showing, it will be hard for you to accidentally run a second copy of Lotus. By the way, this solution isn't limited to Lotus; it can be used with any program you start with a batch file.

A second problem

I like to perform an incremental backup at the end of every day using the XCOPY command. However, there are certain files that get modified every day that I don't need to back up. They are:

MIRROR.FIL. This file is updated by MS-DOS 6 every time I boot by a command in my AUTOEXEC.BAT file. It contains information about the file allocation table that DOS uses to unformat the hard disk and unerase files.

*.BAK. I'm backing up the original files, so I don't need backups of the backup files.

386SPART.PAR. This is my Windows permanent swap file and is modified each time I run Windows.

I need a backup batch file that first removes the archive setting for these files and then performs the incremental backup.

The solution

The first step is to make sure the computer is in the root directory of the current drive. After that, it takes three lines to remove these archive settings. The operational segment of PREPARE.BAT, which does just this, is as follows:

```
CD\
ATTRIB -A MIRROR.FIL
ATTRIB -A *.BAK /S
ATTRIB -A 386SPART.PAR
```

You could also add one more line, XCOPY *.* A: /S /M, to perform the actual backup from the same batch file. Once again, this batch file is nothing more than the same commands you'd enter at the command line to perform the task. However, once you've figured out how to do it once, you can record the commands in a batch file and forget about it because the batch file remembers everything for you. And entering the name of the batch file takes far fewer keystrokes than entering all those commands.

Summary

Batch files can be nothing more than a series of commands to the operating system, in many cases identical to the commands you'd enter on the command line. You can create batch files by writing down the commands you use at the command-line prompt and then entering them into a batch file.

Proper formatting can make batch files more readable without affecting the computer's ability to execute them. However, the formatting allowed in a batch file is very limited since they must be ASCII files. Consistent capitalization, blank lines between parts of a batch file, and indenting the commands within a section all contribute to a readable batch file.

You can write very useful batch files without using a single special batch command.

4

Documentation

One of the worst possible feelings a programmer can have is going back to an old program and not understanding how it works. BASIC programmers even have a name for the type of code most likely to cause this condition. They call is "spaghetti code" because it twists, turns, and winds around like cooked spaghetti.

In any programming language, it's important to document your work using both written documentation and documentation inside the program. If you look at the source code for any well-written program, you'll see lots of documentation, shown as comments. Comments are lines of text inside the program that have nothing to do with the execution of the program. They're simply intended to help you understand the surrounding code, especially when you haven't seen the program for six months.

Internal documentation for a batch file consists of remark lines, started with the REM command. (Novell DOS 7 also treats any batch file line started with a semicolon followed by a space as a remark.)

If you start a line with REM followed by a space, you can enter almost anything you want to. The only thing you can't use are the redirection and piping characters. The computer will skip the remark line, so the information on that line can consist of information for anyone who has to go back to modify the code. Take a look at the following DR DOS batch file:

```
@ECHO OFF
:START
ERASE %1.BAK
COPY %1.DOC B:
COPY C:\WORD\NORMAL\%1.STY B:
ERASE C:\WORD\NORMAL\%1.BAK
COPY C:\WORD\%1.CMP B:
SHIFT
IF (%1)==() GOTO END
GOTO START
:END
```

This example includes some commands you haven't learned yet, but that isn't the important part. The important thing is that %1 takes the place of a filename while the batch file is running. Given that, do you know what the file is doing? Probably not. Now consider the same batch file, properly documented:

```
@ECHO OFF
REM YESDOC.BAT
REM Batch File To Copy New Files To Floppy Disk
REM :START Is Top Of Loop
:START
    REM Erase The .BAK Backup File
    ERASE %1.BAK
    REM Copy The Document File To Floppy
    COPY %1.DOC B:
    REM Copy The Associated Style Sheet To Floppy
    COPY C:\WORD\NORMAL\%1.STY B:
    REM Erase .BAK Backup Of Style Sheet
    ERASE C:\WORD\NORMAL\%1.BAK
    REM Copy Document Dictionary To Floppy
    COPY C:\WORD\%1.CMP B:
    REM Get Next Name
    SHIFT
    REM Test For Another Name, Exit If Not Found
    IF (%1)==() GOTO END
    REM Loop Through Next Name
GOTO START
:END
```

It's the same batch file; none of the working commands are any different. But now you can probably understand the batch file without my explaining the commands I haven't yet covered.

This isn't a made-up example, the first batch file is an actual working batch file. The author of the batch file could probably modify it, but it isn't likely that anyone else could. The point is that batch files aren't so simple that you can skip documentation. No one ever suffered from too much documentation.

All the remark command does, therefore, is allow you to add comments to your batch file. The syntax is REM followed by a space and then your comments. In the next chapter, you'll see how to keep remark lines from showing when you run your batch files.

A Warning

Remember that REM is a command. That means it must abide by all the rules DOS or OS/2 place on commands. To begin with, the line length must be 127 characters for DOS and 255 characters for OS/2. You should also avoid using pipes and redirection characters (>, >>, <, and ¦) with the REM command because they can have unexpected effects. These are discussed in more detail in Chapter 15.

Written Documentation

You can also use written documentation, one example of this being the longer tabular batch files in this book. The code is on the left, and a detailed explanation is on the right. Of course, you probably won't need to document your batch files in this level of detail; you could just print out a listing and write notes in the margins.

Another form of documentation is a printed user's manual. If you use a lot of batch files on your system, you might find it useful to keep a listing of your programs. You might also want to keep this sort of documentation on the utility programs you add to your system.

Self-Documentation

MS-DOS 5 had added a nifty new feature to most of its commands. If you're not sure what a certain command does or how to use it, start it with a /? switch and get a screen of helpful information. This makes it quick and easy for users to find out what a program does or what input it needs. Other operating systems support similar features.

Implementing this kind of feature in a batch file is fairly easy. A section of code near the top of each of the batch files can test to see if the user entered a /?. If so, the batch file will display a help screen and exit rather than performing its usual function. In Chapter 18, you'll see the details of how to add this to batch files.

Special Information at the Top

Some information is important enough to be contained in every batch file, preferably at the top:

Name. The first line of the program should give the name of the batch file. This isn't crucial because you should already know the name from the filename, but it's useful information, especially if your editor doesn't display the name of the file you're editing.

Purpose. The second line of a program should give the purpose of the batch file. In this book's sample programs, I've kept the purpose line fairly short and used multiple lines for a longer purpose in order to make the tables look good. For reasons you'll see later in the book, you should use as descriptive a purpose statement as possible, but keep the line length under 80 characters, although this isn't absolutely necessary. It's okay to use multiple lines for the purpose, as long as each line begins with REM PURPOSE:.

Version. The first version of a program is 1.0. A tiny change would make it 1.0, a larger change would make it 1.1, and a major change would make it 2.0. Because programs tend to evolve over time, this line is a good indicator of how long a batch file has been in use. You might notice that many of the batch files in this book are version 1.0. This isn't because I write perfect programs each time but rather because my programs undergo extensive beta testing before they're added to my book. As is common with many software vendors, I begin numbering my beta copies at 0.0 and mark them as 1.0 only after they're ready to go into the book. As a result, they don't get a number higher than 1.0 unless I enhance them, fix a bug, or go back and figure out a better way to do something.

Date. This is the date of the last modification to the program. A program that hasn't been updated for a very long time is either very stable or not used very often. Following this scheme, the top of a typical batch file will look something like this:

```
REM NAME:     I.BAT
REM PURPOSE: Perform An Incremental Backup
REM VERSION: 1.00
REM DATE:     February 15, 1992
```

Revision. Recently, I've started adding a fifth line of documentation below the date, called Revision. When I make a change to a batch file, I now not only update the version and date, but I add a note about the reason for the update. That makes it easier to follow how my batch files change over time. This is a recent addition, so not all the batch files on the CD-ROM have this line (none of the ones that are version 1.0 would because they haven't been revised) and those that do might not have notes back to 1.0 because changes were made before I started doing this. Following this modified scheme, the top of a typical batch file would look something like this:

```
REM NAME:       I.BAT
REM PURPOSE:   Perform An Incremental Backup
REM VERSION:   1.04
REM DATE:       November 25, 1992
REM REVISION: 1.01: Added *.OBJ To Ignored Files
REM REVISION: 1.02: Added *.INI To Ignored Files
REM REVISION: 1.03: Added Processing Messages To Batch File
```

If you study the sample programs that come with this book, you'll see that almost all of them follow this documentation scheme.

Summary

- Remark lines starting with the REM command make your batch files much easier to understand and follow.

- Written documentation is important to both the users of your batch files and anyone who later wants to modify the batch file.

- Batch files should be able to explain their purpose to a user who starts them with a /? switch on the command line. How to do this is covered later in the book.

- Adding some standard information to the top of each batch file is a good way to begin documenting your batch files and will allow batch files introduced later in this book to access that information in a useful fashion.

Keeping It Quiet

Let's take a moment to recreate the batch file called A.BAT written earlier that performed a directory of the A drive. This time, you'll use what you learned in the last chapter to include some documentation at the top of that batch file. Your resulting batch file might look like this:

```
REM NAME:    A.BAT
REM PURPOSE: Directory Of A Drive
REM VERSION: 1.00
REM DATE:    May 8, 1992
DIR A:
```

Now, run that batch file. Go ahead and do this now because the rest of the chapter will make more sense once you see this batch file run. If you don't want to type in the file, a copy can be found in the \BAT-FILE\DOS\A\CHAP-05 subdirectory of the CD-ROM. If you're an OS/2 user, look in \BAT-FILE\OS2\A\CHAP-05.

While the batch file runs properly and you'll get the information you want, the screen is very unattractive. As the batch file runs, every command in the batch file shows up on the screen, even when the user doesn't need or want this information. In addition, if you ran the batch file under OS/2, Windows, or Windows 95, the contents of the screen would disappear before you had a chance to read the information. We'll deal with the unattractive screen in this chapter and the information disappearing before you can read it in Chapter 8.

Back in Chapter 1, I introduced the concept of a batch file being a script followed by the computer. Well, the computer has a bad habit of reading everything in the script. Take the following dialog out of a bad play, for example:

Sally: I'm leaving you.
Billy: Sally, you can't leave me. I need you.
Sally: (Opens door and walks out.)

The play's author expects Sally to open the door and walk out, not read the line like part of the dialog. While running a tax program, you don't expect to see:

```
Line Input A$
SalesTax = Income * .04 - (State * 2.3)
```

When you use a word processor or spreadsheet, you never see the code that runs the program. Why should a batch file be any different?

Command Echoing

The process of showing commands on the screen while they're being executed is called *echoing* or *command echoing*. When echoing is on, you see commands as they execute. When echoing is off, you don't see commands as they execute. Every batch file starts with echoing turned on.

You can turn off echoing in two different ways, and each method has its own uses. Normally, you can add an ECHO OFF command at the top of the batch file, which turns command echoing off for the entire batch file and any batch file that batch file runs (a process examined later in the book), although not for any other batch files that execute after the batch file terminates. So, as a general rule, you need an ECHO OFF command at the top of each batch file.

The ECHO OFF command turns off command echoing but doesn't turn off messages from the operating system or from other programs the batch file executes. If you copy a file, you'll see the "1 File(s) copied" message. If you use a batch file to start a program, you'll still see that program on the screen. All ECHO OFF affects is the display of batch file commands while that specific batch file is running.

The second way to turn off command echoing affects only a single line. When a line in a batch file is preceded by an @ sign, that single line executes without being echoed to the screen, even if command echoing is on. Since command echoing is not off until after the ECHO OFF command executes, most users combine the two methods and add the command @ECHO OFF as the first line of their batch files. You can now modify A.BAT to present a much clearer screen:

```
@ECHO OFF
REM NAME:    A.BAT
REM PURPOSE: Directory Of A Drive
REM VERSION: 1.00
REM DATE:    May 8, 1992
DIR A:
```

Only the first line has changed. Go ahead and modify your batch file and then run it. As you can see, with command echoing off, the screen is much clearer.

For almost all batch files, you can safely add an @ECHO OFF command to the top and forget about it. As you'll see in the next chapter, you can communicate with the user in spite of command echoing being off. Additionally, operating system messages find their way to the screen in spite of command echoing being off. However, when you start working with ANSI in Chapter 21, portions of some of the batch files will need to have command echoing on. Once command echoing is turned off, it can be turned back on with the ECHO ON command.

Summary

- Batch files start with command echoing on, where commands are displayed on the screen before being executed.
- ECHO OFF turns command echoing off for an entire batch file and any other batch files it runs.
- Preceding a batch file command with an @ sign prevents command echoing for that command, regardless of the status of command echoing.
- Most users start each batch file with an @ECHO OFF command.
- On the rare occasion when you need command echoing on in a portion of a batch file, you can turn it back on with ECHO ON.

6

Communicating with Users

The ECHO command has three different functions. In the last chapter, you saw that, when combined with an ON or OFF, the ECHO command can be used to change the status of command echoing. When used by itself, the ECHO command displays the status of command echoing. The third use for the ECHO command is to display messages on the screen.

Displaying Messages

When the ECHO command is followed by a space and then a message, that message is displayed on the screen. When command echoing is turned on, the message is actually displayed twice. It gets displayed once when the command is issued by the batch file (due to command echoing) and a second time when the command is carried out. When command echoing is off, the message is displayed only once. Type in this brief batch file segment and then run it:

```
@ECHO OFF
CLS
ECHO Hello World
ECHO I Am A Brand New Batch File!
```

When you run the file, the screen clears and the two ECHO messages are displayed, one per line. There are several good reasons to echo messages in a batch file, as described in the following sections.

Telling users what's going on

Any time a batch file is doing something for users, you should let them know what is going on, especially if the process takes a long time. Messages like "Defragmenting

The Hard Disk: This Takes Two Hours" or "Backing Up To Tape Drive: This Takes 20 Minutes," or even "Attempting To Log Onto Network: Please Wait" can go a long way to comfort users when the computer doesn't immediately respond. After all, you don't want users rebooting because they think the computer has locked up.

Not all commands take a long time to run, but it's still nice to keep users informed. For example, my AUTOEXEC.BAT file takes only about a minute to run, but I still have several messages in it to remind me what's going on. Here's a shortened version of the file:

```
@ECHO OFF
ECHO Setting Prompt and Environment
CALL C:\BAT\NICEPROM.BAT
CALL C:\BAT\SETS
CALL C:\BAT\SETPATH

ECHO Delete the .TMP Files In My Word Subdirectory
IF EXIST C:\WORD\*.TMP DEL C:\WORD\*.TMP

ECHO Loading CD ROM Driver
C:\CDROM\MSCDEX /D:MSCD210 /M:4 /L:F /V
C:\CDROM\MSCDINFO

ECHO Saving Hard Disk Information
IMAGE C: /SAVE

ECHO Turning NumLock Off
LOCKEYS N:OFF

ECHO Loading TSR Software
LOADHIGH FASTCONS
LOADHIGH DOSKEY /BUFSIZE=2500
```

Most of the commands run software utilities. The lines beginning with CALL run other batch files. However, what's important is all the ECHO commands. Some of the batch file commands execute very quickly; others take 10 to 15 seconds. Regardless, you can always look at the screen and know what the computer is doing at that moment.

Giving users instructions

Sometimes the computer needs users to either physically do something or provide some information. Messages displayed from within the batch file are an excellent way to provide users with additional information on what to do. The following batch file is an improved version of I.BAT for performing incremental backups:

```
@ECHO OFF
REM NAME:     I.BAT
REM PURPOSE: Perform Incremental Backups
REM VERSION: 2.00
REM DATE:     May 9, 1992

ECHO This Batch File Performs An Incremental Backup
ECHO Using The XCOPY Command
ECHO Insert A Freshly Formatted Disk In The A Drive
ECHO And Then Press Any Key When Ready
```

```
ECHO Note: If The Disk Fills Up, The XCOPY Command Will Abort
ECHO Without Finishing
ECHO If That Happens, Run The Batch File Over With
ECHO Another Freshly Formatted Disk To Copy The Files
ECHO That Were Missed The First Time
PAUSE

XCOPY C:\*.* /S /M A:
```

With the extra information provided by the ECHO commands, even someone who has never performed an incremental backup would know what to do.

Making Your Messages Attractive

Probably the single most important aspect of writing attractive messages is to make sure the message you echo to the screen is no wider than the screen. When a message is too long for the screen, it goes to the end of the screen and then wraps to the next line without regard for meaning. If the break occurs in the middle of a word, then the line is broken in the middle of a word.

This is only a minor problem under DOS, where the screen is 80 characters wide. However, when running DOS in a window under Windows or Windows 95, the screen can be narrower, and OS/2 can display a command prompt in a window of almost any size. This can make it difficult to gauge just how long to make your messages. My solution is to avoid long messages in general. It has been my experience that messages of 40 or fewer characters across are much easier to read than messages that go all the way across the screen. Additionally, these shorter messages are less likely to cause problems when the batch file runs in a window.

You can center titles by putting additional spaces between ECHO and the message. Of course, you need to know how wide the screen is before you can center the message, so this generally works only under DOS. When I have several screens of information, I tend to display a title first on each screen and center that title with a blank line under it.

Where appropriate, I also use subtitles. For these, I display a blank line above and below the subtitle, and underline the subtitle by displaying a series of dashes equal in length to the subtitle. Both items help to draw attention to the subtitle, as well as breaking up the lines of text on the screen.

Blank lines

As I just mentioned, I oftentimes use blank lines in my screen messages to call attention to certain portions of the message or just to break up long messages. However, displaying a blank line isn't as simple as it sounds. You might expect that putting an ECHO on a line by itself would skip a line, but it actually displays the status of command echoing.

Due to a bug in DR DOS 5, the ECHO command followed by a single space redisplays the last message that was echoed to the screen. Under DR DOS 6, the ECHO command followed by two spaces will display a blank line. This method isn't recommended, however, as it's not compatible with other versions of DOS.

You can choose from four different ways to display a blank line, and the one you select depends on several different factors.

Use an almost blank line. The easiest way to display a blank line is to use commands like these:

```
ECHO !
ECHO .
```

Both of these commands display a printable character that's fairly inconspicuous. Most users will either not notice or else ignore the single inconspicuous character. This approach is the easiest, but also the least attractive.

Use an undocumented trick. You can easily display a blank line under many versions of DOS using the command:

```
ECHO.
```

with no space between the ECHO and the period. This is quick and easy, but it relies on an undocumented quirk in ECHO that might not be supported in future versions. This is best reserved for quick-and-easy batch files that aren't likely to be used for too long.

Use a high-order ASCII character. High-order ASCII characters are special characters supported by the computer but not shown on the keyboard. I'll explain more about them in Chapter 7. However, one of them is perfect for displaying blank lines. The high-order ASCII character with a value of 255 looks like a space on the screen, even though it isn't, so it's treated like any other character. Thus, if I represent this character with a <255>, the command:

```
ECHO <255>
```

will display a blank line on the screen. To create this high-order ASCII character, hold down the Alt key and enter 255 from the keypad with NumLock on (Alt–255). Note that using the numbers at the top of the keyboard won't work.

Some editors and word processors either don't accept high-order ASCII characters or make the process of entering them difficult. There's an easy solution to this problem. From the command line, enter the command:

```
COPY CON 255 Alt-255^Z
```

to include an Alt–255 and nothing else in a file called 255. Now, import that into your word processor and paste it wherever you need it in the file.

Use a utility. One of the files on the CD-ROM that comes with this book is a batch file utility called Batch Commander, written by Doug Amaral of hyperkinetix. One function of this program is to easily display a blank line on the screen under DOS and Windows by using the SL (skip line) command:

```
BATCMD SL
```

Note that you must include BATCMD.EXE in your path somewhere. Full documentation for Batch Commander is provided in Chapter 38.

What You Can and Can't Echo

While the ECHO command is very flexible, there are a few things you either can't display using ECHO or that are more difficult than displaying most characters.

Pipes and redirection

If you try to include the symbols <, >, >>, or ¦ in an ECHO statement, they won't be displayed properly. Rather, the text to be displayed by the ECHO command will be piped into a file or alternative device rather than being displayed on the screen. Piping is examined in more detail in Chapter 15.

There is, however, a tricky way to display these characters in an ECHO statement. The trick is a little complex to introduce at this stage in the book, so rather than trying to explain it I'll point you to the solution. The batch file SHOWPIPE.BAT on the CD-ROM that comes with this book explains how to display these symbols in an ECHO message, and includes an example. After reading Chapter 15, you might want to run this batch file and examine its contents should you need to display one of these special symbols in a batch file ECHO message.

Percent sign

You can't directly include a percent sign in an ECHO statement because the operating system tries to interpret a single percent sign as a variable. If you need a percent sign in your ECHO statement, include a double percent sign (%%). The operating system will display this as a single percent sign.

On/Off

You can't echo any message that begins with an *on* or *off* because the operating system interprets this as an ECHO ON or ECHO OFF command. You can solve this in two ways. The easiest way is to rewrite the message so that the words *on* or *off* aren't the first words in the message. If rewriting the message isn't possible, then begin the message with an Alt–255, described in a previous section. Because the high-order Alt–255 is treated as a character, *on* or *off* are no longer the first words in the message.

Longer and Fancier Messages

As I mentioned earlier, Windows, Windows 95, and OS/2 can all run a batch file in a window. Not only can this make the screen narrower, it can make the screen shorter, so it displays less than 24 lines. This can be a particular problem when you need to display several screens of information or when designing fancy screens. Since a batch file cannot force the operating system to use a full-sized window, I suggest you place a prompt at the beginning of those batch files that depend on a full-sized screen, asking the user to switch to full-screen mode. All three systems can switch to full-screen mode while the batch file is running without having to abort the batch file.

Where practical, you might also want to design your screens and messages to use less than 80 columns and fewer than 24 lines. That way, if the user does run the batch file in a window, there will be less of a problem. When you must display a lot of text or when you want fancier formatting, you have several possibilities:

- Place the text in a separate file and use the Type command to send it to the screen. See Chapter 20 for more detail.

- Use ANSI commands to improve the appearance of the text (examined in Chapter 21).

- Use a screen compiler to turn each screenful of text into a stand-alone program (see Chapter 20).

- Use one of the utilities discussed in Chapters 35 and 38.

Background Operation

When a batch file is running in the foreground, it's easy for it to display an error message or otherwise grab the user's attention by displaying a message with the ECHO command. It might need some of the techniques discussed in this book to make it more eye-catching, but those are fairly easy to include.

The problem is that OS/2, Windows, and Windows 95 allow users to minimize batch files and run them in the background where nothing they write to the screen is visible. Batch files can't force themselves to the foreground when there's a problem, so how can a batch file with a problem make users aware of the problem?

As it turns out, the solution is again the lowly ECHO command. When a Ctrl–G character (^G) is included in an ECHO message, it beeps the bell once. The bell beeps even if the batch file is running in the background. So replacing the error message:

```
ECHO XCOPY Ran Out Of Floppy Disk Space
```

with the message:

```
ECHO XCOPY Ran Out Of Floppy Disk Space^G^G^G
```

means the user will always know the batch file has run into problems, even when it's running in the background. The ^G character doesn't display on the screen when the ECHO command executes, so you can place it anywhere in an existing message without changing the formatting. Even so, I generally place the Ctrl–Gs at the end of a message. The faster your machine, the quicker the beep, so the more Ctrl–Gs you'll need. Experiment to see what's best for your machine.

Summary

- The ECHO command can turn command echoing on or off, display the status of command echoing, and display a message on the screen, all depending on how it's used.
- Displaying messages via the ECHO command is useful to tell users that the batch file is running a process that takes a very long time, to tell users what the batch file is doing, and to give users additional instructions.
- ECHO messages shouldn't be too wide in order to prevent unexpected wrapping on the screen.
- Shorter ECHO messages are easier to read than longer messages.
- You can center ECHO messages by adding additional spaces between ECHO and the message.
- You can display nearly blank lines by printing a single inconspicuous character on a line.
- You can display a blank line by using the undocumented command of placing a period directly after ECHO without a space in between, by echoing the high-order ASCII character Alt–255, or by using the Batch Commander SL (skip line) option to display a blank line.
- Piping symbols cannot be displayed in an ECHO command.
- In order to display a single percent sign, the ECHO command must have two percent signs side by side.
- The words *on* and *off* cannot be used as the first word of an ECHO message.
- Batch files running in the background can use Ctrl–G to call attention to their error messages.

7

Using High-Order ASCII Characters

PCs can use 256 different characters, each one having an associated ASCII value, from 0 to 255. Most users concern themselves only with the values below 128 because these are the values you can enter by pressing a key on the keyboard. However, ASCII 128 and higher values offer some nice formatting tools for batch files.

If you want to draw a box without high-order ASCII characters, you'd have to use colons for the vertical bars (remember, the pipe symbol, ¦, can't be used in ECHO messages), plus signs for the corners, and hyphens for the horizontal bars. However, with the high-order ASCII characters, nice boxes are easy.

HI-ASCII.BAT illustrates this. The lines that appear to be an ECHO by itself also have an Alt–255 character to produce a blank line. A copy of HI-ASCII.BAT is on the CD-ROM, and you can run it to see how the boxes look on your screen.

If you ever need to quickly look up an ASCII value while running DOS or Windows, you don't have to look for your copy of this book. Just copy ASCII.EXE from the enclosed CD-ROM to a subdirectory in your path, and then enter ASCII at the command-line prompt to get a display of all the ASCII characters with values 30 to 255. (Values below 30 are used mostly for control functions, so most of them won't display on the screen anyway.) ASCII.EXE requires very little memory, so chances are good you can run it while shelled out from your favorite editor or word processor. Of course, you can also run ASCII.EXE in a DOS session under OS/2, Windows, or Windows 95. You'll find a copy in the \UTILITY\DOS\ASCII subdirectory on the CD-ROM.

Entering High-Order ASCII Characters

If you're using the COPY command to create your batch files, then entering high-order ASCII characters is easy. Follow these steps:

1. Make sure the NumLock key is on. (This isn't always required; check your system to be sure.)

2. Hold down the Alt key.

3. Type the three-digit code for the character using the number pad. (The numbers at the top of the keyboard won't work.)

4. Release the Alt key.

5. Repeat steps 2 to 4 for any additional characters you want to enter.

This method isn't limited to just high-order ASCII characters; you could use Alt–68 to enter a capital D, for example. However, using the keyboard for the low-ordered ASCII characters is much easier.

Some programs make it easy to enter the box-drawing characters. Microsoft Word, for example, has a line-drawing utility that draws using single or double lines as you move around the screen, and automatically inserts the proper joint when the lines cross.

Many word processors make it difficult to enter high-order ASCII characters. Microsoft Word, for example, uses the Alt key to pull down its menus, so sometimes you have to enter the high-order ASCII character several times before Word figures out you're entering a character and not requesting a menu. Some versions of Word-Star require you to enter Ctrl–P and then the three-digit code, rather than using the Alt–key combination. If the Alt–key combination doesn't work in your editor or word processor, check your manual to see what your program expects.

Entering High-Order ASCII Characters When Your Program Won't Let You

A few editors and word processors make it difficult or impossible to enter high-order ASCII characters into your batch files. There's an easy solution that works with almost every program. Take these steps:

1. From the command-line prompt, enter the command COPY CON *file*, only replace *file* with the name of the file to use. I found it handy to create one file per character for each character I use a lot, and use the ASCII number as the filename.

2. Hold down the Alt key and type in the ASCII code for the high-order ASCII character to include in the file.

3. Press F6.

4. Press Enter.

The file now exists and contains the high-order ASCII character. To get this character into your file, just import it into the file using the editor's or word processor's import command. If it doesn't have one, open this file first and copy the character to the "paste buffer" (the area where you store characters to paste into other files). If your editor or word processor can't import a file and doesn't have a paste buffer, you might want to consider finding another editor.

Summary

- High-order ASCII characters make it easy to draw attractive boxes inside a batch file.
- ASCII.EXE on the enclosed CD-ROM displays an ASCII chart of most characters on the screen.
- Many editors let you enter high-order ASCII characters by holding down the Alt key and entering the associated number from the number pad.
- If your editor or word processor won't let you enter high-order ASCII characters, you can pipe them to a file and then read that file into your editor or word processor.

8

Hold That Batch File!

Imagine you're running the following batch file segment:

```
@ECHO OFF
CLS
ECHO Warning: The Following Program Will Do Damage
ECHO.
ECHO          It Erases All Documents
ECHO          It Damages .EXE Programs In This Subdirectory
ECHO          And It Removes The \BAT Subdirectory
ECHO.
RUNIT
```

This batch file presents a fairly stern warning to users, but doesn't allow them to do anything about it. By the time users can read the warning, the program has already started running! It's unlikely you'll ever run such a damaging program, at least intentionally. However, the purpose of a warning is to give users the time to read it and react to it.

What if you had a lot of information to display on the screen, and it was going to take 60 ECHO commands to do it? Using the commands you've learned so far, all you could do is put one ECHO command after another in a batch file. However, unless the computer was very slow, the messages would scroll by too fast for the user to read.

Pausing a Batch File

The PAUSE command is the solution to this dilemma. When a batch file comes to a PAUSE, it stops and displays a "Press any key to continue . . ." or similar message. The batch file then waits until the user presses any key. Keystrokes like Alt, Shift, Ctrl, NumLock, or others that don't produce a character on the screen won't cause a batch file to resume while waiting on a PAUSE command.

If the user presses Ctrl–Break, the batch file will respond with a "Terminate batch job (Y/N)?" or similar message. Using this, you can build an escape clause into your batch files. If the user responds with a no, the batch file will resume on the next line.

Both DR DOS 5 and 6 have a significant bug in the way they handle a no response to the "Halt batch process (Y/N)?" message. When the user responds with a no, control is supposed to return to the batch file line immediately following the line being processed when Ctrl–Break was pressed. DR DOS tries to do this, but the batch file quickly aborts, often with an error message like "Filename too long" that has nothing to do with the real problem. The only way to avoid this problem is to always respond yes to the "Halt batch process (Y/N)?" message. If the user responds with a yes, the batch file stops executing.

Let's reconsider the first batch file with a PAUSE command used as an escape clause:

```
@ECHO OFF
CLS
ECHO Warning: The Following Program Will Do Damage
ECHO.
ECHO          It Erases All Documents
ECHO          It Damages .EXE Programs In This Subdirectory
ECHO          And It Removes The \BAT Subdirectory
ECHO.
ECHO To Skip Running The Program, Hold Down The Control Key
ECHO And Press The Break Key
ECHO When The Computer Asks "Terminate batch job (Y/N)?"
ECHO Respond With A Y
PAUSE
RUNIT
```

The batch file now tells users how to abort processing and has a PAUSE that gives them a chance to think about the messages on the screen and decide how to respond.

PAUSE is useful even if users don't need to press Ctrl–Break; it simply gives them time to read the message and think about it before continuing. If you're going to display several different screens of information, then you need a PAUSE followed by CLS on the next line to ensure that users can read all the information.

Aborting a Batch File

As mentioned previously, you can use a Ctrl–Break to stop a batch file immediately and display a "Terminate batch job (Y/N)?" message. If you respond with a Y, control is immediately returned to the operating system. If you respond with an N, control returns to the batch file.

This makes it easy for users to abort a batch file prior to running a dangerous command. Later on, in Chapter 19 and again in Chapter 34, you'll see a better approach to giving the user an escape clause.

Summary

- PAUSE stops a batch file until the user presses any printable keystroke.
- If users press Ctrl–Break at a PAUSE command or any other point in the batch file, they can stop the batch file.

While it might not seem so, you've covered a tremendous amount of material. You've learned how to write simple batch files that contain a mixture of operating system commands and a few batch subcommands. What follows are three quick problems. Take a few moments and try to solve them. If you get stuck, glance back through the first few chapters. It's important that you have the skills necessary to solve these problems before you go on; otherwise, you'll find continuing difficult.

There are a number of ways to tackle each of these problems. My solutions are shown in Appendix A in the back of the book. It isn't important that you match my answers; if you developed a working solution to the problem, your solution is just as good as mine and maybe even better.

Problem 1

Write a batch file to format a floppy disk that's in the A drive. Assume that FORMAT.COM has been renamed to XYZ.COM. Use plenty of ECHO statements to tell the users what to do, and be sure to turn command echoing off so they won't see the XYZ command and be tempted to run the program directly. Once the disk is formatted, restart the menu program with the command MENU. You can assume that XYZ.COM is in the path. Also, you must make sure to be in the root directory of the C drive sometime prior to restarting the menu.

Problem 2

Write an AUTOEXEC.BAT (or CONFIG.SYS under OS/2) file that performs the following tasks:

- Sets the path to include the following subdirectories:
  ```
  C:\
  C:\DRDOS
  ```

```
C:\NORTON
C:\123
C:\WP
C:\UTILITY
C:\BAT
C:\MENU
```

- Creates the following environmental variables:

```
TEMP=C:\TEMP
DOSONLY=YES
LIB=D:\BLDLITE
OBJ=D:\BLDLITE
```

- Runs a program called Noprtscr in the C:\UTILITY subdirectory to turn off screen printing.

- Starts a menu program in the C:\MENU subdirectory using the command MENU. OS/2, Windows, and Windows 95 users can skip this part.

While order generally doesn't matter, remember that if the path doesn't point to a subdirectory, then you must change to that subdirectory before running a program. Also, loading the menu program must be the last command in the batch file.

Problem 3

Your system has three accounting programs—DAILY.EXE, WEEKLY.COM, and ANNUAL.EXE—that can be run on your computer only by authorized people. Write an informational batch file called ACCTHELP.BAT to give the users information about these programs. That information should include:

- The names of the programs.
- The people authorized to run the programs.
- The fact that passwords are required.
- The name of the person to contact for help with these programs.

Finally, note how important it is to perform a backup after running one of these programs and how a copy of the backup must be sent to the appropriate department at corporate headquarters. Make up the names and numbers you need for this problem.

10

Replaceable Parameters

Batch files would be useful if they did nothing more than what's been covered so far. However, one big limitation of the commands that you've looked at is that they're "written in stone." If you want to erase a file with a batch file that uses just these commands, you'll need to physically enter the filename in the batch file code. This is called *hardwiring*. Sometimes you want to hardwire filenames. If you want to copy all your *.WK4 spreadsheet files to a floppy disk as backup, then hardwiring the command:

```
COPY *.WK4 A:
```

is appropriate. Other times, however, you want the flexibility to have the batch file process different files. Replaceable parameters offer just such flexibility.

You need to know two things in order to use replaceable parameters: how to give the values for the replaceable parameters to the batch file and how to code the replaceable parameters in the batch file.

Sending Replaceable Parameters to a Batch File

Giving the values of the replaceable parameters to the batch file is easy. Replaceable parameters are entered after the batch file name and before you press Enter. For example, the command:

```
BATCH One Two Three Four
```

will run BATCH.BAT and pass it One through Four as replaceable parameters. Each parameter must be separated by either a space, comma, or semicolon. How many replaceable parameters does the previous line have? The obvious (and wrong) answer is four. Batch files count their names as a parameter, so there are five replaceable parameters on this line. Just to make things confusing, they're %0, %1, %2, %3, and %4 and not the %1 through %5 you'd expect.

This notation leaves me with a dilemma in writing this book. Do I refer to %1 as the first replaceable parameter or the second? It truly is the second, but that causes confusion for two reasons. First, most readers associate second with 2 and not 1, so they expect the second replaceable parameter to be %2. Second, %1 is actually the first piece of information you enter for the batch file to use, so you really intend it as the first replaceable parameter. You just have to enter the name of the batch file first in order to run it. Thus I've decided that, throughout this book, I'll refer to %1 as the first replaceable parameter, %2 as the second, %3 as the third, and so on. When I need to talk about %0, I'll refer to it by the name %0.

The general rule is that everything you enter on the command line prior to the space becomes %0, everything between the first and second spaces becomes %1, and so on. This means that the name of the batch file becomes %0. This is stored exactly as you enter it on the command line, so if you run BATCH.BAT with the command BATCH, %0 contains BATCH, with that capitalization and without the .BAT extension. If you run it with the command BATCH.BAT, then %0 contains BATCH.BAT—just as you entered it.

When you boot your computer, DOS automatically runs the AUTOEXEC.BAT file in the root directory without the name being entered on the command line. When AUTOEXEC.BAT is run in this fashion, the %0 variable is equal to nul. Note that some versions of MS- and DR DOS have problems if you test on the %0 variable when the AUTOEXEC.BAT file is run during a boot, so be careful. However, when one batch file runs another batch file with the CALL command, the %0 variable for that second batch file is its name, even though its name isn't entered on a command line.

However, there is an exception to this rule of %0 containing everything you entered before the first space exactly as you entered it. Many programs expect command line parameters to be entered with a slash, like the command DIR/W. DOS doesn't care if you place a space between the DIR and the /W; it knows that DIR is the command and the /W is a parameter. DR DOS handles batch files the same way. If you run BATCH.BAT with the command BATCH/H, BATCH becomes %0 and /H becomes %1. However, MS DOS works differently and treats everything until the first space as %0. This can make writing batch files to run under either operating system difficult. We will revisit this issue when we look at logic testing.

This can be quite confusing so let's look at a couple of examples. For each of these examples, we will need a batch file. SHOWREPL.BAT is shown below and handles the job nicely:

```
@ECHO OFF
REM NAME:    SHOWREPL.BAT
REM PURPOSE: Show Replaceable Parameters
REM VERSION: 1.00
REM DATE:    May 12, 1992

ECHO %%0 = %0
ECHO %%1 = %1
ECHO %%2 = %2
ECHO %%3 = %3
```

```
ECHO %%4 = %4
ECHO %%5 = %5
ECHO %%6 = %6
ECHO %%7 = %7
ECHO %%8 = %8
ECHO %%9 = %9
```

Before running SHOWREPL.BAT, you should note that the ECHO commands with the %%0 are used to display a %0. In order to display a percent sign using an ECHO command, DOS requires the ECHO to have two percentage signs. This batch file will run as-is under Windows and will run under OS/2 if you rename it to SHOWREPL.CMD.

SHOWREPL.BAT is expanded later, and that expanded version is included on the disk. However, that expanded version works fine for these examples, so you don't need to key in the batch file. If you run SHOWREPL.BAT with the command:

```
SHOWREPL/H/I/J One
```

then the replaceable parameters are:

%0   SHOWREPL/H/I/J
%1   One

Note that the three switches /H/I/J are not separated from the SHOWREPL. MS DOS does this consistently. Under DR DOS, the replaceable parameters are as follows:

%0   SHOWREPL
%1   /H/I/J
%2   One

When SHOWREPL.BAT is started with the command:

```
SHOWREPL /H /I /J One
```

then the replaceable parameters are:

%0   SHOWREPL
%1   /H
%2   /I
%3   /J
%4   One

If you are still confused, you might want to run SHOWREPL.BAT several times with different combinations of replaceable parameters to make sure you understand how your version of DOS is translating your command lines into replaceable parameters. A copy of SHOWREPL.BAT is included on the enclosed disk for that purpose.

Using Replaceable Parameters in Your Batch Files

Replaceable parameters are global variables and are available to any command in the batch file. However, once the batch file terminates, the values of the replaceable parameters are terminated as well. When a batch file runs a second batch file, the replaceable parameters are not available to that second batch file unless they are specifically passed to that second batch file by the command that runs it. This is covered in the chapter on subroutines. However, once the second batch file terminates and control returns to the original batch file, its replaceable parameters are once again available to it.

Batch files use replaceable parameters as if they don't exist. That sounds like an extreme statement, but the supporting logic is solid. Everywhere you see a replaceable parameter, the batch file sees the value of that parameter. That statement will make more sense if we look at an example.

First, we need a batch file. I've modified the SHOWREPL.BAT batch file we used earlier to include some REM commands at the bottom of the batch file along with a PAUSE command.

```
@ECHO OFF
REM NAME:     SHOWREPL.BAT
REM PURPOSE: Show Replaceable Parameters
REM VERSION: 1.00
REM DATE:     May 12, 1992

ECHO %%0 = %0
ECHO %%1 = %1
ECHO %%2 = %2
ECHO %%3 = %3
ECHO %%4 = %4
ECHO %%5 = %5
ECHO %%6 = %6
ECHO %%7 = %7
ECHO %%8 = %8
ECHO %%9 = %9
ECHO
ECHO Now, Watch These Remark Statements
ECHO After I Turn Command Echoing On
ECHO ON
REM This Batch File Shows The Values
REM For The First Ten Replaceable
REM Parameters (%0-%9) Entered On
REM The Command Line
@PAUSE
```

Before running SHOWREPL.BAT, you should note that the next to last REM line has two replaceable parameters in it. Because command echoing is on when the batch file reaches this point, we will want to notice how the batch file treats this line. Go ahead and run the batch file. Be sure to enter some replaceable parameters when you run it.

Notice that, when a batch file executes with command echoing on—beginning in the middle of the batch file—each command in the batch file is preceded by the command line prompt. In other words, the operating system treats the commands in the batch file exactly like it would if you entered them from the command line prompt. This is consistent with our idea of a batch file being a script the computer follows.

Now, notice the next to last REM line. In the batch file, it reads "REM Parameters (%0–%9) Entered On." When I ran this batch file, I ran it with the command:

```
showrepl One 2 Three Four 5 6,7,8 Nine
```

so "showrepl" became %0 and "Nine" became %9. If you do the same, in the REM line on the screen, you can see that the batch file has replaced the %0–%9 in the batch file with "showrepl-Nine."

With the single exception of a %%0, everywhere there's a %0 in the batch file, the batch file sees the value of the first replaceable parameter. Except for %%1, everywhere there's a %1 in the batch file, the batch file sees the value of the second replaceable parameter, and so on. In fact, they are called replaceable parameters for exactly that reason. Because the values come from the command line, you can replace them with new values each time you run the batch file.

Limiting the Number of Replaceable Parameters

The operating system does not directly place a limit on the number of replaceable parameters you can specify on the command line. However, it does place an indirect limit. A command line is limited to 127 characters under DOS and 255 characters under OS/2, and the name of the batch file and the first replaceable parameter—as well as each set of replaceable parameters—must be separated by a space, comma, or semicolon. If you run a batch file with a single character name, like A.BAT, and you give it only single character replaceable parameters, you will have room for 63 replaceable parameters under DOS and twice that many under OS/2. However, only the replaceable parameters %0–%9 are valid in your batch file. We will see a way around this problem in the next chapter.

Some Uses for Replaceable Parameters

Back in Chapter 1, we looked at the following batch file segment to start Microsoft Word:

```
C:
WORD
CD\
MENU
```

At the time, we didn't give it a name, so let's call it WP.BAT. Like many programs, Microsoft Word gives you the ability to immediately begin editing a file by specifying the name of that file on the command line. If you start Word with the command:

```
WORD CHAP-10
```

you not only start Word, you cause it to load CHAP-10.DOC so that you can begin to edit it. (If CHAP-10.DOC doesn't yet exist, Word will warn you and then create the document for you.) Using replaceable parameters and the commands we have learned since Chapter 1, we can make this a much more useful batch file:

```
@ECHO OFF
REM NAME:    WP.BAT
REM PURPOSE: Run Microsoft Word
REM VERSION: 2.00
```

```
REM DATE:    May 12, 1992
C:
CD\WORD
WORD %1
CD\
MENU
```

Now, when the user starts this batch file with the command:

```
WP CHAP-10
```

the batch file both starts Word and tells Word to load the CHAP-10.DOC document. (Note: Word doesn't require you to enter the extension; it automatically uses .DOC.)

You might wonder what happens when you start WP.BAT without a replaceable parameter. In that case, %1 has no value. DOS performs an exact replacement of the value of %1, so the batch file line WORD %1 is treated by DOS as "WORD."

In other words, no replaceable parameter was entered so the batch file treats that line as though the %1 does not exist. That gives you the flexibility of using the same batch file both when you want to specify a file name and when you don't.

Replaceable Parameters as Commands

DOS and OS/2 are extremely literal in replacing the replaceable parameters with their values and treating those values as though they were hardwired in the batch file. So literal, in fact, that replaceable parameters can even be used as commands. For example, this batch file:

```
@ECHO OFF
REM NAME:     COMMANDS.BAT
REM PURPOSE: Show Using Replaceable Parameters
REM          As Commands
REM VERSION: 1.00
REM DATE:    May 12, 1992
%1
%2
%3
```

would treat the first three replaceable parameters as commands. If you ran the batch file with the command:

```
COMMANDS DIR/W CHKDSK/F MENU
```

it would first perform a DIR/W, then run CHKDSK/F and finally run the menu program. Of course, just because this works doesn't mean it is a good idea. When you allow the user to enter the command, you lose the control the batch file was designed to provide. So, as a general rule, using replaceable parameters as commands is not a good idea.

A Couple of Examples

Let's create a couple of example batch files using replaceable parameters. As I introduce additional commands for working with replaceable parameters as well as general batch file commands, we will revisit these batch files to make improvements to them. They are on the disk that comes with this book.

This first batch file—A.BAT—performs a directory of the A drive. It uses a single replaceable parameter. When you run it without a replaceable parameter, it gives you all the files on the A drive. You can enter a replaceable parameter like "*.DOC" to narrow the search. It can be found in the \BAT-FILE\DOS\A\CHAP-10 subdirectory. If you are an OS/2 user, substitute "OS2" for "DOS."

```
@ECHO OFF
REM NAME:    A.BAT
REM PURPOSE: Directory Of A Drive
REM VERSION: 1.00
REM DATE:    May 12, 1992

DIR A:%1 /P
```

This second batch file—RONNYMD.BAT or Ronny's MD command—will create a subdirectory branching off the current subdirectory and then change to that subdirectory. It can be found in the \BAT-FILE\DOS\RONNYMD\CHAP-10 subdirectory. If you are an OS/2 user, substitute "OS2" for "DOS."

```
@ECHO OFF
REM NAME:    RONNYMD.BAT
REM PURPOSE: Make And Change To A Subdirectory
REM VERSION: 1.00
REM DATE:    May 12, 1992

MD %1
CD %1
```

A.BAT runs fine if you don't enter a replaceable parameter—you just get a listing of all the files. RONNYMD.BAT has a small problem. The "MD %1" becomes "MD" when no replaceable parameter is entered—resulting in a "Requires parameter missing" error message. Without a replaceable parameter, the "CD" command just displays the current subdirectory. One of the enhancements we will be making to these batch files in the chapters that follow is error-checking to avoid problems.

While A.BAT runs fine without a replaceable parameter and RONNYMD.BAT has a problem with one line, this final batch file—TOA.BAT—has significant problems when used with the wrong number of replaceable parameters. It can be found in the \BAT-FILE\DOS\TOA\CHAP-10 subdirectory. If you are an OS/2 user, substitute "OS2" for "DOS."

```
@ECHO OFF
REM NAME:    TOA.BAT
REM PURPOSE: Copy .CMP And .DOC Files To A-Drive
```

```
REM           While Deleting .BAK Files
REM VERSION: 1.00
REM DATE:    May 12, 1992

DEL %1.BAK
COPY %1.DOC A:
COPY %1.CMP A:

REM %2 - %8 Are Handled In A Similar Fashion
REM I've Removed Their Code From The Figure
REM For The Sake Of Space

DEL %9.BAK
COPY %9.DOC A:
COPY %9.CMP A:
```

TOA.BAT is designed to be run followed by exactly nine replaceable parameters. Each replaceable parameter designates a document to be copied to the A drive and must be entered without the .DOC extension. The batch file performs three steps for each replaceable parameter:

1. Deletes the .BAK backup file.
2. Copies the .DOC document file to the A drive.
3. Copies the .CMP user dictionary for that file to the A drive.

As written, this batch file has several significant problems. In fact, I've included it because it has many of the problems associated with using replaceable parameters in batch files. The problems with this batch file are as follows:

- It doesn't check to make sure that nine replaceable parameters were entered. If only six were entered, then %7, %8, and %9 don't exist. For each of these, the DEL .BAK, COPY .DOC A:, and COPY .CMP A: commands generate a DOS "Invalid directory specified" error message. The filename is missing because the replaceable parameter is empty, and DOS treats the period before the extension as part of a path.

- It ignores replaceable parameters beyond %9.

- It doesn't check to see if the .BAK file exists before it tries to delete it.

- It doesn't check to see if the .DOC and .CMP files exist before it tries to copy them.

In the chapters to come, you'll see how to avoid each of these problems.

When Running a Batch File from the Desktop in OS/2

With OS/2 being a graphical user interface and so many batch files being run from the desktop, you probably want to know whether or not you can incorporate replaceable parameters by clicking on an icon.

You can, and the process is very simple. In the Settings notebook on the program page, enter a pair of square brackets with a space between them ([ ]) in the Parameter field of the Optional section. If you want the batch file to prompt the user for specific information, place a prompt inside the square brackets. For example, [Enter the filename to erase]. Now, each time you click on the icon to run this batch file, OS/2 brings up a box and prompts you for replaceable parameters. You can press Return to skip the replaceable parameters or enter as many as the batch file expects.

This is also a very handy way to enter replaceable parameters under the OS/2 environment because you don't have to remember what the batch file wants and enter it on the command line. There is, however, one quirk involving replaceable parameters and running a batch file from the desktop that you need to be aware of.

If you run a batch file from the command line, the %0 variable contains the name of the file just as you entered it—except if you followed the name with a forward slash (/) and one or more switches, then those switches are moved to the %1 replaceable parameter. So if you start SHOWREPL.CMD with the command SHOWREPL, then the %0 replaceable parameter contains SHOWREPL just as you entered it on the command line. However, if you run SHOWREPL.CMD from the desktop, then the %0 variable contains the fully specified path to the batch file, in all uppercase and inside quotation marks. So running SHOWREPL.CMD would cause the %0 replaceable parameter to contain "F:\BAT\SHOWREPL.CMD".

Of course, the path would match the one on your system. The quotation marks are needed because an OS/2 fully qualified name needs the quotation marks around it in case of embedded blanks in the name under the high-performance file system (HPFS).

Most of the time, having the full path in the %0 replaceable parameter won't cause the batch file to operate any differently, but if you're working with the %0 replaceable parameter you need to be aware of this quirk. Having quotation marks around the filename won't cause any problems at all because they're always allowed under HPFS and OS/2 knows how to handle them.

Summary

- A replaceable parameter is information you enter on the command line after the name of a batch file when you run that batch file. They must be separated by a space, comma, or semicolon on the command line. They're global variables that are available anywhere in the batch file.

- Replaceable parameters are used in a batch file as %0 through %9. %0 is the name of the batch file, %1 is the first replaceable parameter, %2 is the second, and so on.

- Everywhere the batch file sees a %1, it replaces it with the value of the first replaceable parameter as entered on the command line.

- DOS and OS/2 place no limit on the number of replaceable parameters you can enter on the command line, other than limiting the length of the command line.

- DOS and OS/2 are flexible enough to allow you to use replaceable parameters as commands inside your batch files.

- A.BAT performs a directory of the A drive. If a file specification is entered on the command line, it uses that as part of the DIR command.

- RONNYMD.BAT first creates a subdirectory branching off the current subdirectory and then changes to that subdirectory. RONNYMD.BAT expects the user to enter a valid subdirectory name and has problems if no name is entered.

- TOA.BAT tries to copy nine .DOC and .CMP files matching the nine replaceable parameters it expects to the A drive, and also deletes the nine associated .BAK files. This batch file has significant problems.

- OS/2 can be configured to request you to enter replaceable parameters when a batch file is run from the desktop.

11

Using More Than
Ten Replaceable Parameters

As I mentioned in the last chapter, there's no limit on the number of replaceable parameters you can specify on the command line. However, there is an indirect limit due to the maximum length of the command line. And no matter how many replaceable parameters you pass to a batch file, only %0 through %9 are valid in your batch file. While the particular set of ten replaceable parameters to which the batch file has access can be altered, a batch file is always limited to accessing only ten replaceable parameters at any given time.

The SHIFT Command

Because a batch file can "see" only ten replaceable parameters, there is the SHIFT command. The SHIFT command discards the %0 parameter, moves the remaining parameters down one value, and brings in a new %9 value if one exists. So after a SHIFT, the value in %1 moves into %0, the value in %2 moves into %1, and so on. This is illustrated in Figure 11.1.

For an example, let's use the SHOWSHIF.BAT (or SHOWSHIF.CMD for OS/2) batch file. This batch file shows the original set of ten replaceable parameters, issues a SHIFT command, and then redisplays the ten replaceable parameters. A section of SHOWSHIF.BAT is as follows:

```
SHIFT
ECHO After First Shift
ECHO ----------------
ECHO %%0=%0 %%1=%1 %%2=%2 %%3=%3 %%4=%4
ECHO %%5=%5 %%6=%6 %%7=%7 %%8=%8 %%9=%9
ECHO
```

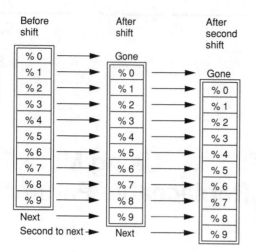

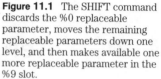

Figure 11.1 The SHIFT command discards the %0 replaceable parameter, moves the remaining replaceable parameters down one level, and then makes available one more replaceable parameter in the %9 slot.

The last line of this section displays a blank line by echoing an Alt–255 high-order character.

What SHIFT Can Do

Take a moment and run SHOWSHIF.BAT with a command like this:

```
SHOWSHIF 1 2 3 4 5 6 7 8 9 10 11 12 13 14 15
```

As you can see, each time the batch file issues a SHIFT, the replaceable parameters move down one level, with the next replaceable parameter becoming %9.

The one thing you can't see is what happens to the value contained in %0 after the SHIFT command. When SHOWSHIF.BAT is first run with the command line just shown, the value in %0 is SHOWSHIF. When the first SHIFT is issued, SHOWSHIF is removed to make room for moving the contents of %1 into %0. That value is unrecoverable. There's no UNSHIFT command. Once you've shifted a value away there's no way to access it, so use SHIFT with care.

Using SHIFT

The SHIFT command has two major purposes. First, by moving the parameters down into a lower replaceable parameter, you can use a single replaceable parameter for all coding by forcing the program to loop through the code. This makes it much easier to update the code when necessary. (Looping is described starting in Chapter 12.) Second, SHIFT allows the batch file to handle more than ten replaceable parameters. Just keep in mind that the total number of replaceable parameters is also constrained by the limitation on the length of the command line and the requirement to separate each replaceable parameter with a space.

Of the three sample batch files introduced in Chapter 10, only TOA.BAT can benefit from the SHIFT command. First, take a quick look back at the original version of TOA.BAT in Chapter 10. Now, compare that to the modified version, shown here. A copy of this file can be found in the \BAT-FILE\DOS\TOA\CHAP-11 and \BAT-FILE\OS2\TOA\CHAP-11 subdirectories.

```
@ECHO OFF
REM NAME:     TOA.BAT
REM PURPOSE: Copy .CMP And .DOC Files To A Drive
REM          While Deleting .BAK Files
REM VERSION: 2.00
REM DATE:    May 12, 1992

DEL %1.BAK
COPY %1.DOC A:
COPY %1.CMP A:
SHIFT
(these four lines are repeated eight more times)
```

With this new version, the SHIFT command is used repeatedly, so TOA.BAT always deals with the same small section of code:

```
DEL %1.BAK
COPY %1.DOC A:
COPY %1.CMP A:
SHIFT
```

which it uses nine times. If there was a way to reuse that code, TOA.BAT would be much shorter. As it turns out, there are two approaches to reusing this section of code: looping and subroutines. Looping is covered in Chapter 12, and subroutines are described in Chapter 22. You'll revisit TOA.BAT in both chapters.

Summary

- There's no limit to the number of replaceable parameters you can enter on the command line, other than the limitation of the length of the command line.

- The SHIFT command discards %0, moves %1 to %0, %2 to %1, and so on. It also brings another replaceable parameter into the %9 slot.

- The SHIFT command is *not* reversible.

12

Looping and Program Flow

So far, the simple batch files you've created have started at the beginning and ended at the end. While that can result in some very useful batch files, it doesn't allow for any decision making. The batch file must follow the exact same sequence of instructions, even if the conditions that exist at the time of execution are different than when the batch file was designed.

The process of designing batch files to react differently to different circumstances will span several different chapters. You'll start by examining several ways to alter the normal top-down progression of a batch file, as well as the GOTO, QUIT, and FOR commands. With these tools, you can create alternative paths for your batch files. Later, you'll build on this concept by introducing decision-making tools to the batch file so it can choose among these different paths depending on conditions. So this chapter shows how to define multiple paths through your batch file, while a later chapter shows how to have the batch file pick a path.

Pseudocode

If you program in a general-purpose computer language like C or Pascal, you generally follow these steps:

1. Start a program as an idea inside your mind.

2. Translate your idea into computer code. (Most programming books recommend you draw a flowchart first, but no one ever does that!)

3. Run a compiler that converts the code you wrote into a program that the computer can understand. With batch files or any language that acts as an interpreter, this step disappears. Batch files don't need to be compiled because the operating system understands the batch file as it is.

4. Once your code is free of enough bugs for the compiler to successfully convert it into a program, you can begin running and testing it.

Pseudocode is really step 1½. Because no one ever does a flowchart, pseudocode is a way of flowcharting without all the hassle. Pseudocode is computer code written in English for later conversion into a programming language. Consider the pseudocode example of a loop:

Mark the top of a loop
Do something
If some test is met, jump out of this loop
Go to top of loop

This program goes around in a continual loop until a certain condition forces it to jump out of the loop. However, the real point of this example is that you understand it without knowing any of the associated batch commands!

Pseudocode is language-independent. If I were to flesh out this example with a few actions and specify the condition for when to jump out of the loop, a BASIC or C programmer could write a program to perform the same task in their respective languages.

Pseudocode is not new. I originally learned pseudocode while learning to program in dBASE II on an Apple II with a CP/M card in 1983. I'll be using pseudocode occasionally in this book to explain the flow of longer batch files because it makes the logic very easy to follow.

Naming Program Lines

The first thing the pseudocode loop requires is that you mark the top of the loop. In a batch file, there's no specific marking for the boundary of a loop. Instead, you just name any line so the batch file can then jump to that line. To name a line, start with a colon and then type in a name with the following characteristics:

- It must follow the colon with no spaces between the colon and the name. While not required, it's a good idea to left-justify the colon and name. Some batch file compilers won't work with a batch file unless the label is left-justified.

- The name should have eight characters or less. Actually, the name can be longer than eight characters; the batch file just ignores everything after the eighth character. That can cause problems if you have labels like GOTOTHIS1 and GOTOTHIS2, because they're identical through the first eight characters. As a result, both GOTO GOTOTHIS1 and GOTO GOTOTHIS2 will cause the batch file to jump to the same label.

- There can be nothing after the name on the same line.

- Capitalization doesn't matter. The labels :END and :End work the same.

- There can be no spaces in the name.

- While you don't have to, it's a good idea to make the name mean something, like TOP or END.

The next two lines in the pseudocode example in the previous section are "do something" and "if some test is met, jump out of this loop." The "do something" line represents your typical commands in a batch file. For example, a segment of the TOA.BAT batch file you've examined over the last two chapters might look like this:

```
:MAINPART
DEL %1.BAK
COPY %1.DOC A:
COPY %1.CMP A:
SHIFT
```

The first line is the label and the next four lines are what the section is discussing. The "if some test is met, jump out of this loop" line represents logic testing. This topic is covered in detail in the next chapter.

The GOTO Command

The last line in the pseudocode example specifies to go to the top of the loop. In a batch file, you jump to another section of the batch file by jumping to a line with a name. Because the line containing the name doesn't perform any action, the batch file behaves as though it jumps to the line following the name.

The command to jump to another line is GOTO, which must be followed by the name of the label to jump to without the colon. GOTO has two specific uses: repeating a series of commands more than once (in other words, *looping*) and transferring control to another section of the batch file. You'll look at both uses.

Looping

One important use of GOTO is to loop through a section of code more than once. You can see this with a couple of simple examples. We'll call the first one ENDLESS.BAT:

```
@ECHO OFF
REM NAME:     ENDLESS.BAT
REM PURPOSE: Demonstrate GOTO Command
REM VERSION: 1.00
REM DATE:    May 13, 1992
:TOP
ECHO Before A GOTO Command
GOTO TOP
ECHO After A GOTO Command
```

There's a copy of ENDLESS.BAT on the CD-ROM that comes with this book. If you run ENDLESS.BAT, you'll see a series of "before a GOTO command" messages scrolling up the screen. You have to press Ctrl–Break to stop ENDLESS.BAT. Let's review the operation of this batch file and you'll see why. The steps in the batch file are as follows:

1. Process the @ECHO OFF command.

2. Skip over the REM commands.

3. Skip over the :TOP label. (Labels are completely ignored except when the batch file is figuring out where to jump to after a GOTO command.)

4. Display the message "ECHO Before A GOTO Command."

5. Jump to the TOP line, causing the batch file to move back to step 3.

Because the batch file jumps back to the :TOP label each time it reaches the GOTO command, it will continue looping until you force it to stop. This is called an *endless loop* because, if left alone, it would never end.

By the way, you can stop ENDLESS.BAT by pressing Ctrl–Break or Ctrl–C and responding Yes to the "Terminate batch job (Y/N)?" message. In the next chapter, you'll see how to add logic testing to batch files so the batch file itself can figure out if it needs to jump out of a loop rather than depending on the user to press Ctrl–Break. You'll almost always need this "stopping logic" when using the GOTO command to construct a loop.

The steps between the :TOP label and the GOTO command in ENDLESS.BAT form a multiline loop. It's standard programming practice to indent everything inside a loop—that is, everything except the top (the label) and the bottom (usually a GOTO command). This helps you visualize the loop as you look at the code and actually forms documentation of sorts. Batch files don't require commands to be indented. It does, however, make the batch file easier for someone to understand when looking at it.

With this information, you can modify the TOA.BAT batch file you've looked at over the past two chapters. Look back at the version in Chapter 11. That version of the batch file performed the same few steps nine times. The new version uses a loop to consolidate the steps inside a single loop. It looks like this:

```
@ECHO OFF
REM NAME:     TOA.BAT
REM PURPOSE: Copy .CMP And .DOC Files To A Drive
REM          While Deleting .BAK Files
REM VERSION: 3.00
REM DATE:    May 12, 1992

:TOP
   DEL %1.BAK
   COPY %1.DOC A:
   COPY %1.CMP A:
   SHIFT
GOTO TOP
```

A copy of this file can be found in the \BAT-FILE\DOS\TOA\CHAP-12 and \BAT-FILE\OS2\TOA\CHAP-12 subdirectories.

The first two versions of TOA.BAT had problems if fewer than nine replaceable parameters were entered because it was designed to handle exactly nine. This third version has a different problem. Because there's nothing in the batch file to cause it to stop, it wants to continue running forever. Of course, it soon runs out of replaceable parameters, and you must press Ctrl–Break to stop it. You'll see how to avoid this in Chapter 16.

Transferring Control

The following batch file is completely legal:

```
@ECHO OFF
GOTO END
ECHO This Message Never Seen
ECHO This Message Skipped Too
:END
```

When the batch file processes the second line, control is immediately transferred to the last line of the batch file and it terminates. It makes little sense because it has lines that are never executed. It often makes good sense, however, for a batch file to jump to different locations depending on conditions. Let's look as the pseudocode for the version of TOA.BAT you'll create in a later chapter:

```
Top Of Loop
        Test For Another Replaceable Parameter Pending
                If No Then Jump To End Of Batch File
                If Yes Then Continue
        Erase The *.BAK File
        Copy The .DOC File To A Drive
        Copy The .CMP File To A Drive
        Shift Replaceable Parameters Down One Level
Go Through Loop Again
```

You haven't yet read about logic testing, so you can't produce this batch file as written, but you can see how the ability to jump out of that loop when the batch file runs out of replaceable parameters is useful.

In general, you'll use this unconditional transfer of control to jump to different sections of a batch file, depending on the conditions the batch file finds when it begins operation. Of course, that means you must write different sections of the batch file to deal with these different conditions.

A Quick Exit with the QUIT Command

Many of the batch files in this book will have one or more GOTO END commands to exit the batch file quickly without processing the remainder of the batch file. Often, this command is issued when the system passes some logic test. When the command is executed to terminate a batch file and not a batch file functioning as a subroutine, however, there's actually a quicker way. In your batch file subdirectory, enter the command:

```
TYPE NOFILE > QUIT.BAT
```

where NOFILE is the name of a nonexistent file. Make sure you don't already have a QUIT.BAT because this command will erase it. This line creates a zero-length file called QUIT.BAT. Then replace the GOTO END commands with the QUIT command. Running QUIT.BAT without CALL will keep control from returning to the original batch file, and because QUIT.BAT has no commands, the batch file immediately terminates.

Since most versions of DOS won't copy a zero-length file, you'll have to recreate QUIT.BAT on every machine where you want to use it. That's why I didn't include a copy on the CD-ROM that comes with this book.

A Handy Formatting Option

When I mentioned looping earlier, I said that you should indent everything between the top and bottom of the loop as a visual aid in debugging and maintaining the batch file. If you do that, the loop from TOA.BAT would look like this:

```
TOP
    DEL %1.BAK
    COPY %1.DOC A:
    COPY %1.CMP A:
    SHIFT
GOTO TOP
```

As you begin developing longer batch files, you'll find them to be very compartmentalized. In many cases, the batch files will have many different sections for handling specific tasks. For example, a "full-blown" version of TOA.BAT might have sections to perform the following:

- Displaying help when the user starts the batch file with a /? switch.

- Displaying an error message when the user fails to enter a replaceable parameter.

- Displaying an error message when the user specifies a filename as a replaceable parameter, and the .DOC version of that file doesn't exist. (Not all files have associated .CMP and .BAK files, so don't give an error message if one of those is missing.)

- Displaying an error message when the target disk is full or if another copying problems occurs.

- Performing the actual copying.

Clearly, you need a method to keep these sections separate, both in execution and visually.

Code Separation

Making sure the batch file executes only the right section of code is fairly easy. You jump into the appropriate section using the GOTO command. At the end of the section, the batch file jumps to the next section of the batch file. You can see the TOA.BAT segment reproduced earlier. It doesn't need to jump into the loop because it reaches it sequentially, but it jumps at the end of the loop.

One way to visually separate sections is to use blank lines. If the section is a loop, then you also have the visual clue of the indenting used inside the loop. I tend to use the same form of indenting with sections that aren't loops. For example, a section of

TOA.BAT to display an error message when the user fails to enter a replaceable parameter might look like this:

```
:NOTHERE
    ECHO You Started TOA.BAT
    ECHO Without A Replaceable Parameter
    ECHO This Information Is Required For TOA.BAT To Run
    ECHO When You Start TOA.BAT
    ECHO List The Names Of The Files
    ECHO To Copy On The Command Line After The TOA Command
GOTO END
```

Now you have a visual clue that this section of code is an integral section of code.

Conditional Execution in Novell DOS 7

Novell DOS 7 allows you to alter the flow of a batch file by making the execution of lines conditional. That is, the batch file will prompt the user prior to executing specified lines. The syntax is:

```
? ["message"] command
```

where *message* is the prompt to display for the user and *command* is the command to execute. If no message is included, the entire command is followed by a (Y/N)? prompt. If a message is included, only the message is displayed and the command isn't shown. Novell DOS 7 is picky about spacing; there must *not* be a space between the question mark and first double quotation mark when a message is included, or the command won't execute properly.

A response is required before the batch file will continue. If the user presses Y, the command is executed; any other key and the command is skipped. This approach is excellent for performing tasks, like loading memory-resident software, where the user might sometimes want to skip that step. The ASK-SKIP.BAT batch file on the CD-ROM included with this book illustrates this. The operational code is as follows:

```
@ECHO OFF
?"Would You Like To See A Directory? (Y/N)" DIR
?"Would You Like To Beep The Speaker? (Y/N)" ECHO ^G
?"Would You Like To See Help For The Batch File? (Y/N)" GOTO HELP
GOTO END
```

The FOR Command

Once I cover logic testing in the next chapter, you'll have everything you need to know to write complex loops using the GOTO command. However, one limitation of looping via GOTO is that you must provide the parameters of the loop when you code the batch file. For example, you can't go through the loop once for each .DOC file or for every file on the B drive. For that, you need the FOR command.

In its simplest form, FOR causes the operating system to loop through a series of files and perform a single action on those files. There are two forms of the command. The first takes a list of files:

```
FOR %%h IN (CHAPTER1.BAK CHAPTER2.BAK) DO ERASE %%h
```

and the second form uses wildcards to calculate all applicable files:

```
FOR %%j IN (*.BAK) DO DEL %%j
```

In general, the command is:

```
FOR %%variable IN (set) DO command
```

The FOR command must be on one line. Under DOS, FOR commands can't be nested, so only one FOR command can be on each line. Under OS/2, FOR commands can be nested. Under OS/2, the following command will count from 000 to 999 when entered all on one line:

```
FOR %%a IN (0 1 2 3 4 5 6 7 8 9) DO FOR %%b in (0 1 2 3 4 5 6 7 8 9)
   DO FOR %%c in (0 1 2 3 4 5 6 7 8 9) DO ECHO %%a%%b%%c
```

The %%*variable* must be a single character, for example %%A through %%Z. In addition, if you reference %%*variable* after the DO command, you must use the same capitalization you used in the beginning. For example:

```
FOR %%J IN (*.*) DO ECHO %%J
```

and:

```
FOR %%j IN (*.*) DO ECHO %%j
```

are valid because both Js are the same case, but the command:

```
FOR %%J IN (*.*) DO ECHO %%j
```

is invalid because one J is uppercase and the other is lowercase. Some versions of DOS will let you use %0 through %9 as variables in the FOR command, but it's a bad programming habit because DOS uses these as replaceable parameters. You can also use the FOR command from the command-line prompt without a batch file. The only change is that you use one percent sign rather than two, so %%*variable* must be %*variable*.

Local variables

When working with replaceable parameters back in Chapter 10, you saw that replaceable parameters were global variables. That is, you could use %1 anywhere in your batch file and the command would have access to the value stored in %1. However, variables created by the FOR command are local variables. Their value is usable only while the batch file is running the FOR command, so the following batch file segment:

```
@ECHO OFF
FOR %%J in (1 2 3) DO ECHO %%J
ECHO %%J
```

wouldn't have a value for %%J to echo when it reached the third line. It would simply echo %J. (Recall that you use two percent signs in an ECHO command to echo a single percent sign.)

FOR command quirks

The FOR command has two quirks, both of which can be useful under certain circumstances. The first quirk is how it processes elements of its set when preceded with a forward slash (/). The variable is split in two with the first element being the first character and the second element being the remainder. For example, if you enter this command from the command line:

```
FOR %J IN (/ABC /XYZ /123) DO ECHO %J
```

you might expect to see three messages, /ABC, /XYZ, and /123, but you'd actually see six: A, BC, X, YZ, 1, and 23. Not only is the first character separated, the forward slash is stripped off as well.

The second quirk involves what the FOR command actually runs after the DO component. Only internal commands and programs are allowed after the DO component—no batch files. You can put a batch file there, but the FOR loop will abort after processing the first element in its set. This makes it difficult to use the FOR command for several steps, like copying a file to a backup floppy disk and then deleting it.

Fortunately, a slight trick lets you run a batch file in a FOR loop. In a batch file, the CALL command is used to run another batch file and the CALL command is an internal command, so:

```
FOR %%J IN (%1) DO CALL BATCH %%J
```

would loop through all the files matching the first replaceable parameter and run BATCH.BAT for each one, passing it the filename as the first replaceable parameter.

This second quirk allows you to avoid one of the major limitations of the FOR command: its inability to run more than one command for each element. By using a batch file, as many commands can be executed for each element as are required. The one thing to notice is that the element must be passed to the batch file in the FOR command since FOR variables are local variables and not available in the batch file. The previous command illustrates this.

Summary

- Pseudocode is the process of outlining programs in English without worrying about which language will be used to create the program. Pseudocode is later turned into a program.

- You can name lines in a batch file by preceding an eight-character or shorter name with a colon.

- The GOTO command causes control to jump from the current line to the line named in the GOTO statement.

- The GOTO command creates a loop or permanently transfers control to another section of a batch file.

- Loops created with GOTO need some logic added to tell the batch file when to stop looping.

- Once the zero-length file QUIT.BAT has been created in a subdirectory in your path, you can use the QUIT command to quickly terminate a batch file without a GOTO END command and corresponding :END label.

- When creating loops with the GOTO command, it's useful to indent everything between the label and the GOTO command to visually represent the loop.

- Novell DOS 7 prompts the user before executing any batch file line that begins with a question mark. These lines can also contain an optional message to be displayed while Novell DOS 7 is waiting on a decision for that line.

- The FOR command constructs a single-line loop that's automatically executed once for each item in the set of items specified with the command.

- The FOR command must be contained on a single line and cannot be nested under DOS. Nesting is allowed under OS/2.

- Due to a quirk in the FOR command, when an element in its set is preceded with a forward slash, that element is split into two components, one containing the first character and the second containing the remaining characters. The forward slash is dropped.

- In order to run a batch file via a FOR loop, the name of the batch file must be preceded with a CALL command.

13

The Environment

The operating system sets aside a portion of memory for storing system-wide variables, called *environmental variables*. In addition to storing the value of environmental variables, this area stores the prompt, path, and other system variables. Technically, the prompt and path are nothing more than environmental variables, although they have such specific functions that they're usually treated differently.

The Prompt

The default prompt is C>, which tells you almost nothing (except that C is the default drive). You can use the PROMPT command to change it to a wide range of prompts. The PROMPT command is normally used just in the AUTOEXEC.BAT file under DOS or the CONFIG.SYS file under OS/2; when used by itself, it resets the prompt to C>.

You can include any printable character string in the PROMPT command. In fact, one of the first tricks most computer users learn is to include their name or company name in the prompt. You can also include special characters in the DOS prompt with the commands in Table 13.1. Table 13.2 shows the more extensive list that can be used with OS/2. The most popular prompt is:

```
SET PROMPT=$P$G
```

**TABLE 13.1 DOS Metacharacters to Use with the
PROMPT Command to Insert Special Characters into Your Prompt**

Command	Action
$$	Displays a dollar sign.
$_	Includes a carriage return and line feed.
$b	Displays a vertical bar.
$d	Displays the date.

TABLE 13.1 Continued

Command	Action
$e	Includes an escape. This is useful for sending ANSI escape sequences via the PROMPT command.
$g	Displays a greater-than sign.
$h	Displays a backspace—thus deleting the prior character.
$l	Displays a less-than sign.
$n	Displays the current drive.
$p	Displays the current subdirectory.
$q	Displays an equal sign.
$t	Displays the time.
$v	Displays the DOS version.

TABLE 13.2 OS/2 PROMPT Metacharacters

Symbol	Action
$$	Displays a dollar sign.
$_	Includes a carriage return and line feed.
$a	Displays an ampersand.
$b	Displays a vertical bar.
$c	Displays an open parenthesis.
$d	Displays the date.
$e	Includes an escape. This is useful for sending ANSI escape sequences via the PROMPT command.
$f	Displays a closed parenthesis.
$g	Displays a greater-than sign.
$h	Displays a backspace—thus deleting the prior character.
$i	Displays a blue bar at top of screen with help and window switching information.
$l	Displays a less-than sign.
$n	Displays the current drive.
$p	Displays the current subdirectory.
$q	Displays an equal sign.
$r	Shows a return code (errorlevel) of last action.
$s	Displays a space.
$t	Displays the time.
$v	Displays the version.

This command adds the current subdirectory to the default disk display. It's important to remember that any prompt you develop is stored in the environmental space, along with the path and environmental variables. A long prompt combined with a long path and an environmental variable might require you to expand your environmental space, as explained later in this chapter.

The Path

The path defines the drives and subdirectories the operating system searches to find programs and batch files. The path is stored in the environment. The syntax for the PATH command is either:

```
SET PATH=C:\;C:\DOS;C:\WINDOWS
```

or:

```
PATH=C:\;C:\DOS;C:\WINDOWS
```

This second approach to creating a path has two advantages over the first. First, paths tend to grow larger and larger, but the path command, like all commands, is limited to 127 characters under DOS and 255 characters under OS/2. (Beginning with MS-DOS 6, command lines in CONFIG.SYS are no longer limited to 127 characters, so longer environmental variables can be created. This allows for a longer path.) Removing the SET (and the space following it) reduces the length of the command and thus allows your path to contain four additional characters.

The second advantage is that paths created with the PATH= command are converted to all uppercase while those created with SET PATH= aren't. This offers batch file authors one way to convert text strings to uppercase without using any utilities. This concept is explored in depth in Chapter 18.

COMSPEC

In an OS/2 session, this variable tells OS/2 what program to load as the command processor. This is usually C:\OS2\CMD.EXE, but you can load an alternative command processor, like 4OS2, by specifying an alternative value for the COMSPEC variable. In a DOS session, the COMSPEC variable points to COMMAND.COM or an alternative command processor like 4DOS.

Environmental Variables

Think of the environment as a scratch pad, where the operating system leaves notes for itself. As you'll see, batch files can also use this scratch pad.

Most programs distinguish between different types of variables. For example, you don't generally use the same type of variable for a string of characters as you do for numbers. The environment doesn't make this distinction. Every environmental variable is treated as a string of characters, even if it's all numbers.

Unlike filenames, environmental variable names aren't limited to a few characters. Therefore, it's a good idea to use descriptive names like SourceDrive and Target-Drive. Of course, these longer names take up more space in the environment and, as you'll see, environmental variable names are converted to uppercase. If an environmental variable is used temporarily by a batch file, it's a good idea for that batch file to delete the environmental variable once it no longer needs it so it doesn't use environmental memory.

Notes on names

A lot of the batch files in this book use environmental variables, and almost every one uses them without concern for the name. That is, they go ahead and use a name without first checking to see if the name is already in use. That's okay for demonstration batch files, but you need to be more careful on your system. If a batch file depends on an environmental variable existing when it runs, then you don't want another batch file altering its contents or even wiping it out!

Since environmental variable names can be long, you can avoid this problem by starting important environmental variable names with the name of the batch file that creates them. So if PASSWORD.BAT creates an environmental variable called AL-LOWED, you could name the environmental variable PASSWORD_ALLOWED. Since every batch file would use its unique name for the first portion of environmental variable names, they'd all be unique.

You can also avoid problems by deciding on some names, like JUNK or TEMP, that you never use for permanent information. That way, they can always be overwritten without concern for their contents.

While you don't want to accidentally overwrite a permanent environmental variable, you also want to avoid filling up your environment with environmental variables you no longer need. It's important that batch files clean up after themselves and delete any environmental variables that aren't needed later. This goes a long way in keeping you from running out of environmental space.

Windows loads a new copy of COMMAND.COM for each batch file it executes. As a result, each batch file receives a fresh copy of the environment. Windows also discards all free environmental space so batch files running under Windows have no free environmental space.

With Windows, you can run batch files without having to worry about running out of environmental memory if you create a .PIF file for the batch file. There are only two settings that require special attention. The first is the Program Filename. This should be set to COMMAND.COM and you should specify the full path to it. The second is the Optional Parameters setting. You'll need two different settings here. The first is /E:xxx, where the xxx represents the size of the environment to create. I've found that a setting of 800 is adequate for most of my work. The second is /C *batch*, where *batch* is the name of the batch file to execute, along with a path if it isn't stored in the path. The /C is a switch for COMMAND.COM that tells it to run the program that follows, the batch file in this case, and then unload. Once the .PIF file is ready, tell Windows to run the .PIF file rather than the batch file.

If you choose to create a .PIF file for any of your batch files, you must also make sure that the remaining settings in the .PIF file are compatible with all of the programs the batch file is going to run.

Additionally, since Windows runs each batch file in a different session, environmental variables created in one session aren't available for the other sessions. This limits the ability of batch files to communicate with each other. Of course, when one batch file executes another batch file, those batch files run in the same session and share a common pool of environmental memory. You can, however, start a DOS session under Windows and run all your batch files in this one session. If you do this, they'll share a common pool of environmental memory but you'll lose the benefits of the graphical user interface.

Like Windows, OS/2 starts each session off with a fresh set of environmental variables and doesn't allow the environment of one session to affect the environment of another session. Also like Windows, you can start one command session and run all your batch files from the command line so they'll share a common pool of environmental memory.

Environmental variables are transient

As mentioned earlier, all systems have a COMSPEC environmental variable, and most have path and prompt environmental variables. Some hardware and software also creates environmental variables when you install them. Windows wants an environmental variable called TEMP to point towards a place for its temporary files. My tape drive creates two, and my CD-ROM creates three. You'll find these added to your AUTOEXEC.BAT file. Usually, the installation program adds them automatically.

Variables in the environment are lost when you turn off or reboot the computer. Although these variables are transient, they can be very useful for communicating between different batch files or for storing information used by more than one batch file.

Putting Variables into the Environment

You can place environmental variables into the environment either with a batch file or interactively from the command-line prompt. Under MS-DOS 6 or later and OS/2, you can also create environmental variables in the CONFIG.SYS file. Either way, the syntax to place an environmental variable into the environment is:

```
SET variable=value
```

Note that the only space is between the SET command and the variable name. Don't use spaces around the equal sign. If you do, the name of your variable and its contents will be corrupted.

Once you store a variable in the environment, you cannot edit its value. However, you can replace the contents of an environmental variable using the same command—thus overwriting the contents of the environmental variable with a new value. You can also delete an environmental variable with the command:

```
SET variable=
```

where nothing follows the equal sign. Finally, you can view the contents of the environment by issuing the SET command by itself from the command line or in a batch file.

Using the Environment in Batch Files

Batch files create and erase environmental variables just as you would from the command line. They can also reference the contents of an environmental variable by surrounding its name with percent signs. For example, a batch file could create an environmental variable called FLOPPY with the command:

```
SET FLOPPY=A:
```

and then copy files to the A drive with the command:

```
COPY *.* %FLOPPY%
```

The batch file would then replace %FLOPPY% with the contents of the FLOPPY environmental variable. This also works from the command line in OS/2, but not DOS. You can use a similar approach to transferring data between environmental variables. For example, if the environmental variable BEFORE contains a value you want to store in the environmental variable AFTER, the command to do this in a batch file is:

```
SET AFTER=%BEFORE%
```

Note that the BEFORE environmental variable is surrounded by percent signs because you want to use its value, but the AFTER environmental variable isn't because you're using that name for a variable. Also, the command doesn't change the contents of the BEFORE environmental variable, so now you have the same information stored under two names. Of course, you could go ahead and work with either environmental variable to alter their contents.

Special Novell DOS 7 System Information Variables

Novell DOS 7 maintains a number of system information variables whose contents can be used in a batch file just like environmental variables. Before exploring system information variables, let's look at their differences from environmental variables:

- They're created automatically by Novell DOS 7 without the user doing anything, and they're kept up to date automatically by Novell DOS 7.
- They aren't displayed when you issue the SET command.
- The user can't change them.

TABLE 13.3 Novell DOS 7 System Information Variables

Variable name	Explanation
AM_PM	Contains an am or pm depending on the current time.
Day	Contains a 01 to 31 representing the day of the month.
Day_of_Week	Contains a Mon, Tue, or so on.
ErrorLevel	Contains the current errorlevel value. Testing on this value (e.g., %ERRORLEVEL%) is easier than testing the actual errorlevel.
Greeting_Time	Contains a Morning, Afternoon, or Evening depending on the current time.
Hour	Contains a 01 to 12 depending on the current hour.
Hour24	Contains a 00 to 23 depending on the current hour.
Minute	Contains a 00 to 59 depending on the current minute.
Month	Contains a 01 to 12 depending on the current month.
Month_Name	Contains a January to December depending on the current month.
NDay_of_Week	Contains a 1 (Sunday) to 7 (Saturday) depending on the day of the week.
OS	Contains the current operating system, e.g., NWDOS. Batch files that need to run only under Novell DOS 7 can test this value to make sure it exists since no other operating systems will have it.
OS_Version	Contains the version of the operating system.
Second	Contains a 00 to 59 dependig on the current second.
Short_Year	Contains a 94, 95, and so on depending on the current year.
Year	Contains a 1994, 1995, and so on depending on the current year.

TABLE 13.4 NetWare System Information Variables

Variable name	Explanation
Login_Name	The user's login name
P_Station	The physical station number
Station	The station number

In spite of these differences, they function much like environmental variables. You'd normally display one by surrounding its name with percent signs, or piping its contents to a file in a similar fashion. Table 13.3 lists the Novell DOS 7 system information variables, and Table 13.4 lists the NetWare system information variables. The SHOW-SIV.BAT batch file included on the CD-ROM illustrates many of these variables in action.

Special OS/2 Environmental Commands

Sometimes you need to make temporary changes to the environment. OS/2 makes that easy. When a batch file issues a SETLOCAL command, OS/2 stores the current status of the environment as well as the current drive and subdirectory. After that, you can use the batch file to make as many changes to either as you want. Once the batch file is ready to restore the environment, drive, and subdirectory, an ENDLO-CAL command returns them all to their exact state before the SETLOCAL command was issued.

If a batch file terminates with a SETLOCAL command in effect, OS/2 behaves as though the last command were an ENDLOCAL and goes ahead and restores the environment when the SETLOCAL command was in effect.

The biggest use of SETLOCAL and ENDLOCAL in a batch file is to return the batch file to its original subdirectory when it's done. It's also important to note that SETLOCAL and ENDLOCAL are two of the few batch file commands that won't run from the command line.

On the CD-ROM, you'll find a batch file called LOCAL.CMD to illustrate these commands. LOCAL.CMD displays the environment, issues a SETLOCAL command, deletes a number of environmental variables, and displays the rest so you can see that a number of changes have been made. After that, it restores the original environment with the ENDLOCAL command and displays the restored environment to the user. It also displays the current subdirectory, changes to the \OS2\INSTALL subdirectory and displays it, then changes back with the ENDLOCAL command and displays that.

What You Can Do with Environmental Variables

Programming languages generally let you perform mathematical operations on variables, but batch files don't have a command to do this on an environmental variable. However, some of the utilities discussed later in this book will perform arithmetic operations on environmental variables. Environmental variables can be used for the following:

Display. You can use a batch file to display the contents of any environmental variable by surrounding its name with percent signs. For example, ECHO %PATH% will display the path. Also, when the expanded line is longer than 127 characters, as it might be with a long path, and you issue the command ECHO My Path Is: %PATH%, then the entire message won't display and the computer might lock up.

Combining strings. Two or more environmental variables can be displayed together. The technique is the same: just surround the respective names with percent signs. For example, if there are environment variables named Drive and File, the command ECHO %DRIVE%%FILE% will display them both side by side.

In place of text. Environmental variables can be used anywhere text would be used. For example, the command PATH=%PATH%;C:\123 would append C:\123 onto the current path because the %PATH% is used just like the batch file entering the current path, and the command COPY C:\AUTOEXEC.BAT %DRIVE%%FILE% would copy your AUTOEXEC.BAT to the drive and filename stored under these environmental variables.

In place of commands. A batch file can run a command stored to an environmental variable if you put that environmental variable, surrounded by percent signs, on a line by itself.

While all these techniques work from within a batch file, none of them work from the command line under DOS. They will, however, work fine under OS/2.

Using the Environment When Shelling Out of a Program

While batch files work with the original or master copy of the environment, every time you start a program the operating system passes that program a full copy of the environment. The program is free to alter its copy of the environment, but when the program terminates, its copy of the environment is also terminated and the changes aren't passed back to the master copy of the environment.

Remember comparing the environment to a scratch pad? Well, when the operating system runs a program, it provides that program with a "photocopy" of its scratch pad in case the program needs any of the information it contains. However, before passing a copy of the environment to a program, DOS trims off as much empty space as possible. It would trim all the free space except that, like all memory blocks, the environment is created and maintained in 16-byte (or one-paragraph) blocks. This trimming therefore results in zero to 15 bytes of free environmental space. OS/2 doesn't restrict the environment when running another program. When the program is finished, both OS/2 and DOS ignore any notes the program has made on its photocopy and just tosses the copy into the memory recycling bin.

The action of the environment while a program is running leads to an interesting problem and a useful shortcut for experimenting with the environment. First the problem, and then the shortcut.

To avoid having the user shell out of Word for Windows and trying to run another program, you might want to add the modification examined in Chapter 3: changing the prompt before starting Word and changing it back after Word terminates. That version of the batch file segment is as follows:

```
@ECHO OFF
C:
CD\WORD
PROMPT Type EXIT To Return To Word $P$G
WORD %1
PROMPT $P$G
```

However, this batch file won't run as expected under Windows. The problem is that Windows discards the free memory from its copy of the environment so there's no more than seven bytes of free environmental space. When Windows loads a second copy of COMMAND.COM, that COMMAND.COM gets a copy of this reduced-size environment. Because the new "Type EXIT To Return To Word PG" prompt is much longer than the existing prompt, it will not fit and you'll get the "Environment full" error message.

This problem is not unique to Windows. If you shell out of Lotus or Word and try to run a batch file that adds information to the environment, it will also fail to run properly. Both Lotus and Word discard free environmental memory in order to have more conventional memory and then pass along this reduced-size environment to COMMAND.COM when you shell out.

Increasing the size of the master copy of the environment won't help. This will just give the programs more free environment space to discard when they start. You can create a .PIF file to give the batch file more environmental space, as discussed earlier, but then you have to worry about making sure the .PIF file is compatible with all the programs the batch file is going to run. For that reason, you need a way to make environmental space available under Windows and when shelled out of a program.

In your AUTOEXEC.BAT file, create a long environmental variable containing a lot of information so, if the file were deleted, you would free up enough environmental space to make the environment usable under other programs. We'll call this variable JUNK, so the AUTOEXEC.BAT file would have a statement like:

```
SET JUNK=AAAAAAAAAAAAAAAAAAAAAAAAAAAA
```

Before adding information to the environment in a batch file designed to run while shelled out of another program, delete the JUNK environmental variable. The modified version of the batch file segment is shown next:

```
@ECHO OFF
C:
CD\WORD
SET JUNK=
PROMPT Type EXIT To Return To Word $P$G
WORD %1
PROMPT $P$G
CD\
EXIT
```

If you're modifying a batch file that will be used both from the command line and from within a program, then deleting the JUNK environmental variable before adding information to the environment is okay. However, the current version of WP.BAT never recreates the JUNK environmental variable. When a program terminates, its copy of the environment is also terminated. Most programs shell out by running COMMAND.COM; this is always the case if you have to type EXIT to return to the original program. When that copy of COMMAND.COM terminates, changes to its environment are lost.

However, when a dual-mode batch file is running from the command line, the environment isn't restored and the contents of the JUNK environmental variable aren't available for other batch files to delete. To avoid that, add a command at the end of any dual-mode batch files to recreate the JUNK environmental variable. That way, when they run by themselves, the environmental variable is recreated properly. When run from inside a program, there might not be enough free memory to recreate the variable, but in that case it doesn't matter.

By following these steps, you'll always have free environmental memory—if your batch file is running directly from DOS or while shelled out of Windows or any other program.

As explained earlier, after you shell out of a program, the changes you make to the environment are lost when you enter the EXIT command to return to the original program. However, as long as you follow the procedures just described to create a dummy environmental variable from your AUTOEXEC.BAT file that you can later delete, you'll have free environmental space while shelled out of a program.

All this makes shelling out of a program the perfect place for testing batch files that modify the environment, especially if your system depends on a well-crafted environment. No matter how many alterations you make to the environment, a simple EXIT command restores the environment to its pristine form.

Using the Environment in a Batch File

The environment is commonly used as a common exchange ground, where one batch file can place information into the environment for another batch file to use. Looking at this in more depth requires an understanding of both the errorlevel and logic testing, so I'll postpone this topic until Chapter 18.

Batch files can use environmental variables just like replaceable parameters, even as filenames or commands. This allows you to use environmental variables as a shortcut.

Imagine you're writing a large database program using Quicksilver. You usually work on one program for most of the day, trying to get out all the bugs. You use batch files to start Microsoft Word in order to edit your program and to run Quicksilver in order to compile the program. If you store the name of the program in the environment as COMPILE, then the batch files can automate much of the work for you.

A batch file segment to compile the program for you, called COMPILE.BAT, would look like this:

```
@ECHO OFF
DB3C -A %COMPILE%
DB3L %COMPILE%
```

The DB3C -A runs the Quicksilver compiler to produce the .OBJ file. It uses the COMPILE environmental variable so the user doesn't have to enter the name of the program each time. The DB3L runs the Quicksilver linker to produce the .EXE file, and again uses the COMPILE environmental variable.

You could write a similar batch file segment, WORD2QS.BAT, to similarly automate loading the program into Microsoft Word for editing. It would look like this:

```
@ECHO OFF
WORD %COMPILE%
```

Because Word defaults to ASCII mode when editing an ASCII file, no special switches are required.

Summary

- The environment is a portion of memory set aside for storing system-wide variables, much like a scratch pad for the operating system.
- There are a number of special metacharacters for creating fancy prompts.
- The path is a list of subdirectories for the operating system to search through for programs.
- The COMSPEC environmental variable tells DOS where to find COMMAND.COM.
- The prompt, path, and COMSPEC are stored in the environment.
- The size of the environment is limited but can be expanded.
- The values of environmental variables are lost when the computer is turned off or rebooted.
- A copy of the environment is provided to each program, but any changes made to it are lost when the program terminates.
- The SET command allows you to store data in the environment. With it, you can also erase or change existing data in the environment.
- You can use batch files to access the contents of the environment by surrounding the environmental variable name with percent signs. You can do the same at the command line under OS/2, but not DOS.
- You can use batch files to display environmental variables, combine them together, and transfer values between them. You can even use them as commands.
- Programs give you very little free environmental space when you shell out to run other programs.
- You can increase the available environmental space when you shell out of a program by creating a dummy environmental variable before you start the program and then deleting it when you shell out.
- You can increase the available environmental space when shelling out of Windows by editing the DOS .PIF file.
- When you return to a program after shelling out to DOS, the environment is restored to its condition prior to your shelling out.
- You can pass information between batch files by using the environment.
- Batch files can use the environment to store data that will be accessed by more than one batch file or that a single batch file needs to access each time it runs.

14

Errorlevel

While a nice place for batch files, the environment is a very inhospitable place for programs to store information to communicate with each other or with a batch file. When a program reads from or writes to the environment, it's dealing with its copy of the environment and not with the original. When the program terminates, its copy of the environment, along with all the changes the program made to it, is destroyed.

The errorlevel was provided to overcome this problem. The errorlevel is a single byte of memory, so it can contain only a single character. (OS/2 sometimes calls the errorlevel the *return code* and DR DOS sometimes calls it the *error code*. Both terms refer to the errorlevel.) Normally, the content of the errorlevel is referred to by its ASCII value rather than its character representation, so ASCII values 0 to 255 are possible.

When a program terminates, it can store a number in the errorlevel to indicate its status at termination. When programs use the errorlevel, the usual rule is to set it to zero for a successful execution and higher values to indicate different types of errors.

The errorlevel isn't stored in the environment, so changes made to it aren't lost when a program terminates. Unlike the environment, there's only one copy of the errorlevel under DOS, and every program changes the same one. Under OS/2, each session has its own errorlevel. The errorlevel doesn't change unless a program changes it, you start another program, or you reboot, so you can perform multiple tests on it. However, the errorlevel is automatically reset to zero each time you start a new program, so each time a program runs, the prior errorlevel value is lost.

Under DOS, the errorlevel isn't reset when you run internal commands. However, most internal commands do reset the errorlevel under OS/2. Some internal batch commands, such as IF, don't reset the errorlevel under OS/2. As a result, batch files that depend on the errorlevel might run differently under DOS than they do under OS/2.

You don't need the errorlevel when running programs from the command line because you see any error messages. However, a batch file doesn't "see" error messages, so the errorlevel gives them a way to respond to errors.

MS-DOS commands that support the errorlevel are BACKUP, CHKDSK, CHOICE, DISKCOMP, DISKCOPY, KEYB, REPLACE, RESTORE, SETVER, and XCOPY. Their errorlevel values are documented in the MS-DOS manual. The errorlevel returned by CHOICE depends on how you configure it; this is discussed in Chapter 19.

OS/2 has eleven commands that are documented to support the errorlevel: BACKUP, CHKDSK, COMP, EAUTIL, FORMAT, GRAFTABL, RECOVER, REPLACE, RESTORE, UNPACK, and XCOPY. OS/2 also has a number of internal commands with undocumented errorlevel support. For example, the DIR command returns an errorlevel of 1 if you use an invalid switch, and an errorlevel of 18 if it doesn't find the file you specify after the DIR command.

OS/2 provides no documentation for any support of the errorlevel by internal commands. I found out about the few I'm familiar with by experimentation. If you need to know about a specific command, include a $R in your prompt and experiment with the command to see if it produces an errorlevel when you use the command incorrectly or get an error message. I also call on IBM to document all the errorlevel values it plans on supporting in future releases.

While DOS and OS/2 make little use of the errorlevel, it's important to become familiar with the errorlevel. Almost every batch utility uses the errorlevel to communicate results back to the batch file.

Summary

The errorlevel is a single byte of information that's common to all programs and batch files. It's used by the vast majority of batch file utilities to report their results.

Punctuation

Command-line punctuation can be very cryptic, which you know if you've ever tried to direct input from one file into a filter and then direct the output to another file. Because punctuation is often used in batch files, I've devoted this chapter to helping you understand the topic.

Piping and Redirection

Normally, you enter input from the keyboard and output goes to the screen, printer, or disk drive. (Input and output is often referred to as I/O.) DOS and OS/2 have the ability to redirect I/O to and from nonstandard locations, called *redirection* or *piping*, depending on how it's performed. When you cause input to come from a nonstandard location, it's *input redirection*; when you cause output to go to a nonstandard location, it's *output redirection*. Anything else, which usually involves taking output from one program and using it as input for another program, is *piping*.

DOS and OS/2 maintain two file handles for I/O, with 0 reserved for input and 1 reserved for output. When you boot, they're both automatically mapped to the console. If you load ANSI.SYS or any ANSI clone in your CONFIG.SYS, then the output file handle is remapped to ANSI. What redirection and piping really does is replace one of these standard file handles with a different file handle for I/O processing.

Available piping symbols

There are four symbols used for either redirection or piping:

>. The greater-than symbol causes output from one location to flow to another location. Many times, it's treated as input by the receiving program. When the alternative location is a file, this causes the file to be overwritten if it exists. For this reason, you must be very careful when using a greater-than symbol in a batch file. You should

always test first, using an IF test, before piping to a file. If the file exists, you can issue an error message and stop, rename the existing file, or pipe to an alternative file after checking to make sure that file doesn't exist.

>>. The dual greater-than symbol is used to route output to alternative locations. It's the same as the greater-than symbol except that, when the alternative location is a file, dual greater-than piping causes the messages to be appended to the end of the existing file. This is a safer alternative if you're storing error messages or other information in a file. Since the dual greater-than symbol is really just a special case of the greater-than symbol, I'll consider just the greater-than symbol for most of this discussion.

<. The less-than symbol causes a program to get its input from the specified device or file.

¦. Instead of creating a permanent file with the greater-than or dual greater-than symbol, the vertical bar creates a temporary file that's read and erased by the following program. A common use is in the command DIR¦MORE. Another use of the vertical bar symbol is to pipe data a program needs to run into that program. For example, ECHO Y¦DEL *.* will erase all the files in the current directory without asking for verification. That's because the confirmation is piped into the DEL command with the ECHO Y command. Basically, the vertical bar means you're using the output of what's on the left as input to what's on the right.

Devices to pipe to/from

Generally, redirection and piping involves either a system device driver or a filename. System device drivers are device drivers that are automatically created by the system. They are:

AUX. This is an auxiliary device that's normally treated as COM1.

CLOCK$. This is the real-time clock.

COM#. This is the serial port. COM1 is the first port and COM2 is the second. You can also use AUX as the default serial port.

CON. Depending on the usage, this is either the screen or the keyboard. When used as the target, it's the screen. When used as the source, CON is the keyboard.

LPT#. This is the printer port. LPT1 is the first port and LPT2 is the second port. You can also use PRN to specify the default printer port.

NUL. This is an output device that causes any output sent to it to be discarded.

PRN. This is the printer and is normally mapped to LPT1.

If the target of a redirection or pipe isn't one of these devices, then the operating system knows it's a filename.

How DOS and OS/2 handle pipes

When the operating system encounters a less-than symbol, it means a program is going to receive its input from the alternative device specified by the pipe. It then closes the standard input device and opens the alternative one specified on the command line because only one input device can be open at a time. This is why when inputs are redirected into a program from a file, that file must contain all the inputs required by the program. Since the file is the only active source of inputs, no others are available.

The receiving program (the one on the left of the less-than symbol) doesn't know data is being redirected to it. All it knows is that data is coming in from the input device. The operating system alters the input device before turning control over to the program.

The most common use of input redirection is to construct small programs. You create a small script with an editor and, once you're very sure the script is correct, you redirect it into DEBUG with a command like `DEBUG<SCRIPT`. Everything has to come from the script file.

You can also use this technique to bypass questions asked by utilities by redirecting answers to them. For example, to bypass the question about formatting another disk in FORMAT, you can create a text file containing the character n and a Return, then format a disk with the command `FORMAT A:<N.TXT`.

Output redirection works in a similar fashion except, of course, it's the output file handle that gets replaced rather than the input file handle. For example, if you issue the command `COPY *.* A:` to copy some files to the A drive, you expect to see each filename scroll by on the screen as it's copied and then to see the "n file(s) copied" message when the copying is done. Now change the command to:

```
COPY *.* A: > NUL
COPY *.* A: > NUL 2 > &1 (Under OS/2)
```

and you'll see absolutely nothing extra appear on the screen as the command works. When it's done, all you'll see to indicate it is the return of your prompt! Don't worry, the files were still copied. The >NUL told the operating system to turn off the standard output device—the console or ANSI—and turn on the alternative output device, NUL in this case. None of this affects the actions of the COPY command itself. This technique is a good way of hiding these sorts of messages from new users in batch files.

If you want to log these messages, you could redirect them to a file with *>filename* for a one-time log or *>>filename* if you don't want to overwrite the log file first. The second approach is particularly useful for accumulating multiple messages in a single file.

When the operating system encounters a vertical bar (¦), it takes the output of one command and passes (or pipes) it on to another command. For example, you can use piping to display directory information one screenful at a time. (Yes, I know DIR/P will do this, but it's a nice easy example.) First, you can get a file listing of your files with the command DIR>*file*. This will direct the output of the DIR command into *file*. Next, you can send this file through the MORE filter (discussed in the following paragraph) with the command TYPE FILE>MORE and you'll get exactly what you want.

However, that takes two steps and there's an easier way. The command DIR¦MORE does the same thing. The operating system runs the DIR command, stores its output in a temporary file, and then passes that temporary file over to MORE for display. The operating system uses one or more temporary files in the process that are created prior to the DIR command, so you might see a strange zero-length file or two if you use this command. I just ran it on my computer and saw AFALBJAE and AFALBJAK in the listing. Don't worry, the operating system erases them automatically for you.

You must use DOS or OS/2 for piping and redirection

As you experiment with redirection and piping, you're going to find circumstances where it looks like you've done everything right but the command doesn't work and all you end up with is a zero-length file. For example, start Lotus with the command 123>LOG and no matter what you do in Lotus, when you exit, LOG will be a zero-length file! Start Lotus with the command 123<LOG and Lotus will still expect input from you and won't accept it from the LOG file—which must exist or the operating system will object and not run the command.

There's nothing wrong here with either the operating system or Lotus, and there's no problem with the way the commands are constructed. Rather, there's confusion about what redirection and piping does.

For output, the operating system offers several character output services. Programs can also use video BIOS routines or they can write information straight to the video buffer. As you might expect, these latter methods are faster and most programs use them. For input, programs can let the operating system read the keyboard for them or they can take the faster approach of using interrupt 16h BIOS services.

Output can be piped only when it goes through the standard output device, and input can be piped only when it comes from the standard input device. Since most programs bypass these, they're immune to piping. However, most system utilities and command-line utilities use standard I/O, so you can pipe these. When a properly constructed pipe fails to work, the flaw is usually that the program bypasses standard I/O.

This also explains why you can't use redirection or piping to capture data intended for the printer into a file. Since the printer isn't the standard output device but an alternative one, piping doesn't affect it.

Filters to use in pipes

DOS and OS/2 include three filters you can use to manipulate the data coming out of or going into a pipe:

FIND. Searches each line of a file for specified text.

MORE. This displays one screen of information, pauses until you press any key, and then displays another screen of information. It continues until all the information has been displayed. You can't scroll backwards. Common usages are DIR¦MORE and TYPE FILE¦MORE.

SORT. This sorts the file (or input) into ASCII order.

The CD-ROM includes several additional REXX filters for use with OS/2. These are discussed in Chapter 32.

Problems with redirection and piping

Redirection and piping can cause problems, the major one being a "hung" computer. If you use piping to tell a program to get its input from a file, then that file must contain all the input the program requires. If it doesn't, you'll either have to reboot or press Ctrl–Break, and either of these will abort the program you're running. In addition, redirection and piping can get around warnings. For example, the command:

```
ECHO Y¦DEL *.*
```

will delete all your files without asking you if you want to because the ECHO command supplies the necessary response. Those warnings are generally in place for a good reason, and it isn't a good idea to avoid them. Another problem crops up when you specify an invalid command, such as:

```
DATE < NUL
PROGRAM < LPT1
```

In the first example, NUL is used as an input device, but NUL can never supply input. In the second case, the printer is used for input and, like NUL, it can't supply input. Unfortunately, the operating system won't spot either of these problems; the programs or commands will wait forever for a response (or until you press Ctrl–Break or reboot).

You can also destroy data by using redirection and piping improperly. For example, if you wanted to take the data in FILE.DAT and sort it using SORT.EXE, you might issue the command:

```
SORT < FILE.DAT > FILE.DAT
```

This tells the operating system to run SORT.EXE and supply it with input from the file FILE.DAT. When SORT.EXE finishes, it's supposed to write the results back to the FILE.DAT file. However, what happens is that FILE.DAT gets erased!

When the operating system processes a command line or batch file command, the first thing it does is replace any environmental variables or replaceable parameters with its values. There are neither in this line. The next thing it does is check for redirection and piping and, if it finds any, it initializes any files. Since this command pipes data into FILE.DAT, the operating system creates FILE.DAT, erasing the existing copy in the process. Since all this happens prior to actually running the command line, data hasn't yet been read out of FILE.DAT and piped into SORT.

This very "feature" is a handy way to create zero-length files if you need them. A zero-length file has a directory entry and valid name but no contents, so it doesn't take up any disk space. By typing a nonexistent file with a command like TYPE NOFILE>TARGET, DOS goes ahead and creates the TARGET file but, since it has nothing to put into that file, it remains a zero-length file.

+

The plus sign is used to perform file concatenation, which is a fancy name for combining two or more files together. For example, the command:

```
COPY File1+File2+File3 File4
```

will copy the first three files into one larger file, File4. This can cause problems if any of the first three files contains an end-of-file (EOF) marker; most editors won't allow you to go beyond the point in a file where the first EOF marker is located.

You can also use file concatenation to append information to the bottom of a batch file without loading an editor. For example, the command:

```
COPY CONFIG.SYS+CON
```

copies the current contents of the CONFIG.SYS file plus whatever you type after issuing this command (press F6 or ^Z to quit entering text) into a new version of the CONFIG.SYS file.

Use this approach to appending text with care. If the file you're appending text to is large, the operation might not work properly. Plus, if the file doesn't end with a Return, you must first press Return, or else the text you enter will be appended to the last line of the file.

:

The colon is used to name lines in a batch file. This is explained in detail in Chapter 12.

.

DOS 3 and later will display a blank line in response to an ECHO. command, so you might see this in batch files you receive from others.

@

The at symbol is used to turn command echoing off for a single command in a batch file, regardless of the global status of command echoing. This was covered in Chapter 5.

%

The single percent sign is used to mark replaceable parameters in a batch file, as covered in Chapter 10. You can also use it to name the variable in a FOR loop when issued from the command line rather than in a batch file. This usage is covered in Chapter 12.

%%

You can use dual percent signs to name the variable in a FOR loop when the FOR loop is used as part of a batch file. See Chapter 12.

%*variable*%

Percent signs surrounding a variable allow the value of that variable to be used in a batch file. This usage was covered in Chapter 13. This command doesn't work from the command line under DOS, but it does work from the command line in OS/2.

=

Use the single equal sign to assign values to environmental variables and to erase those values. This usage was covered in Chapter 13.

==

Dual equal signs are used in IF tests to test to see if two strings are equal. This usage will be covered in Chapter 16.

Special OS/2 Operators

OS/2 offers three very useful command-line operators that aren't available in DOS: &, &&, and ¦¦. The ampersand allows you to place two commands on the same line and have them both executed, so the command:

```
ECHO First Line & ECHO Second Line
```

is functionally equivalent to these two lines:

```
ECHO First Line
ECHO Second Line
```

The double ampersand is similar to the single ampersand, but the second command is executed only if the first command is successful. So the command:

```
ECHO First Line && ECHO Second Line
```

is equivalent to the previous two lines, but the second command in the following line:

```
DIR Z*.* && ECHO Z*.* Found
```

would execute only if the current subdirectory contained a file matching the Z*.* file specification.

The ¦¦ operator allows you to place two commands on the same line, where the second command is executed only if the first command fails. So, with the command:

```
DIR Z*.* ¦¦ ECHO Z*.* Not Found
```

only the first or second line would execute, but not both. If a file matching the Z*.* file specification exists, the first command would execute; otherwise, the second command would execute.

In order to display these symbols in an ECHO statement, they must be preceded with a caret. The batch file SHOWPIPE.CMD, following, illustrates using these commands in a batch file:

```
@ECHO OFF
ECHO Showing ^¦^¦ Command
ECHO Runs Command Only If Prior Command Failed
DIR A*.* ¦¦ ECHO No A*.* Files Found
DIR Z*.* ¦¦ ECHO No Z*.* Files Found
DIR ZQZ*.* ¦¦ ECHO No ZQZ*.* Files Found

ECHO Showing ^& Command
ECHO Runs One Command After Another On Same Line
ECHO 1 & ECHO 2 & ECHO 3 & ECHO 4 & ECHO 5

ECHO Showing ^&^& Command
ECHO Runs Another Command On Same Line
ECHO Only If First Successful
ECHO 1 && ECHO 2 && ECHO 3 && ECHO 4
```

I found that these three symbols didn't work consistently when used in conjunction with an IF test, so I don't recommend using them in that context.

Summary

- With piping, the operating system can get input from alternative sources and send output to alternative locations.

- The greater-than sign causes the operating system to pipe output to an alternative location. When that location is a file, the file is overwritten.

- Dual greater-than signs also cause the operating system to pipe output to an alternative location. When that location is a file, the file isn't overwritten.

- The less-than sign cause a program to obtain its input from an alternative location.

- The vertical bar causes the output of one program to be sent to another program without creating a permanent file.

- Devices that can be used as alternative sources for pipes include the console (CON), printer (LPT or PRN), serial port (COM), nothing (NUL), and a file.

- DOS and OS/2 include three filters for use with pipes: FIND for locating specific text, MORE for displaying text one screen at a time, and SORT for placing data in order.

- Improper use of piping can cause files to be overwritten.

- OS/2 has three unique operators. The ampersand allows you to enter two commands on one line and have both execute, the double ampersand allows you to enter two commands on one line and have the second execute only if the first is successful, and the double vertical bar allows you to enter two commands on one line and have the second execute only if the first fails.

16

Logic Testing

Basically, logic testing in a batch file means that you can specify a statement and then have the batch file react differently depending on whether the statement is true or false. The IF test allows a batch file to accomplish this. The basic syntax of the IF test is:

```
IF statement action
```

If the statement being tested is false, then the batch file will skip to the next line and continue processing. If the statement is true, then the batch file will process the rest of this line.

The *action* portion of the IF test can be a GOTO command. Using GOTO allows the batch file to take different paths through the batch file, and thus do different things, depending on the conditions the batch file finds while it's running. Logic testing can take the form of one of the following four questions:

- Are the two values the same?
- What is the errorlevel?
- Does a file exist?
- Does a subdirectory exist? (This is just a special case of testing to see if a file exists.)

When you compare two strings of characters, you can acquire these strings from several different sources: they could come from replaceable parameters or from the environment, or be hardwired into the batch file.

Are the Two Values the Same?

Batch files can only test to see if two character sets are the same; they cannot perform numeric calculations to see if two equations are equal. A set of characters is called a string, and comparing two strings is called a string comparison. The format of the IF test when used for string comparisons is:

```
IF string1==string2 action
```

where *string1* is the source of the first string, *string2* is the source of the second string, and *action* is the command to be formed when the two strings are the same. Notice that two equal signs are used, not one. If you forget and use a single equal sign, you'll get a "Syntax error" error message.

One of the strings in this comparison almost always comes from either a replaceable parameter or the environment, with replaceable parameters being by far the most common source. The other string is generally hardwired into the batch file. I generally place the replaceable parameter on the left side of the two equal signs and the hardwired value on the right side.

One of the things you'll use this for throughout the remainder of the book is to add help to batch files. You'll use /? to be consistent with MS-DOS 6, but let's look at a problem associated with using the older form of /H. When the user starts the batch file with an /H, you want to briefly display a help message and then have the user exit the batch file. You might think the command to do this is:

```
IF %1==/H GOTO HELP
```

and this indeed might work. However, it suffers from two problems—one minor and one more serious.

The minor problem is that string comparisons in a batch file are case-sensitive. Recall that a batch file simply replaces the replaceable parameters with the values entered on the command line. When the user starts this batch file with /H, the test becomes:

```
IF /H==/H GOTO HELP
```

which is true. However, when the user starts the batch file with /h, the test becomes:

```
IF /h==/H GOTO HELP
```

which is not true. The solution to this problem is to test for both possible values, so the test becomes:

```
IF %1==/H GOTO HELP
IF %1==/h GOTO HELP
```

In this case, if the user enters /H, the first test passes and the batch file jumps to the help section without ever reaching the second test. If the first test fails because the user enters /h, the batch file runs the second test and now finds the two strings equal, jumping to the help section. Of course, if the user enters some other replaceable parameter, both tests fail and the batch file continues without executing either GOTO command.

While it's not difficult to check different capitalizations for a single letter, it can become burdensome when multiple letters are involved. For example, if the first replaceable parameter was Daily, Weekly, or Monthly, then it would take nine IF tests to test for just the likely capitalization combinations of all lowercase, all uppercase, or first letter capitalized. The disk that comes with this book includes several utilities to deal with this. They're explored later in the book.

Also, recall from Chapter 10 that, when there's not a space between the batch file name and the slash on the command line, MS-DOS doesn't split the /H apart from the batch name. To make matters worse, DR DOS *will* split these apart, making it difficult to write batch files that run under both operating systems. You'll look at possible solutions to this problem when examining adding help in Chapter 18.

When you compare strings where one or both of the values comes from replaceable parameters, you'll have more problems dealing with the way a batch file treats replaceable parameters. Recall from Chapter 10 that everywhere you enter a %1 in the batch file, the batch file replaces it with the first replaceable parameter entered on the command line. Thus, if you have the test:

```
IF %1==/H GOTO HELP
```

and the user enters a replaceable parameter, then the test works properly, as shown earlier. Unfortunately, batch files aren't very smart in making these comparisons. When the user doesn't enter a replaceable parameter, the batch file substitutes nothing for %1 and the comparison becomes:

```
IF ==/H GOTO HELP
```

When this happens, the batch file thinks you left off part of the IF test and issues a "Syntax error" message. The solution to this minor dilemma is simple: surround the comparison with a set of symbols so the batch file will always compare something to something. I use parentheses. The advantage to surrounding both items to compare with a set of parentheses is that you allow a single test to compare the two strings, while avoiding any problems when one or even both of the strings in the comparison are empty. It even allows testing for an empty string because ()==() is a valid test. Thus, the command:

```
IF (%1)==() GOTO NONE
```

would successfully test for a blank first replaceable parameter and return the correct result. In addition to testing the replaceable parameters, you can use the same IF test to test environmental variables. The only difference is that the environmental variable must be surrounded by percent signs. So the IF test to see if the prompt is PG is this:

```
IF (%PROMPT%)==($P$G) ECHO Prompt Is $P$G
```

The percent signs around PROMPT tell the batch file to replace it with the value of the PROMPT environmental variable, so you don't need percent signs around the PG. Of course, like all other IF tests, this one is case-sensitive.

What Is the Errorlevel?

As you saw in Chapter 14, the errorlevel has room for only one byte, so only an ASCII value of 0 to 255 can be stored in it. Using the statement:

```
IF ERRORLEVEL #
```

a batch file can test the contents of errorlevel and make decisions based on that content. Unfortunately, the test isn't straightforward. The test IF ERRORLEVEL 5 doesn't test to see if the errorlevel is equal to 5, as you might expect from the section on string comparisons. Rather, it tests for an errorlevel of 5 or higher, so any number from 5 to 255 will result in a true response to this test.

Because the IF errorlevel test is a greater-than-or-equal test, you must always test from the highest possible errorlevel value to the lowest. In addition, you must branch away from the testing after the first match. CHECKERR.BAT is a batch file that tests for every possible errorlevel value and displays that value on the screen. A small segment of CHECKERR.BAT is shown here:

```
@ECHO OFF
IF ERRORLEVEL 255 ECHO 255
IF ERRORLEVEL 255 GOTO END
IF ERRORLEVEL 254 ECHO 254
IF ERRORLEVEL 254 GOTO END
IF ERRORLEVEL 253 ECHO 253
IF ERRORLEVEL 253 GOTO END

--and so on--
```

Notice how CHECKERR.BAT operates. It first tests for a value of 255. Because the maximum value of the errorlevel is 255, this first test is an equality test rather than the normal greater-than-or-equal test. If the value is 255, it displays that information and jumps to the end of the batch file. If the value is not 255, it tests for 254. The errorlevel is not 255 because the batch file has reached this point, so the normal greater-than-or-equal test again functions as an equality test. If the value is 254, it displays that value and jumps to the end of the batch file. If not, it tests for 253, 252, and so on down the line. By testing from the highest to the lowest possible value, you can avoid the problems associated with the greater-than-or-equal errorlevel test.

While CHECKERR.BAT is very long, most batch files can test every possible errorlevel value while remaining fairly short. None of the DOS or OS/2 commands has a possible errorlevel value higher than 10 or so. DOXCOPY.BAT follows. It performs an XCOPY and reports which errors it encountered. Notice that DOXCOPY.BAT tests for all possible errorlevel values from the XCOPY command, but is still fairly short.

```
@ECHO OFF
REM NAME:     DOXCOPY.BAT
REM PURPOSE: Run Xcopy Program And Report Errors
REM VERSION: 1.00
REM DATE:     May 16, 1992

XCOPY %1 %2 %3 %4 %5 %6 %7 %8 %9

IF ERRORLEVEL 5 GOTO 5
IF ERRORLEVEL 4 GOTO 4
IF ERRORLEVEL 2 GOTO 2
IF ERRORLEVEL 1 GOTO 1
GOTO 0

:0
   ECHO Normal Completion
GOTO END

:1
   ECHO No Files Found To Copy
GOTO END

:2
   ECHO User Pressed Ctrl-Break
GOTO END

:4
   ECHO Not Enough Memory
   ECHO Or Not Enough Disk Space
   ECHO Or Invalid Drive Specified
   ECHO Or Syntax Error
GOTO END

:5
   ECHO Disk Write Error
GOTO END

:END
```

Does a File Exist?

The third possible type of IF test tests to see if a file exists. The format for the command is:

```
IF EXIST filename action
```

so the command:

```
IF EXIST C:\AUTOEXEC.BAT ECHO AUTOEXEC.BAT File Exists
```

will check to see if an AUTOEXEC.BAT file exists in the root directory of the C drive and display a message if it does. The IF test has no problem testing to see if a file exists, even if the replaceable parameter used in the test doesn't have a value. Thus, the test:

```
IF EXIST %1 action
```

needs nothing special to protect it in case the user doesn't enter a replaceable parameter. If fact, putting the replaceable parameter inside parentheses would cause the test to always fail. The IF test can use wildcards, so:

```
IF EXIST C:\BAT\*.BAT ECHO Batch Files Found
```

would be true if at least one .BAT file existed in the C:\BAT subdirectory. If no path is specified in the IF EXIST test, it looks only for the file in the current subdirectory on the current drive. If you like, you can specify the full path to the file, as is the case in the earlier tests.

Does a Subdirectory Exist?

The EXIST command is not designed to check to see if a subdirectory exists, but there are two different tricks for dealing with that. First, the command:

```
IF EXIST C:\TESTSUB\*.*
```

will check for any file in C:\TESTSUB, and the test will pass only if the subdirectory exists. However, it won't pass if the subdirectory exists but is empty. If you modify this test slightly to:

```
IF EXIST C:\TESTSUB\NUL
```

the command will use the NUL device to test the subdirectory, where the test passes even if the subdirectory is empty.

Earlier Batch Files Revisited

Back in Chapter 10, you looked at three batch files: A.BAT, RONNYMD.BAT, and TOA.BAT. A.BAT worked fine, but the other two had problems. You've looked at TOA.BAT a couple of times since then, but it still has some problems. You now have enough tools to revisit these three files and put them into final form.

A.BAT

When you last examined A.BAT, it looked like this:

```
@ECHO OFF
REM NAME:    A.BAT
```

```
REM PURPOSE: Directory Of A Drive
REM VERSION: 1.00
REM DATE:    May 12, 1992

DIR A:%1 /P
```

This batch file runs fine, but you can make it better. You can add command-line help and, assuming that if the user enters a %2 then the user wants to specify the switches, you can leave off the /P. In writing the command-line help, assume the user will always enter a space between the name of the batch file and the switch; then you can ignore the problem mentioned in Chapter 10 of the /? being part of %0. The resulting version of TOA.BAT is as follows:

```
@ECHO OFF
REM NAME:    A.BAT
REM PURPOSE: Directory Of A Drive
REM VERSION: 2.00
REM DATE:    May 12, 1992

IF (%1)==(/?) GOTO HELP
IF (%2)==() DIR A:%1 /P
IF (%2)==() GOTO END

DIR A:%1 %2 %3 %4 %5

:HELP
  ECHO Performs A Directory Of The A Drive
  ECHO Allows You To Specify Files And Switches
  ECHO On The Command Line
GOTO END

:END
```

This new version has a line added at the top to jump to a help section if the user requests help, plus four lines to display that help. It has an IF test added to the front of the old DIR line, which it performs only when the user enters a single replaceable parameter. The next line exits the batch file if the user enters a single replaceable parameter. Finally, it performs a directory using five replaceable parameters. It reaches this point only if the user enters two or more replaceable parameters; if the user enters less than five, the extra ones in the batch file are ignored. A copy of this file can be found in either the \BAT-FILE\DOS\A\CHAP-16 or the \BAT-FILE\OS2\A\CHAP-16 subdirectories of the CD-ROM.

RONNYMD.BAT

When you last looked at RONNYMD.BAT, it appeared like this:

```
@ECHO OFF
REM NAME:    RONNYMD.BAT
REM PURPOSE: Make And Change To A Subdirectory
REM VERSION: 1.00
REM DATE:    May 12, 1992

MD %1
CD %1
```

The major problem with this batch file is that it doesn't confirm that the user entered the name of a subdirectory to create. A minor problem, which you can now completely solve, is that it also fails to check to see if the user specified a subdirectory that already exists.

Checking to see that the user entered a replaceable parameter is fairly easy. Checking to see if the subdirectory name the user specified already exists follows a technique shown earlier. The resulting, and final, version of RONNYMD.BAT is:

```
@ECHO OFF
REM NAME:     RONNYMD.BAT
REM PURPOSE: Make And Change To A Subdirectory
REM VERSION: 2.00
REM DATE:     May 12, 1992

IF (%1)==(/?)    ECHO Makes And Changes To A Subdirectory
IF (%1)==(/?)    GOTO END
IF (%1)==()      ECHO No Subdirectory Specified
IF (%1)==()      GOTO END
IF EXIST %1\NUL ECHO %1 Subdirectory Exists
IF EXIST %1\NUL GOTO END

MD %1
CD %1

:END
```

A copy of this file can be found in the \BAT-FILE\DOS\RONNYMD\CHAP-16 and \BAT-FILE\OS2\RONNYMD\CHAP-16 subdirectories of the included CD-ROM.

The most interesting aspect of this modified batch file is the way it handles help and errors. Rather than jumping to a special section, it uses two IF tests: the first displays a brief message and the second jumps to the end of the batch file. This approach works when your messages are short. When you need more than one or maybe two lines of messages, you're better off jumping to a special section to handle it.

TOA.BAT

When you last saw TOA.BAT back in Chapter 12, it looked like this:

```
@ECHO OFF
REM NAME:     TOA.BAT
REM PURPOSE: Copy .CMP And .DOC Files To The A Drive
REM          While Deleting .BAK Files
REM VERSION: 3.00
REM DATE:     May 12, 1992
:TOP
   DEL %1.BAK
   COPY %1.DOC A:
   COPY %1.CMP A:
   SHIFT
GOTO TOP
```

This batch file performs its assigned tasks of deleting .BAK files and then copying .DOC and .CMP files to the A drive for the first replaceable parameter. The SHIFT command then brings the next replaceable parameter into the %1 slot and the process is repeated. The one problem is that the batch file doesn't know when to stop. Even after using all the replaceable parameters, it continues trying to use nonexistent replaceable parameters to copy nonexistent files until the user presses Ctrl–Break.

Fixing TOA.BAT is as easy as adding two lines. First, it needs a label at the end of the batch file to jump to, and it needs an IF test to jump to the end label when the batch file runs out of replaceable parameters. The corrected version of TOA.BAT is shown next; a copy of this file can be found in the \BAT-FILE\DOS\TOA\CHAP-16 and \BAT-FILE\OS2\TOA\CHAP-16 subdirectories.

```
@ECHO OFF
REM NAME:     TOA.BAT
REM PURPOSE: Copy .CMP And .DOC Files To The A Drive
REM          While Deleting .BAK Files
REM VERSION: 4.00
REM DATE:    May 12, 1992

:TOP
   IF (%1)==() GOTO END
   DEL %1.BAK
   COPY %1.DOC A:
   COPY %1.CMP A:
   SHIFT
GOTO TOP

:END
```

The only thing missing is command-line help with the /? switch, which the CD-ROM version has. Notice that the batch file tests for a blank replaceable parameter at the top of the loop before any processing. That's important, in case the user starts the batch file without any replaceable parameters. If the logic testing were at the end and the user started the program without a replaceable parameter, the first journey through the loop would generate error messages.

Summary

- You can use the IF test to perform logic testing in a batch file.
- The IF test can test to see if two strings are the same, what the errorlevel is, or if a file exists.
- Batch file string comparisons are case-sensitive.
- In a string comparison, the variables on both sides of the dual equal signs should be surrounded by parentheses to avoid problems when one of the strings is empty.
- An IF test can test the errorlevel value, but the test is a greater-than-or-equal test and not an equality test.
- Because the IF test of the errorlevel is a greater-than-or-equal test, errorlevel tests must go from largest to smallest.
- The IF test can test to see if a single file, a group of files specified with a wildcard, or a subdirectory exists.
- You can add command-line help by either jumping to a special section to display the help or having an IF test display the help and a second IF test exit the batch file.

17

Review

You now know how to get information into a batch file from the command line, how to use that information in a batch file (no matter how much of it was entered on the command line), how to loop, and how to perform logic testing.

Take a few moments and try to work the following three problems out. If you get stuck, glance back through the last few chapters. You need to have the skills necessary to solve these problems before you continue through the book; otherwise, you'll run into difficulty. The answers to the problems are in Appendix A.

Problem 4

A friend of yours has a new computer. He's going away for the weekend, but he wants to run the computer continually while he's gone. He purchased a diagnostic program called Check-It-Out; the command to run the program is CHKITOUT. This program performs a complete diagnostic on the computer. It creates a file containing a full report and sets the errorlevel to 1 when it encounters a problem, but it doesn't display any information on the screen.

Your friend asks you to write him a batch file to run CHKITOUT continually. Each time CHKITOUT terminates with an errorlevel of 1, the batch file should display an error message on the screen.

Problem 5

Your boss is having problems with her computer. It has a C and a D drive, but sometimes she has to reboot the computer several times before the D drive is operational. She has found a utility program called BOOT.COM that reboots the computer, and she has asked you to write a batch file she can call from her AUTOEXEC.BAT file to reboot the computer if the D drive isn't operational. That way, the computer will automatically reboot itself until the D drive is operational.

Problem 6

You did such a good job on the last problem that your boss has asked you for another favor. It seems that she spends a lot of time on bulletin board systems and acquires a lot of ASCII files to read. Normally, she reads them with the command:

```
TYPE file | MORE
```

but the method is difficult when she has a lot of files to read. She has asked you for a batch file that loops through and displays all the files she specifies on the command line. She has also mentioned she's considering giving you a raise.

Chapter 18

Advanced Logic Testing

In Chapter 16, you began looking at logic testing in batch files, and saw that batch files could test for the following four conditions in a batch file:

- Whether or not two strings of characters are identical.
- What the errorlevel is.
- Whether or not a file exists.
- Whether or not a directory exists.

When you compare two strings of characters, you can acquire them from several different sources:

- Hardwired into the batch file.
- From replaceable parameters.
- From the environment.

In this chapter, you'll examine logic testing in even more detail. Included in this text is your first look at some of the utilities included on the CD-ROM that comes with this book. As you'll see, these utilities will make your batch files extremely powerful.

NOT

The NOT modifier reverses an IF test. If an IF EXIST test is true, then the corresponding IF NOT EXIST test is false. If an IF EXIST test is false, then the IF NOT EXIST test is true. For example, the batch file segment:

```
IF EXIST C:\AUTOEXEC.BAT ECHO AUTOEXEC.BAT Exists
IF NOT EXIST C:\AUTOEXEC.BAT ECHO AUTOEXEC.BAT Missing!
```

will tell users about their AUTOEXEC.BAT file whether or not it exists.

Interbatch Communications

You can have batch files communicate with each other by placing values into the environment. ACCOUNT1.BAT performs monthly closing, and CLOSE.EXE sets the errorlevel to show whether or not it ran without errors. ACCOUNT1.BAT needs to communicate that information to ACCOUNT2.BAT. It could depend on the errorlevel, but that could be reset if you ran another program in between the two batch files. To avoid that problem, ACCOUNT1.BAT places a value into the environment. The portion of ACCOUNT1.BAT that handles running the closing program and creating the environmental variable is shown here:

```
CLOSE
IF ERRORLEVEL 1 SET ACCOUNT=NO
IF ERRORLEVEL 1 GOTO END
IF ERRORLEVEL 0 SET ACCOUNT=YES
```

ACCOUNT2.BAT then checks for that value and won't run without a correct setting. The portion of ACCOUNT2.BAT that handles this is shown next:

```
IF (%ACCOUNT%)==() GOTO ERROR
IF (%ACCOUNT%)==(NO) GOTO NO
CLOSE2
GOTO END

:ERROR
  ECHO Run Account1 First
  PAUSE
  GOTO END

:NO
  ECHO Warning: Close Did Not Run Successfully
  ECHO Fix These Errors Before Running Account2
  PAUSE
  GOTO END

:END
SET ACCOUNT=
```

Capitalization is not a problem here because ACCOUNT1.BAT always creates the variables in uppercase. Also note that ACCOUNT2.BAT resets the ACCOUNT environmental variable after running, which keeps ACCOUNT2.BAT from being run twice.

A logical question is "Why didn't CLOSE.EXE set the information into the environment itself?" Well, each program is passed a copy of the environment when it starts. When the program terminates, that copy of the environment is erased. So CLOSE.EXE couldn't set the environment directly because those changes would have been lost when CLOSE.EXE terminated. The errorlevel isn't stored in the environment, so it isn't lost when CLOSE.EXE terminates.

Capitalization

Managing capitalization in batch files is a real pain. As I said in Chapter 16, just testing for the likely capitalization of three possible replaceable parameters—Daily,

Monthly, and Annual—takes nine IF tests. That means the code to handle just the most likely types of capitalization takes up nine lines, where three would work if capitalization weren't a problem.

Even this elaborate scheme, however, won't respond properly to replaceable parameters such as DAIly. There are a number of ways of dealing with the capitalization problem quickly without a lot of extra code. Each method has unique advantages, so we'll look at each in more detail.

GOTO %1

The first way to avoid the capitalization problem is to use a replaceable parameter as a label for the GOTO command, because labels are case-insensitive. Keep in mind that a batch file always replaces replaceable parameters with their value. Take a look at this batch file segment:

```
GOTO %1

:DAILY
    DAILY
GOTO END

:MONTHLY
    MONTHLY
GOTO END

:ANNUAL
    ANNUAL
GOTO END

:END
```

If you run the batch file with the following command line:

```
BATCH daily
```

the batch file will replace the line GOTO %1 with GOTO daily and the batch file will run properly, no matter what capitalization you use. This method is, however, only a partial solution. If the user starts the batch file with an invalid parameter, yearly, for example, the batch file will abort on the GOTO yearly line with a "Label not found" or similar error message. Because the batch file stops working after a GOTO %1 command if the specified label doesn't exist, no commands are necessary under GOTO %1 other than the sections that are being jumped.

While there's no absolute protection against invalid labels when using this approach, there is partial protection. Each section can use multiple labels with all the labels the user is likely to use. For example, the Annual section might look like this:

```
:ANNUAL
:ANNUALLY
:YEAR
:YEARLY
:ENDOFYEAR
    ANNUAL
    GOTO END
```

This helps prevent the "Label not found" message by putting as many possible labels in the batch file as the user is likely to use. Because label lines aren't executed, having the batch file jump to the :ANNUAL or :ENDOFYEAR line has the same effect on the execution of the batch file.

Environmental variables

A second method is to store the selected option in the environment as an environmental variable. The next batch file segment illustrates this:

```
SET DAILY=
SET MONTHLY=
SET ANNUAL=
SET %1=YES

IF %DAILY%==YES GOTO DAILY
IF %MONTHLY%==YES GOTO MONTHLY
IF %ANNUAL%==YES GOTO ANNUAL
GOTO ERROR

:DAILY
   DAILY
GOTO END

:MONTHLY
    MONTHLY
GOTO END

:ANNUAL
    ANNUAL
GOTO END

 :ERROR
  ECHO You Entered An Invalid Parameter
GOTO END

 :END
```

Each possible environmental is deleted and then the line SET %1=YES creates a single environmental variable with the name of the replaceable parameter and a value of YES.

This method works well for most replaceable parameters and avoids the missing label problem associated with the GOTO %1 method, but it has a minor problem of its own. If the replaceable parameter the user enters can be a number, the batch file will end up making unexpected tests. Suppose you wanted to run Lotus 1-2-3 and the user could be expected to use 123 as a replaceable parameter. The SET %1=YES line would work properly. In order to run Lotus, you'd need a test line of IF %123%==YES, but the batch file would translate the %1 portion of this test as the first replaceable parameter. This is, however, a fairly minor problem that you can usually avoid by restricting the user from using keywords that begin with a number.

The path (DOS only)

The path is the only environmental variable DOS converts to uppercase. You can use this to convert a replaceable parameter to uppercase by performing the following steps:

1. Store the current path under another variable name.

2. Set the path equal to the replaceable parameter. Note that you must use a PATH= statement and not SET PATH= because DOS won't convert the path to uppercase using the SET PATH= method.

3. Store the replaceable parameter now stored under the path to another variable name.

4. Restore the proper path using the holding variable created in step 1.

5. Clear out the holding variable created in step 1.

The following batch file segment illustrates this:

```
SET OLDPATH=%PATH%
PATH=%1
SET VARIABLE=%PATH%
PATH=%OLDPATH%
SET OLDPATH=
IF (%VARIABLE%)==(DAILY)    GOTO DAILY
IF (%VARIABLE%)==(MONTHLY)  GOTO MONTHLY
IF (%VARIABLE%)==(ANNUAL)   GOTO ANNUAL
GOTO ERROR
```

This method handles all possible inputs without problem, but requires the most environmental space; you must store the path under a different name before you store the replaceable parameter to the path variable, so at this point DOS must store two versions of the path in environmental memory at once. Since most paths are long, this takes a lot of memory.

Running a program

I became so frustrated trying to deal with capitalization that I wrote a program to deal with this problem. As you'll see, the REXX language made this easy for OS/2. Just about any user could easily learn REXX well enough to write simple utilities like this. REXX is included free with OS/2. The DOS program was written using Builder Lite. The Builder Lite language is available on a disk accompanying the book *Builder Lite: Developing Dynamic Batch Files* from McGraw-Hill.

OS/2's REXX

OS/2 includes an advanced and very powerful batch-like language called REXX. Chapter 32 provides you with an introduction to the power of REXX and my *Writing OS/2 REXX Programs* book, also available from McGraw-Hill, covers it in detail. The only thing of interest for this book, however, is that REXX lets you write utilities to overcome the limitations of the OS/2 batch language.

Don't worry; you don't have to write REXX programs or even understand them. In fact, I'm not even going to show you a listing of the REXX programs in this chapter. I've already written the programs so all you need to know is how to use them. You'll find all the programs on the CD-ROM that comes with this book.

In order to use these utility programs, they need to be in a subdirectory that's in your path. On my system, I created a special \REXX subdirectory and added it to my path.

If you had a program called BatUtil that you wanted to run as part of a batch file, you'd just need to add the command BATUTIL to a line by itself in your batch file. That works with programs, but REXX programs aren't really programs. Rather, they're a cross between programs and batch files. If you have a REXX program called BAT-UTIL.CMD, you must run it with the command CALL BATUTIL. Other than that, they run just like other programs. You'll see more about the CALL command in Chapter 22.

CAPITAL.CMD

CAPITAL.CMD is a REXX program that takes a single word as an input, converts it to all uppercase, and stores the results in the environment under the environmental variable name RETURN. CAPITAL.CMD is able to do this because REXX programs work with the master copy of the environment rather than being passed a copy of the environment by OS/2 like other programs.

CAPITAL.CMD works on only one word at a time. Send it more than one word, and it ignores everything after the first word. This is true even if everything is enclosed inside quotation marks. Since filenames are case-insensitive, CAPITAL.CMD doesn't need to be compatible with them. The next batch file segment illustrates using CAPITAL:

```
CALL CAPITAL %1
IF (%RETURN%)==(DAILY)    GOTO DAILY
IF (%RETURN%)==(MONTHLY)  GOTO MONTHLY
IF (%RETURN%)==(ANNUAL)   GOTO ANNUAL
GOTO ERROR
```

Of course, somewhere near the end of the batch file you'd want a SET RETURN= command to reset this variable once you no longer needed it.

DOS's Builder Lite

CAPITAL.EXE is a Builder Lite program that takes a single word as an input, converts it to all uppercase, and stores the results in the environment under the environmental variable name RONNY. Before you use this program, a couple of notes are in order.

Normally, a program like CAPITAL doesn't have access to the master copy of the environment, so if CAPITAL were to just place the results in its copy of the environment, that information would be lost as soon as CAPITAL terminated. That is clearly not what you want. The only remaining "usual" way to pass the information back to the batch file is via the errorlevel, but that value is limited to one byte. CAPITAL avoids the problem by searching through the computer's memory to find the master copy of the environment. It then makes its changes there. This is the same approach taken by most batch utilities that work with the environment.

Since CAPITAL expects to store the results in the environment, it won't be able to run if there isn't enough free environmental space. Also, CAPITAL works on only one word at a time. Send it more than one word, and it will abort and display an error message. The next batch file segment illustrates using CAPITAL:

```
CAPITAL %1
IF (%RONNY%)==(DAILY)    GOTO DAILY
IF (%RONNY%)==(MONTHLY)  GOTO MONTHLY
IF (%RONNY%)==(ANNUAL)   GOTO ANNUAL
GOTO ERROR
```

Of course, somewhere near the end of the batch file you'd want a SET RONNY= command to reset this variable once you no longer needed it.

Capitalization conclusion

Each of these approaches has good and bad points. The one you select really depends on your needs. However, I find that most of my batch files can be written using either the GOTO %1 or CAPITAL.CMD/CAPITAL.EXE approach. I use GOTO %1 when I have a lot of possible labels, and CAPITAL when there are fewer labels.

Multiple IF Tests

You can combine several IF tests to handle a complex decision or to help overcome the case problem associated with string comparisons. The format of a two-deep multiple IF test is:

```
IF statement IF statement2 action
```

When the first IF test fails, control flows to the next line in the batch file as it normally would. When the first IF statement is true, control passes to the remainder of the command, only in this case the remainder of the command is another IF test. If the second IF test fails, control flows to the next line in the batch file, but if the second IF test is true the *action* command is executed. So each IF test acts as a gate, and the *action* is executed only when every IF test before it is true. If just one of the IF tests is false, the entire test will fail and the *action* won't be executed.

A batch file doesn't place a direct limit on the number of IF tests you can combine in this fashion. You can use three or four or even five if you like. However, the command must be shorter than the limit the operating system places on the command line. In addition, the logic must clear enough that the batch file author and anyone who later needs to maintain the batch file can understand it.

Novell DOS 7

Novell DOS 7 offers several IF test advancements. It can recognize both = and == as a valid operator in the IF test. This eliminates a major source of syntax errors. It also allows you to more easily combine multiple IF tests with the AND operator. For example, the MS-DOS test of:

```
IF (%1)==(1) IF (%2)==(2) IF (%3)==(3) ECHO 1 2 3 Entered
```

can be replaced with the more logical:

```
IF (%1)==(1) AND (%2)==(2) AND (%3)==(3) ECHO 1 2 3 Entered
```

When combined with the first change, this can be written even more succinctly as:

```
IF (%1)=(1) AND (%2)=(2) AND (%3)=(3) ECHO 1 2 3 Entered
```

In addition to the AND operator, the OR operator is supported, making testing for different capitalizations easier. For example, %1 could be checked for a value of Ronny with the following:

```
IF (%1)=(Ronny) OR (%1)=(ronny) OR (%1)==(RONNY) GOTO OKAY
```

which is much easier than using three different IF tests, one per each capitalization. It also executes more quickly. The LOGIC-N7.BAT batch file illustrates this in a simple example. Its operational code is as follows, and the batch file is included on the CD-ROM that comes with this book:

```
@ECHO OFF
IF (%1)=(1) OR (%2)=(1) OR (%3)=(1) ECHO At Least One Parameter
 (%%1-%%3) Is 1
IF (%1)=(1) AND (%2)=(1) AND (%3)=(1) ECHO All Parameters (%%1-%%3)
 Are 1
GOTO END
```

A Short Way to Show the Errorlevel

Consider the following example:

```
IF ERRORLEVEL 3 IF NOT ERRORLEVEL 4 ECHO Errorlevel Is 3
```

Three conditions are possible: the errorlevel is less than 3, the errorlevel is greater than 3, or the errorlevel equals 3. When the errorlevel is less than 3, the first IF test fails and the batch file moves on to the next line. When the errorlevel is greater than 3, the first IF test passes. When an IF test passes, the batch file executes the remainder of the line, which in this case contains another IF test. For this second IF test, the test IF ERRORLEVEL 4 is true, but the NOT modifier changes the results to false. Thus, the second IF test fails and the batch file continues on to the next line.

When the errorlevel is equal to 3, the first IF test passes and again the batch file moves on to the remainder of the IF test. In this case, the test IF ERRORLEVEL 4 is false because the errorlevel is 3, so this test fails. However, the NOT modifier changes the results to true. Having passed both IF tests, the batch file moves on the next portion of the line and displays the errorlevel value. In general, the IF test:

```
IF ERRORLEVEL n IF NOT ERRORLEVEL n+1 action
```

is true only for an errorlevel value of exactly n. Take a look at CHECKER1.BAT, a brief segment of which follows (this batch file takes advantage of these multiple IF tests to considerably reduce the number of lines needed to display all possible errorlevel values over CHECKERR.BAT in Chapter 16):

```
IF ERRORLEVEL 255                       ECHO 255
IF ERRORLEVEL 254 IF NOT ERRORLEVEL 255 ECHO 254
IF ERRORLEVEL 253 IF NOT ERRORLEVEL 254 ECHO 253
IF ERRORLEVEL 252 IF NOT ERRORLEVEL 253 ECHO 252
--and so on--
```

While CHECKER1.BAT is shorter, it takes much longer to run, especially when the errorlevel is a high number. When CHECKERR.BAT processes a high errorlevel number, say 250, it has to go through only a few IF tests before it finds a match. For a value of 250, it would go through 12 IF tests before jumping out of the batch file. However, for each errorlevel value, CHECKER1.BAT processes all 255 of the first IF tests. In addition, it processes the second IF test for all errorlevel tests with test values lower than the errorlevel value. That is, for errorlevel test values of 0 to 250, CHECKER1.BAT must move on to the second IF test because the first is true. For 250, CHECKER1.BAT would end up processing 305 IF tests rather than the 12 CHECKERR.BAT required, and so run more slowly.

A Shorter Way to Show the Errorlevel (DOS Only)

While writing my *Dr. Batch File's Ultimate Collection* book, I developed an extremely short and fast batch file for displaying the errorlevel. I've found it so useful that I keep it in my utility subdirectory and find myself using it all the time. Because it's so useful, I want to share it with you now.

An easier way to find the errorlevel is to test each of the three digits individually. First, find out if the left digit is a 0, 1, or 2. This takes only one FOR loop. The next batch file segment does this:

```
FOR %%J IN (0 1 2) DO IF ERRORLEVEL %%J00 SET ERROR=%%J
ECHO Left Digit Was %ERROR%
```

In addition to displaying the left digit, it also stores it in the environment under the environmental variable name ERROR. That is required for the remaining steps. The next step is to find out if the middle digit is from 0 to 9, which also takes only one FOR loop. The following batch file segment does this:

```
FOR %%J IN (0 1 2 3 4 5 6 7 8 9) DO IF ERRORLEVEL
 %ERROR%%%J0 SET ERROR=%ERROR%%%J
ECHO Left Two Digits Are %ERROR%
```

(Please note that the first line had to be continued, with the continuation line indented one space, due to the width of the page.) The variable ERROR is being built as you go, from left to right. The right portion of the first line might look confusing, but DOS interprets it properly. Let's look at this line in more detail:

FOR %%J IN (0 1 2 3 4 5 6 7 8 9) DO. This is the typical beginning of a FOR loop, which causes it to loop through the numbers 0 to 9.

IF ERRORLEVEL. This specifies that, for each FOR loop, an IF test on the errorlevel value will be performed.

%ERROR%. This is replaced by the environmental variable value, which is the left digit of the errorlevel value—usually a 0.

%%J. This is replaced by the value of the loop counter variable on each loop.

0. Because you're testing for the middle variable, a place holder for the last variable is needed. Zero is the smallest value, so it's used.

SET ERROR=. When the test passes, the value of the test is stored in the environment.

%ERROR%%%J. When the value is stored to the environment because the IF test passed, %ERROR is replaced by the current value of the left digit stored in the environment, and %%J is replaced by the loop counter value. Testing for the right digit works the same way. The next batch file segment does this:

```
FOR %%J IN (0 1 2 3 4 5 6 7 8 9) DO IF ERRORLEVEL
 %ERROR%%%J SET ERROR=%ERROR%%%J
ECHO ERRORLEVEL is %ERROR%
```

(Note that the first line had to be continued due to the amount of material and width of the page.) The FOR loop in this batch file works much like the previous one. This method works properly for errorlevel values from 0 to 199, but there's a problem for errorlevel values 200 and over. There are no restrictions in the batch file, so when the first digit is a 2, the remaining segments end up testing for values 256 to 299. The maximum errorlevel value is 255 and DOS doesn't handle tests above 255 properly, so we need some complex branching.

If the first digit is a 2, the batch file must branch to a separate test to make sure the test on the second digit doesn't exceed 5. If the second digit is a 5, it must branch again to make sure the test on the final digit doesn't exceed a 5. That way, the batch file never tests for an errorlevel greater than 255. In addition, there's no advantage in using separate batch files for each digit, so all three batch files can be combined into one. The resulting batch file is SAYERROR.BAT, and the operational code for it is as follows:

```
@ECHO OFF
SET ERROR=
FOR %%J IN (0 1 2) DO IF ERRORLEVEL %%J00 SET ERROR=%%J
IF %ERROR%==2 GOTO 2
IF %ERROR%==0 SET ERROR=
FOR %%J IN (0 1 2 3 4 5 6 7 8 9) DO IF ERRORLEVEL
 %ERROR%%%J0 SET ERROR=%ERROR%%%J
IF %ERROR%==0 SET ERROR=
```

```
FOR %%J IN (0 1 2 3 4 5 6 7 8 9) DO IF ERRORLEVEL
 %ERROR%%%J SET ERROR=%ERROR%%%J
GOTO END

:2
FOR %%J IN (0 1 2 3 4 5) DO IF ERRORLEVEL %ERROR%%%J0
 SET ERROR=%ERROR%%%J
IF %ERROR%==25 GOTO 25
FOR %%J IN (0 1 2 3 4 5 6 7 8 9) DO IF ERRORLEVEL %ERROR%%%J
 SET ERROR=%ERROR%%%J
GOTO END

:25
FOR %%J IN (0 1 2 3 4 5) DO IF ERRORLEVEL %ERROR%%%J
 SET ERROR=%ERROR%%%J
GOTO END

:END
ECHO Errorlevel Is %ERROR%
```

(Again, please note that several lines in this batch file had to be continued, with the continuation lines indented one space. Although there would normally be indents elsewhere in the batch file, they've been left out for clarity's sake.)

SAYERROR.BAT quickly tests the errorlevel values. The test takes under a second for every errorlevel value. In addition to displaying the errorlevel value, SAYERROR.BAT also stores the value in the environment under the name ERROR, which allows you to retain the errorlevel value while running another program. It also makes testing on the errorlevel value much easier. While the usual errorlevel test of IF ERRORLEVEL n is a greater-than-or-equal test, the test IF %ERROR%==n is an equality test. This reduces the number of IF statements required to test for any value in half.

This batch file won't work under OS/2, even if you rename it to SAYERROR.CMD. The reason for this is that the FOR internal command resets the errorlevel under OS/2, so SAYERROR.CMD always reports an errorlevel of zero.

Setting the Errorlevel (DOS)

Testing the errorlevel value can be difficult. When I first started working with errorlevel IF tests, I did things like using XCOPY and leaving the drive open to force an errorlevel value into DOS. Then I received my copy of Batcmd. Batcmd is a program designed to be run from inside a batch file. The general format of the command is:

```
BATCMD keyword [prompt]
```

where *keyword* is a two-letter command abbreviation that tells Batcmd what to do and *prompt* is an optional message to tell the user what information to enter. I'll talk about Batcmd in more detail in Chapter 38. One of Batcmd's nicer features is its ability to force any value into the errorlevel. The command to do that is:

```
BATCMD EX number
```

where *number* is a number from 0 to 255 to be forced into the errorlevel. Being able to force any value, 0 to 255, into the errorlevel makes it easy to test batch files. It's also handy for resetting the errorlevel after an XCOPY or other command has failed and stored a value in the errorlevel. A copy of Batcmd is included on the CD-ROM that comes with this book.

Setting the Errorlevel (OS/2)

The SETERROR.CMD REXX program that comes with this book will set the errorlevel to any value you like, from 0 to 255. Just start the program with the number to set the errorlevel to as a replaceable parameter.

Help

Back in Chapter 16, I hinted at batch file help while exploring the capitalization problem associated with IF test string comparisons. Now's the time to look at batch file help in more detail.

Beginning with version 5, MS-DOS allowed you to get quick summary information about most programs by running the program with a /? switch. When you do this, the program displays summary information and then exits to the command line without doing anything other than displaying help. That way, you can read about a program without having to run it. You can add this to batch files. The general format in pseudocode is:

If the user requested help
   Display the help information
   Exit the batch file

The second and third lines of the pseudocode are easy. You display help information using a series of ECHO commands and you exit the batch file by having a line labeled :END at the end of the batch file and using a GOTO End command.

There are basically two ways a user can run a batch file and request help: BATCH/? and BATCH /?. If you're running DR DOS 5 or 6 exclusively, then you don't have a problem because DR DOS 5 and 6 will automatically split the batch file name from the switch, so %0 would be BATCH and %1 would be /?, no matter which way the user entered the information. However, MS-DOS doesn't do this. If you run BATCH/? under any version of MS-DOS, then %0 is BATCH/? and %1 is empty.

So running a batch file called BATCH.BAT under MS-DOS and checking for a /? switch requires the following to test for just the most likely types of capitalization:

```
IF (%1)==(/?) GOTO HELP
IF %0==BATCH/? GOTO HELP
IF %0==batch/? GOTO HELP
IF %0==Batch/? GOTO HELP
```

And even this won't catch unusual types of capitalization. Note that I didn't use parentheses around %0. I omitted them because %0 always has a value.

To avoid this problem, I wrote the program NEEDHELP.EXE for DOS using Builder Lite. It's on the CD-ROM that comes with this book. To use NeedHelp, just pass it your %0 and %1 variables with a space between them. It checks to see if the %1 variable or the last two characters of %0 are /?. If so, it sets the errorlevel to 1; otherwise, it sets it to 0. In other words, an errorlevel of one indicates that the user requested help, while an errorlevel of zero indicates that the user didn't request help.

If you don't pass NeedHelp a parameter, it sets the errorlevel to 255. It does this because %0 always exists, so not receiving a parameter means you made an error. It doesn't object to only one parameter because %1 might not have a value.

To use NeedHelp, place these following lines near the top of your batch file:

```
NEEDHELP %0 %1
IF ERRORLEVEL 1 GOTO HELP
```

Now your batch files will work the same under MS-DOS as they do under DR DOS, without you having to worry about how the specific operating system handles command-line switches. You also no longer have to worry about the capitalization of the batch file name.

NEEDHELP.CMD is a REXX program that performs the exact same function in the same manner under OS/2. That way, you can write your batch files the same way under DOS and OS/2 and they'll work the same.

Don't use NeedHelp (either version) in any batch file that depends on the errorlevel being set when it starts running, because NeedHelp resets the errorlevel. When I first wrote NeedHelp, I added it to all the batch files I included with one of my books—including SAYERROR.BAT. Since NeedHelp resets the errorlevel, that version of SAYERROR.BAT always reported an errorlevel of zero!

This warning holds true for any batch file utility, not just NeedHelp. If your batch file depends on the errorlevel being set when it starts, don't run any program until the batch file is finished using the preset errorlevel value.

Summary

- The NOT modifier reverses the decision of any IF test.
- By creating environmental variables, batch files can communicate with each other, even when there's a time lapse between each of them running.
- One way to deal with the capitalization of replaceable parameters is with a GOTO %1 command.
- When using GOTO %1 to deal with the capitalization of replaceable parameters, the batch file bombs if the label doesn't exist. You can reduce the chance of this happening by using multiple labels.
- Another way to deal with the capitalization of replaceable parameters is by creating an environmental variable with the name of the replaceable parameter, because environmental variable names are always converted to uppercase.
- A third way to deal with the capitalization of replaceable parameters under DOS is to temporarily store the replaceable parameter to the path because the path is converted to uppercase.

- A final way to deal with the capitalization of replaceable parameters is to run the CAPITAL program included on the CD-ROM that comes with this book.

- When multiple IF tests are combined on a single line, the *action* command isn't executed unless all the IF tests are true. When multiple IF tests are combined, their length must not exceed 127 characters.

- Novell DOS 7 supports the AND and OR operators in IF tests. It will also treat the = operator the same as the == operator, eliminating a common source of syntax errors.

- The SAYERROR.BAT batch file on the CD-ROM that comes with this book quickly displays the errorlevel as well as storing it to the environment under the name ERROR.

- The Batcmd program on the CD-ROM that comes with this book allows you to set the errorlevel to any value from 0 to 255 under DOS. SETERROR.CMD provides the same function under OS/2.

- The NeedHelp program on the CD-ROM that comes with this book checks to see if the user requested help using the same commands under DOS. NEEDHELP.CMD provides the same function under OS/2.

19

An Advanced Way to Get Information from Users

The errorlevel is one of the most useful items available to batch file authors, yet it's also one of the least used. Part of the reason it's avoided is because of its idiotic name, which tells the user nothing about what it actually does and probably scares off a lot of potential users. In fact, the OS/2 documentation usually refers to it as a *return code* rather than the errorlevel. The other reason it's rarely used is that, prior to MS-DOS 6, MS-DOS didn't give you any tools to take advantage of the errorlevel.

So far, you've seen only two ways to get information from the user: replaceable parameters and Ctrl–Break. With replaceable parameters, users must remember the questions in advance, before running the batch file, in order to enter that information on the command line. That's asking for a lot! I have trouble remembering which batch file I need to run, much less what questions they're going to ask me. And the questions often change each time the batch file runs. "Do you really want to delete these files?" can take a lot of different meanings depending on which files you're referring to.

Pausing the batch file and asking the user to press either any key to continue or Ctrl–Break to stop is one way of getting a yes/no response. It's inelegant, but it works. However, because the batch file stops in response to a Ctrl–Break, it can't perform any other tasks if the user wants to stop the operation.

All in all, the tools that MS-DOS 5 and earlier give you to query the user are a pretty sorry lot, but utility programs can overcome this problem. In this chapter, you'll look at the utility programs that are native to the various operating systems, and in Chapter 34 you'll review stand-alone utilities to perform the same function. Keep in mind that a number of the utility sets in Chapter 38 also offer this function.

MS-DOS 6 includes CHOICE.COM, a small "errorlevel asker" program (a term I coined in my *Batch File Utilities* book to describe programs that ask the user to select a single-character response in a batch file and then make that response available to the batch file via the errorlevel).

Novell DOS 7 and PC DOS 6.2 also include a version of CHOICE that has the same syntax as the MS-DOS 6 version. Just like the MS-DOS version, these are external programs rather than internal commands. The format for using the CHOICE command is:

```
CHOICE [/C[:keys]] [/N] [/S] [/T[:default,time]] [prompt]
```

The /C, when used by itself, causes the user to select between a Y and an N. You can have the user select between any keys you like by listing the keystrokes to accept. They should be bunched together without anything between them, and capitalization doesn't matter unless you use the /S.

The /N will cause CHOICE to not display the valid keys, but the prompt is still displayed. This might be useful for prompting for a password. The /S will cause CHOICE to be case-sensitive. By default, CHOICE ignores case and treats a and A equally. That saves you the trouble of having to deal with capitalization. The only time you should need this option is when you want the user to select more than 36 options (26 letters and 0 to 9).

The /T specifies a time for CHOICE to wait for users to press a key and a default key to use if they don't make a selection in the allowed time. The time is specified in seconds, with a value of 0 to 99.

When you run CHOICE, it shows the prompt you specify followed by a list of allowable characters inside square brackets and separated with commas—unless you use the /N switch, in which case it shows only the prompt. Since the allowable characters are listed after the prompt, you should always end your prompt with a space. Additionally, if you load ANSI.SYS in your CONFIG.SYS file, the prompt can contain the ANSI escape sequences discussed in Chapter 20.

When the user makes an invalid selection, one that isn't on the list of allowed characters, CHOICE just beeps and continues waiting for an allowable character. Once an allowable character has been selected, CHOICE sets the errorlevel to indicate the position of the character in the allowable list. The first character gets an errorlevel of 1, the second 2, and so on.

So you can see CHOICE in action, the CD-ROM contains a demonstration batch file called PICKDEMO.BAT. Just run it and it will show you some of the power of CHOICE. Just remember that this demonstration requires a version of DOS containing CHOICE.

OS/2 doesn't include any utilities to ask the user questions in a batch file. However, several of these tools, discussed in Chapter 32, are included on the CD-ROM. These tools were written in REXX, the native programming environment for OS/2, but you don't have to know anything about REXX or programming to use them.

Summary

The CHOICE command lets you get information from the user and place it in the errorlevel. CHOICE accepts a prompt and list of acceptable characters and, when run, requires the user to enter one of these acceptable characters. Unless a special switch is used, CHOICE is case-insensitive. There are also switches to hide the list of acceptable characters and to cause CHOICE to make a default selection after 0 to 99 seconds.

20

Advanced Screen Design I

The main tool for displaying messages in a batch file is a series of ECHO commands, which works well for a few messages, but soon gets old if your batch file has to display a lot of information. Fortunately, you have several alternatives. You can:

- Create a text file and use the TYPE command to send that file to the screen
- Write a custom program
- Use a screen compiler
- Use ANSI

Creating a Text File

Probably the easiest way to quickly display a screen of information is to use an editor or your word processor to create each screen as a separate ASCII file. That way, you can add blank lines where you want them, center text, and otherwise visually arrange the elements on the screen. Once the files look the way you want, just type them to the screen from your batch file. Of course, you'll need a PAUSE command between each screen. Using this method, a batch file might look like this:

```
@ECHO OFF
TYPE C:\TEXT\INTRO.TXT
PAUSE
TYPE C:\TEXT\SCREEN1.TXT
PAUSE
TYPE C:\TEXT\SCREEN2.TXT
PAUSE
```

Notice that this batch file segment specifies the full path to each text file. Because batch files are usually designed to run from anywhere on your hard disk, you can't depend on the batch file and the associated text files being in the same subdirectory from which the batch file is executed.

This method is easier than a series of ECHO commands, but it has several drawbacks. One is simply remembering to send copies of all the associated text files when you send someone a copy of the batch file. A second drawback is that anyone who wants to run your batch file must have a subdirectory of the same name you used to store your text files and must copy the text files to that subdirectory. That's a lot to expect users to do. Of course, you could write a batch file to install the batch file. Finally, this method doesn't allow you to control the screen color.

Writing a Program

You can also display text by using a high-level programming language. Writing high-level programs to display text is beyond the scope of this book, however, so I won't cover it in any detail. Most high-level programs compile to an executable .EXE file, so all you have to do to display the text is include the name of the .EXE file in a batch file. In addition, most high-level languages can control the screen color and execute very quickly.

This approach means you don't need a specific directory in which to store the file. As long as the resulting screen is anywhere in the path, it will execute whenever the batch file issues the command to run the program. However, while you've solved one problem, you've introduced another—namely the programming tools and abilities this approach requires, which many readers lack.

Using a Screen Compiler

It would be nice to have a method of creating screen display programs as nice as those you can create with a programming language, without having to buy a programming language and learning to use it. Well, the CD-ROM that comes with this book has just that (in the \UTILITY\DOS\BATSCREN subdirectory). It contains a screen compiler called BatScreen. BatScreen was written especially for this book by Doug Amaral of hyperkinetix, the makers of the Builder batch file compiler. The BatScreen screen compiler combines the ease of creating an ASCII file with the power of writing a program.

BatScreen takes an ASCII text file and converts it to a small .COM file. When you enter the name of the .COM file at the command-line prompt or in a batch file, the file will flash up on the screen almost immediately.

To run BatScreen, first create the screen with any ASCII editor. Arrange the text in the file the way you want it to appear on the screen. Feel free to use high-order ASCII characters. Once the screen is ready, change to the subdirectory containing the ASCII file and enter BS at the command-line prompt. BatScreen will present a screen showing all the nonblinking color choices, with a box around the currently selected color combination. Use the cursor to select the color combination you want. If you want the text to blink, press PgDn to select from the blinking text in the same fashion.

Next, BatScreen will prompt you for the name of an ASCII file. To completely fill the screen, the ASCII file should contain 80 columns and 24 rows. If the file is larger, BatScreen will ignore the extra. Finally, BatScreen will ask you if you want to clear the screen when the program displays. If you answer Yes, the .COM file will clear the entire screen, set it to the colors you selected, and display the contents of the ASCII file. If you answer No, the .COM file will clear off only enough lines to display the message. Using blinking text and not clearing the screen is perfect for error messages and other occasions where you want to grab the user's attention. Full-screen solid colors are great for menus and general-purpose text.

The original ASCII file isn't modified and doesn't need to be present for the .COM file to operate, so you can modify and recompile it if you ever need to change the screen. Additionally, once you've created the .COM file, you don't need BatScreen to display the screen.

BatScreen makes excellent menus. You can also use it to display a blank screen just to reset the screen colors, and display warning messages in bright or unusual colors. After you try out BatScreen, I'm sure you'll agree that Doug has produced an excellent tool for batch file menus and screens. In fact, I use it almost exclusively for my screens.

Using ANSI

Because ANSI is such a large topic, I've devoted all of the next chapter to it. At the moment, I'll just say that ANSI allows you to control almost every aspect of the appearance of the screen but also requires loading the device driver ANSI.SYS—something most users do not do.

Summary

- You can display a screen of information with a series of ECHO commands.
- Another way to display a screen of information is by creating an ASCII file and typing it to the screen.
- Using an ASCII file to display text when the batch file is shared with other users requires that you also share the text files and that users install the text files in the same subdirectory as was used on the original system.
- Another way to display a screen of information is by writing your own program. This requires programming tools and experience with a programming language.
- If you use a program to display a screen of information, you must share the program with other users of the batch file; it can still be placed in any subdirectory along the path, though.
- Another way to display a screen of information is to create an ASCII file and compile it with the BatScreen screen compiler.
- When you create a screen program with BatScreen and share the batch file with other users, you must also share the screen program and install it in a subdirectory along the path.
- The final way to display a screen of information is by using ANSI commands. ANSI is covered in Chapter 21.

21

Advanced Screen Design II

In the last chapter, you examined using text files and the TYPE command, writing custom programs, and using a screen compiler to design screens. Another method of screen design is ANSI (an abbreviation for the American National Standards Institute). Because ANSI is such a complex program, I'll cover it here in a separate chapter instead of including it with the other methods.

ANSI under DOS

The device driver ANSI.SYS gives you an incredible amount of power over the appearance of the screen, allowing you to produce very attractive and eye-catching screens and messages in your batch files. However, writing batch files for others using ANSI is asking for problems because so few users load ANSI. Nothing looks worse than seeing ANSI escape sequences stream across a screen when ANSI isn't running. The reason for ANSI's lack of popularity is that it's saddled with the worst user interface of any program on the market! ANSI makes the old Edlin look user-friendly!

To use ANSI, you must first load it in your CONFIG.SYS file with a statement like this:

```
DEVICE=C:\DOS\ANSI.SYS
```

Of course, be sure to use the subdirectory where you have ANSI stored. This is generally your DOS subdirectory. ANSI uses around 4K of memory, which is actually very little memory to sacrifice for the power that ANSI gives you.

ANSI under OS/2

Things are a little better under OS/2. ANSI still has its terrible interface, but ANSI support is automatically included in OS/2, so you don't have to worry about the user loading ANSI.SYS. It can, however, be turned off with the ANSI OFF command. If you're writing batch files for others, it's a good idea to add an ANSI ON command to any batch file using ANSI commands.

Getting Started with ANSI

Before reading about ANSI, you might want to try a little experiment. Configure your computer to load ANSI and reboot if you run DOS and don't normally use ANSI. Under OS/2, simply issue the ANSI ON command. Once you've done that, run the AN-SIDEMO.BAT or ANSIDEMO.CMD batch file. ANSIDEMO.BAT is explained in detail in Figure 21.1.

If you have a color display, ANSIDEMO.BAT will give you a blue background with bright white letters for the text. There's a flashing red title at the top of the menu and a bright yellow message at the bottom telling you to make your selection. Now, to see the real power of ANSI, issue a CLS command.

With other utilities that set the color of the display, clearing the screen will return the display to white characters on a black background. However, ANSI color assignments are permanent, at least until you reboot or issue a new ANSI command, so the CLS command retains the blue background with bright white lettering. Because AN-SIDEMO.BAT used nothing but ANSI commands, this batch file will run on any computer that loads ANSI. As a result, you don't have to worry about the user owning a utility program to be able to change colors or position the cursor. You also don't have to worry about any supporting files.

Batch File Line	Explanation
@ECHO OFF	Turn command-echoing off.
REM NAME: ANSIDEMO.BAT REM PURPOSE: Show ANSI.SYS Power REM To Control The Screen REM VERSION: 2.00 REM DATE: July 22, 1991	Documentation remarks.
NEEDHELP %0 %1 IF ERRORLEVEL 1 GOTO HELP	Use the NeedHelp utility program to check and see if the user requested help.
REM Change The Screen Colors REM Bright White On Blue	Documentation remarks.
ECHO ESC[37m	Send an ANSI sequence to set the foreground color to white. (Note: the batch file uses an ASCII 27 escape character, not ESC.)
ECHO ESC[44m	Send an ANSI sequence to set the background color to blue.
ECHO ESC[1m	Send an ANSI sequence to set the foreground color attribute to bright.
REM Clear the Screen REM Set Colors First So CLS REM Would Use New Colors	Documentation remarks.

Figure 21.1 ANSIDEMO.BAT demonstrates some of the formatting power of ANSI.SYS. Before running ANSIDEMO.BAT, you must load ANSI.SYS in your CONFIG.SYS file and reboot.

`ECHO ESC[2J`	Send an ANSI sequence to clear the screen.
`REM Change To Flashing Red` `REM Display Message And Reset`	Documentation remarks.
`ECHO ESC[1;30HESC[31mESC[5mA Very Special` `    MenuESC[0mESC[37mESC [44mESC[1m`	Send the following ANSI sequences: ESC[1;30H to position the cursor on row 1 and column 30. ESC[31m to set the foreground color to red. This affects only the text that is written to the screen after this. ESC[5A to set the foreground text to blinking. At this point, a message is written to the screen. ESC[0m to reset the screen display to white on black. This affects only future text and is used here to stop the blinking. ESC[37mESC[44m ESC[1m to set the display to bright white on blue.
`REM Position Cursor & Display Options`	Documentation remark.
`ECHO ESC[6;20H1.  Run Word Processing`	Position the cursor on row 6 at column 20 and write text.

`ECHO ESC[7;20H2.  Run Spreadsheet`
`ECHO ESC[8;20H3.  Run Database`
`ECHO ESC[9;20H4.  Play Games`
`ECHO ESC[10;20H5.  Format A Disk`
`ECHO ESC[11;20H6.  Backup Hard Disk To Floppies`
	Write the remaining menu options to the screen.

`ECHO ESC[15;20HESC[33mPress The Number of`
`The`
`    Program You WantESC[37m`
	Position the cursor on row 15 and column 20, change the foreground color to yellow, write text to the screen, and reset the foreground color.

`ECHO`
`PAUSE`
`GOTO END`
	Pause until the user presses a key and then exit the batch file.

`:HELP`
` ECHO This Batch File Is A`
` ECHO Demonstration Of ANSI`
` ECHO It Requires That You Load`
` ECHO ANSI.SYS In Your CONFIG.SYS File`
`GOTO END`
	Section that displays help when the user starts the batch file with a /? or a ? as the first replaceable parameter.

`:END`	Label marking the end of the batch file.

If you like what you saw, read on: what follows is a tutorial on ANSI. ANSI functions fall into four broad categories:

Screen control. You've already seen this in the example. ANSI controls screen colors nicely and allows you to display different text on the screen in different colors. It also allows you to make your prompt far fancier than those you can design without ANSI.

Cursor control. ANSI allows you to position the cursor anywhere on the screen. AN-SIDEMO.BAT uses this to center text and otherwise control its position on the screen without needing to pad with spaces or issue a specific number of ECHO commands to move the cursor down the screen.

Video control. ANSI allows you to easily change the display mode and attributes.

Keyboard control. ANSI lets you remap your keyboard and write keyboard macros.

First a warning: ANSI is very difficult to learn to use, due to the poor explanation in the manual and the unusual user interface. Plan on spending a lot of time studying this chapter and the manual for your operating system, and doing a lot of experimenting, before you can consider yourself an ANSI master.

Entering ANSI Commands

Every ANSI command starts with an escape followed by a left square bracket. The ANSI command to clear the screen, for example, is ESC[2J. (For all the commands and batch file listings that follow, I use ESC to stand for the escape character so you can read it. However, the batch file or command must have the actual escape character, which has an ASCII value of 27 and a hexadecimal value of 1B.) Because the first character in an ANSI command is always an escape, the commands are often called *escape sequences*.

From the description so far, you should immediately see the first problem with ANSI: you can't enter any ANSI commands from the keyboard because, when you press the Esc key, the operating system thinks you want to abort the current command. Typing Alt–27 on the number pad won't bypass this problem; it's just another way of entering an escape.

So you can experiment, I've included a batch file called SENDANSI.BAT on the CD-ROM that comes with this book. It has command-line help and remarks, so it's fairly long, but the only command it uses is ECHO ESC[%1. To use it, enter the ANSI command you want to run without the escape and left bracket that begins the command. SENDANSI.BAT will add those two characters and issue the command. SENDANSI.BAT won't work with ANSI keyboard reassignment commands or any other ANSI commands that include a semicolon or require more than one "word" of commands.

Word processors, editors, and escaping

Many word processors and editors make it difficult to create batch files with ANSI commands because they refuse to let you enter an escape character into a file. There's a trick, however, to get around that. When you enter the CLS command, the operating system responds with an ESC[2J command, even if ANSI isn't loaded. You can redirect that to a file with the command CLS>file and then edit that file with your word processor. While many word-processing programs don't allow you to enter an escape, most will edit a file containing an escape without any problem. Just copy the escape character anywhere you need it.

Entering ANSI Commands by Typing a File

While ANSI is loaded, all the text written to the screen through the operating system is processed by ANSI. ANSI watches for the ESC[sequence. Anything beginning with ESC[is treated as an ANSI command, and anything else is sent to the screen. That gives you a number of ways to send ANSI sequences to the screen. To see that, issue the following two commands:

```
CLS > TEMP.BAT
TYPE TEMP.BAT
```

(If you're using OS/2, change TEMP.BAT to TEMP.CMD.) If you look at the file TEMP.BAT with an editor, you'll see that it contains the text sequence ESC[2J, but if you try to display it with the TYPE command ANSI will see the sequence beginning with ESC[as a command and execute it. So, in addition to echoing ANSI commands to the screen with the ECHO command, you can put them in an ASCII file and type them to the screen. You can also copy these ASCII files to the screen with the command:

```
COPY TEMP.BAT CON
```

Entering ANSI Commands Using the Environment

To continue with the experiment, load TEMP.BAT into an editor. Add the command SET TEMP= in front of the ANSI sequence so the line looks like this: SET TEMP= ESC[2J. Then exit and run the batch file. Because you didn't turn command echoing off, the operating system tries to echo the command to the screen, and again ANSI intercepts it and executes it. However, the environmental variable was successfully created.

Now enter the SET command. The operating system will display the other environmental variables properly, but when it reaches the TEMP variable and tries to display its contents, ANSI again intercepts and executes the escape sequence. This gives you another way to issue ANSI commands. It also turns out that this is the easiest way.

Entering ANSI commands via the prompt

Most environmental variables are rarely displayed. There is, however, one exception. The prompt is an environmental variable that's displayed after every command when using the command line. It's also displayed for each batch file command if command echoing is on. The prompt is particularly useful for ANSI commands. The metacharacter $e issues an escape, so you avoid the problem of having to get an escape into the sequence. In addition, the prompt command has other metacharacters to spice up a prompt. Prompt metacharacters were listed in Table 13.1 and Table 13.2.

You can see an example of the fancy prompts ANSI is capable of generating by issuing the following command from the command-line prompt with ANSI loaded:

```
PROMPT=$e[s$e[1;1H$e[K$d  $t   $p$e[u$p$g$e[44m$e[37m$e[ 1m
```

This prompt shows the day of the week, the date, the time, the drive, and the subdirectory on the top line of the screen. It also sets the screen colors to bright white on blue.

This prompt uses a couple of ANSI sequences I haven't yet mentioned, but you can see how to combine elements of the prompt metacharacters and ANSI to produce an exceptional prompt. In case you don't want to take the time to enter and debug this complex prompt, the batch files NICEPROM.BAT and NICEPROM.CMD on the CD-ROM that comes with this book will issue it for you.

There are, unfortunately, two problems with using the prompt to send ANSI escape sequences in a batch file. Normally, the first command of a batch file is @ECHO OFF, to turn command echoing off. However, this also causes the operating system to stop displaying the prompt, which prevents ANSI escape sequences stored in the prompt from being sent to the screen so they can be processed. The solution is to issue an ECHO ON command when you want to send ANSI escape sequences with the prompt. After sending the ANSI escape sequence, you can reissue an ECHO OFF so the batch file will execute cleanly.

ANSIHIDE.BAT illustrates this. First, it configures the display for a white-on-black screen with the following sequence:

```
ECHO ON
PROMPT=$e[0;40;37m
ECHO
@ECHO OFF
```

Notice that command echoing is turned on before changing the prompt to issue the ANSI color command. The line that appears to be just an ECHO command actually echoes a blank line, displaying the prompt in the process with the high-order 255 space character. Once the colors have been changed, command echoing is turned back off. Next, the batch file displays several messages using the ECHO command, which are visible.

At this point, ANSIHIDE.BAT changes the color to black on black with the following sequence:

```
ECHO ON
PROMPT $e[0;30;40m
ECHO
@ECHO OFF
```

After that, it displays several more messages using the ECHO command, only this time the user can't read them because the text is the same color as the background. Finally, ANSIHIDE.BAT returns the colors to white on black.

Prompts used to send ANSI escape sequences tend to be much longer than standard prompts. Because your prompt is stored in the environment, you must make sure you have enough free environmental space for these longer prompts.

I created a batch file called SENDANS2.BAT so you can experiment with all the combinations of ANSI commands you like. To run it, enter the command:

```
SENDANS2 command1 command2 . . .
```

at the command line. SENDANS2.BAT adds the ESC[to the beginning of each command, so leave this off all commands. It also builds a large environmental variable containing the entire command string and issues it all at once so there are no linefeeds between commands. However, that means your environment must be large enough to store all the commands you plan on issuing, plus the ESC[that SENDANS2.BAT adds to the beginning of each command. Finally, because SENDANS2 strips off one character from each parameter (the leading space) and adds two characters (ESC[), the environmental variable will be longer than the command you issue. If that causes it to exceed the command-line character limit, the computer could lock, reboot, or misbehave in some other unpredictable manner. If you keep your commands to 80 characters or less, this won't affect you.

Like SENDANSI.BAT, you can't use SENDANS2.BAT to send ANSI commands containing a semicolon because the operating system treats the semicolon as a divider and strips it off before passing the replaceable parameter to the batch file. As a result, there's no way to get the colon on the command line into the batch file.

Screen Control

The most common ANSI command is the command to change colors. It's ESC[#m, where # is the number of the foreground or background color to use. The color numbers are all two digits; all foreground colors start with a 3 and all background colors start with a 4. The colors are as follows:

0	Black
1	Red
2	Green
3	Yellow
4	Blue
5	Magenta
6	Cyan
7	White

So the command ESC[44mESC[37m sets the screen to white letters on a blue background. Table 21.1 shows all of the associated ANSI escape sequences. Two notes are in order here:

- The clear screen command ends with an uppercase J, while the color command ends with a lowercase m. Most ANSI commands are case-sensitive, so pay attention to case while writing them.

TABLE 21.1 ANSI Color Escape Sequences

Escape sequence	Function
ESC[30m	Sets foreground color to black.
ESC[31m	Sets foreground color to red.
ESC[32m	Sets foreground color to green.
ESC[33m	Sets foreground color to yellow.
ESC[34m	Sets foreground color to blue.
ESC[35m	Sets foreground color to magenta.
ESC[36m	Sets foreground color to cyan.
ESC[37m	Sets foreground color to white.
ESC[40m	Sets background color to black.
ESC[41m	Sets background color to red.
ESC[42m	Sets background color to green.
ESC[43m	Sets background color to yellow.
ESC[44m	Sets background color to blue.
ESC[45m	Sets background color to magenta.
ESC[46m	Sets background color to cyan.
ESC[47m	Sets background color to white.

- An m ends every ANSI attribute-setting command, but you need only one per line. Thus, the previous command could be shortened to ESC[44;37m. The m terminates the command. You don't have to reissue the ESC[after the 44; the ANSI command isn't terminated because there's no m.

Being able to control screen colors leads to two somewhat useful utilities. BLANK .BAT uses ANSI sequences to blank the screen at the command-line prompt by converting the screen to black text on a black background:

```
@ECHO OFF
ECHO ESC[0m
ECHO ESC[30m
ECHO ESC[40m
CLS
```

This will keep amateur snoops from looking at your files. BLANK.BAT and UN-BLANK.BAT, however, are ineffective under Windows, Windows 95, and OS/2, where the user can simply switch to another session to avoid the effects.

Note that a blank screen is really blank only at the command line and in the few programs that use ANSI color settings. Most programs, however, display fine while ANSI is set for a blank screen. Of course, users must be able to load the program without seeing the prompt of the commands being entered. Typing UNBLANK runs UNBLANK.BAT, shown here:

```
@ECHO OFF
ECHO ESC[37m
ECHO ESC[44m
ECHO ESC[1m
CLS
```

UNBLANK.BAT uses ANSI commands to restore the screen to bright white letters on a blue background. (You must, of course, be able to run UNBLANK.BAT without being able to see the screen.) Note that the batch files on your disk have more documentation and command-line help. However, this does not aid in the explanation here, so I haven't reproduced it. ANSI also provides for several types of screen erasing:

ESC[0J. Erases the screen from the cursor position to the end of the screen. (Note: Not all versions of ANSI support this command.)

ESC[0K. Erases the line the cursor is on, but only from the cursor position to the right.

ESC[1J. Erases the screen from the cursor position to the top of the screen. (Note: Not all versions of ANSI support this command.)

ESC[1K. Erases the line the cursor is on, from the beginning of the line to the current cursor position. (Note: Not all versions of ANSI support this command.)

ESC[2J. Clears the entire screen, like a CLS command. In fact, the CLS command causes the operating system to issue an ESC[2J command.

ESC[2K. Erases the entire line that the cursor is currently on. (Note: Not all versions of ANSI support this command.)

Cursor Control

ANSI gives you the ability to position the cursor anywhere on the screen and move the cursor around the screen as you see fit. In their simplest form, the commands to move around the screen are:

ESC[A	Moves the cursor up one row
ESC[B	Moves the cursor down one row
ESC[C	Moves the cursor to the right one column
ESC[D	Moves the cursor to the left one column

If you precede the A through D with a number, the cursor moves that many times, so ESC[5A would move the cursor up five rows. The command ESC[r;cH would move the cursor to row R and column C, ESC[1;1H would move the cursor to the top left corner of the screen, and ESC[24,80H would move it to the bottom right corner. One note: the lowercase f works the same as the uppercase H, so ESC[10;10H and ESC[10;10f do the same thing.

With ANSI, you can also save the current cursor position with the command ESC[s. This saves only one cursor position, though, so each time you use it you overwrite the prior position it has saved. The ESC[u command returns to the position saved with the ESC[s command. You can also have ANSI report the cursor position with an ESC[6n command. This is generally used by programs and is of little value in a batch file.

Video Control

The MODE command allows you to control the video mode, but ANSI does an even better job. For example, the ESC[=1h command configures the screen for 40×25 color mode so the text appears very large, and ESC[=3h returns the screen to 80×25 mode. The format of the command is slightly unusual because it has an equal sign in the middle. Assuming your display supports them, the ANSI commands to change the display mode are as follows:

ESC[=0h	40×25 monochrome text
ESC[=1h	40×25 color text
ESC[=2h	80×25 monochrome text
ESC[=3h	80×25 color text
ESC[=4h	320×200 four-color graphics
ESC[=5h	320×200 monochrome graphics
ESC[=6h	640×200 two-color graphics
ESC[=13h	320×200 16-color graphics (EGA and VGA only)
ESC[=14h	640×200 16-color graphics (EGA and VGA only)
ESC[=15h	640×350 monochrome graphics (EGA and VGA only)
ESC[=16h	640×350 16-color graphics (EGA and VGA only)
ESC[=17h	640×480 two-color graphics (VGA only)
ESC[=18h	640×480 16-color graphics (VGA only)
ESC[=19h	320×200 256-color graphics (VGA only)

ANSI also has several commands to control other aspects of how the screen appears:

ESC[=7h. Causes lines longer than 80 characters to wrap around to the next line. This is the default mode.

ESC[=7l. Causes lines longer than 80 characters to be truncated so they don't wrap. Note that the last character is a lowercase L and not a 1.

ESC[0m. Turns off all screen attributes, returning the screen to white on black.

ESC[1m. Turns on high-intensity foreground colors.

ESC[2m. Returns the foreground colors to normal intensity.

ESC[4m. Turns on underlining on a monochrome display.

ESC[5m. Causes the foreground text to blink.

ESC[7m. Converts the display to inverse video.

ESC[8m. Blanks the screen by setting the foreground color to the background color. As you can see, ANSI offers a lot of control over video attributes.

Keyboard Control

With ANSI, you can also reconfigure your keyboard. This topic is unrelated to batch files, so I'll cover it only briefly. The general format of the command is:

```
ESC[Key1;Key2p
```

The Key1 variable contains the ASCII value of the key to reassign, and Key2 the ASCII value the key is to take on. If you like, you can enclose the actual value in double quotation marks. While using the command line, you use parentheses more than brackets (although the left bracket gets a workout under ANSI). You can switch them with the following commands:

```
ECHO ESC[91;40p
ECHO ESC[93;41p
ECHO ESC[40;91p
ECHO ESC[41;93p
```

The reassignment works at the command line, but not in programs like Microsoft Word that bypass the operating system for keystrokes. To reset the keyboard reassignments, issue the commands:

```
ECHO ESC[91;91p
ECHO ESC[93;93p
ECHO ESC[40;40p
ECHO ESC[41;41p
```

You could have started remapping these using the actual keystrokes. The first command would have been:

```
ECHO ESC["[";"("p
```

but after remapping the square brackets to parentheses, you wouldn't have been able to type them into the second two commands to map the parentheses to square brackets because they had been turned into something else. Using ASCII values avoids this problem.

The CD-ROM that comes with this book has two batch files to help you experiment with ANSI keyboard reassignments. The first is ANSIKEY1.BAT or its OS/2 equivalent, ANSIKEY1.CMD. It takes pairs of numbers associated with the various keystrokes: the first number is the keystroke to modify, and the second is its new value. It issues the ANSI command necessary to make the first assignment, issues two

SHIFT commands, and checks to see if another pair of numbers is waiting. It's shown next without internal documentation and command-line help:

```
:TOP
   IF (%2)==() GOTO END
   ECHO _[%1;%2p
   SHIFT
   SHIFT
GOTO TOP
```

To remap the square brackets and parentheses mentioned earlier, enter the command:

```
ANSIKEY1 91 40 93 41 40 91 41 93
```

and to restore the keys to their original value, enter:

```
ANSIKEY1 40 40 41 41 91 91 93 93
```

The second batch file is ANSIKEY2.BAT or ANSIKEY2.CMD. It's similar to AN-SIKEY1.BAT, only it accepts the actual keystrokes rather than the numbers. It's shown next without internal documentation and command-line help:

```
:TOP
   IF (%2)==() GOTO END
   ECHO _["%1";"%2"p
   SHIFT
   SHIFT
GOTO TOP
```

To remap the square brackets and parentheses mentioned earlier, enter this command:

```
ANSIKEY1 ( [ ) ] [ ( ] )
```

Because none of the keys are remapped until the command is issued, you'll have no trouble issuing all the commands on the command line. To restore the keys to their original value, enter:

```
ANSIKEY1 ( ( ) ) [ [ ] ]
```

Both batch files will accept over 25 reassignments on a single line, making it easy to reassign a lot of keys at once. If you find yourself using the same reassignment command more than once or twice, you might want to write a custom batch file to either issue the ANSI commands or store the commands you use to call one of these batch files.

In addition to remapping standard keys, you can also remap extended keystrokes like Ctrl–F1. These keystrokes have a two-digit code that starts with 0—the number, not the letter. They're entered like any other keystroke, thus to remap Ctrl–F1 to issue a DIR command:

```
ECHO ESC[0;94;"DIR";13p
```

Because this type of assignment involves one number and one character string, you can't issue it with either ANSIKEY1.BAT or ANSIKEY2.BAT, although either could easily be modified to handle it. Table 21.2 shows many of the ASCII and extended keystrokes you can use.

TABLE 21.2 Extended ANSI Keystrokes

ANSI Keystroke	Key code	ANSI Keystroke	Key code	ANSI Keystroke	Key code
Alt–;	0;131	Alt–L	0;38	Del	0;83
Alt–0	0;129	Alt–M	0;50	Down arrow	0;80
Alt–1	0;120	Alt–N	0;49	End	0;79
Alt–2	0;121	Alt–O	0;24	F1	0;59
Alt–3	0;122	Alt–P	0;25	F10	0;68
Alt–4	0;123	Alt–Q	0;16	F2	0;60
Alt–5	0;124	Alt–R	0;19	F3	0;61
Alt–6	0;125	Alt–S	0;31	F4	0;62
Alt–7	0;126	Alt–T	0;20	F5	0;63
Alt–8	0;127	Alt–U	0;22	F6	0;64
Alt–9	0;128	Alt–V	0;47	F7	0;65
Alt–A	0;30	Alt–W	0;17	F8	0;66
Alt–B	0;48	Alt–X	0;45	F9	0;67
Alt–C	0;46	Alt–Y	0;21	Home	0;71
Alt–D	0;32	Alt–Z	0;44	Ins	0;82
Alt–dash	0;130	Ctrl–F1	0;94	Left arrow	0;75
Alt–E	0;18	Ctrl–Left arrow	0;115	NUL	0;3
Alt–F	0;33	Ctrl–Right arrow	0;116	PgDn	0;81
Alt–F1	0;104	Ctrl–End	0;117	PgUp	0;73
Alt–F10	0;113	Ctrl–F10	0;103	Right arrow	0;77
Alt–F2	0;105	Ctrl–F2	0;95	Shift–F1	0;84
Alt–F3	0;106	Ctrl–F3	0;96	Shift–F10	0;93
Alt–F4	0;107	Ctrl–F4	0;97	Shift–F2	0;85
Alt–F5	0;108	Ctrl–F5	0;98	Shift–F3	0;86
Alt–F6	0;109	Ctrl–F6	0;99	Shift–F4	0;87
Alt–F7	0;110	Ctrl–F7	0;100	Shift–F5	0;88
Alt–F8	0;111	Ctrl–F8	0;101	Shift–F6	0;89

TABLE 21.2 Continued

ANSI Keystroke	Key code	ANSI Keystroke	Key code	ANSI Keystroke	Key code
Alt–F9	0;112	Ctrl–F9	0;102	Shift–F7	0;90
Alt–G	0;34	Ctrl–Home	0;119	Shift–F8	0;91
Alt–H	0;35	Ctrl–PgDn	0;118	Shift–F9	0;92
Alt–I	0;23	Ctrl–PgUp	0;132	Shift–Tab	0;15
Alt–J	0;36	Ctrl–Print Screen	0;114	Up arrow	0;72
Alt–K	0;37				

As you can see, ANSI gives you a great deal of control over the screen. It's also difficult to learn; once you learn ANSI, though, it's fairly easy to use. Table 21.3 summarizes many frequently used ANSI commands.

TABLE 21.3 ANSI Escape Sequences

ANSI command sequence	Function
ESC[#,#p	Reassigns the key defined by the first pound sign to the value of the second pound sign.
ESC[#A	Moves the cursor up the number of rows specified by the number that replaces the pound sign.
ESC[#B	Moves the cursor down the number of rows specified by the number that replaces the pound sign.
ESC[#C	Moves the cursor left the number of rows specified by the number that replaces the pound sign.
ESC[#D	Moves the cursor right the number of rows specified by the number that replaces the pound sign.
ESC[=0h	Sets the display mode to 40×25 monochrome text.
ESC[=13h	Sets the display mode to 320×200 16-color graphics.
ESC[=14h	Sets the display mode to 640×200 16-color graphics.
ESC[=15h	Sets the display mode to 640×350 monochrome graphics.
ESC[=16h	Sets the display mode to 640×350 16-color graphics.
ESC[=17h	Sets the display mode to 640×480 2-color graphics.
ESC[=18h	Sets the display mode to 640×480 16-color graphics.
ESC[=19h	Sets the display mode to 320×200 256-color graphics.
ESC[=1h	Sets the display mode to 40×25 color text.
ESC[=2h	Sets the display mode to 80×25 monochrome text.
ESC[=3h	Sets the display mode to 80×25 color text.
ESC[=4h	Sets the display mode to 300×200 4-color graphics.
ESC[=5h	Sets the display mode to 320×200 monochrome graphics.
ESC[=6h	Sets the display mode to 640×200 2-color graphics.

TABLE 21.3 Continued

ANSI command sequence	Function
ESC[=7h	Turns line wrap on.
ESC[=7l	Turns line wrap off.
ESC[?7h	Turns line wrap on. This is needed only if line wrap has been turned off.
ESC[?7l	Turns line wrap off. When line wrap is off, once the cursor reaches the end of the line, each succeeding character is printed on top of the last one at the end of the line.
ESC[0h	Sets the display mode to 40×25 monochrome.
ESC[0J	Erases the screen from the cursor position to the end of the screen. (Not all versions of ANSI support this command.)
ESC[0K	Erases the current line from the cursor position right.
ESC[0l	Sets the display mode to 40×25 monochrome.
ESC[0m	Resets the screen display to white on black.
ESC[1h	Sets the display mode to 40×25 color.
ESC[1J	Erases the screen from the cursor position to the top of the screen. (Not all versions of ANSI support this command.)
ESC[1K	Erases the line the cursor is on, from the beginning of the line to the cursor position. (Not all versions of ANSI support this.)
ESC[1l	Sets the display mode to 40×25 color.
ESC[1m	Sets the foreground text to bold.
ESC[2h	Sets the display mode to 80×25 monochrome.
ESC[2J	Clears the screen.
ESC[2K	Erases the entire line that the cursor is on. (Not all versions of ANSI support this.)
ESC[2l	Sets the display mode to 80×25 monochrome.
ESC[2m	Returns the foreground colors to normal intensity.
ESC[30m	Sets foreground color to black.
ESC[31m	Sets foreground color to red.
ESC[32m	Sets foreground color to green.
ESC[33m	Sets foreground color to yellow.
ESC[34m	Sets foreground color to blue.
ESC[35m	Sets foreground color to magenta.
ESC[36m	Sets foreground color to cyan.
ESC[37m	Sets foreground color to white.
ESC[3h	Sets the display mode to 80×25 color.
ESC[3l	Sets the display mode to 80×25 color.
ESC[40m	Sets background color to black.
ESC[41m	Sets background color to red.
ESC[42m	Sets background color to green.
ESC[43m	Sets background color to yellow.
ESC[44m	Sets background color to blue.
ESC[45m	Sets background color to magenta.

TABLE 21.3 Continued

ANSI command sequence	Function
ESC[46m	Sets background color to cyan.
ESC[47m	Sets background color to white.
ESC[4h	Sets the display mode to 320×200 color graphics.
ESC[4l	Sets the display mode to 320×200 color graphics.
ESC[4m	Sets the foreground text to underlined on a monochrome display. On a color display, this sets the foreground to blue.
ESC[5A	Sets the foreground text to blinking.
ESC[5h	Sets the display mode to 320×200 monochrome graphics.
ESC[5l	Sets the display mode to 320×200 monochrome graphics.
ESC[5m	Sets the foreground color to blinking.
ESC[6h	Sets the display mode to 640×200 monochrome graphics.
ESC[6l	Sets the display mode to 640×200 monochrome graphics.
ESC[6n	Reports the cursor position.
ESC[7m	Sets the display to reverse video, black text on a white background.
ESC[K	Erases the current line from the cursor position right.
ESC[r,cf	Positions the cursor on row number r and column number c.
ESC[r,cH	Positions the cursor on row number r and column number c.
ESC[s	Stores the current cursor position.
ESC[u	Returns to the cursor position stored by the ESC[s command.
ESC8m	Blanks the screen by setting the foreground color equal to the background color.

An Example

You can use ANSI keyboard remapping to construct a very useful batch file. Often, computer magazines print debugging scripts for you to enter to create small utilities. Since these are in hexadecimal, the numbers to enter range from 0 to 9 and A through F, but not all of these are on your numeric keypad. ENTERHEX.BAT or EN-TERHEX.CMD remaps the /, *, -, +, =, and Del keys that surround the number pad as A through F, so you can quickly enter the letters as well as the numbers. While this remapping works with Edlin and COPY CON, it doesn't work inside most editors. The code for the operational portion of ENTERHEX.BAT follows:

```
ECHO Esc["/";"A"p
ECHO Esc["*";"B"p
ECHO Esc["-";"C"p
ECHO Esc["+";"D"p
ECHO Esc["=";"E"p
ECHO Esc[0;83;"F"p
ECHO Number Pad Ready For Hex Entry
```

UNENTER.BAT or UNENTER.CMD will restore the keys to normal. The code for the operational portion follows:

```
ECHO Esc["/";"/"p
ECHO Esc["*";"*"p
ECHO Esc["-";"-"p
ECHO Esc["+";"+"p
ECHO Esc["=";"="p
ECHO Esc[0;83;0;83p
ECHO Number Pad Back To Normal
```

Summary

- You can display a screen of information by using ANSI commands.
- With ANSI, you can control the screen, cursor, video, and keyboard.
- You can use ANSI escape sequences to change the foreground and background colors.
- When using ANSI to change the color of the screen, a CLS command doesn't reset the colors to white on black.
- ANSI commands are called *escape sequences*.
- You can't enter ANSI commands from the keyboard because they start with the escape character.
- If you can't enter an escape character in a file with your word-processing program, pipe the CLS command to a file and incorporate the escape from that file in your document.
- ANSI processes any line that's sent to the screen that begins with an escape character followed by an open bracket, no matter how the characters are displayed.
- You can display ANSI escape sequences by using the ECHO command.
- You can display ANSI escape sequences by storing them in an ASCII file and typing that file to the screen.
- You can display ANSI escape sequences by storing them in environmental variables and then using the SET or ECHO commands to display one or more environmental variables.
- You can display ANSI escape sequences by using the PROMPT command, which has a built-in escape character.
- When displaying ANSI escape sequences in a batch file via the PROMPT command, you must turn command echoing on while the prompt is being used to send the ANSI commands.
- ANSI provides several different ways to erase different portions of the screen.
- ANSI lets you move the cursor in any direction, as well as save and recall the cursor position.
- You can use ANSI to set the video mode.
- ANSI also allows you to remap the keyboard, although the remapping won't work with many programs that avoid the operating system to get their keystrokes.

22

Batch File Subroutines

In programming, a subroutine is a special type of program. When a program calls a subroutine, control is passed to the subroutine. When the subroutine is finished, control is passed back to the program that called the subroutine. The calling program continues from the point where it passed control to the subroutine. This is illustrated in Figure 22.1.

Subroutines are a way of writing a section of code once, storing it, and reusing it as many times as needed. In a batch file, this often makes the logic much easier to follow and the batch file easier to write and debug. For example, if you want to perform multiple commands based on the errorlevel value, you must have a series of IF tests for each possible errorlevel value. Each IF test must jump to a different section of the batch file to perform the multiple commands, and then the sections must reconverge. With subroutines, the batch file would have a single command for each IF test, where each command runs a subroutine. Look at this example:

```
IF ERRORLEVEL 3 SUB-3
IF ERRORLEVEL 2 SUB-2
IF ERRORLEVEL 1 SUB-1
IF ERRORLEVEL 0 SUB-0
```

What Is a Subroutine?

A subroutine is nothing more than one or more lines of batch file commands, exactly like any other batch file commands. The question isn't "What is it?" but rather "How do you use it?" You can store the subroutine either as a separate batch file or inside the original batch file and use IF tests to jump to it.

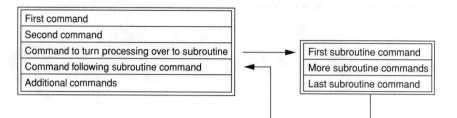

Figure 22.1 When one program or part of a program calls another program, the part being called is called a subroutine.

As a separate batch file

The easiest way to write a subroutine is as a stand-alone batch file. The method's biggest advantage is that it allows multiple batch files to call on a common subroutine; its worst disadvantage is that it uses more hard disk space because each batch file is allocated a full cluster of space no matter how small it is. Of course, this isn't an issue if you use disk compression or you have a lot of free space.

Prior to MS-DOS 3.3

Early versions of MS-DOS (prior to 3.3) didn't support a batch file running other batch files as subroutines. With those older versions of the operating system, once a batch file passed control to another batch file, control never passed back to the original batch file. This isn't how a batch file behaves when it passes control to a program. When that program finishes, control is passed back to the calling batch file. It's possible to "trick" DOS into running one batch file from another batch file and then returning control to the original batch file, but these older versions of MS-DOS are now so out of date and so rarely used that I won't go into that trick here.

DOS 3.3 and later

DOS 3.3 added the CALL batch subcommand. Thus, a batch file can call another batch file with the command CALL *batch*, where *batch* is the name of the batch file. Once the subroutine batch file terminates, control automatically returns to the batch file that called the subroutine.

OS/2 also uses the CALL command to run batch files as subroutines. Interestingly, when an OS/2 batch file runs a REXX program as a utility program, the REXX program must also be executed with the CALL command if control is to return to the batch file once the REXX program terminates.

An Example

To illustrate this, we'll look back to TOA.BAT. TOA.BAT was a batch file in Chapter 10 that allowed you to copy .DOC and .CMP files to the A drive, and delete the associated .BAK file when the user entered just the filename. This batch file evolved over the next several chapters, reaching its ultimate form in Chapter 16:

```
@ECHO OFF
:TOP
    IF (%1)==() GOTO END
    DEL %1.BAK
    COPY %1.DOC A:
    COPY %1.CMP A:
    SHIFT
GOTO TOP

:END
```

The purpose of this batch file is to copy the modified versions of files to a floppy disk to be transported to another location, but it doesn't enforce it. If a .DOC file has been modified, then—on my system using Microsoft Word—a .BAK file always exists. Suppose you wanted to add the logic necessary to skip copying the file if a .BAK file doesn't exist. The new version of TOA.BAT might look like this:

```
@ECHO OFF
:TOP
    IF (%1)==() GOTO END
    IF NOT EXIST %1.BAK ECHO %1 Not Modified So Not Copied
    IF NOT EXIST %1.BAK GOTO SKIP
    DEL %1.BAK
    COPY %1.DOC A:
    COPY %1.CMP A:
:SKIP
    SHIFT
GOTO TOP

:END
```

Now suppose you wanted to add logic to the COPY portion of the batch file to detect minor copying errors, like a full diskette, and warn the user. And say you wanted to make sure users enter the name correctly by warning them if the .DOC file doesn't exist. As you can imagine, the original three lines of the batch file that handled the repetitive tasks of copying and deleting files, shown here, are going to become very complex:

```
DEL %1.BAK
COPY %1.DOC A:
COPY %1.CMP A:
```

Predictably, because this chapter covers subroutines, the solution is to place these three commands in a separate batch file and treat them as a subroutine. The original version of TOA.BAT has these three lines stripped out and a single command added to call the subroutine. Within TOA.BAT, the files to be copied are known as %1. However, this replaceable parameter is global while inside TOA.BAT and isn't available to the subroutine, called TOA-SUB.BAT. In order to make the name of the file available to TOA-SUB.BAT, you must pass it to that batch file as a replaceable parameter. The resulting TOA.BAT looks like this:

```
@ECHO OFF
:TOP
    IF (%1)==() GOTO END
```

```
        CALL TOA-2SUB %1
        SHIFT
GOTO TOP

:END
```

A version of TOA.BAT with internal documentation and command-line help is included on the CD-ROM that comes with this book in either the \BAT-FILE\DOS \TOA\CHAP-22 or \BAT-FILE\OS2\TOA\CHAP-22 subdirectories. TOA-SUB.BAT looks like this:

```
@ECHO OFF
DEL %1.BAK
COPY %1.DOC A:
COPY %1.CMP A:
```

Two notes about this subroutine are important. First, it doesn't need to test to see if %1 exists because TOA.BAT takes care of that prior to calling the subroutine. Second, the @ECHO OFF command isn't really necessary because command echoing is always off when a batch file with command echoing turned off calls another batch file as a subroutine. You'll see why I added it later.

Because this subroutine is shorter and isn't convoluted by the looping performed in TOA.BAT, you can add additional checks without the batch file becoming as complicated as TOA.BAT would have become. First, let's add the logic to test and make sure the file has been modified by testing to see if the .BAK file exists. The pseudocode for this is:

If the .BAK file doesn't exist, tell user and exit subroutine
If the .BAK file exists, continue normally

The resulting subroutine looks like this:

```
@ECHO OFF

IF NOT EXIST %1.BAK ECHO File Not Modified, Not Copied
IF NOT EXIST %1.BAK GOTO END

DEL %1.BAK
COPY %1.DOC A:
COPY %1.CMP A:

:END
```

Next, you want to make sure the file actually exists before trying to copy it. If the file was created by Lotus or dBASE, a .BAK file might still exist. If the .DOC file doesn't exist, you want to exit without copying anything; if the .CMP file doesn't exist, you simply want to skip that COPY command because not all documents have .CMP files. The pseudocode for this is:

If the .DOC file doesn't exist, warn user and exit subroutine
If the .CMP file exists, copy it to the diskette

and the resulting subroutine looks like this:

```
@ECHO OFF

IF NOT EXIST %1.BAK ECHO File Not Modified, Not Copied
IF NOT EXIST %1.BAK GOTO END

IF NOT EXIST %1.DOC ECHO %1.DOC File Not Found
IF NOT EXIST %1.DOC GOTO END

DEL %1.BAK
COPY %1.DOC A:
IF EXIST %1.CMP COPY %1.CMP A:

:END
```

Because the second set of IF tests makes sure the .DOC file exists, no IF test is used in front of the COPY command. However, when it's time to copy the .CMP file, the batch file hasn't verified that it exists, so this COPY command is preceded by an IF test.

As the last modification to the logic, you want to make sure that the file was successfully copied to the A drive. Because COPY doesn't set the errorlevel, you must perform this test manually. The pseudocode for this is "If the file is on the current drive but not the A drive, warn the user." The resulting subroutine looks like this:

```
@ECHO OFF

IF NOT EXIST %1.BAK ECHO File Not Modified, Not Copied
IF NOT EXIST %1.BAK GOTO END

IF NOT EXIST %1.DOC ECHO %1.DOC File Not Found
IF NOT EXIST %1.DOC GOTO END

DEL %1.BAK
COPY %1.DOC A:
IF EXIST %1.CMP COPY %1.CMP A:

IF NOT EXIST A:%1.DOC ECHO %1.DOC Not Copied Successfully
:END
```

This test will spot occasions when the file was too big to fit on the A drive, but won't handle situations were there was a version of the file already on the A drive and some other problem prevented the successful copying—all because the batch file finds that the file A:%1.DOC exists. While COPY doesn't set an errorlevel value, XCOPY does. A zero represents a successful copy and a higher value represents some sort of problem. You can therefore use XCOPY and errorlevel tests to modify the subroutine in order to spot any copying problems. The resulting subroutine looks like this:

```
@ECHO OFF

IF NOT EXIST %1.BAK ECHO File Not Modified, Not Copied
IF NOT EXIST %1.BAK GOTO END

IF NOT EXIST %1.DOC ECHO %1.DOC File Not Found
IF NOT EXIST %1.DOC GOTO END
```

```
DEL %1.BAK
IF EXIST %1.CMP XCOPY %1.CMP A:
XCOPY %1.DOC A:

IF ERRORLEVEL 1 ECHO %1.DOC Not Copied Successfully
:END
```

In addition to converting the COPY commands to XCOPY and converting the final IF EXIST test to IF ERRORLEVEL, I also reversed the copying order of the .CMP and .DOC files. The errorlevel used in the IF ERRORLEVEL test is the final errorlevel value, and the .DOC document file is far more important than the .CMP dictionary file. So by copying the .DOC file last, its errorlevel is the one tested. You might want to add tests on both values if the first XCOPY has a problem.

These are all the modifications the subroutine needs if it's to function as a stand-alone subroutine. However, users might try and run it to see what it does. You can help avoid this by adding command-line help for the now familiar /? switch, but this time have it also display help if the batch file is started without a replaceable parameter. This final test works because TOA.BAT always calls the subroutine with a replaceable parameter, and the batch file knows it's being run improperly if it doesn't receive a replaceable parameter. The final version of the batch file is:

```
@ECHO OFF
IF (%1)==()   GOTO HELP
IF (%1)==(/?) GOTO HELP

IF NOT EXIST %1.BAK ECHO File Has Not Been Modified, Not Copied
IF NOT EXIST %1.BAK GOTO END

IF NOT EXIST %1.DOC ECHO %1.DOC File Not Found
IF NOT EXIST %1.DOC GOTO END

DEL %1.BAK
IF EXIST %1.CMP XCOPY %1.CMP A:
XCOPY %1.DOC A:

IF ERRORLEVEL 1 ECHO %1.DOC Not Copied Successfully
GOTO END

:HELP
    ECHO This Batch File Is A Subroutine Used By TOA-2.BAT
    ECHO It Is Not Designed To Be Run By The User
GOTO END

:END
```

This version of TOA-SUB.BAT is included on the CD-ROM that comes with the book. That version includes some additional internal documentation.

By now, you should also see why I included the @ECHO OFF command in the subroutine, although it's not needed when the batch file runs as a subroutine. If a user runs the batch file from the command line to find out what it does, the help section will take care of that, but everything would look very unattractive without @ECHO OFF.

Inside the Calling Batch File

Each batch file you write takes up a minimum of one cluster of disk space. Depending on several factors, that can be up to 8K and will most likely be at least 2K, unless you use disk compression. If you're running very short of hard disk space, that can seem like a large price to pay for a relatively small subroutine. You can avoid this by bundling all your subroutines within the main batch file.

When you include subroutines inside a batch file, it ends up running itself; in other words, it's *recursive*. Recursive batch files have two advantages over batch files that call separate subroutines. First, as mentioned earlier, the resulting batch file is generally smaller than the separate batch file and subroutines. This is generally true in spite of the requirement of additional IF tests to direct the recursive batch file to continue processing.

The second advantage of a recursive batch file is how easy it is to transfer to different systems. If you need to copy a recursive batch file to another system, then that batch file is all you need to take to the new machine. If you want to transfer a batch file with external subroutines, then you have to remember to copy all the files, something I have trouble remembering to do.

There is, however, one very significant drawback to recursive batch files. The resulting batch file is longer and more complex and, without the proper approach, can be much more difficult to write. This additional complexity is an important consideration—one you shouldn't overlook.

Storing Subroutine Commands within a Batch File

A replaceable parameter signals the batch file if it's being called by itself as a subroutine. When that signal is missing, the batch file knows it's being called from the command line. A series of IF tests at the beginning of the batch file direct it to the appropriate section of the batch file depending on the flag it receives as a replaceable parameter. That way, the batch file can contain more that one internal subroutine.

We'll start with TOA.BAT, include TOA-SUB.BAT as an internal subroutine, and call the resulting batch file TOA-3.BAT. TOA-3.BAT needs to run exactly like TOA.BAT when it first starts, but when TOA.BAT would be calling TOA-SUB.BAT as a subroutine, TOA-3.BAT needs to call itself. We'll use %2 as a flag to TOA-3.BAT that it's running as a subroutine; specifically, when TOA-3.BAT calls itself as a subroutine, it will pass XYZ123ABC as %2.

That means you have to have several IF tests at the top of TOA-3.BAT. One will direct the batch file to help if /? is entered, and another will direct the batch file to the subroutine section if %2 is XYZ123ABC. Because TOA-3.BAT provides this replaceable parameter, capitalization isn't a problem. The end of the subroutine section is a GOTO END command, so the subroutine copy of the batch file will exit and return control to the calling copy of TOA-3.BAT. Otherwise, the subroutine section is identical. The resulting batch file is:

```
@ECHO OFF
:TOP
```

```
        IF (%1)==() GOTO END
        IF (%1)==(/?) GOTO HELP
        IF (%2)==(XYZ123ABC) GOTO SUB
        CALL TOA-3 %1 XYZ123ABC
        SHIFT
GOTO TOP

:HELP
    ECHO This Batch File Requires You To Enter Filenames
    ECHO Without The Extension. For Each Name, It Erases
    ECHO The Associated .BAT File, Then It Copies The
    ECHO Associated .DOC And .CMP Files To The A Drive
GOTO END

:SUB
  IF NOT EXIST %1.BAK ECHO File Not Modified, Not Copied
  IF NOT EXIST %1.BAK GOTO END

  IF NOT EXIST %1.DOC ECHO %1.DOC File Not Found
  IF NOT EXIST %1.DOC GOTO END

  DEL %1.BAK
  IF EXIST %1.CMP XCOPY %1.CMP A:
  XCOPY %1.DOC A:

  IF ERRORLEVEL 1 ECHO %1.DOC Not Copied Successfully
GOTO END

:END
```

A copy can be found on the CD-ROM that comes with this book in the \BAT-FILE\DOS\TOA\CHAP-22 subdirectory.

TOA-3.BAT calls itself as a subroutine. It also illustrates the best approach to writing recursive batch files. Because the individual files approach is easier to write, that's what I used here. Only after TOA.BAT and TOA-SUB.BAT were finished did I begin working on the single recursive batch file that incorporated both files.

This example also illustrates the reason for a habit you might be wondering about. I usually close out the last section of the batch file, generally the help section, with a GOTO END command, even when the next line is the :END label. By doing that, I avoid introducing problems when I rearrange the logic of the batch file—as I did when I created TOA-3.BAT by modifying TOA.BAT to include the subroutine.

You can also reorder the IF tests in TOA-3.BAT to make it run more quickly. Because TOA-3.BAT calls itself as a subroutine for each file, it's likely to run as a subroutine more often than as a stand-alone batch file. As written, when running as a subroutine it has to first pass through the two IF tests relating to command-line help. By putting the subroutine IF test first, the two IF tests are avoided when TOA-3.BAT runs as a subroutine. In general, when using branching IF tests in a batch file, you should order them from the most likely to be true to the least likely.

DR DOS 6 and Novell DOS 7

DR DOS 6 introduced four batch subroutine commands that make building subroutines into a main batch file a snap, and these were retained in Novell DOS 7. However, these commands aren't supported by MS- or PC DOS, so use them only if you're certain your batch file won't be run under MS-DOS. In addition, because most batch file compilers, like Builder and Builder Lite, support only the MS-DOS format for commands, DR DOS 6 subroutine batch subcommands won't compile properly. These batch files also won't run under DR DOS 5. The four subroutine batch subcommands are as follows:

EXIT. Causes a batch file to immediately terminate. This is useful in any batch file where it can replace the GOTO END commands. While Novell DOS 7 doesn't document the EXIT batch command, it does continue to work.

GOSUB. Turns control over to a subroutine with the name that follows the GOSUB command. The subroutine must be included inside the batch file and marked with a label giving the name of the subroutine. Subroutine labels are assigned identically to the labels used with the GOTO command.

RETURN. Marks the end of a subroutine and causes control to return to the line in the batch file immediately following the GOSUB command.

SWITCH. Allows the user to select the subroutine to jump to from the command line. This is usually used to construct a menu, so it's discussed in Chapter 26.

Only GOSUB and RETURN are needed to bundle a subroutine within a batch file. The EXIT command lets you skip a lot of extra GOTO END commands, so it's useful. The SWITCH command is useful for developing menus. The modified version of TOA.BAT, now called TOA-DR6.BAT, is as follows:

```
@ECHO OFF
:TOP
   IF (%1)==() EXIT
   IF (%1)==(/?) GOTO HELP
   GOSUB SUB
   SHIFT
GOTO TOP

:HELP
   ECHO This Batch File Requires You To Enter Filenames
   ECHO Without The Extension. For Each Name, It Erases
   ECHO The Associated .BAT File And Then Copies The
   ECHO Associated .DOC And .CMP Files To The A Drive
EXIT

:SUB
   IF NOT EXIST %1.BAK ECHO File Not Modified, Not Copied
   IF NOT EXIST %1.BAK EXIT

   IF NOT EXIST %1.DOC ECHO %1.DOC File Not Found
   IF NOT EXIST %1.DOC EXIT

   DEL %1.BAK
   IF EXIST %1.CMP XCOPY %1.CMP A:
   XCOPY %1.DOC A:
   IF ERRORLEVEL 1 ECHO %1.DOC Not Copied Successfully
   IF ERRORLEVEL 1 EXIT
RETURN
```

One of the commands used in TOA-DR6.BAT is EXIT. Under DR DOS 6, this causes the batch file to immediately terminate. This command can be easily simulated under DR DOS 5 and all versions of MS and PC DOS. Simply create a zero-length file called EXIT.BAT in your batch subdirectory. When the batch file issues an EXIT command, it will run EXIT.BAT. Because EXIT.BAT is run without CALL, control doesn't return to the original batch file. EXIT.BAT, because it has no commands, will run quickly.

Summary

- A subroutine is reusable code that one or more batch files can access when needed to perform some specific function.

- You can store subroutines as separate batch files and run them with the CALL command.

- Storing subroutines as stand-alone batch files is the easiest way to write and debug subroutines, but it takes up more disk space and you must remember to provide all the subroutines when you give a batch file to another user.

- When you use the CALL command to access another batch file, the called batch file doesn't have access to the replaceable parameters of the original batch file, so it must be passed any information it needs.

- It's important for stand-alone batch file subroutines to protect themselves from being run from the command line. The safest form of protection is to test for a specific replaceable parameter provided by the batch file that's supposed to call the subroutine batch file.

- Storing the subroutine inside the original batch file saves space and makes it easier to transport the batch file, but it also makes the resulting batch file more complex.

- You can store subroutines inside the original batch file by using a series of IF tests to direct the batch file to the appropriate location.

- If you're writing a subroutine that can be called by more than one batch file, it makes sense to create that subroutine as a stand-alone batch file. That way, all the batch files can access a single subroutine. If the subroutine will be used by only one batch file, then it makes more sense to create that subroutine as part of the original batch file.

- DR DOS 6 and Novell DOS 7 offer several batch file commands designed especially for writing subroutines. These commands are not duplicated under MS- and PC DOS.

23

When Batch Files Don't Work

By now, you should have a good understanding of the basics of writing and using batch files. You should be able to create a batch file that uses standard operating system commands, as well as batch-specific commands and even some Batcmd commands. You should also know how to use replaceable parameters and IF tests to control the flow of the batch file. As you begin to use this knowledge in your computing, however, you're going to occasionally have a batch file that doesn't work properly, so you need to know what to do.

If your batch file is in a loop or doesn't appear to be doing anything, hit ^C or ^Break. This should stop the batch file and give you a "Terminate batch job (Y/N)?" or similar prompt. Answer Y for yes and press Enter. This is the only way to stop a batch file. If it doesn't work under DOS, you'll have to reboot. If the problem batch file is running under Windows, Windows 95, or OS/2, you might be able to close the problem session. Once you stop the batch file, you need to locate the problem. You can list the file on screen with the command:

```
TYPE file.BAT
```

However, you'll need to use an editor to make changes, so you might as well load it into an editor to begin with. While it's impossible to provide a checklist of everything you should do when your batch file fails, what follows is a list of what I've found to be the most common troubleshooting approaches.

Possible Error Messages

If you're lucky, the operating system will tell you why your batch file isn't working properly. However, the message is likely to be cryptic and difficult to understand. Listed next are some of the error messages you're likely to see, along with their causes and possible solutions. The specific wording of these messages will depend on which operating system you're using.

Syntax error

This is the nastiest error to deal with because it gives you so little information. Generally, it means that a command like IF has the wrong syntax. The solution is to turn command echoing on so you can see which line is the problem line and then review the syntax for that command to see where the problem is. Far and away, the two most common problems here are using a single equal sign for an IF test and testing a replaceable parameter like this:

```
IF %1==A
```

without first making sure the replaceable parameter has a value. You can avoid this error by always surrounding the replaceable parameter you're testing and the test value with parentheses, so there's never a nul value on either side of the test. Thus, this test should be rewritten as:

```
IF (%1)==(A)
```

Bad Command or File Name
Command or File Name Not Recognized

The batch file is trying to run a program that isn't in the current subdirectory or path. This is usually caused by misspelling the name of a program or batch subcommand or forgetting to change subdirectories or drives before running a program from a subdirectory not in your path. The solution is to verify the spelling of the program or batch subcommand or make sure the batch file changes to the proper drive and subdirectory. You should always have a batch file access the proper drive before changing to a subdirectory because you never know for sure if the user has changed drives before running the batch file.

Label Not Found

This means that a batch file issued a GOTO command, but the label listed after GOTO doesn't exist. The solution is to rewrite the batch file to include the specified label.

Abort, Retry, Ignore, Fail?
Abort, Ignore, Retry?
Abort, Retry, Fail?
Data Error
Drive Not Ready
Physical Media Error
Sector Not Found

These error messages indicate that the batch file, or a program being run by the batch file, is unable to read from or write to the drive it's trying to use. The most common cause is trying to read from or write to a floppy disk drive without a diskette in it, with the drive door open, or with an unformatted diskette in the drive. The second most common cause is a defective disk.

If you forgot to insert a diskette, go ahead and insert it and press R for Retry. However, *never* change disks while one is being read from or written to. For any other problem, press F for Fail and troubleshoot from the operating system. If you have a defective diskette, replace it. If you have a defective hard disk, you can generally correct the problem with a utility program like the Norton Utilities or PC Tools.

Access Denied

This means that the file you're trying to access is a read-only file. If you want to modify it, you must change the read-only flag with the ATTRIB command.

```
Batch File Missing
Batch File name Missing. Retry [Y/N]?
```

The operating system can read batch files only one line at a time. After executing one line, it goes back to the batch file to read the next line. When the operating system can't find the batch file in order to read the next line, you get this error message. The most common cause is a batch file that deletes itself. For example, BATCH.BAT:

```
@ECHO OFF
DEL BATCH.BAT
DIR
```

will generate this error message. When the operating system reads the DEL BATCH.BAT line it knows there's another line, but after deleting the batch file it goes back to read the next line and the batch file isn't there. Other less common reasons for this error message are batch files that rename themselves, substitute drives containing the batch file, or swap a floppy disk that contains the batch file for a different disk.

The solution is simple. Review the logic of the batch file and make sure that nothing causes the operating system to "lose" the batch file. It's usually easy to find the problem line. Just turn command echoing on and look to see which is the last line the batch file executes; that's generally the problem line.

If you want a batch file to delete itself, you can have it do so without generating this error message. Because the resulting batch file runs only once, however, it's usually easier to just ignore the error message. In order for the operating system to delete the batch file without complaining about it being missing, absolutely nothing must follow the DEL BATCH.BAT command, not even a Return. The easiest way to make sure this is the case is to enter the batch file from the command line via the COPY CON BATCH.BAT command and press F6 or ^Z immediately after entering DEL BATCH.BAT, without pressing Return first.

Batch Files Nested Too Deep

One batch file can call another batch file with the CALL command. When this happens, the second batch file is said to be *nested* inside the first. That second batch file can then call a third batch file, and so on. If these batch files become nested too deeply, they'll abort with this error message. The solution is to reduce the number of nested batch files.

Not Enough Memory
Not Enough Memory for . . .
Not Enough Memory to . . .

These mean that a batch file is trying to load a program but there isn't enough memory to run that program. The solution is to increase available memory by removing unnecessary device drivers or memory-resident software.

Not Ready Error

This error message indicates that the device the batch file is trying to access (e.g., LPT1, CON, or COM1) isn't ready, the disk drive isn't ready to use, or the hard disk has failed. For nondrive devices, try rebooting. If the problem continues, verify that the requested device is actually installed. If it is, the computer needs to be repaired. For a disk drive, try inserting a new, formatted disk and making sure the drive door is shut. For a hard disk, try using a utility program like PC Tools or Norton Utilities to repair the drive. If you don't have experience in this area, get help.

Cannot Start Command, Exiting
No Free File Handles
Too Many Files Open
Too Many Open Files

These error messages mean that the operating system is trying to open more files than is allowed. This generally happens when running a second batch file with the command:

```
COMMAND/C batch
```

rather than using CALL. The solution is to either rewrite the batch file or increase the values for the FILE switch in the CONFIG.SYS file and reboot.

Environment Full

The batch file is trying to create an environmental variable, but it doesn't have enough room. The solution is to either delete unwanted environmental variables or expand the size of the environment.

Environment Error

The operating system can't find the current environment. The only solution is to reboot.

Filename Too Long

DOS supports filenames of only eight characters or less and extensions of three characters or less. The solution is to shorten the filename to an acceptable length. You won't see this problem under OS/2 unless you use very large filenames or if you're using the FAT system rather than HPFS.

Disk Full

The batch file is trying to copy or otherwise write to a disk that either has no more room or (when writing/copying to the root directory) has no more room in the file allocation table for directory entries. The solution is to erase unwanted files.

Write Protect Error

The diskette the batch file or application is trying to write to is write-protected. The solution is to remove the write-protection.

File Sharing Conflict

This error occurs only on a network. The action of the batch file or application running from within the batch file conflicts with actions of another network user, for example trying to delete a file that's in use by another user. The solution is to rewrite the batch file to avoid conflicting with other users.

On or Off Parameter Required

The batch file issued a BREAK following by something other than an on/off switch. These two switches, or using BREAK by itself, are the only three valid ways to issue a BREAK command. The solution is to rewrite the batch file to use BREAK properly.

Invalid Path or Path Not Found
Invalid Path Specified: Check Path

The batch file issued a command that requires the operating system to search the path. While searching the path, the operating system found an invalid entry in the path. This is a problem with your path, not the batch file that's running. The solution is to make sure your path contains only valid subdirectories.

Other errors

Many other error messages are possible because any application your batch file runs can itself trigger an error message from the operating system. In addition, these programs might display their own error messages. When you see an error message you don't recognize while your batch file is running, check the back of your operating system manual to see if it's listed there along with possible solutions. If not, check the manual for the software your batch file runs to see if it lists that error message and possible solutions.

Check the Spelling

It's very easy to make a spelling error when writing batch files, especially when you're copying a file from the console. Sometimes it's difficult to spot a word that's slightly misspelled, like ECHE for ECHO. I use Microsoft Word, a word processor that lets you specify your own dictionaries, so I've developed a dictionary of batch commands and the common commands and messages I use in batch files. If your dictionary allows custom dictionaries, you might try the same thing.

You can also try an old proofreading trick. When reading anything forwards, you tend to get interested in the content and anticipate the words or spelling that should be there. That makes it harder to catch errors. The solution is to read backwards, or in the case of batch files, where lines usually can't be split up, from the last line to the first. While you won't be able to follow the logic (that's the idea), you're much more likely to spot spelling errors.

Look More Closely

Sometimes it's hard to follow the execution of a batch file. With command echoing turned off and a fast computer, it can be very hard to follow your batch files as they run. When I have this problem, I remove the @ECHO OFF line and slow my computer down to its slowest speed before running the batch file. If you're running Windows or OS/2, you can also start up other programs to slow the computer down even more. The CD-ROM includes the program SLOWDOS in the \OTHER\SLOWDOS subdirectory, which you can also use for this purpose.

Step Through the Batch File

MS-DOS 6.2 adds a nice feature for debugging batch files that's also supported by PC DOS but not Novell DOS 7. When you start a batch file with the command:

```
COMMAND /Y /C file
```

MS-DOS will load a second command processor and let you step through the batch file line by line. For each line, it will ask you if you want to execute that line. This is controlled by the /Y switch. The /C switch causes the second copy of COMMAND.COM to unload when the batch file finishes. If you use a /K switch rather than /C, COMMAND.COM doesn't unload. Note that the /Y switch must come before the /C switch.

To make debugging batch files easier, the CD-ROM contains a batch file called BATDEBUG.BAT. It includes command-line help and checks to make sure it's passed a replaceable parameter and isn't running under Novell DOS 7, but otherwise simply runs COMMAND.COM. To debug a batch file, simply issue the command:

```
BATDEBUG file
```

The batch file takes care of everything else.

Isolate the Problem

As you begin taking a closer look at your batch file, you'll most likely find that most of it runs fine but that it breaks down at some particular point. Once I've isolated the problem to a particular section of the batch file, I turn command echoing off for the rest of the batch file and just turn it on for that section. I also insert several PAUSE commands in the problem section so I can take my time examining the information on the screen while the problem section runs.

Separate the Problem Section

Occasionally, a particular section just seems so wrong that nothing I do will make it work. When that happens, I remove the problem section and make it a separate batch file. That way, I can run it by itself, supplying the input it needs, without the rest of the batch file getting in the way. I can add ECHO commands to see the values of variables and any number of PAUSE commands to review the screen. When I finally get this batch file working, I merge it back into the original batch file.

Diagram the Logic

When you have a problem involving logic testing, the best solution to resolving the problem is to map out the logic of the batch file. That way, you can make sure all the paths end up where they should and none of them are dead-ends. It's been my experience that dead-end paths are one of the major sources of logic errors.

Put It Aside for a While

When nothing seems to work, sometimes the best thing you can do is put the batch file aside and then come back to it. A number of times, I've put aside a batch file with what seemed to be an impossible task only to come back to it later and see an obvious problem. This approach works for many problems, not just batch files.

Start Over

If all else fails, the final solution is to erase the problem batch file or batch file segment and start over. Often, the second attempt will turn out better than the first.

Summary

- If your batch file generates an error message, that message can help you find the problem with your batch file.
- If your batch file appears to lock up, you can often regain control by pressing Ctrl–Break.
- After looking for error messages, the next thing to check when a batch file doesn't work is to check the spelling of the commands.

- When checking the spelling doesn't resolve the problem, try turning command echoing on and adding PAUSE commands to watch command execution closer.

- You can also try isolating the problem portion of the batch file into a separate batch file.

- When the batch file problem involves logic testing, try drawing a map of the logic.

- As a last resort, put the problem batch file aside for a while, or start over.

24

Review

Take a few moments and try to figure out solutions to the following three problems. It's important that you have the skills necessary to solve them before you go on. The answers are in Appendix A.

Problem 7

A friend of yours is always copying files between two different machines. Several times, she has made the mistake of copying a file to a floppy disk when another version of that very file was already on the floppy disk. She has asked you to write a batch file to copy all the files she specifies on the command line to the A drive, but only if the file doesn't already exist there.

The complete filename with the extension will be provided on the command line, so don't make any assumptions about the name. When wildcards are used, the batch file should copy all the files to the A drive that don't exist there, while skipping the ones that do. Keep the user informed of the process.

Problem 8

You're working with a program you don't normally use, and you find yourself entering the same long command over and over. You'll be using this program for only a few weeks, so you first elected not to construct a batch file to issue this one command. However, you change your mind and decide to write a batch file to handle it.

When you run this new batch file with the command after its name, it should store that command in the environment and then run it. When you run the batch file alone, it should issue the command stored in the environment. The command is very long, so you want to avoid limiting the command length to nine pieces, corresponding to %1 through %9. You have a lot of free environmental space, so you aren't worried about running out.

Problem 9

Your friend from problem 7 likes your batch file but asks you for a modification. Sometimes she wants to overwrite the file on the disk with the one on the hard disk. Rather than just skipping all the files that exist on the floppy disk, she wants the batch file to show her information on both versions and ask her what to do.

25

An Automated Batch
File Help System

One problem with having a lot of batch files is that it's difficult to remember which batch file does what. One way around this is with a menu. Menus are nothing more than a list of available options, along with some method of selecting the various options. Menus are discussed in detail in the next chapter, but if you write a menu system with an entry for every one of your batch files you're going to have to work through a lot of menus to find one particular batch file.

One way around this problem is to install the batch files to a graphical user interface, such as Windows or OS/2. The longer descriptions allowed on the desktop by these environments, plus the ability to attach custom icons and group similar programs into folders, can go a long way towards making sure you can find the specific batch file you need.

This chapter lists several batch file approaches to solving the problem of locating a specific batch file. They work well under DOS and you can also use them to manage lesser-used batch files in a graphical environment, where you don't want to clutter up your desktop with batch files you use only occasionally.

Help Files

One approach is to write your own help file, like HELP.BAT. It's shown here, without documentation and command-line help (the CD-ROM version has both):

```
@ECHO OFF
CLS
ECHO DISCARD.BAT
ECHO ------
ECHO Will Move All Unwanted Files
ECHO To A Directory For Holding
```

```
ECHO SYNTAX: DISCARD FILE1 FILE2
BATCMD SL

ECHO MAINTAIN.BAT
ECHO ------
ECHO Will Erase Temporary Files,
ECHO Sort Files, And Run Your
ECHO File Defragmentation Program
ECHO SYNTAX: MAINTAIN
ECHO WARNING: Takes Two Hours To Run
BATCMD SL

ECHO PRINT.BAT
ECHO -----
ECHO Will Print ASCII Files Automatically
ECHO SYNTAX: PRINT FILE1 FILE2 FILE3
ECHO WARNING: Make Sure Printer Is On
ECHO Or Computer Will Lock Up
```

It displays the purpose of each batch file. Once you've accumulated a lot of batch files, however, it can be time-consuming to read through all these messages looking for a specific file. When you reach this point, you can use IF tests to make batch file help somewhat context-sensitive.

A segment of HELP1.BAT might help to illustrate this. The command CAPITAL %1 converts the first replaceable parameter to all uppercase and stores it in the environment under the name Ronny. After that, the batch file jumps to the section entered by the user, which gives help on only the requested topic. The segment of HELP1.BAT shown here also includes the section displayed when the user requests help on utilities:

```
CAPITAL %1

IF %RONNY%==UTILITY GOTO    UTILITY
IF %RONNY%==UTILITIES GOTO UTILITY
IF %RONNY%==PRINTING GOTO   PRINTING
IF %RONNY%==PRINT GOTO      PRINTING
IF %RONNY%==BACKUP GOTO     BACKUP
IF %RONNY%==BACK GOTO       BACKUP
IF %RONNY%==MISC GOTO       MISC
GOTO WRONG

:UTILITY
    ECHO DISCARD.BAT
    ECHO -----------
    ECHO Will Move All Unwanted Files
    ECHO To A Directory For Holding
    ECHO SYNTAX: DISCARD FILE1 FILE2...
GOTO END
```

Customized Help

While writing menus or custom help batch files works, it's a difficult system to maintain. Each time you write a batch file or discard an existing batch file, you must update everything to reflect that change. Otherwise, your help system gets out of "sync" with your batch files and gives outdated information.

One approach allows you to add and delete batch files at will and never gets out of sync, but it requires some special consideration when you create your batch file. First, it helps if you store all your batch files in a common subdirectory. I use C:\BAT for this, although the name doesn't matter. If you use a different subdirectory name, however, you'll need to modify these batch files to work with your subdirectory name.

While you don't need to keep all your batch files in one subdirectory, it makes the help system work much better. If you have your batch file arsenal scattered across multiple subdirectories, the help system can give you information on only one subdirectory at a time. Also, for these batch files to work across different subdirectories, you'll need to modify them to either take the subdirectory as an input or always use the current subdirectory.

Second, you must create batch files with the proper internal documentation and consistent capitalization, although readers with OS/2 or a later version of DOS, where FIND can be configured to ignore capitalization, can ignore this consideration. This requirement affects only the first five lines of the batch file, and every batch file should begin with these same first five lines:

```
@ECHO OFF
REM NAME:
REM PURPOSE:
REM VERSION:
REM DATE:
```

HELPBAT.BAT, shown in Figure 25.1, uses this documentation to display custom help about each batch file. It begins with a FOR loop that loops through each batch file in the C:\BAT subdirectory. (The OS/2 versions of these batch files are in the F:\BAT subdirectory.) For each batch file, it calls itself with a special flag that causes HELPBAT.BAT to jump to a special routine the second time through.

That special subroutine displays the name of the batch file and underlines it. It has access to the name because it's passed to the subroutine as a replaceable parameter. After displaying the name, it types the batch file using the TYPE command and pipes the information to the FIND filter, which then displays only the purpose line. This is the reason for my recommendation in Chapter 4 to put your entire purpose statement on one line; that way, this display will completely explain the purpose of the batch file.

If you must use multiple lines for your purpose statement, you could start each one with PURPOSE: to make sure these help batch files display the entire purpose. That does, however, tend to make the help screen look cluttered. After that, control returns to the original version of HELPBAT.BAT, which loops through to the next batch file, if any remain.

On a 16-MHz 80386 this system runs slow enough that I can read all the lines as they scroll on the screen, but on a 66-MHz 80486 the lines scroll by too fast to read. If that happens to you, replace the ECHO %1 line with TYPE %1 ¦ FIND "NAME:". That will cut the speed of the display in half because the batch file now has to type the batch file twice and use the FIND filter twice to locate specific text. If it still runs too fast, you can add lines to display the version and last modified date. If you display all four pieces of information, that version of HELPBAT.BAT will run at one-fourth the speed of the original version.

Batch File Line	Explanation
`@ECHO OFF`	Turn command-echoing off.

`REM NAME:    HELPBAT.BAT`
`REM PURPOSE: Display .BAT Purpose`
`REM VERSION: 1.00`
`REM DATE:    November 6, 1991`
	Documentation remarks.

`IF (%2)==(DISPLAY) GOTO DISPLAY`	This line checks to see if the second replaceable parameter is a DISPLAY, indicating the batch file is calling itself as a subroutine. If so, it jumps to the subroutine section.
`NEEDHELP %0 %1` `IF ERRORLEVEL 1 GOTO HELP`	Use the NeedHelp utility program to check and see if the user requested help.
`FOR %%J IN (C:\BAT\*.BAT) DO` `            CALL HELPBAT %%J DISPLAY`	When running as the main routine, loop through each batch file in the C:\BAT subdirectory and call this batch file as a subroutine. Pass it the batch filename and a flag to indicate its subroutine status. If you keep batch files in a different location, change the C:\BAT to the name of that subdirectory. To work in the current directory, change the first portion of the command to FOR %%J IN (*.BAT).
`GOTO END`	After looping through all the batch files in the main routine, exit the batch file.
`:DISPLAY`	Label marking the beginning of the subroutine.
`   ECHO %1`	Display the name of the batch file by echoing the %1 replaceable parameter, which contains the name since it was passed when the batch file called itself as a subroutine.
`   ECHO ─────────`	Underline the name of the batch file to set it off from the purpose.
` TYPE %1	FIND "PURPOSE:"`	Type the batch file and use the Find filter to search for the line containing the phrase PURPOSE:. In most batch files, this line will be the purpose line, although a few batch files—like this one—will have PURPOSE as part of a command. When that happens, two lines will be displayed.
`   BATCMD SL`	Use the Batcmd utility to display a blank line.
`GOTO END`	The subroutine is finished, so exit the batch file. Control will return to the version of HELPBAT.BAT running as the main routine.

`:HELP`
`   ECHO Reads Batch Files & Displays`
`   ECHO The Name And Purpose Line`
`GOTO END`
	Display a help screen and exit the batch file when the user requests help.

`:END`	Label marking the end of the batch file.

Figure 25.1 HELPBAT.BAT displays the name of each batch file and its purpose line.

If you don't want all this additional information, you can use the SLOWDOS program in the \OTHERS\SLOWDOS subdirectory of the CD-ROM to slow down the batch file. Experiment with the delay parameter until you find the setting that's right for your system.

When you delete a batch file, it ceases to exist and the FOR loop bypasses any reference to it. When you add a new batch file, it contains all the information required by HELPBAT.BAT and the FOR loop automatically includes it. As a result, the system is automatically current when you modify your batch files.

For OS/2 users, there's a VX-REXX program called BATHELP.EXE in the \UTILITY \OS2\BATHELP subdirectory of the CD-ROM that performs all these functions in a graphical environment. To use it, copy the VREDIT.DLL file to a subdirectory in your path. BATHELP.EXE gathers up all the files ending with the .CMD extension in the current subdirectory and all the subdirectories branching off the current subdirectory. Thus, if you run it from the root directory, it will show all the files on your hard disk. This means you don't have to put all your batch files in one subdirectory if you don't want to.

For each file, BATHELP shows the filename, complete path to the file, and purpose line. Scrolling is handled automatically, so you can move around the file list reading the descriptions of each file. Since it processes all .CMD files, it displays help on both your batch and REXX program files. OS/2 users will find BATHELP.EXE to be very useful.

Context-Sensitive Help

While HELPBAT.BAT is a very effective method of displaying general batch file help, it can be overpowering when you have a lot of batch files. For example, I have over 1,000 batch files for all the books I've written. Finding a specific batch file using HELPBAT.BAT would take a long time and a lot of reading.

Fortunately, narrowing the search is fairly easy. You simply need to add a filter to the line that types the batch files, as shown in HELPBAT2.BAT. When you don't enter any text, you get all the purpose lines, as you do with HELPBAT.BAT. However, when you enter a phrase, HELPBAT2.BAT displays the purpose line for only those batch files that contain that phrase.

HELPBAT2.BAT is very similar to HELPBAT.BAT, but it differs in two areas. First, you must construct the phrase to search on as an environmental variable. Second, this phrase must appear on the purpose line, and it must be worded correctly. If the purpose line was:

```
REM PURPOSE: Runs The Menu Program
```

then the phrases Menu, Menu Program, and The Menu would all display this line, but the phrases Run The Menu, Runs Menu, and Menu Program Now wouldn't. The section of batch file code that constructs the environmental variable is as follows:

```
:TOP
   IF NOT (%FIND%)==() SET FIND=%FIND% %1
   IF (%FIND%)==() SET FIND=%1
   IF NOT (%FIND%)==() SET BLANK=NO
   SHIFT
```

```
    IF (%1)==() GOTO RUN
GOTO TOP
```

This code loops around, constructing the FIND environmental variable, by adding one word at a time until it runs out of replaceable parameters. After that, it's used as an additional search parameter:

```
:DISPLAY
    IF %BLANK%==YES GOTO BLANK
    ECHO %1
    ECHO ----------
    TYPE %1 ¦ FIND "%FIND%" /I ¦ FIND "PURPOSE:" /I
    BATCMD SL
GOTO END
```

Notice how it skips the additional searching by jumping to a different section if there's no replaceable parameters, but includes a second FIND filter search if replaceable parameters are entered. It's required because using a FIND filter to search on an empty replaceable parameter would cause none of the lines to match.

While HELPBAT2.BAT displays the purpose line for only those batch files that contain the text the user specifies on the command line, it displays the underlined filenames of every batch file in the subdirectory. You can avoid this, but it requires several steps. First, pipe the results of the FIND search into a file. If the FIND search is successful, this file will contain the purpose line; otherwise, it will be a zero-length empty file. Second, check the file (called JUNK.@@@) with IsItZero to see if it's a zero-length file. If so, the batch file currently being processed doesn't match the search criteria, so it's skipped.

I originally checked for a zero-length file by copying JUNK.@@@ to a new name and then seeing if the new file existed. This worked because MS-DOS won't copy a zero-length file. However, other versions of DOS do copy zero-length files, so I wrote the IsItZero utility to work with all DOS versions. There's also an ISITZERO.CMD REXX program for OS/2 users.

If it isn't a zero-length file, then you can display the name of the batch file and the purpose line by typing JUNK.@@@ to the screen. HELPBAT3.BAT accomplishes this. First, it searches for the text with the command:

```
TYPE %1 ¦ FIND "%FIND%" /I ¦ FIND "PURPOSE:" /I > JUNK.@@@
```

which pipes the results of the search to a temporary file. Note that this line can cause problems if the text you're searching on is so long that it causes the line to exceed the command-line length limit. Next, it finds out if it's a zero-length file with the commands:

```
ISITZERO JUNK.@@@
IF ERRORLEVEL 4 GOTO END
```

If the batch file makes it past these two lines, then it's not a zero-length file, so the search was successful. Finally, it displays the batch file and purpose line with the commands:

```
ECHO %1
ECHO ----------
TYPE JUNK.@@@
```

Depending on how many batch files you have, you'll find either HELPBAT.BAT or HELPBAT3.BAT a big help in figuring out which batch file does what. I use HELP-BAT3.BAT constantly on my system.

Summary

- One way to keep track of all your batch files is to access them through a menu system.

- If you track your batch files with a menu system, you must update the menu system every time you add or delete a batch file.

- Another way to track your batch files is to write yet another batch file to provide help on existing batch files. This can be noncontext-sensitive like HELP.BAT, or context-sensitive like HELP1.BAT.

- Before you can write a more advanced help system, you must store your batch files in a common subdirectory and construct them with the proper internal documentation.

- HELPBAT.BAT automatically displays the purpose line for each batch file. It doesn't require any modifications when you add or delete batch files.

- HELPBAT2.BAT uses the FIND filter to display the purpose line for only batch files that contain a specified piece of text. However, HELPBAT2.BAT still displays the name of all the batch files.

- HELPBAT3.BAT uses the FIND filter to display the purpose line for only batch files that contain a specified piece of text. By using several tricks, HELPBAT3.BAT avoids displaying the names of batch files that don't match the search criteria.

26

DOS Batch File Menus

Back in 1983, the company I worked for got its first few computers. They were shared by over 20 users, most of whom didn't know much about computers at the time. After answering the question "How do I start Lotus?" constantly for several weeks, I developed a menu system very much like the first menu system I'll describe in this chapter. I placed it on the most frequently used computer. The MIS manager saw it and laughed at it, saying that no one would ever use it. Several days later, I saw him copying it onto the other computers! He thought it wasn't necessary, but the users loved it.

The purpose of a menu system is to handle much of the overhead involved in performing routine tasks with a hard disk, like changing subdirectories and starting programs. Menus are becoming much less popular than they have been in the past, however, because graphical environments like Windows, Windows 95, and OS/2 eliminate the need for them. For that reason, this chapter discusses implementing menus only under DOS.

It's still important to study batch file-based menus. You're likely to run into this type of menu system on older machines that lack the power to run Windows or OS/2. Menus are revisited in Chapter 36, where you'll look at utility programs designed to make menus even easier to write and use.

Introduction to Menus

A menu is nothing more than a list of options on the screen, and it allows you to select these options by typing a letter or number. Menu options can do more than just automatically run a program; they can also control how dangerous programs are used. For example, if you try to format a floppy disk without the drive specification (FORMAT, for instance), you could erase your entire hard disk with some older versions of DOS. You can avoid this by formatting disks from the menu. The menu option to format a disk runs a batch file, thus preventing the user from entering the command incorrectly.

Displaying a Menu

The menu itself is nothing more than text on the screen, displayed using any of the methods explored in Chapters 20 and 21. For all the examples in this chapter, I'll be using .COM files produced by the BatScreen screen compiler. Refer to Chapter 20 for documentation on this program. Menus fall into four very broad categories:

- Nonresident nonnested menus
- Resident nonnested menus
- Nonresident nested menus
- Resident nested menus

The first menu type is called *nonresident* because, after displaying the menu screen, it removes itself from memory—leaving you with nothing but the operating system. Entering a selection, say 1, to run a word-processing program with a nonresident menu does nothing by itself; you must also create a batch file called 1.BAT to perform the action under the first option in the menu. Entering 1 runs 1.BAT. In addition to running the word processor, 1.BAT would typically contain a final command to redisplay the menu.

The first menu type is also called *nonnested* because none of the menu items call other menus. When one of the menu items calls another menu, the menu being called is nested inside the first menu. Menus can be nested as deeply as you like.

The second menu type is called a *resident* menu because the menu remains in memory, watching over your selection and then executing that selection. The advantage of this approach is the menu can monitor users and make sure they don't enter invalid selections. The disadvantage of this approach is that the batch file driving a resident menu is much more complex.

Memory usage isn't a problem with a resident menu system. Unlike traditional memory-resident software that uses a lot of memory, a batch file needs only a few bytes for use as a pointer while another program is running.

Nested menus, the third and fourth menu types on the list, are duplicates of the first two, only they have additional menus nested inside them. These types of menus are much more complex. A single menu screen can comfortably display 40 or more options in two columns, or even 60 in three columns, so it's rarely necessary to write nested menus. If you need menus this complex, you're usually better off using one of the commercial or shareware menu development packages rather than depending on batch files. For this reason, this chapter contains only a very general description of nested menus.

Nonresident Nonnested Menus

You'll develop a complete nonresident nonnested menu system as an example in this chapter. Figure 26.1 shows the hard disk structure you'll be using, and Figure 26.2 shows how the menu will look.

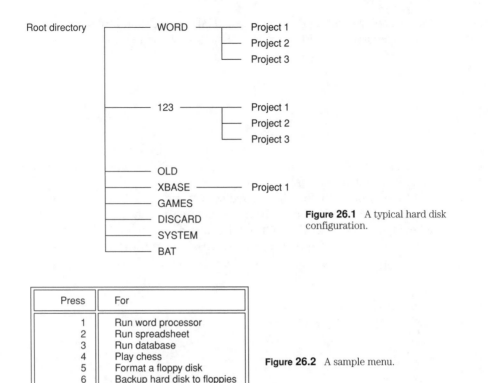

Figure 26.1 A typical hard disk configuration.

Press	For
1	Run word processor
2	Run spreadsheet
3	Run database
4	Play chess
5	Format a floppy disk
6	Backup hard disk to floppies

Figure 26.2 A sample menu.

All the files for this demonstration system are stored in the \BAT-FILE\DOS\MENU1 subdirectory on the CD-ROM that comes with this book. In order to allow you to experiment with the nonresident nonnested menu system, I've included slightly altered copies of the batch files shown in the book on the CD-ROM. The modifications are as follows:

- The batch files would normally return to the root directory, but because the files are stored in a subdirectory I've commented out this line. Since the action takes place in the MENU.BAT subdirectory, you need to make this change in only one location to make it operational.

- The batch files don't automatically return to the C drive; instead, they remain on whatever drive you ran them from. Each batch file changes to the drive containing the application it's running, while MENU.BAT takes care of returning to C:\, so you'll need to modify each batch file to make the system operational.

- Because there are no applications to run on the CD-ROM, the batch files that run the applications merely simulate running them by displaying a screen and pausing until you press a key. Of course, on your own system you'd want to modify the batch files to run your specific applications.

As mentioned previously, a nonresident nonnested menu is nothing more than a method of displaying the menu screen and a batch file to run each option. The batch file to display the menu screen is called MENU.BAT and is shown next without command-line help and without most of its internal documentation:

```
@ECHO OFF

REM C:
REM CD\
SCREEN1
```

As you can see, the only thing it does is change to the appropriate drive and subdirectory and then display the menu via SCREEN1. This runs SCREEN1.COM, a compiled copy of the screen.

The location of the batch files and screen compiler .COM files that drive this system is important. They must be in a subdirectory that's always in your path. I keep all my files in my C:\BAT batch subdirectory along with all my other batch files.

Now let's create the first batch file, 1.BAT, to run the word-processing program. The entire batch file is shown here because you need to look at it fairly closely:

```
@ECHO OFF
REM NAME:     1.BAT
REM PURPOSE: Run Word Processor
REM VERSION: 1.00
REM DATE:    June 2, 1992

NEEDHELP %0 %1
IF ERRORLEVEL 1 GOTO HELP

REM C:
REM CD\WORD
PROMPT EXIT To Return To Word
REM WORD
REM Delete The Next Two Lines
WORD
PAUSE
PROMPT $P$G
MENU

:HELP
    ECHO Runs Word Processor
GOTO END

:END
```

After the internal documentation checks to see if the user requested help, the batch file changes to the drive and subdirectory containing the word-processing program, changes the prompt (as mentioned earlier, to remind users shelling out that the program is loaded in memory), and then runs the program. In this batch file, the command WORD runs WORD.COM on the disk—another screen created with BatScreen to simulate a word processor. Users planning on converting this batch file for use on their system should remove the REM and PAUSE commands.

After running the applications, the batch file resets the prompt and then runs MENU.BAT to redisplay the menu. However, it runs MENU.BAT without the using CALL, so control never returns to 1.BAT. At this point, MENU.BAT picks up, returning to the appropriate subdirectory and redisplaying the menu. The other batch files, 2.BAT through 6.BAT, run in a similar fashion. The batch files for formatting a floppy disk and making a backup can run easily from any location on the hard disk, so they skip changing location. Because these programs don't allow you to shell out, they also skip changing the prompt.

The real advantage of this sort of system is its flexibility. If you want to run the spreadsheet and remember that 2.BAT can do that, you can issue the 2 command anywhere and load the spreadsheet. You don't have to load the menu program and you don't have to change to a specific location on the hard disk. Since 2.BAT is in your path, it works automatically when you issue the 2 command.

This is the very system I installed back in 1983, only back then I displayed the menu options with ECHO commands in the batch file. I upgraded the system to replace the ECHO commands with output from an earlier version of the screen compiler, and it's still in use today. As you can imagine, for an organization to continue using this type of application for almost 12 years through four generations of computers, it must be powerful and easy to use. I'll explain resident nonnested menus in detail and briefly cover nested menus, but I'm absolutely convinced that this approach creates the best menus you're going to find.

Resident Nonnested Menus

With a nonresident menu, the batch file displays the menu and then quits running. With a resident menu, the batch file hangs around and waits for the user to press a key. The advantage of this approach is that the batch file can monitor users, making sure they don't push the wrong key. The disadvantage is that writing such a batch file is more difficult, plus the system can be more complex to use. Because you're trading off extra "hand holding" against more complex development and use, I recommend this approach only when you're developing a system that will be used by inexperienced users.

There are two approaches when writing resident menus: the hybrid batch file and the stand-alone batch file. With a hybrid batch file, the menu system stays in memory to validate your selection, but then calls on stand-alone batch files to run the menu selection. With a stand-alone batch file, a single batch file validates the user's selection, executes that selection, and then redisplays the menu.

Both of these approaches require something the nonresident menu doesn't: an Exit or Quit command as part of the menu. Occasionally, someone will want to issue a command or run a program that's not on the menu. Because the nonresident menu simply leaves you at the command-line prompt after displaying the menu, that's simple. However, the resident menu keeps you within the cocoon of the batch file, so you need a specific command to exit the menu to get to the command-line prompt.

Hybrid batch file

In this section, you'll be developing a complete hybrid resident nonnested menu system. All the files for this demonstration system are stored in the \BAT-FILE\DOS\ MENU2 subdirectory on the CD-ROM that comes with this book. In order to allow

Batch File Line	Explanation
@ECHO OFF	Turn command-echoing off.
REM NAME: MENU2.BAT REM PURPOSE: Display Menu And Position DOS REM In Proper Location & Validate REM User Selections REM VERSION: 1.00 REM DATE: June 2, 1992	Documentation remarks.
NEEDHELP %0 %1	Use the NeedHelp utility program to check and see if the user started the batch file with a /? switch.
IF ERRORLEVEL 1 GOTO HELP	If the user requested help, jump to a special section to display that information.
REM C: REM Change Line Below To CD\ On Your System CD\MENU2	Change to the appropriate drive and subdirectory on your system.
SCREEN2	Display the screen.
:RETRY	Label used to loop when the user makes an invalid selection.
BATCMD GN	Use the Batcmd command to obtain a number from the user.
IF ERRORLEVEL 7 GOTO WRONG	If the user entered 7-9, that is an invalid selection so jump to an error-handling section. Because errorlevel tests for greater-than or equal values, the possible values from Batcmd (0-9) must be tested from largest to smallest.
IF ERRORLEVEL 6 6 IF ERRORLEVEL 5 5 IF ERRORLEVEL 4 4 IF ERRORLEVEL 3 3 IF ERRORLEVEL 2 2 IF ERRORLEVEL 1 1	If the user entered 1-6, that is a valid selection corresponding to a batch file so run that batch file. Since the batch file is run without the CALL command, control does not return directly to MENU2.BAT; however, each batch file calls MENU2.BAT as its last command.
IF ERRORLEVEL 0 GOTO END	If the user selected zero, he wants to exit the menu system to leave the batch file.
:WRONG	Label marking the beginning of the error-handling section. The batch file reaches this section and beyond only via a GOTO command.
BATCMD PC 19 1	Position the cursor using the Batcmd program.
ECHO Invalid Selection	Display an error message.
BATCMD BE	Beep the speaker using the Batcmd program.
GOTO RETRY	Go back through the user selection loop again.
:HELP ECHO Displays The Menu GOTO END	Display a help screen and exit the batch file when the user requests help.
:END	Label marking the end of the batch file.

Figure 26.3 MENU2.BAT drives a hybrid nonnested menu system.

you to experiment with the hybrid resident nonnested menu system, I've slightly modified the batch files for the CD-ROM. These modifications are the same mentioned earlier for the nonresident nonnested menu system.

As explained before, the hybrid system uses the same batch files to run the menu selection as does the nonresident system. For that reason, none of the batch files to run the software are printed in this chapter, although all of them are included on the CD-ROM.

The difference comes in with MENU.BAT, now called MENU2.BAT. After displaying the menu, it stays in memory, waiting for the user to enter a keystroke. When the user makes a selection, MENU2.BAT first verifies that the selection was valid. If so, it simply runs the proper batch file. Because that batch file will reload MENU2.BAT, it runs the batch file without the CALL command. If the user makes an invalid selection, MENU2.BAT displays an error message and waits for the user to make another selection. MENU2.BAT is shown in detail in Figure 26.3.

As you can see from Figure 26.3, MENU2.BAT is only somewhat more complex than MENU.BAT. Additionally, 1.BAT through 6.BAT will still function as stand-alone batch files. So you have additional error-checking of resident menu systems, and the nonresident system advantage of the batch files working from anywhere without having to run the menu. Thus, at the expense of a slightly more complex menu batch file, a hybrid menu system offers all the advantages of both the nonresident and resident systems without the complexities of the full resident menu system. That makes the hybrid system well suited for those applications where you want the control of a resident system without the added complexity.

Stand-alone batch file

In this section, you'll be developing a sample complete stand-alone resident nonnested menu system. All the files for this demonstration system are stored in the \BAT-FILE\DOS\MENU3 subdirectory on the CD-ROM that comes with this book. In order to allow you to experiment with the stand-alone resident nonnested menu system, the batch files shown in the book have been slightly modified on the CD-ROM. These modifications are the same modifications explained for the nonresident nonnested menu system earlier.

A stand-alone resident nonnested menu is one where a single batch file displays the menu and handles both user selection validation and running all the applications. They tend to be massive batch files that are difficult to write and harder to maintain. The stand-alone approach is useful under three circumstances:

Compilers. If you plan on compiling the batch file using a batch file compiler, like Builder or Builder Lite, you can use stand-alone batch files. However, most batch file compilers offer their own menuing options that are usually much more powerful than those in batch files, so here you're usually better off using the native language to develop the menu than you are the batch language. A few compilers (like Bat2Exec) offer no native menu support, so you must write them in the batch language.

Space. If your hard disk is very pushed for space, you can often save a little by using one massive batch file rather than several smaller ones. However, this approach requires the presence of a utility like Batcmd to get information from the user. If you have that on your hard disk anyway, it's not a consideration. If you don't, then the combination of Batcmd and the large batch file can exceed the space required for the individual batch files.

Security. If you want to control who runs the applications or how they run them, then building that security into a central batch file is much easier than building it into each individual batch file. Also, not being able to run individual batch files adds security. In fact, this is the best justification for the stand-alone approach to resident menus.

While the batch file that drives a stand-alone resident menu is long and complex, it possesses one secret that makes it easier to write and debug. MENU3.BAT, shown in Figure 26.4, is the same batch file used for the hybrid menu, only instead of running another batch file for valid selections, it runs one of its own internal routines by using the GOTO command.

To create MENU3.BAT, I took MENU2.BAT (Figure 26.3) and modified the error-level tests to go to a separate section of the batch file rather than running a separate batch file. For each of these six sections, I imported 1.BAT through 6.BAT, stripped off the documentation and command-line help, and added a GOTO command to the bottom. Once I finished those two steps, MENU3.BAT was finished and ready to use.

Nested Menus

A nested menu is nothing more than one menu where one or more of its menu items calls additional menus, or submenus, rather than a program. Nested menu systems are difficult to set up using stand-alone or hybrid batch files. The reason is numbering. Suppose the menu you've been working on had option 4, Play Chess, replaced by Play Games, and that menu selection brought up a selection of the different games you have installed on your system. The first menu used options 1 to 6, corresponding to 1.BAT to 6.BAT, so this second menu can't easily reuse these numbers. This second menu might use A to G corresponding to A.BAT to G.BAT. Now, if you add a third and fourth menu, what are you going to use to select the items?

You might try A to G for the first menu, H to M for the second, and N to S for the third. But what do you do when you need to add a menu item to the first menu? If you make it H, all the menus have to be renumbered and the commands the users have learned will no longer work the same. If you use T because it's the next available letter, then the menu items aren't numbered sequentially. There's no good solution to this problem with stand-alone batch files.

You'll have the same problem with a hybrid system if you want the menu options used within the hybrid system to correspond to the batch files—that is, if selecting option 1 runs 1.BAT. If you're willing to give that up and have option 1 run a batch file like WP.BAT, then nesting menus with a hybrid system is no more difficult than it is with a stand-alone system. However, this sacrifices the advantage of a hybrid system because knowing the menu option used inside the hybrid system doesn't allow you to run that program from anywhere on the hard disk without working through the menu first.

Batch File Line	Explanation
`@ECHO OFF`	Turn command-echoing off.

`REM NAME:     MENU3.BAT`
`REM PURPOSE: Stand-Alone Resident`
`REM          Non-Nested Menu`
`REM VERSION: 1.00`
`REM DATE:    June 2, 1992`
	Documentation remarks.

`NEEDHELP %0 %1`	Use the NeedHelp utility program to check and see if the user started the batch file with a /? switch.
`IF ERRORLEVEL 1 GOTO HELP`	If the user requested help, jump to a special section to display that information.
`:TOP`	Label marking the top of the menu portion of the batch file. As each menu option terminates, it will jump here to redisplay the menu.

`REM C:`
`REM Change Line Below To CD\ On Your System`
`CD\MENU3`
	Change to the appropriate drive and subdirectory on your system.

`SCREEN2`	Display the screen.
`:RETRY`	Label used to loop when the user makes an invalid selection.
`BATCMD GN`	Use the Batcmd command to obtain a number from the user.
`IF ERRORLEVEL 7 GOTO WRONG`	If the user entered 7-9, that is an invalid selection so jump to an error-handling section. Since errorlevel tests for greater-than or equal values, the possible values from Batcmd (0-9) must be tested from largest to smallest.

`IF ERRORLEVEL 6 GOTO 6`
`IF ERRORLEVEL 5 GOTO 5`
`IF ERRORLEVEL 4 GOTO 4`
`IF ERRORLEVEL 3 GOTO 3`
`IF ERRORLEVEL 2 GOTO 2`
`IF ERRORLEVEL 1 GOTO 1`
	For each of these valid selections, jump to a separate section of the batch file to handle the selection.

`IF ERRORLEVEL 0 GOTO END`	If the user selected zero, he wants to exit the menu system so leave the batch file.
`:WRONG`	Label marking the beginning of the error-handling section. The batch file reaches this section and beyond only via a GOTO command.
`BATCMD PC 19 1`	Position the cursor using the Batcmd program.
`ECHO Invalid Selection`	Display an error message.
`BATCMD BE`	Beep the speaker using the Batcmd program.
`GOTO RETRY`	Go back through the user selection loop again.

Figure 26.4 MENU3.BAT drives a stand-alone nonnested menu system.

Batch File Line	Explanation

:1
   REM C:
   REM CD\WORD
   PROMPT EXIT To Return To Word
   REM WORD
   REM Delete The Next Two Lines
   WORD
   PAUSE
   PROMPT PG
GOTO TOP
	Section to handle the first menu option. Notice how these commands exactly mirror the commands in 1.BAT. That makes it fairly easy to convert a hybrid system to a stand-alone system.

:2
   REM C:
   REM CD\123
   PROMPT EXIT To Return To 1-2-3
   REM 123
   REM Delete The Next Two Lines
   123
   PAUSE
   PROMPT PG
GOTO TOP
	Section to handle the second menu option.

:3
   REM C:
   REM CD\XBASE
   PROMPT EXIT To Return To XBASE
   REM XBASE
   REM Delete The Next Two Lines
   XBASE
   PAUSE
   PROMPT PG
GOTO TOP
	Section to handle the third menu option.

:4
   REM C:
   REM CD\GAMES
   PROMPT EXIT To Return To Chess
   REM Chess
   REM Delete The Next Two Lines
   Chess
   PAUSE
   PROMPT PG
GOTO TOP
	Section to handle the fourth menu option.

:5
   FORMAT-1 A:
   PAUSE
GOTO TOP
	Section to handle the fifth menu option.

:6
   BACKUP-1 C:\ A: /S
   PAUSE
GOTO TOP
	Section to handle the sixth menu option.

:HELP ECHO Displays The Menu GOTO END	Display help and exit the batch file when the user requests help.
:END	Label marking the end of the batch file.

Figure 26.4 Continued.

Because everything is built into a stand-alone system, the numbering scheme used for one menu can't interfere with the number scheme used for another menu, so you're free to reuse numbers or letters at will. That makes developing nested menus much easier in a stand-alone system.

I must warn you that programming nested menus with batch files is difficult, and the more complex the menu structure the more difficult it is. Your best approach if you have a lot of programs to run is to try to fit all the options on one, or at most two, menus. By using short descriptions and a multicolumn format, you can easily list 60 or more menu options on a single screen. By using the 26 letters and ten single-digit numbers, the most programs you can run with a single-digit command is 36, which will easily fit on a two-column screen with room left for instructions and formatting.

If you need more menu items than this, you're probably better off using a dedicated menu system rather than batch files. One of the better dedicated menu systems is Automenu from Magee Enterprises. It's a shareware program, so you'll find it on many bulletin board systems.

DR DOS 6 and Novell DOS 7 Menus

DR DOS 6 introduced the SWITCH command. While intended to allow the selection of subroutines from the command line, its primary usefulness is in designing menus. Novell DOS 7 retains the SWITCH command. Of course, batch files using the SWITCH command will run only on a DR DOS 6 or Novell DOS 7 system. The format of SWITCH is:

```
SWITCH Label1, Label2, Label3, . . . , Label9
```

where the SWITCH command is followed by up to nine labels, separated by commas. When the batch file encounters a SWITCH command, it pauses and waits for the user to press a key, ignoring any keys other than the numbers 1 through 9. When the user presses a valid key, the batch file jumps to the associated label using the equivalent of a GOSUB command. If the user presses the number 3, for instance, the batch file would act as if a *GOSUB LABEL3* command was issued.

SWITCH-M.BAT in Figure 26.5 illustrates the SWITCH command with a working batch file. Before SWITCH-M.BAT is operational, however, you'd need to modify it to issue the commands needed to run these applications rather than simply displaying messages. One interesting note about SWITCH-M.BAT is that it's completely self-contained; it needs no utility to get a keystroke from the user nor any other batch files to run, and it handles all text display itself. As a result, you could easily share SWITCH- M.BAT with other users.

If less than nine labels are listed on the line, it will ignore numbers higher than the number of labels on the line. For example, with the command:

```
SWITCH WP SPREAD DATABASE
```

Batch File Line	Explanation
@ECHO OFF	Turn command-echoing off.
REM NAME: SWITCH-M.BAT REM PURPOSE: Show Select Command REM VERSION: 1.00 REM DATE: June 11, 1992	Documentation remarks.
NEEDHELP %0 %1	Use the NeedHelp utility program to check and see if the user started the batch file with a /? switch.
IF ERRORLEVEL 1 GOTO HELP	If the user requested help, jump to a special section to display that information.
:TOP	Label marking the top of the menu loop.
CLS	Clear the screen.

ECHO 1 = Run Word Processor
   ECHO 2 = Run Spreadsheet
   ECHO 3 = Run Database
   ECHO 4 = Play Chess
   Echo 5 = Format A Floppy Disk
   ECHO 6 = Backup Hard Disk To Floppy
   ECHO 9 = Exit
	Display the menu.

SWITCH WP, LOTUS, DATABASE, CHESS,
        FORMAT, BACKUP, INVALID,
        INVALID, END
	Use the DR DOS 6 SWITCH command to select a section to function as a subroutine. Pressing 1 selects Wp, pressing 2 selects Lotus, and so on. Notice that the Invalid section is used twice. This is a quick way to handle invalid selections. Notice also how the Exit option selects the End section and exits the batch file.

GOTO TOP	After returning from the subroutine, loop through the menu again.

:HELP
   ECHO Show Using The Select Command
   ECHO To Build A Menu
   ECHO Only Works With DR DOS 6 And
   ECHO Novell DOS 7
GOTO END
	Display a help screen and exit the batch file when the user requests help.

:CHESS
   ECHO Playing Chess
   PAUSE
RETURN
	Section to handle the chess game option on the menu. Notice the section ends with a Return command and the sections do not have to appear in the batch file in the same order they appear after the Select command.

:FORMAT
   ECHO Formatting A Floppy Disk
   PAUSE
RETURN
	Section to handle formatting a disk. In all of these sections, you would want to replace the existing commands with the commands needed to run the software on your system.

:BACKUP
   ECHO Backing Up Hard Disk
   PAUSE
RETURN
	Section to handle performing a backup.

Figure 26.5 SWITCH-M.BAT illustrates using the DR DOS/Novell DOS SWITCH command to write a menu.

Batch File Line	Explanation
| ```
:INVALID
   ECHO Invalid Option Selected
   ECHO Press Any Key To Try Again
   PAUSE > NUL
RETURN
``` | Section to handle an invalid selection. Notice it displays an error message, pauses so the reader can read the error message and then use a Return command to go back to the menu. |
| ```
:WP
   ECHO Running Word Processor
   PAUSE
RETURN
``` | Section to handle running the word processor. |
| ```
:LOTUS
   ECHO Running Spreadsheet
   PAUSE
RETURN
``` | Section to handle running the spreadsheet. |
| ```
:DATABASE
   ECHO Running Database
   PAUSE
RETURN
``` | Section to handle running the database. |
| ```
:END
``` | Label marking the end of the batch file. Notice that this label is referenced in the SWITCH command for the option to exit the menu. |

DR DOS 6 and Novell DOS 7 will ignore any number higher than 3 because there are no labels beyond the third label. Several other structural considerations are important:

- The SWITCH command has no built-in facilities for displaying options. As a result, you have to handle that in the batch file prior to issuing the SWITCH command. You can, of course, use ECHO commands for this.

- Like all resident menus, the one displayed by the SWITCH command needs an Exit option. This is shown in SWITCH-M.BAT as the :END label, which is the last label in the SWITCH command. I almost always have Exit as option 9 in these menus.

- It can be confusing for the user to press a number and have nothing happen. I usually avoid this by having a single section handle invalid selections. Because I always have the exit option as number 9, I use this invalid selection section to pad all the selections between the last acceptable selection and the number 9 selection. Again, you can see this in SWITCH-M.BAT in Figure 26.5.

- You'll normally want to stay in a resident menu until the user selects the Exit option, so SELECT needs to be followed by a GOTO to cause the batch file to loop through the menu again.

- The SWITCH command is specific to DR DOS 6 and Novell DOS 7. It won't work under DR DOS 5 or any version of MS- or PC DOS. It also won't work when you're using a batch file compiler.

While SWITCH-M.BAT is a stand-alone menu and this section has focused on stand-alone menus, you can also develop a hybrid menu using the SWITCH command. To do that, each section in the batch file would need to call a stand-alone
```

batch file to perform the work. For example, the WP section of SWITCH-M.BAT could be replaced with:

```
:WP
    CALL 1.BAT
RETURN
```

By modifying all the sections in a similar fashion, SWITCH-M.BAT would run as a hybrid resident menu system.

Because the SWITCH command always uses the numbers 1 through 9, it isn't possible to develop a hybrid nested menu system because the batch file would need to call on batch files named other than 1.BAT through 9.BAT in order to handle all the menu options. While it still uses external batch files, that difference in names would prevent the user from using the same keystroke inside and outside the menu system.

Summary

- The purpose of a menu system is to handle much of the overhead involved in running programs and other routine tasks.

- The four types of menus are nonresident nonnested, resident nonnested, nonresident nested, and resident nested.

- A nonresident menu displays the menu option and then leaves the user at the command-line prompt to make a selection, while a resident menu displays the menu option and then remains in memory to validate the user's selection. Resident menus are more complex than nonresident menus.

- In a nonnested menu, none of the menu items is an additional menu, while in a nested menu, one or more of the menu items brings up additional menus.

- A nonresident menu displays text on the screen and then depends on batch files to run the menu options.

- A nonresident nonnested menu lets you run the menu options from anywhere on the hard disk, even if the menu isn't displayed.

- A hybrid resident menu turns over the execution of menu options to other batch files after it has validated the selection.

- A stand-alone resident menu handles menu display, selection validation, and option execution.

- Nested menus are more difficult in nonresident and hybrid systems because of the difficulty of arranging for different batch file names for each menu option. Nested menus are easier in a stand-alone system, but if you need to nest more than one or two menus, you're probably better off with a dedicated menu system.

- The SWITCH command in DR DOS 6 and Novell DOS 7 makes it easy to construct menus without a utility program to get a keystroke from the user.

27

A Document Archival System

What I'm going to describe in this chapter is a complete system for making sure that you never again lose an important file. Because it consists of several major sections, you can adopt only those sections that are necessary for your own applications. The major sections to the system are listed next.

Do periodic backups. Absolutely nothing is more important than periodically backing up your hard disk or important floppy disks. This is the only part of this plan that I recommend to everyone. In fact, without periodic backups, the rest of the system is fairly useless. If you don't care enough about your data to protect it with a backup, then why waste time protecting it in any other fashion?

Systematically copy crucial data files. Many important data files undergo routine revisions. Prior to making a major revision, I copy the file to be revised to a special holding subdirectory.

Never delete old files. Never erase an old file. Instead, copy it to a special holding subdirectory. When that subdirectory is full, copy the files to a disk and erase them from the subdirectory. Then store the disk in a safe place.

Index document files. Use a commercial indexing package to index your word-processed documents so you can find them faster.

Periodic Backups

Back when everyone used floppies, the most damage you could do was losing a few data files. Like mistakes, bad disks or defective hardware rarely damaged very much data. Large hard disks, however, now give us the ability to damage massive amounts of data with one mistake, or as the result of an errant command or defective hardware.

I insure my computer with a company called Safeware. Recently, they sent out a newsletter listing some of the more unusual claims they had paid. This list included the following:

- A man carried some work home with him. He kept the disks in a box that looked like his cat's litter box. As you might expect, the cat used the disk box to relieve himself and destroyed all the data on the disks.

- A boy was hiding behind the family computer during a game of hide-and-seek. When a friend found him, the boy made a dash to avoid being tagged. In doing so, he tripped over the power cord, which sent a shock through the computer that caused the hard disk to crash.

- A motorist collided with a fire hydrant, sending a column of water into the air. That water entered a nearby office building, damaging several computers.

- A man knocked his fish tank over, spilling all the water onto his computer.

- A man had his laptop out near the pool. The family dog bumped the table and sent the computer into the pool.

As you can see, computers can be damaged by a number of unexpected events. While an insurance policy like the one from Safeware can protect your hardware and even your programs, it's up to you to protect your data.

In the 1992 presidential campaign, there was a graphic reminder of the importance of backups on CNN. CNN reported a break-in at the campaign headquarters of Ross Perot. The only damage reported was the erasure of a file containing the names of 17,000 supporters. As you can imagine, this was potentially a tremendous amount of damage, especially if the names had been those of Perot's more generous supporters. In a close race, it could even have determined the outcome! However, at the close of the report, the CNN reporter noted that the Perot campaign had a backup disk.

Many small businesses maintain all their records—all the payroll records, tax information, bid information, and more—on a single microcomputer. Imagine the impact to that business if those records were lost. I know of one company who had their three computers stolen. To make matters worse, they didn't have backups. They were so desperate for the data that they ran ads saying that the thieves could keep the computers and they wouldn't press charges if they could just get the data back. They never did, and ended up going out of business.

I currently have about 20 articles in progress, the final version of my dissertation, a copy of this book, the related batch files, eight other finished books, and several books in progress on my hard disk. Until recently, I made a daily incremental backup and two full weekly backups. One backup is stored at home and the other is stored at my office.

Is this carrying things too far? I don't think so. An incremental backup takes about two minutes, and the two full backups take less than half an hour. So I spend about an hour a week on backups, this hour being insurance. It would take an experienced typist over 20 hours to retype just my dissertation, and it would take me thousands of hours to redo the research if I lost the hard disk copy and couldn't locate a printed copy. Even my notes are on the hard disk. Now add in the time to redo all the other files, and you'll begin to see why I make backups.

As I said, that was my approach until recently. I now have a very fast tape drive that can perform a full backup on both my hard disks in about 20 minutes, which is so fast that I've forgone incremental backups. I now make two full backups daily (one during supper and one after I quit for the night), and I keep the three latest versions of these two backup sets. I keep one set at home and the other at the office.

Which files to back up?

You should have copies of most of your software on the original distribution disks, so you don't need to back up these files very often. Just keep the originals in a safe place so they can't be damaged. Even in case of fire or theft, you can always replace your software by buying a new copy, so you can't lose it.

Except during installation, programs don't often change. The software is "tied together" with system files that include batch, AUTOEXEC.BAT, CONFIG.SYS, and .INI files. You can safely go a long time between backups of these files. They generally change only when you install new software or remove existing software. If damaged, you can replace these system files with files from an old backup or the original distribution disks.

However, things aren't that simple with your data files. You create them and then usually modify them quite often. It's important, therefore, to back them up frequently.

Types of backup

Your first hard drive backup should be a full backup. This gives you a good copy of installed software and system files, as well as a copy of your data files. When you change a data file, your operating system automatically changes an archive flag it maintains to indicate that a current backup no longer exists. At the end of the day (or week, if you want to live dangerously), you can make an incremental backup. The backup software looks through your hard disk for files with the archive flag. It then backs up those files and resets the flags.

This process is fairly painless because incremental backups are very quick. As you continue making incremental backups, the disks will begin to pile up. If you're constantly updating a 300K database, then you'll create a new copy of this file on disk every day because most backup software don't remove earlier versions of files from the backup disks during an incremental backup. Another problem is that files you've erased from the hard disk still exist on the backup disks, and files that have been re-named exist on the backup disks under both names. If you have to restore from backup disks, you can end up with a lot of extra files.

You can reduce these minor problems by using LISTFILE.BAT, shown here without command-line help or internal documentation (the CD-ROM version has both):

```
@ECHO OFF
C:
CD\
ATTRIB *.* /S > C:\CHANGED.TXT
```

All LISTFILE.BAT does is create a file containing a list of all the files on the hard disk. On my 386/20 with a packed 105MB hard disk, it takes less than two minutes to run. To avoid tying up your computer, you can easily run LISTFILE.BAT while running an errand or taking a break.

If you run it before backing up, you'll also back up this list file, even if it's an incremental backup—because you just changed it. If you must restore, you can compare the files that exist after you restore to LISTING.TXT. Any files that exist on the hard disk but not in LISTING.TXT were either erased or renamed, so they can be deleted.

While incremental backups are quick, restoring from them can be cumbersome if they've been going on too long. At some point you'll have so many disks from incremental backups that it will be time to erase them and make another full backup.

These types of backups will protect you from hardware problems and mistakes, but not from theft, fire, or other types of damage. For that, you need a second backup set stored off-site. In order to create a second incremental backup, your backup program must give you the option of not resetting the archive flag, and not all of them do.

Many organizations with crucial files maintain their three or so most recent incremental backups. These are often called the grandparent, parent, and child. The purpose of these multiple backups is that you can recreate changes to important files.

Multiple backups also give you a way to recover if your primary backup fails. I once needed to restore from a backup made by a major backup program. The program hadn't displayed any error messages when making the backup, but when I went to restore not a single file on the backup was recoverable. I sent the diskettes to the software company and they couldn't recover any data either. Luckily, I had a full backup from the day before, and it restored properly, so all I lost was one day's work. Without that second backup, all my data would have been lost.

Systematically Copy Crucial Data Files

If you need multiple backups for only a few files, there's a better way than running your backup program several times a day. I have a subdirectory called C:\OLD just for old copies of files. Every time I make a major change to a file, I copy it to this subdirectory with a number extension. So the first version of this chapter is CHAP-27.001, the second is CHAP-27.002, and so on. This way, I can always go back to an earlier version if I decide I don't like the changes I've made.

This chapter will use the same sample hard disk configuration that was shown back in Chapter 26 in Figure 26.1. COPYBACK.BAT automates copying important files to the backup subdirectory, with limited error checking. It expects to be passed the name of the file to be archived as the first replaceable parameter, and the archive name as the second replaceable parameter. If the file to be archived isn't in the current subdirectory, COPYBACK.BAT must be passed its full path. The operational code for COPYBACK.BAT is:

```
IF EXIST C:\OLD\%2 GOTO EXISTS
COPY %1 C:\OLD\%2/V
GOTO END

:EXISTS
   ECHO %2 Already Exists!
   ECHO Select Another Name And Try Again
GOTO END
```

Note that COPYBACK.BAT checks to make sure the target filename doesn't exist before copying. As these files continue to accumulate, you have a choice. You can erase older versions of the now modified (several times over) files, or you can copy them to floppy disks.

Never Delete Old Files

One of the things I learned a long time ago is that, just as soon as you erase a file, you end up needing it. As a result, I never completely erase a file unless I can easily recreate it. There are a lot of files on your hard disk that you can easily recreate, such as these:

.BAK files. With most word processors, every time you save a file, the prior version is saved under the same name with a .BAK extension. Because I save all crucial versions to a special subdirectory (as I explained previously), I routinely erase these files.

.OBJ files. When you run most compilers, they first turn your source code into .OBJ files, and then they turn the .OBJ files into .EXE files. If you have the source code, you can easily recreate the .OBJ files by running the compiler again.

.PRN files. These are ASCII files created when you print a spreadsheet file as a document. You can easily recreate them by reprinting the spreadsheet.

.$$$ and .TMP files. These are working files created by some commercial packages. They're usually erased by the package when you exit, but a reboot or disk problem can leave them on your hard disk.

Commercial program files. These are the files that come on your software disks. If you need to recreate these, you can copy them from the original disks.

These are about all the files I erase. I copy the rest of my files, when I'm finished using them, to a holding subdirectory called C:\DISCARD, and then I erase the original. Figure 27.1 shows DISCARD.BAT, the batch file I use for this. It copies all the files I list on the command line. Prior to copying, it checks to make sure that a file doesn't already exist in the \DISCARD subdirectory with the same name. After successfully copying the file, it erases the original.

Once I get a lot of files in the C:\DISCARD subdirectory, I copy them to a floppy disk and then delete them from the hard disk. Each of my floppy disks is numbered. After copying the files to a floppy disk, I perform three steps. First I erase the copied files from the hard disk. Next, I create a list of the files on the floppy disk. This list

Batch File Line	Explanation
`@ECHO OFF`	Turn command-echoing off.

`REM NAME:     DISCARD.BAT`
`REM PURPOSE: Moves Files To \DISCARD`
`REM VERSION: 1.00`
`REM DATE:    June 3, 1992`
	Documentation remarks.

`NEEDHELP %0 %1`	Use the NeedHelp utility program to check and see if the user started the batch file with a /? switch.
`IF ERRORLEVEL 1 GOTO HELP`	If the user requested help, jump to a special section to display that information.
`:TOP`	Label marking the top of the main loop.
`    IF (%1)==() GOTO END`	Once there are no more replaceable parameters, exit the batch file.
`    IF EXIST C:\DISCARD\%1 GOTO ERROR`	If the file to be discarded already exists in the discard subdirectory, jump to an error-handling routine.
`    COPY %1 C:\DISCARD\%1 /V`	If it reaches here, the file is not in the discard directory so copy it there.
`    IF EXIST C:\DISCARD\%1 DEL %1`	If the copy was successful, erase the original file.
`    SHIFT`	Move all the replaceable parameters down one level.
`GOTO TOP`	Continue looping.

`:ERROR`
`   ECHO %1 Already Exists In C:\DISCARD`
`   ECHO You Must Decide Which File To Keep`
`GOTO END`
	Display an error message and exit when the file already exists in C:\DISCARD.

`:HELP`
`   ECHO Moves Files To \DISCARD`
`   ECHO List Files To Move After Name`
`GOTO END`
	Display a help screen and exit the batch file when the user requests help.

`:END`	Label marking the end of the batch file.

Figure 27.1 DISCARD.BAT is a batch file to copy files to a discard subdirectory.

stays on the hard disk for easy retrieval when I want to search for a file. Finally, I index the document files on the hard disk.

Deleting all the files on the hard disk that were copied to the discard floppy disk would be easy if I copied all of them—it would just take a DEL *.* command. However, sometimes I have more files than will fit on a single floppy, but not enough to justify two. The problem is then to delete only those files that were actually copied to the discard floppy disk. DELOLD.BAT does just that. While it contains a number of lines to handle command-line help and internal documentation, the operational command is:

```
A:
FOR %%j IN (*.*) DO DEL C:\DISCARD\%%j
C:
```

The batch file changes to the A drive first because it would be more difficult to write this batch file to run from the C drive. To create a file on the hard disk containing a listing of all the files on the floppy disk, I change over to the C:\DIRECTORY subdirectory and issue the command:

```
DIR A: > 99.DIR
```

replacing 99 with the number of the current floppy disk. By maintaining a directory of all my discard floppy disks on my hard disk, I can rapidly search them for a file.

This might sound like overkill, especially if you rarely go back to a file after you're finished with it. The advantage to this system is that it's dirt cheap. In my area, 1.44MB floppy disks currently cost about $10 for a box of ten. So I have less than $125 invested in storing every one of my old files. The way I figure it, being able to recover just one of those files saves me much more than $125. I've been using this system for several years now, and I'm very pleased with the results. In fact, I find these disks so useful that I recently started using DISKCOPY to make duplicates to keep off-site for safety.

Index Document Files

Currently, a number of good word-processing index programs are available. These programs take a word-processed or ASCII file and create an index of it. They aren't indexes like you'd find in the back of a book; rather, they allow you to search for every document that contains a specific phrase.

ZyIndex is such a package. It will index most word-processed documents, using their native format. All you have to do is tell ZyIndex what it is. I use ZyIndex to index all the text files on my discard floppy disks so I can rapidly locate information on them. A big drawback to ZyIndex, and all other indexing programs, is that it indexes only text information; it won't index dBASE database files or Lotus spreadsheet files. To get around that problem, I create a small text file with the same name but a different extension that explains what the attached file does. For example, I create .WKT files to explain worksheet (spreadsheet) files. So HP.WKT explains in ASCII text what the file HP.WK1 does. I use .DBT files to explain the function of .DBF dBASE database files.

ZyIndex lets you assign names up to 30 characters long to floppy disks. These names can't include spaces, so I use an underscore to simulate a space. Because all the floppy disks are numbered, I give them the same name combined with their unique number. Disk number 43 is DISCARD_DISK_43.

INDEX.BAT runs the indexing program, shown here without the command-line help or internal documentation of the version on the CD-ROM:

```
@ECHO OFF

IF (%1)==() GOTO NONE

CD\ZYINDEX
IF EXIST A:*.DOC ZYINDEX D:\ZYINDEX\ A:*.DOC/03 DISCARD_DISK_%1
IF EXIST A:*.WKT ZYINDEX D:\ZYINDEX\ A:*.WKT/01 DISCARD_DISK_%1
IF EXIST A:*.DBT ZYINDEX D:\ZYINDEX\ A:*.DBT/01 DISCARD_DISK_%1
```

```
GOTO END

:NONE
   ECHO You Did Not Enter A Number
   ECHO For The Floppy Disk
GOTO END

:END
```

It knows the name should include the DISCARD_DISK_ specification, so I don't have to enter that. It also knows a number should be entered, so it checks to make sure that one was.

Summary

By following all four steps outlined in this chapter, you can be sure that you'll never lose an important data file. Additionally, you'll have the tools and techniques to quickly locate any single data file in your set of floppy disks that you use to store old data files. I'd like to hear from any users who have success with this system or who find ways to improve it.

The major steps in this plan are making periodic backups, duplicating crucial data files before modification, copying old files to floppy disks rather than erasing them, and indexing data files with a commercial indexing program. Also discussed in this chapter were the following:

- Periodic backups are crucial to the health of your data.

- Regular full backups and daily incremental backups will ensure the safety of your data.

- For further protection, keep rolling backups where you keep the last two or more backups.

- For full protection, keep both on-site and off-site copies of all your backups.

- Program files and batch files that support the operation of your system need to be backed up far less frequently than your data files.

- LISTFILE.BAT makes sure that every incremental backup includes a list of all the files currently on the hard disk.

- If you make a backup copy of crucial data files before modifying them by copying the file to a new name in a backup subdirectory, you can always revert to the prior version if you decide you don't like the changes you made.

- COPYBACK.BAT automates copying important files to the backup subdirectory so you can keep multiple copies of them when you make modifications. This allows you to revert to earlier versions as needed.

- For additional protection, as this subdirectory of prior versions of crucial files grows, you can copy it to floppies rather than simply deleting files.

- You can safely delete program files because you can restore them from the distribution diskettes.

- You can safely delete data files that are easily recreated, such as .PRN and .OBJ files.

- Move all other old data files to a holding subdirectory rather than deleting them.

- As this holding subdirectory fills up or when you need additional space on the hard disk, you can copy the files to floppy disks and then delete them from the hard disk.

- Maintain a list of files for each floppy disk on the hard disk to make locating a specific file quicker.

- Use a commercial program to index the data files on floppy disks to speed file location even more.

28

Simulating DOSKEY with Batch Files

Ever since version 5, MS-DOS has come with a wonderful keyboard enhancement program called DOSKEY. This memory-resident program gives you three major command-line enhancements:

- Command-line macros
- Command-line recall
- The ability to run multiple commands

When I talk to DOS users who've switched to OS/2, far and away the most common complaint I hear is about having to give up DOSKEY. I've also heard complaints from some network users that DOSKEY is incompatible with a few network drivers. Additionally, DOSKEY is a memory-resident program that significantly reduces available memory, something that some people can't afford.

Well, I have a solution for you. In this chapter, you'll see how to write batch files that give you most of the functionality of DOSKEY without any memory-resident component. They'll work on any operating system, including OS/2. In some cases, the batch files even out-perform DOSKEY!

Command-Line Macros

With a command-line macro, you enter a macro name and a command or series of commands on the command line. Unlike a command-line recorder, a macro isn't run immediately after it's created; it's merely stored in memory for later use. After that, every time you enter the macro name on a command line, DOSKEY replaces it with the command assigned to it.

DOSKEY stores these assignments in memory. That means they're lost when you turn the computer off or reboot. While you can save them to a file, you can't use that file to restore the macros to memory without first editing it.

In order to recreate command-line macros with a batch file, the batch file has to be able to do the following things:

Store a new macro. It can do this by piping the commands entered on the command line to a batch file.

Run a macro stored in a file. It can do this by running the batch file containing the macro.

Display the available macros. It can do this by simply typing the contents of each macro to the screen.

MACRO.BAT, in Figure 28.1, does all this. It restricts you to the macro names of 0 to 9, but you can easily modify this. It also limits your commands to nine "words" because %1, which contains the name of the macro, is shifted down to %0. You can easily modify this as well.

Batch File Line	Explanation
`@ECHO OFF`	Turn command-echoing off.

`REM NAME:    MACRO.BAT`
`REM PURPOSE: Run Macros From File`
`REM VERSION: 1.00`
`REM DATE:    November 6, 1991`
	Documentation remarks.

`NEEDHELP %0 %1` `IF ERRORLEVEL 1 GOTO HELP`	Use the NeedHelp utility program to check and see if the user requested help.
`IF NOT EXIST C:\MACRO\NUL MD C:\MACRO`	If the subdirectory used by this batch file to store macros does not exist, create it.
`IF (%1)==()   GOTO MISSING`	If the user failed to tell the batch file what to do, jump to an error-handling section.
`IF (%1)==(D) GOTO DISPLAY` `IF (%1)==(d) GOTO DISPLAY`	If the user requested a listing of the available macros, jump to a section to handle that.
`IF (%1)==(ABC123XYZ) GOTO SHOWTHEM`	If the first replaceable parameter is a subroutine flag, jump to that section.
`IF (%2)==()   GOTO RUN`	If the second replaceable parameter is blank, the user wants to run a macro so jump to that section.
`FOR %%J IN (0 1 2 3 4 5 6 7 8 9) DO` `     IF (%1)==(%%J) GOTO DEFINE`	At this point, the user wants to define a macro. Loop through the acceptable names and jump to that routine if the user entered a valid name.
`GOTO ERROR1`	At this point, the user entered an invalid macro name so jump to an error-handling routine.

`:ERROR1`
`   ECHO You Entered An Invalid Code On`
`   ECHO The Command Line`
`   ECHO`
`GOTO MISSING`
	When the user enters an invalid macro name, display an error message then jump to another section.

Figure 28.1 MACRO.BAT allows you to define, view, and run keyboard macros.

Batch File Line	Explanation

```:ERROR2```
   ```ECHO The Command You Entered Was Too```
   ```ECHO Long And Everything After The```
   ```ECHO %9 Is Missing From The Macro```
   ```ECHO```
   ```ECHO Try To Shorten Your Command```
```GOTO END```
	When the user tries to create a macro with more than nine "words," display a warning then exit the batch file.

```:ERROR3```
   ```ECHO The Macro You Selected (%1) Does```
   ```ECHO Not Exist```
   ```ECHO```
```GOTO MISSING```
	When the user tries to run a macro that does not exist, warn the user then exit the batch file.

```:RUN``` ```IF NOT EXIST C:\MACRO\%1.BAT GOTO ERROR3```	Make sure the requested macro exists. If not, jump to an error-handling routine.
```C:\MACRO\%1.BAT```	Run the macro. Without the CALL command, control does not return to this batch file.
```GOTO END```	Control does not return, so this is used only for formatting to close the loop.

```:MISSING```
   ```ECHO To Define A Macro, Enter The Number```
   ```ECHO Followed By The Macro Defination```
   ```ECHO```
   ```ECHO Numbers 0-9 Are Allowed```
   ```ECHO```
   ```ECHO To Run An Existing Macro, Enter```
   ```ECHO The Number Of That Macro```
   ```ECHO```
   ```ECHO The Available Macros Are:```
```GOTO DISPLAY```
	When a required value is missing, display an error message and exit the batch file.

```:DISPLAY```
   ```FOR %%J IN (0 1 2 3 4 5 6 7 8 9) DO```
      ```CALL MACRO ABC123XYZ %%J```
```GOTO END```
	Loop through the ten possible macro names. For each one, call MACRO.BAT as a subroutine, passing it the batch file name, then exit.

```:SHOWTHEM``` ```IF NOT EXIST C:\MACRO\%2.BAT GOTO END```	If this particular macro does not exist, exit the subroutine.
```ECHO -%2-```	Display the macro name.

```TYPE C:\MACRO\%2.BAT|FIND /V "@ECHO OFF"```
   ```ECHO```
```GOTO END```
	Type the batch file and display the line without the @ECHO OFF followed by a blank line, then exit subroutine.

```:DEFINE``` ```SHIFT```	Move all replaceable parameters down one level. This makes the macro name %0.
```ECHO @ECHO OFF > C:\MACRO\%0.BAT```	Pipe an @ECHO OFF to the macro.
```ECHO %1 %2 %3 %4 %5 %6 %7 %8 %9 >>``` ```C:\MACRO\%0.BAT```	Pipe the commands entered on the command line to the macro.
```SHIFT```	Move all the replaceable parameters down one level.
```IF NOT (%9)==() GOTO ERROR2```	If %9 still exists, then something was left out of the macro so jump to an error-handling section.
```GOTO END```	Exit the batch file.

Batch File Line	Explanation
| ```
:HELP
    ECHO MACRO.BAT Allows You To Define
    ECHO Up To Ten Macros (0-9) That Are
    ECHO Stored On Disk So They Do Not
    ECHO Use Any Memory
GOTO END
``` | Display a help screen and exit the batch file when the user requests help. |
| `:END` | Label marking the end of the batch file. |

Figure 28.1 Continued.

If you enter MACRO D, it will display all the available macros. If you enter MACRO #, it will run the macro stored under the number you enter on the command line. And if you enter MACRO # *commands*, it will store the commands in a macro without executing them. Macros are stored in the C:\MACRO subdirectory, which should *not* be in your path. They will remain there until you overwrite them or manually erase them, so macros are retained between sessions.

If you're interested in implementing this system but are concerned about being allowed to enter just one line of commands, note that, once MACRO.BAT has created a macro, nothing prevents you from going behind it and enhancing the macro batch files it creates because they're nothing but regular batch files. Additionally, there's nothing preventing you from creating one or more of the macro batch files yourself without using MACRO.BAT. You'll still be able to use MACRO.BAT to display and run the resulting batch file.

Command Line Recall

I really dislike the way DOSKEY, and every other keyboard program I've seen, stores old command lines. Every single command line gets stored. I tend to enter a lot of short commands, like DIR or D:, and I prefer not to have to search through all these looking for one or two long commands. That's the nice thing about a batch file approach: only those command lines you enter via the batch file are stored, so you control which ones are stored. If you enter a command normally, it will bypass the macro program, which is just perfect for short commands. If you enter the command after the batch file name, the command will be executed *and* stored for later use, which is just perfect for longer commands.

Like the macro batch file, old command lines are kept in batch files so they aren't affected by rebooting or turning the computer off. In addition, for especially complex command lines, you can edit the batch file directly. In fact, the command-line recorder is very similar to the macro recorder. But it does have three differences:

- After storing a command line, that command line is immediately executed.

- You assign macro names, but command lines are stored under the next available name.

- After all the names have been used, the oldest command line is discarded and the remaining ones are moved down one name to make room for the new command line.
```

As it turns out, all three of the differences are easy to accomplish with a batch file. To run a command line after storing it requires only one additional line in the batch file: a line to run the just-created batch file. Assigning the name to the command line requires that you search for the first available name; if none is found, 0.BAT is deleted, the remaining batch files are renamed to a number one lower, and then the current command line is stored in 9.BAT. Beyond this, the batch file, called CL.BAT, is very similar to MACRO.BAT, explained earlier. CL.BAT is reviewed in detail in Figure 28.2.

Batch File Line	Explanation
`@ECHO OFF`	Turn command-echoing off.

`REM NAME:    CL.BAT`
`REM PURPOSE: Store Command Lines`
`REM         Using Files Not Memory`
`REM VERSION: 1.00`
`REM DATE:    November 6, 1991`
	Documentation remarks.

`IF (%1)==(ABC123XYZ) GOTO SHOWTHEM`	If it is being called as a subroutine, jump to the subroutine portion of the batch file.
`SET USE=`	Reset the environmental variable used by the batch file.
`NEEDHELP %0 %1` `IF ERRORLEVEL 1 GOTO HELP`	Use the NeedHelp utility program to check and see if the user started the batch file with a /? switch.
`IF (%1)==(D)  GOTO DISPLAY` `IF (%1)==(d)  GOTO DISPLAY`	If the user requested the display of the available command lines, jump to a section to handle that.
`IF NOT EXIST C:\CL\*.* MD C:\CL`	If the subdirectory to store command lines does not exist, create it.
`FOR %%J IN (0 1 2 3 4 5 6 7 8 9) DO` `       IF (%1)==(%%J) GOTO RUN`	Loop through the ten available macros to see if the user has requested running one. If so, jump to a section to run it.
`FOR %%J IN (9 8 7 6 5 4 3 2 1 0) DO IF NOT` `       EXIST C:\CL\%%J.BAT SET USE=%%J`	At this point, the user is entering a command line to store and run so find the first available slot.
`IF NOT (%USE%)==() GOTO USE`	If a slot was found, jump to the section that processes the command.
`GOTO ALLUSED`	If no slot was available, jump to a section to create one.

`:RUN`
`   C:\CL\%1.BAT`
`GOTO END`
	Section that runs the command line selected by the user. Since the Call command is not used, the GOTO command is used for formatting and is never executed.

`:USE`	Label marking the beginning of the section that stores a command line and then runs it.
`   SHIFT`	Move all the replaceable parameters down one level.
`   ECHO @ECHO OFF > C:\CL\%USE%.BAT`	Pipe an @ECHO OFF to the batch file that was selected to store the command line.
`   ECHO %0 %1 %2 %3 %4 %5 %6 %6 %7 %8 %9 >>` `       C:\CL\%USE%.BAT`	Pipe the commands to the batch file that was selected to store the command line.

Figure 28.2 CL.BAT stores, displays, and reruns command lines.

Batch File Line	Explanation
`C:\CL\%USE%.BAT`	After creating the batch file to store the command line, run it.
`GOTO END`	Since the batch file was run without the CALL command, control never returns to this batch file so this command is used only for formatting.

`:ALLUSED`
`    DEL C:\CL\0.BAT`
`    REN C:\CL\1.BAT 0.BAT`
`    REN C:\CL\2.BAT 1.BAT`
`    REN C:\CL\3.BAT 2.BAT`
`    REN C:\CL\4.BAT 3.BAT`
`    REN C:\CL\5.BAT 4.BAT`
`    REN C:\CL\6.BAT 5.BAT`
`    REN C:\CL\7.BAT 6.BAT`
`    REN C:\CL\8.BAT 7.BAT`
`    REN C:\CL\9.BAT 8.BAT`
`    SET USE=9`
`GOTO USE`
	When all the available slots have been used, erase the oldest command line file, move the remaining ones down one level, and use the last slot to store the current command line.

`:DISPLAY`
`    FOR %%J IN (0 1 2 3 4 5 6 7 8 9) DO`
`        CALL CL ABC123XYZ %%J`
`GOTO END`
	When user requests displaying the command lines, loop through and display them by calling CL.BAT as a subroutine.

`:SHOWTHEM` `    IF NOT EXIST C:\CL\%2.BAT GOTO END`	If this particular command line does not exist, exit the batch file subroutine.
`    ECHO ─%2─`	Display the command line name.
`    TYPE C:\CL\%2.BAT ¦ FIND /V "@ECHO OFF"`	Display the contents of the batch file.
`    ECHO` `GOTO END`	Display a blank line by echoing an Alt-255 and then exit the batch file.

`:MISSING`
`    ECHO You Did Not Enter Anything`
`    ECHO After The Name So CL Does`
`    ECHO Not Know What To Do!`
`    ECHO`
`GOTO EXPLAIN`
	Display an error message when the user does not tell the batch file what to do and jump to another section.

`:EXPLAIN`
`    ECHO Enter CL D To Display The`
`    ECHO Existing Command Lines`
`    ECHO`
`    ECHO Enter CL # To Reuse One Of`
`    ECHO The Existing Command Lines`
`    ECHO Where # Is The Number Of`
`    ECHO The Command Line To Reuse`
`    ECHO`
`GOTO DISPLAY`
	Explain what the batch file does then jump to another section to display additional information.

Figure 28.2 Continued.

Batch File Line	Explanation

:HELP
   ECHO Enter CL D To Display The
   ECHO Existing Command Lines
   ECHO
   ECHO Enter CL # To Reuse One Of
   ECHO The Existing Command Lines
   ECHO Where # Is The Number Of
   ECHO The Command Line To Reuse
GOTO END
	Display a help screen and exit the batch file when the user requests help.

:END	Label marking the end of the batch file.

Running Multiple Commands

MULTI.BAT, shown in Figure 28.3, allows you to enter as many commands as you like on a command line, up to the limit the operating system places. It constructs an environmental variable containing the command by looping through the replaceable parameter and adding each one to the environmental variable until it reaches a replaceable parameter that's a caret (^); the caret tells it that the command is complete. At that point, it executes the command, resets the environmental variable, and starts over. Because replaceable parameters must be separated by spaces, the caret must have a space on each side.

Batch File Line	Explanation
@ECHO OFF	Turn command-echoing off.
REM NAME: MULTI.BAT REM PURPOSE: Issue Multiple DR DOS REM Commands On a Single Line REM VERSION: 1.10 REM DATE: May 7, 1991	Documentation remarks.
NEEDHELP %0 %1 IF ERRORLEVEL 1 GOTO HELP	Use the NeedHelp utility program to check and see if the user started the batch file with a /? switch.
SET COMMAND=	Reset the environmental variable used by this batch file.
IF (%1)==() GOTO ERROR	If the user did not tell the batch file what to do, jump to an error-handling routine.
IF (%1)==(^) GOTO ERROR	If the first replaceable parameter is a caret, the user specified the command wrong so jump to an error-handling routine.
:TOP	Label marking the top of the main loop.
SET COMMAND=%COMMAND% %1	Add the current word on to the end of the environmental variable that contains the command to run.
SHIFT	Move all the replaceable parameters down one level and make available another replaceable parameter as %9.

Figure 28.3 MULTI.BAT lets you enter multiple commands on a single command line.

Batch File Line	Explanation
`IF (%1)==() GOTO RUNLAST`	If there are no more replaceable parameters then the batch file has reached the end of the last command, so jump to a section to run it.
`IF (%1)==(^) GOTO RUN`	If the next replaceable parameter is a caret then the batch file has reached the end of a command with another one following, so jump to another section to run this command.
`GOTO TOP`	Continue looping.
`:RUN`	Beginning of the section that runs a command with other commands pending.
`    SHIFT`	Shift to move the caret that separated the commands out of the %1 position.
`    CALL %COMMAND%`	Run the command. When the command is a program, the CALL command is ignored but when the command is a batch file, the CALL command allows this batch file to regain control.
`    SET COMMAND=`	Reset the environmental variable that contains the command now that the command has been executed.
`GOTO TOP`	Continue looping.
`:RUNLAST`	Label marking the beginning of the section that handles running the last command.
`    %COMMAND%`	Run the last command. Since the CALL command is not used, control does not return to this batch file if the command is a batch file; however, control does return if the command is a program.
`GOTO END`	Exit the batch file.

`:ERROR`
`ECHO Invalid Commands Specified`
`ECHO The Command Is Multi Followed`
`ECHO By Command Lines`
`ECHO Each Line Must Be Separated By ^`
`PAUSE`
`GOTO END`
	Display an error message and exit the batch file.

`:HELP`
`    ECHO MULTI.BAT Runs Multiple`
`    ECHO Commands Entered On The`
`    ECHO Command Line`
`    ECHO`
`    ECHO ----------------------`
`    ECHO To Run, Enter:`
`    ECHO MULTI Command ^ Command`
`    ECHO Where The Commands Are`
`    ECHO Separated By A ^ With`
`    ECHO Spaces Around It`
`GOTO END`
	Display a help screen and exit the batch file when the user requests help.

`:END`	Label marking the end of the batch file.
`SET COMMAND=`	Reset the environmental variable used by the batch file before exiting.

Figure 28.3 Continued.

I used the caret because it's not likely to be used on the command line and because there's no lowercase version of it to complicate testing. If you need to use the caret surrounded by spaces in commands, you can substitute another unused symbol.

MULTI.BAT uses a nifty trick and has one limitation you need to be aware of. It executes all of its commands with:

```
CALL %COMMAND%
```

MULTI.BAT must do this so it can regain control if the command you enter executes a batch file. Interestingly, CALL has no impact if the command is not a batch file, so CALL DIR and DIR will perform exactly the same function.

The limitation of this construction is piping. DOS and OS/2 process pipes before handing processing over to MULTI.BAT, so the pipes will never even get to MULTI.BAT. As a result, none of the commands you execute using MULTI.BAT can use pipes. Otherwise, commands execute the same under MULTI.BAT as they do when run from the command line.

Summary

MACRO.BAT, CL.BAT, and MULTI.BAT provide most of the functions of the DOSKEY program without using any memory. And with MACRO.BAT and CL.BAT, you can automatically store information between sessions.

Chapter 29

Smaller Batch File Applications

This chapter presents a number of shorter batch file applications, some mundane and others unique. This diversity has two purposes. First, you can see how to use fairly simple batch files to solve everyday problems. Second, by examining batch files that are used for unusual purposes, you can see how to solve your own unique problems with batch files.

Maintaining Your C:\BAT Subdirectory

In several places in this book I've recommended you keep all your batch files in the C:\BAT subdirectory. In fact, the help system discussed in Chapter 25 requires this to work properly. However, it can make it difficult to create and modify batch files "on the fly" since you first have to change to the C drive and then the \BAT subdirectory. EDITBAT.BAT automates editing batch files in the C:\BAT subdirectory without having to leave your current subdirectory!

While the batch file contains a number of commands for error checking and help, its single operational line is:

```
EDIT C:\BAT\%1.BAT
```

Since this command automatically creates or edits the file in the C:\BAT subdirectory, you don't have to change to it first. EDIT doesn't create a .BAK backup file for you, but you could add that with the following line (placed before the EDIT line):

```
IF EXIST C:\BAT\%1.BAT COPY C:\BAT\%1.BAT C:\BAT\%1.BAK
```

Of course, you'll want to replace the EDIT command in EDITBAT.BAT with the name of the editor your operating system uses.

Screen Saver

A screen saver is a program that either blanks or places a colorful picture on the screen until you press a key, and you can construct your own screen saver with a very short batch file. NOBURN.BAT does just this. While it has lines for documentation and command-line help, its two operational lines are:

```
CLS
PAUSE > NUL
```

The CLS blanks the screen and the PAUSE > NUL keeps the prompt from reappearing until you press a key. NOBURN.BAT isn't as fancy as the commercial programs, but it's free and requires no memory when you aren't using it.

Is Windows Running?

Certain commands, like CHKDSK/F, shouldn't be issued while Windows is running. You can use either a utility like IsItWin or a few batch commands. When Windows 3.1 is running, it creates an environmental variable called windir, only it creates it differently than DOS. Windows creates windir as a lowercase environmental variable. The contents of windir is the location of the Windows program.

Microsoft's reason for having Windows create windir as a lowercase environmental variable is to keep you from altering its contents and pointing Windows to the wrong subdirectory. Because it's lowercase, the command ECHO %windir% won't display its contents, and the command SET windir=new will create a whole new environmental variable called WINDIR, while leaving windir unaltered.

Nevertheless, your batch file can find out if windir exists! CHECKWIN.BAT on the disk does just that. The operational commands for CHECKWIN.BAT are:

```
SET ¦ FIND "windir" > JUNK.1
ISITZERO JUNK.1
IF ERRORLEVEL 4 ECHO Windows Not Running
IF ERRORLEVEL 4 GOTO END
IF ERRORLEVEL 3 ECHO Windows Running
IF ERRORLEVEL 3 GOTO END
```

Basically, it uses the FIND filter to search for a line containing windir and pipes that line to a file named JUNK.1. If Windows is running, that file will contain information; otherwise, it will be a zero-length file. The batch file then uses the IsItZero program to inspect the file. This batch file is shown more for illustrative purposes since you can use IsItWin to see if Windows is running without creating any temporary files.

Changing Subdirectories

Many users have a very complex directory structure that's nested several levels deep. They often need to leave one subdirectory to check something in another subdirectory and then switch back, and are looking for a way to automate this.

You can actually attack this problem in a couple of different ways. The best way is probably using a quick directory changing program like NCD of Norton Utilities. If you need or want to tackle the problem with batch files, you have a couple of alternatives. If you're always switching between just a couple of subdirectories, you can write a custom batch file to change to each subdirectory. For example, you could write a batch file called 0-9.BAT with the single command:

```
CD\D\LOTUSFIG\0-9
```

to change to that subdirectory. I use this method to change back to my home directory on the network at the office, because entering CD\D\USERS\MKTEVAL\RICHARDS is a bit much.

Of course, this can be a complex solution if you have a lot of subdirectories to change between. You can write a batch file to partially solve this problem. This batch file marks the current directory as home and builds a second batch file to always return you to the home directory. The next time you run this batch file, it creates a new home directory and a new batch file to change you there. The batch file RETURN.BAT:

```
COPY C:\BAT\RETURN C:\BAT\RETURNTO.BAT
CD >> C:\BAT\RETURNTO.BAT
```

copies a file called RETURN to the batch file named RETURNTO.BAT. RETURN contains the single line, CD ^z, where ^z is an end-of-file marker. Because there's no return in the file, when the next line of RETURN.BAT pipes in the subdirectory, it gets added to the same line as the CD. The result is a line similar to this:

```
CD C:\D\LOTUSFIG\0-9
```

Even though this path includes the drive, it won't change drives under most DOS versions. That is, if you're trying to change to the \D\LOTUSFIG\0-9 subdirectory on the C drive, but issue this command from the D drive, DOS will remained logged onto the D drive and won't change to the appropriate subdirectory.

Because the batch file must be in a subdirectory in the path in order for it to work, RETURN.BAT is configured to always use the C:\BAT subdirectory. For that reason, every time you run RETURN.BAT, it overwrites RETURNTO.BAT with a new version. You can expand RETURN.BAT to handle multiple subdirectories by using a replaceable parameter on the command line and creating RETURN1.BAT, RETURN2.BAT, and so on. I'll leave this up to you.

If you don't want to create a custom batch file, you can use the batch file RETURN2.BAT as follows:

```
@ECHO OFF
CD %HOME%
```

There's no way to pipe the current subdirectory into the environment, so this batch file requires you to manually issue the command:

```
SET HOME=\D\LOTUSFIG\0-9
```

to tell RETURN2.BAT which subdirectory is home. The only real drawback to RE-
TURN2.BAT is that you have to manually type the home subdirectory into the environment. This method also has trouble changing drives under most DOS versions.

You can avoid having to enter the home subdirectory into the environment with
RETURN3.BAT, which stores the home subdirectory in the environment under the
name HOME. When RETURN3.BAT first starts, it checks to see if it was passed a replaceable parameter. If not, it assumes the user wants to change to the home subdirectory, so it does that and quits. Otherwise, it changes to the subdirectory passed to
it as the first replaceable parameter and stores that in the environment as the home
subdirectory. The operational code is:

```
IF (%1)==() GOTO GOHOME

CD\%1
    SET HOME=%1
GOTO END

:GOHOME
    CD %HOME%
GOTO END
```

Using RETURN3.BAT to change to a subdirectory (which you must do anyway)
automatically records that subdirectory into the environment. When you use RE-
TURN3.BAT without a subdirectory, it changes back to the last subdirectory you
changed to, using RETURN3.BAT with a subdirectory name. If you like, you can
modify RETURN3.BAT to record multiple home subdirectories in the environment.

If you routinely change between only a few subdirectories, it's possible to duplicate the power of Norton Utilities' NCD program with a batch file. RCD.BAT is a sample batch file that illustrates this. Run RCD.BAT by including the nickname of a
subdirectory to change to after the batch file name. RCD.BAT uses a GOTO %1 to
jump to that label, where it issues a command to change to that subdirectory. Because you can have multiple labels together in a batch file, it's possible to assign multiple shortcut names to a single subdirectory.

Some of the operational code for RCD.BAT follows. You can, of course, add as
many nicknames and subdirectories as you like.

```
GOTO %1

:BAT
    C:
    CD\BAT
GOTO END

:SYSLIB
:DOS
    C:
    CD\SYSLIB
GOTO END

:BOOKBAT
    D:
    CD\BATFIG\BAT
GOTO END
```

The problem with RCD.BAT is that you must manually append each new subdirectory. Also, if you specify a shortcut name that doesn't exist, the batch file will abort with a "Label not found" error message. Unlike the previous methods, RCD.BAT has no trouble changing drives because you can easily program that into the batch file.

Running Inflexible Programs

At an office where I used to work, we used one computer for all our communications, logging onto a remote database that supplied us with custom communications software. Because of the unique features of this database, we had to use the custom software. One of its limitations was that it stored the account number, password, and other information in a file called MENU.INF. Two people used this database, and they both had different account numbers, passwords, and so on, but the communications software couldn't handle multiple users. The vendor suggested keeping two versions in two different subdirectories. We used batch files to create a better solution.

The first user ran the configuration program to create MENU.INF with his information. We then copied MENU.INF to a file called RONNY.INF. The second user ran the configuration program, and we once again copied MENU.INF to a file, this time DAVID.INF.

This database software required just this one special file, MENU.INI, for each user. We created several versions of that special file under different names. The batch file in Figure 29.1, STARTDAT.BAT, copies the appropriate one to MENU.INF.

Batch File Line	Explanation
@ECHO OFF	Turn command-echoing off.
REM NAME: STARTDATA.BAT REM PURPOSE: Allow Two Users To REM Access Database REM VERSION: 1.00 REM DATE: April 15, 1991	Documentation remarks.
NEEDHELP %0 %1 IF ERRORLEVEL 1 GOTO HELP	Use the NeedHelp utility program to check and see if the user started the batch file with a /? switch.
IF (%1)==() GOTO NOTHING	If the user did not enter his name, jump to an error-handling routine.
CAPITAL %1	Use the Capital utility to convert this value to uppercase and store it in the environment under the variable name Ronny.
IF %RONNY%==DAVID GOTO OK IF %RONNY%==RONNY GOTO OK	If the user entered a valid name, jump to a section to run the database program.
GOTO ERROR	If the batch file reached this point, jump to an error-handling routine.

:NOTHING
   ECHO Enter Your Name After
   ECHO The STARTDAT Command
GOTO END
	When the user does not enter a name, display an error message and exit.

Figure 29.1 STARTDAT.BAT activates different setups for a database program.

Batch File Line	Explanation

`:ERROR`
   `ECHO Invalid User Name`
   `ECHO Try Again Or See Manager`
`GOTO END`
	When the user enters an invalid name, display an error message and exit.

`:OK`	Label marking the beginning of the section to run the database program when a valid name is entered.
`COPY %1.INF MENU.INF`	Copy the appropriate configuration file to the file MENU.INI, the name used by the database.
`MENU /1200/5551212`	Start the database, giving it the baud rate and phone number.
`GOTO END`	After running the database, exit the batch file.

`:HELP`
   `ECHO This Batch File Allows Ronny`
   `ECHO Or David To Access Remote`
   `ECHO Database`
   `BATCMD SL`
   `ECHO Enter STARTDAT RONNY/DAVID`
   `ECHO To Start The Database`
`GOTO END`
	Display a help screen and exit the batch file when the user requests help.

`:END`	Label marking the end of the batch file.

Figure 29.1 Continued.

You can use this same technique with any program that stores default values in a special file. For example, Microsoft Word stores the document you're working on, your place, and several optional settings in a file called MW.INI. STARTWOR.BAT, for example, is a sample batch file that Ronny and David could both use to maintain their own versions of MW.INI. There's only one major difference between START-WOR.BAT and STARTDAT.BAT: Microsoft Word allows you to change defaults while running the program, so each user's defaults are copied back to the holding file when that user exits Word.

Several readers of prior versions of this book have told me that they use this same method with Ventura Publishing by using multiple copies of its VP.INI file. Rather than using this trick for multiple users, however, they report using it to store multiple configurations of Ventura for a single user.

Finding Files

While batch files aren't as flexible as some commercial programs, you can use it as a fast file-searching program. The DOS and OS/2 ATTRIB (short for *attribute*) program was designed to change the attributes of files. It works across subdirectories with the /S switch. Because running ATTRIB without any switches causes it to list all the files it finds matching your file specification, you can use ATTRIB as a file-finding utility. Its operational code is:

```
IF (%1)==()    GOTO NOFILE
GOTO FILE

:NOFILE
   ECHO No File Entered On Command Line
   ECHO Syntax Is C>FASTFIND File
   ECHO Where File Is The File You
   ECHO Want To Find
GOTO END

:FILE
   ATTRIB \%1 /S ¦ MORE
GOTO END
```

For OS/2 users, there's a FASTFIND.CMD on the disk. However, the FF.CMD REXX program performs this function even more powerfully than the FASTFIND.CMD batch file. While FF.CMD is included on the CD-ROM, its operation isn't explained here because it's a REXX program and not a batch file. Since FF.CMD uses OS/2 advanced REXX functions, it will work only if you installed REXX when you installed OS/2.

Running Commands Occasionally

If you use your computer to store important data, you should make daily incremental backups. If your data is less important, you might decide to forgo daily backups in favor of less frequent backups. The problem is remembering to do them.

Many people think of batch files as being like either the AUTOEXEC.BAT file, which is run every time you turn your computer on, or a stand-alone batch file that's run only when you enter its name. However, there are some things you want your computer to do occasionally, like make a backup.

OCCASION.BAT in Figure 29.2 illustrates this concept. To run this from your AUTOEXEC.BAT file (OS/2 doesn't use an AUTOEXEC.BAT file, so you must add it to the CONFIG.SYS file), you'll need a CALL OCCASION.BAT statement. This batch file maintains a counter in the form of a zero-length file. When the batch file first starts, it creates COUNT.00. The next time it runs it renames this file COUNT.01, the next time it renames it COUNT.02, and so on. When it encounters COUNT.09, it renames the file COUNT.00 and performs the task it's supposed to perform occasionally—the backup, in this example.

The batch file counts reboots, not days. If you're working with problem software that frequently locks up, therefore, it could end up running backups several times a day. If you leave your computer on for days at a time or use it infrequently, ten reboots could end up taking several weeks.

OCCASION.BAT has two interesting tricks in it. The first trick is the counter test on the second line. The batch file needs to perform ten IF EXIST COUNT.00 GOTO 00 tests for the values 00 through 09. Because these tests will be exactly the same except for the digit used, all ten tests are combined into a single FOR loop. The second trick is the zero-length file.

Batch File Line	Explanation
`@ECHO OFF`	Turn command-echoing off.

`REM NAME:    OCCASION.BAT`
`REM PURPOSE: Run Programs Occasionally`
`REM VERSION: 1.00`
`REM DATE:    April 15, 1991`
	Documentation remarks.

`NEEDHELP %0 %1` `IF ERRORLEVEL 1 GOTO HELP`	Use the NeedHelp utility program to check and see if the user started the batch file with a /? switch.
`FOR %%J IN (00 01 02 03 04 05 06 07 08 09)` `        DO IF EXIST COUNT.%%J GOTO %%J`	Loop through ten values. If a file named COUNT exists with that extension, jump to a section corresponding to the extension.
`GOTO NOFILE`	If the batch file reaches this point, COUNT does not exist with the ten acceptable extensions so jump to a section to create it.

`:00`
`   REM All Work Done Here`
`   BACKUP C:\ A:`
`   REN COUNT.00 COUNT.01`
`GOTO END`
	When the file COUNT.00 exists, perform the backup and rename the file to COUNT.01 to increment the counter.

`:01`
`   REN COUNT.01 COUNT.02`
`GOTO END`
	Increment the counter and exit the batch file.

`:02`
`   REN COUNT.02 COUNT.03`
`GOTO END`
	Increment the counter and exit the batch file.

`:03`
`   REN COUNT.03 COUNT.04`
`GOTO END`
	Increment the counter and exit the batch file.

`:04`
`   REN COUNT.04 COUNT.05`
`GOTO END`
	Increment the counter and exit the batch file.

`:05`
`   REN COUNT.05 COUNT.06`
`GOTO END`
	Increment the counter and exit the batch file.

`:06`
`   REN COUNT.06 COUNT.07`
`GOTO END`
	Increment the counter and exit the batch file.

`:07`
`   REN COUNT.07 COUNT.08`
`GOTO END`
	Increment the counter and exit the batch file.

`:08`
`   REN COUNT.08 COUNT.09`
`GOTO END`
	Increment the counter and exit the batch file.

`:09`
`   REN COUNT.09 COUNT.00`
`GOTO END`
	Increment the counter and exit the batch file.

`:NOFILE`
`   REM Restore Counter File`
`   REM Then Restart Process`
`   TYPE NOFILE > COUNT.00`
`GOTO 00`
	When the counter file does not exist, create it by typing a file that does not exist and piping the results to the counter file. After this, jump to the section that performs the backup.

Figure 29.2 OCCASION.BAT backs up the hard disk once every ten times the computer is rebooted.

Batch File Line	Explanation

`:HELP`
   `ECHO OCCASION.BAT Demonstrates How`
   `ECHO Commands Can Run Occasionally`
   `ECHO By Performing A Backup Every`
   `ECHO Tenth Time It Is Run`
`GOTO END`
	Display a help screen and exit the batch file when the user requests help.

`:END`	Label marking the end of the batch file.

You can create a zero-length file by typing a file that doesn't exist and piping the results to a file. Because there's nothing to type, the resulting file is empty. The file has a length of zero, so it doesn't take up any disk space and you get to use the name as a counter holder without any disk space penalty.

You can use occasional batch files for other kinds of applications. For example, my disk testing program has two levels. The first is the quick mode that takes only a few minutes to run. The complete mode spots more errors but takes much longer to run. The batch file that runs the program normally runs it in quick mode, but it occasionally runs it in complete mode. You can have as many different occasional batch files as you need. The only trick is to remember to use a different name for each counter.

The approach in OCCASION.BAT works if you have a fairly short time period. If you want a longer interval, having a separate section for each possible value of the counter would make for a long and slow batch file. However, it's possible to avoid this, as OCCASIN2.BAT in Figure 29.3 illustrates.

Batch File Line	Explanation
`@ECHO OFF`	Turn command-echoing off.

`REM NAME:     OCCASIN2.BAT`
`REM PURPOSE: Run Programs Occasionally`
`REM VERSION: 1.00`
`REM DATE:    June 5, 1991`
	Documentation remarks.

`NEEDHELP %0 %1` `IF ERRORLEVEL 1 GOTO HELP`	Use the NeedHelp utility program to check and see if the user started the batch file with a /? switch.
`SET MATH=`	If the Math environmental variable already exists, reset its value.
`FOR %%J IN (0 1 2 3 4 5 6 7 8 9) DO IF EXIST` `COUNT.%%J SET MATH=%%J`	Loop through the acceptable counter values. If the file COUNT exists with that extension, store the value to the Math environmental variable. To increase the period, just add more items to the loop.
`IF (%MATH%)==(0) GOTO 00`	If the Math environmental variable equals 0 then jump to the section that performs the backup.
`IF (%MATH%)==() GOTO NOFILE`	If the Math environmental variable does not exist, jump to a section to create the counter variable.

Figure 29.3 OCCASIN2.BAT also backs up the hard disk once every ten times the computer is rebooted only it is shorter than OCCASION.BAT in Figure 33.6.

Batch File Line	Explanation
`IF (%MATH%)==(9) REN COUNT.9 COUNT.0` `IF (%MATH%)==(9) GOTO END`	If the Math environmental variable equals the maximum value for the counter, reset the counter and exit the batch file. These lines must also be changed to increase the period.
`SET NOW=%MATH%`	Store the value of the Math environmental variable to the Now environmental variable.
`BATCMD AD`	Use Batcmd to increase the value of the Math environmental variable by one.
`REN COUNT.%NOW% COUNT.%MATH%`	Increase the counter by one by renaming the counter file.
`GOTO END`	Exit the batch file.

`:00`
`    REM All Work Done Here`
`    BACKUP C:\ A:`
`    REN COUNT.0 COUNT.1`
`GOTO END`
	When the counter reaches the proper value, perform the backup, reset the counter, and exit.

`:NOFILE`
`    REM Restore Counter File`
`    REM Then Restart Process`
`    TYPE NOFILE > COUNT.0`
`GOTO 00`
	When the counter file does not exist, create it and jump to the section to perform the backup.

`:HELP`
`    ECHO OCCASION.BAT Demonstrates How`
`    ECHO Commands Can Run Occasionally`
`    ECHO By Performing A Backup Every`
`    ECHO Tenth Time It Is Run`
`GOTO END`
	Display a help screen and exit the batch file when the user requests help.

`:END`	Label marking the end of the batch file.

Figure 29.3 Continued.

OCCASIN2.BAT first jumps to other sections if the value of the counter is 0 or if the file is missing. Then it uses two IF tests to handle the special case of the last counter value, where the counter has to be reset to zero. After that, all that's needed is to increment the counter value by 1. It's possible to compute this new counter value by using Batcmd to add one to the environmental variable that's storing the counter that matched the extension. Because Batcmd strips off the leading 0 when it performs addition, OCCASIN2.BAT doesn't use the leading 0 in the counter the way OCCASION.BAT did. For longer intervals, this approach is much faster.

Since Batcmd is designed to run only under DOS, there's no version of OCCASIN2.BAT for OS/2.

Using the Volume in a Batch File

When you format a floppy or hard disk, DOS gives you the option of assigning an 11-digit volume label to the disk. Occasionally, it can be useful to access this volume label in a batch file. For example, if you sent the user three disks of data to install and a batch file to handle the installation, checking the volume label is one way to make sure the user inserted the correct disk at each stage of the installation. (Checking for a unique filename on each disk is another approach that's much easier.)

DOS doesn't give you any built-in functions to access the volume label from within a batch file. In fact, all it has is the VOL command to display the volume label on the screen. You can use this as the first of several steps to make the volume available to the batch file. Using the VOL command, you can pipe the information DOS displays into a file with the command:

```
VOL > STOREVOL.BAT
```

in a batch file called GETVOL.BAT. The VOL command only displays information and doesn't need input like the date or time, so you don't need to use piping to send a Return to the command.

If you run VOL from the keyboard, you'll see a message like "Volume in drive C is RICHARDSON." When you pipe this to a batch file, the batch file contains the same information.

The trick now is to run STOREVOL.BAT. You can automate this by including a STOREVOL command as the last command in GETVOL.BAT. STOREVOL.BAT immediately issues the command "Volume in drive C is RICHARDSON," which runs VOLUME.BAT and passes it the following information:

```
%1    in
%2    drive
%3    C
%4    is
%5    RICHARDSON
```

So VOLUME.BAT can place the volume into the environment with this command:

```
SET VOLUME=%5
```

To summarize, the steps in the process are as follows:

1. Run GETVOL.BAT. This file first pipes the volume label into STOREVOL.BAT, and then runs STOREVOL.BAT. Because the CALL command isn't used, control never returns to GETVOL.BAT.

2. STOREVOL.BAT runs and enters the single command VOLUME to run VOLUME.BAT. The volume label is passed as %5. The CALL command isn't used, so control never returns to STOREVOL.BAT.

3. VOLUME.BAT runs and places the contents of the volume label into an environmental variable.

So far, the process has been fairly simple, but you must consider one major complication: Volume labels can have spaces in them. If your volume label were A B C D E F, which has five spaces in it, only the first part of the volume label, A, would be placed into the environment. Although GETVOL.BAT and STOREVOL.BAT can remain the same, VOLUME.BAT must be modified to handle volume labels with spaces.

The operational code of VOLUME.BAT with the necessary modifications is as follows:

```
IF (%5)==() SET VOLUME=No Volume Label
IF (%5)==() GOTO END

SHIFT
SHIFT
SHIFT
SHIFT
SET VOLUME=%1

:TOPLOOP
   SHIFT
   IF (%1)==() GOTO END
   SET VOLUME=%VOLUME% %1
GOTO TOPLOOP
```

This version issues four SHIFT commands to move the first component of the volume label into the first replaceable parameter position. VOLUME.BAT then loops through all the remaining replaceable parameters, appending a space and the next component onto the VOLUME environmental variable.

Even this method is less than perfect. When components of a volume label are separated by more than one space, this method reduces the spacing to one space. The reason is that spaces are used as dividers for the replaceable parameters and the operating system treats multiple spaces as a single divider.

When a disk doesn't have a volume label, DOS displays a "Volume in drive C does not have a label" message. Because nothing in VOLUME.BAT limits the volume label to 11 characters, it ends up creating a "does not have a label" environmental variable, which is what you might want when the drive doesn't have a volume.

Of course, once you get the volume label into the environment, you need something to do with it. Typically, it's tested to see if it matches some predefined value. You could do this with a standard IF test. It's important to remember that many after-market utilities allow volume labels with lowercase letters, so you can't make any assumptions about the capitalization. However, if you're testing disks you created, then you know what capitalization to expect.

Because getting the volume label is so difficult in a batch file, Batcmd includes a function to make it easy. Just enter the command:

```
BATCMD VO drive
```

where *drive* is the drive you want to find the volume label of (Batcmd will accept only drives A through E). Batcmd stores its volume label in the environment under the name BATCMD, using the same capitalization as that of the volume label. There isn't a version of these batch files for OS/2.

Batch File Floppy-Disk Catalog

You can use batch files to catalog disks fairly well if you have only a few disks. If you have more than a few, however, you're probably better off buying one of the many shareware disk cataloging programs because the batch file method is fairly slow and lacks important error checking. Be careful when you use it and make frequent backups.

Figure 29.4 shows CATALOG.BAT, the batch file that creates the catalog. Notice that it lacks any error checking at all; I'll leave this to you to add. The batch file should determine that it's logged into the proper drive and subdirectory before running. As written, the batch file makes sure the user enters a name and then uses the FOR loop to cycle through all the files on the A drive. This would be a good application for grabbing the volume label and including it in the ECHO command.

Batch File Line	Explanation
`@ECHO OFF`	Turn command-echoing off.

`REM NAME:     CATALOG.BAT`
`REM PURPOSE: Cataloging Floppy Disks`
`REM VERSION: 2.00`
`REM DATE:     November 15, 1991`
	Documentation remarks.

`REM Assumes You Are Using The B drive`
`REM For The Floppies And The C drive`
`REM For The Catalog.`
	More documentation remarks.

`NEEDHELP %0 %1` `IF ERRORLEVEL 1 GOTO HELP`	Use the NeedHelp utility program to check and see if the user started the batch file with a /? switch.
`IF (%1)==()  GOTO NONAME`	If the user did not enter a name for this catalog entry, jump to an error-handling routine.
`C:` `CD\CATALOG`	Change to the appropriate drive and subdirectory.
`ECHO Insert Disk To Catalog In A Drive` `ECHO And Press Any Key When Ready`	Tell the user what to do next.
`PAUSE>NUL`	Pause the program until the user presses a key.

`FOR %%j in (B:\*.*) DO ECHO %%j %1 %2 %3 %4`
`%5`
`        %6 %7 %8 %9 >> C:CATALOG.TXT`
	For each file on the B drive, pipe the file name, some spaces and the first nine words of the catalog entry name into the catalog file.

`GOTO END`	Exit the batch file.

`:NONAME`
`   ECHO You Must Enter Catalog Name`
`   ECHO Where Name Describes The Disk`
`GOTO END`
	When the user does not enter a catalog name, display an error message and exit the batch file.

`:HELP`
`   ECHO Creates A Catalog In The`
`   ECHO C:\CATALOG Subdirectory That`
`   ECHO Lists All The Files In the`
`   ECHO B Drive Along With The Name`
`   ECHO You Enter On The Command Line`
`GOTO END`
	Display a help screen and exit the batch file when the user requests help.

`:END`	Label marking the end of the batch file.

Figure 29.4 CATALOG.BAT creates a catalog of files on a floppy disk.

Figure 29.5 shows REMOVE.BAT, a batch file for removing entries. It also lacks much error checking, but it's impossible to add enough error checking with batch commands. The basic problem is using the FIND command to select lines to delete. If you start the batch file with the replaceable parameter OFFICE, it will delete not only the lines with the added label OFFICE, but also the file OFFICE.TAX and any other line containing the line OFFICE. For this reason, use this cataloging method with a great deal of care and frequent backups.

Batch File Line	Explanation
`@ECHO OFF`	Turn command-echoing off.

`REM NAME:     REMOVE.BAT`
`REM PURPOSE: Removes Entries From Catalog`
`REM VERSION: 2.00`
`REM DATE:    November 15, 1991`
	Documentation remarks.

`NEEDHELP %0 %1` `IF ERRORLEVEL 1 GOTO HELP`	Use the NeedHelp utility program to check and see if the user started the batch file with a /? switch.
`IF (%1)==() GOTO NoName`	If the user did not enter a name for this catalog entry, jump to an error-handling routine.
`SET FIND=%1`	Store the first word of the catalog title to search file in the environment.
`SHIFT`	Move all the replaceable parameters down one level.
`:TOPLOOP`	Label marking the top of the loop to process any remaining words in the catalog title.
`    IF (%1)==() GOTO CONTINUE`	Once there are no more words in the catalog title to process, jump out of this processing loop.
`    SET FIND=%FIND% %1`	When the batch file reaches this point, more words exist for the catalog title so append this word onto the existing environmental variable.
`    SHIFT`	Move all the replaceable parameters down one level.
`GOTO TOPLOOP`	Continue looping.
`:CONTINUE`	Label used to jump out of the above loop.

`ECHO All Floppy Catalog Entries Containing`
`ECHO %FIND% Will Be Deleted`
`ECHO If This Is Not OK, Press Control-Break`
`ECHO Otherwise, Press Any Other Key`
`PAUSE`
	Tell the user what will happen next.

`C:` `CD\CATALOG`	Change to the appropriate drive and subdirectory.
`COPY CATALOG.TXT CATALOG.BAK`	Make a backup copy of the catalog before modifying it.

Figure 29.5 REMOVE.BAT will remove entries from the catalog.

Batch File Line	Explanation
TYPE CATALOG.TXT|FIND/V "%FIND%" > JUNK.TMP	Type the catalog, use the Find filter to search for all lines not containing the catalog text to delete, and pipe the results to an output file.
DEL CATALOG.TXT	Delete the current catalog.
REN JUNK.TMP CATALOG.TXT	Rename the temporary file to make it the catalog file.
GOTO END	Exit the batch file.

:HELP
   ECHO This Batch File Deletes The
   ECHO Entries From The Disk Catalog In
   ECHO The C:\CATALOG Subdirectory That
   ECHO Contain The Name You Enter On The
   ECHO Command Line
GOTO END
	Display a help screen and exit the batch file when the user requests help.

:END	Label marking the end of the batch file.

Adding to and Deleting from Your Path (DOS Only)

Most people simply include every subdirectory they need DOS to search through in the path and forget it. There are occasions, however, when you might want to have two separate paths (for example, if you're testing a new program and you don't want DOS to search anywhere other than the current subdirectory, if you've added a subdirectory for a special program and you want it in the path for only a short period of time, or if you have so many subdirectories to search that you want to have a separate path for each task). The plan of attack is the same for each of these problems. The steps are as follows:

1. Store the current path to a variable in the environment.
2. Replace the path with a new path or modify the existing path.
3. Restore the old path from the environment.

You can use a batch file to store the current path to another environmental variable with the command:

```
SET OLDPATH=%PATH%
```

Of course, at this point, two versions of your path exist, one stored under OLDPATH and one stored under PATH, so you'll need an expanded environment if you have a long path.

If you want to create a new path, it will be easier to either write a custom batch file for each alternative path or simply enter it from the command line. However, if you have two or three alternative paths that you use a lot, you might want to have a batch file that uses a replaceable parameter to let you select among them. For example:

```
@ECHO OFF
IF (%1)==(1) SET PATH=C:\;C:\DBASE
IF (%1)==(2) SET PATH=C:\;C:\WORD
IF (%1)==(3) SET PATH=C:\;C:\NORTON
```

would let you select rapidly from three different paths. You could even use this same batch file to restore the original path with two modifications:

```
@ECHO OFF
IF (%1)==()  SET PATH=%OLDPATH%
IF (%1)==()  SET OLDPATH=
IF (%1)==(1) SET PATH=C:\;C:\DBASE
IF (%1)==(2) SET PATH=C:\;C:\WORD
IF (%1)==(3) SET PATH=C:\;C:\NORTON
```

You can also use a batch file to remove subdirectories from your path, although the process is a little tricky. A batch file has access to the %PATH% environmental variable, but has no way to strip it into its component parts. However, the different subdirectories in a path are separated by semicolons, which DOS treats as legal dividers for replaceable parameters. If you issue the command:

```
BATCH %PATH%
```

and have DOS treat %PATH% as the environmental variable, then the first subdirectory in the path would be %1, the second would be %2, and so on. Unfortunately, you can't use environmental variables on the command line in this fashion. Luckily, batch files can, so if one batch file invokes another with this exact same command, the subdirectory components are passed as separate replaceable parameters, just as you'd expect.

Putting all this together, you can have a very nice set of batch files for editing the path. The first is called EDITPATH.BAT. While it contains command-line help and internal documentation, its single operation line is:

```
EDIT2 %PATH%4
```

which calls EDIT2.BAT and passes it the path on the command line. This causes EDIT2.BAT, shown in Figure 29.6, to be passed the entire path as a series of replaceable parameters.

EDIT2.BAT loops through the subdirectories one at a time and asks users if they want to keep that subdirectory in the path. If they answer yes, it stores that subdirectory in an environmental variable. If they answer no, it doesn't store that subdirectory. When all of the subdirectories have been processed, EDIT2.BAT constructs the new path.

As you elect to keep each subdirectory, EDIT2.BAT stores that subdirectory in a temporary environmental variable called P. Only when you finish making all your selections is the contents of the PATH environmental variable replaced with the contents of the P environmental variable.

Batch File Line	Explanation
`@ECHO OFF`	Turn command-echoing off.

`REM NAME:    EDIT2.BAT`
`REM PURPOSE: Selectively Delete`
`REM          Path Subdirectories`
`REM VERSION: 3.00`
`REM DATE:    December 14, 1992`
	Documentation remarks.

`NEEDHELP %0 %1` `IF ERRORLEVEL 1 GOTO HELP`	Use the NeedHelp utility program to check and see if the user requested help.
`IF (%1)==() GOTO HELP`	Since EDIT2.BAT is not designed to run from the command line it should never run with a value for %1, so when that happens jump to a help section.

`REM The Environmental Variable`
`REM P Will Contain The New Path`
`REM We Must Maintain Old Path`
`REM So Utilities Will Work`
`REM P Is Used So "SET P=" Is As`
`REM Close In Length To "PATH="`
`REM As Is Possible`
	Documentation remarks.

`SET P=`	Make sure the environmental variable is empty.

`REM MATH Environmental Variable`
`REM Used To Track Additions Since`
`REM First Addition To Path Must`
`REM Skip Leading SemiColon`
	Documentation remarks.

`SET MATH=0`	Set the flag environmental variable to zero.
`:TOP`	Label marking top of loop.
`   IF (%1)==() GOTO ENDLOOP`	Once there are no more replaceable parameters, jump out of the loop.
`   BATCMD SL`	Skip a line on the screen using Batcmd.
`   BATCMD YN Keep %1 in PATH (Y/N)`	Ask a question using Batcmd.
`   IF NOT ERRORLEVEL 1 GOTO SKIP`	If the user answered "no" then skip keeping the subdirectory.
`   BATCMD AD`	Increase the flag value by one.
`   IF %MATH%==1 SET P=%1`	If the flag has a value of one (0+1), then this is the first directory in the path, so do not precede it with a semicolon.
`   IF %MATH%==1 GOTO SKIP`	If the flag has a value of one, then nothing else is needed, so jump to end of loop.
`   SET P=%P%;%1`	The path already has at least one directory so append this one and precede it with a semicolon.
`:SKIP`	Label used to bypass part of the code in the loop.
`   SHIFT`	Move all the replaceable parameters down one level.
`   GOTO TOP`	Continue looping.
`:ENDLOOP`	Label marking the end of the loop.

Figure 29.6 EDIT2.BAT lets you decide whether or not to keep each subdirectory in your path.

Batch File Line	Explanation
PATH %P%	Set the path equal to the contents of the P environmental variable.
ECHO PATH Now Set To: PATH	Tell the user the new path. Since the path could be very long, it is displayed separately. Including it in the ECHO command might make the command too long.
SET MATH= SET P=	Reset the environmental variables used by the batch file.
GOTO END	Jump to the end of the batch file.

:HELP
    ECHO This Batch File Is Used By
    ECHO EDITPAT2.BAT To Edit The Path
    ECHO *DON'T RUN FROM COMMAND LINE**
GOTO END
	Display a help screen and exit the batch file when the user requests help.

:END	Label marking the end of the batch file.

Figure 29.6   Continued.

There are two problems that EDIT2.BAT has to avoid. The first subdirectory added to the path isn't preceded by a semicolon, while all the remaining subdirectories are. Also, the length of any command line cannot exceed 127 characters, but the path itself can be 122 characters. (Five characters are needed for the PATH command and space following it that precedes the path when you create it.)

When I first started writing this batch file, I tried to avoid adding the semicolon before the first subdirectory with these two IF tests:

```
IF NOT (%PATH%)==() SET PATH=%PATH%;%1
IF (%PATH%)==() SET PATH=%1
```

This approach works well as long as the path is fairly short. However, the PATH environmental variable is used twice in the first IF test, so a moderately long path would cause this statement to exceed the 127-character limit DOS places on the command line. EDIT2.BAT avoids this problem by setting the MATH environmental variable to 0 and then incrementing it with Batcmd for every subdirectory added. The leading semicolon is avoided only when MATH has a value of 1.

EDIT2.BAT constructs a second environmental variable called P to contain the modified path until the end of the batch file when the path is replaced with the contents of the P environmental variable. The reason for this is that, if you reset the path at the beginning of the batch file and reconstruct it in the batch file rather than using P, Batcmd wouldn't run because it's no longer in your path!

OS/2 allows a much longer path than DOS, so there aren't OS/2 versions of these batch files.

Password Protection (DOS Only)

One way to keep casual users from accessing your hard disk is to add password protection. Password protection ranges from simple programs that require you to enter a password to complex systems that encrypt the file allocation table (FAT) and won't access the hard disk at all until the proper password is entered. If all you need is light protection, then you can put together a batch file password system that's very effective.

The password application we'll be looking at is simply a batch file that requires a password. Once the user enters a password, it terminates. You could add the commands to the batch file to run a specific application or you could add this code to the top of your AUTOEXEC.BAT file. Keep in mind that this system won't keep a user from booting off a floppy disk and then accessing your hard disk. In addition, because you can't encrypt the batch file, anyone with access to the hard disk can look at the batch file and figure out your password. They will have to have some experience to do this though, since the password is stored using its ASCII value. With that caveat in mind, let's construct the password system.

The password batch file, PASSWORD.BAT, is shown in Figure 29.7. It uses Batcmd to get the first character of the password. If that character is correct, it uses Batcmd to get the second character. If the first character is incorrect, it increments a counter and asks again. It repeats this process for the second and third character. Any time an incorrect character is entered, the program begins prompting for the password from the beginning. Once the counter reaches three, which is after you've entered three incorrect passwords, the batch file enters an endless loop and appears to lock up.

Batch File Line	Explanation
@ECHO OFF	Turn command-echoing off.
REM NAME: PASSWORD.BAT REM PURPOSE: Batch Password REM VERSION: 1.51 REM DATE: March 25, 1991	Documentation remarks.
NEEDHELP %0 %1 IF ERRORLEVEL 1 GOTO HELP	Use the NeedHelp utility program to check and see if the user requested help.
CLS	Clear the screen.
CTTY NUL	Turn off the console. While this is in effect, the keyboard does not work and nothing shows up on the screen without piping.
SET COUNTER=1	Create a counter variable that will be used to count the number of password attempts.
ECHO Enter Password > CON	Tell the user to enter the password. This show up on the screen only because it is piped there.
REM Enter Three Digit Password Here REM A=ASCII Value Of First Digit REM C=ASCII Value Of Second Digit REM E=ASCII Value Of Third Digit REM Run FINDPASS.BAT To Find These REM If You Are Not Sure What To Use	Documentation remarks.
REM ———————— REM Change These Numbers REM To Change Password REM ————————	Documentation remarks.

Figure 29.7 PASSWORD.BAT requires the user to enter the correct password (which is RON at the moment, as currently set up) in three tries or less.

Batch File Line	Explanation
SET A=82 SET C=79 SET E=78	Create the three variables that contain the ASCII values of the three digits of the password.
REM ―――――――― REM Need To Develop The Second Number REM To Use In The Dual If Tests	Documentation remarks.
SET MATH=%A% BATCMD AD SET B=%MATH% SET MATH=%C% BATCMD AD SET D=%MATH% SET MATH=%E% BATCMD AD SET F=%MATH% SET MATH=	The dual If tests need both the ASCII value of the password digit and the value one higher—for the IF NOT ERRORLEVEL portion of the test. Rather than having the user enter a value one higher, this section uses the addition abilities of Batcmd to calculate those values.
:TOP	Label marking the top of the section that gets the first digit of the password.
BATCMD GK<CON	Use the Batcmd to obtain any character from the user. This works only because the input is piped from the keyboard.
IF ERRORLEVEL %A% IF NOT ERRORLEVEL %B% GOTO SECOND	If the user entered this digit properly, jump to the section to get the second digit.

IF %COUNTER%==1 GOTO 1
   IF %COUNTER%==2 GOTO 2
   IF %COUNTER%==3 GOTO 3
	Jump to a section to increment the counter. This section also automatically returns the user to the section to enter the first digit of the password.

GOTO TOP	The batch file never reaches this point, this line is just used to having a closing point for the loop.
:SECOND	Label marking the top of the section that gets the second digit of the password.
ECHO X>CON	Display an X on the screen to represent the first digit of the password.
BATCMD GK<CON	Use the Batcmd to obtain input from the user.
IF ERRORLEVEL %C% IF NOT ERRORLEVEL %D% GOTO THIRD	If the user entered this digit properly, jump to the section to get the third digit.

IF %COUNTER%==1 GOTO 1
   IF %COUNTER%==2 GOTO 2
   IF %COUNTER%==3 GOTO 3
	Jump to a section to increment the counter.

GOTO SECOND	The batch file never reaches this point, this line is just used to having a closing point for the loop.
:THIRD	Label marking the top of the section that gets the third digit of the password.
ECHO XX>CON	Display an XX on the screen to represent the second digit of the password.
BATCMD GK<CON	Use the Batcmd to obtain input from the user.
IF ERRORLEVEL %E% IF NOT ERRORLEVEL %F% GOTO CORRECT	If the user entered this digit properly, jump to the section to leave the batch file.

Figure 29.7 Continued.

Batch File Line	Explanation
IF %COUNTER%==1 GOTO 1 IF %COUNTER%==2 GOTO 2 IF %COUNTER%==3 GOTO 3	Jump to a section to increment the counter.
GOTO THIRD	The batch file never reaches this point, this line is just used to having a closing point for the loop.

:1
   ECHO Wrong Password, Start Over>CON
   SET COUNTER=2
GOTO TOP
	Section to handle the first time the user enters the password wrong. Increments the counter by one, tells the user about the mistake, and jumps to the top of the password routine.

:2
   ECHO Wrong Password, Start Over>CON
   SET COUNTER=3
GOTO TOP
	Section to handle the second time the user enters the password wrong. Increments the counter by one, tells the user about the mistake, and jumps to the top of the password routine.

:3	Label marking the top of the section used to lock up the computer for an invalid password.
CLS > CON	Clear the screen. The piping makes this work.
BATCMD PC 12 38 > CON	Position the cursor with Batcmd. Again, the piping makes this work.
ECHO —DEATH— > CON	Pipe a message to the screen.
:DEATH GOTO DEATH	This endless loop locks up the computer. Since the keyboard is not working, the user cannot break out.
:CORRECT	Label marking the beginning of the section where the user entered the password properly.
FOR %%J IN (A B C D E F COUNTER) DO SET %%J=	Reset the environmental variables used by the batch file.
CTTY CON GOTO END	Turn the console back on and exit the batch file.

:HELP
   ECHO This Demonstration Batch File
   ECHO Requires The User To Enter A
   ECHO Password Before It Continues
   ECHO And The User Cannot Break Out
   ECHO By Pressing Control-Break Or
   ECHO Any Other Method
   BATCMD SL
   ECHO The Demonstration Password Is
   ECHO RON And The Capitalization
   ECHO Must Match Exactly
GOTO END
	Display a help screen and exit the batch file when the user requests help.

:END	Label marking the end of the batch file.

With any batch file, you have the problem of the user pressing Ctrl–Break to stop the batch file. PASSWORD.BAT avoids this problem almost completely by using the CTTY NUL command at the top. This turns the console off so the computer won't accept most inputs from the keyboard, and won't write output to the screen. It's interesting to note that the batch file will still accept the Ctrl–Break, but won't accept the Y response to the "Halt Batch Process (Y/N)" message, thus effectively locking the computer. After the correct response is entered, the batch file restores the screen and keyboard with the CTTY CON command.

Because the keyboard and screen don't respond to the batch file under the CTTY NUL command, the batch file forces them to work by piping output to the screen with the >CON piping command and grabbing input from the keyboard with the <CON piping command.

If you add the password to the top of your AUTOEXEC.BAT file, anyone booting the computer from the hard disk will have to enter a password. It should be at the very top of the AUTOEXEC.BAT file so the user won't have time to enter Ctrl–Break before the password part of the AUTOEXEC.BAT file takes over. You should also create a stand-alone batch file with a name like LOCK.BAT, so you can lock your computer but leave it running when you have to leave it.

Since Batcmd is designed to work under DOS, there are no OS/2 versions of these batch files.

Which Codes to Use with the Password Batch File (DOS Only)

One of the problems of using PASSWORD.BAT is you have to know the ASCII values of the three digits of the password in order to configure the batch file. You could use an ASCII chart, but a batch file can automate the process. FINDPASS.BAT will prompt you for the three characters you want to use as a password and tell you the values to enter into PASSWORD.BAT to configure it for the desired password. It does this simply by using Batcmd to prompt you for the three letters, setting the error-level, and then calling on SAYERROR.BAT to display the current errorlevel.

Batcmd is designed to work under DOS, so there are no OS/2 versions of these batch files.

Summary

- EDITBAT.BAT lets you keep all your batch files in the C:\BAT subdirectory, yet still easily edit them on the fly.

- NOBURN.BAT is a simple screen saver that runs from DOS and requires so little memory that you can run it while shelled out of another program.

- CHECKWIN.BAT tells you if Windows is running without needing a utility program.

- One way to change subdirectories quickly is with a special utility like NCD of Norton Utilities.

- Another way to change to a single subdirectory quickly is with a custom batch file.

- A batch file like RETURN.BAT can store the current subdirectory in a batch file for instant return.

- A batch file like RETURN2.BAT can store a single subdirectory in the environment for quick changes.

- A batch file like RCD.BAT can switch between a number of subdirectories quickly.

- You can run programs that inflexibly store their configuration in a single file in different configurations by making multiple copies of the configuration file and using batch files to activate different copies.

- Combining the ATTRIB command with a batch file will give you a quick and powerful file-location program.

- By having the AUTOEXEC.BAT count reboots by using the name of a zero-length file, you can run programs occasionally by running them only after a certain number of reboots.

- A batch file like GETVOL.BAT can pipe the volume label into the environment, where you can perform IF tests on it to verify that the proper floppy disk has been inserted in the drive.

- Passing the path between batch files as a replaceable parameter gives the second batch file access to the subdirectories in the path as individual replaceable parameters.

- A batch file like EDITPATH.BAT can let you pick subdirectories to either keep in or discard from the path.

- A batch file like PASSWORD.BAT can set up a surprisingly powerful password protection program.

30

Review

You've now finished most of the book that's devoted to writing batch files. All that re-mains are advanced topics and batch file utilities. Take a few moments and try to solve the following four problems. If you have difficulty with any of them, look back through the book. Appendix A contains the answers to these problems.

Problem 10

A friend asks you if it's possible to put together a telephone database using batch files. She's looking for a system where she can run the batch file followed by a nick-name of the person to call and have her modem dial the number for her. As she sees it, the command PHONE MOM should call her mother.

You decide to put together a mock-up with just a few numbers, like information and 911, to make sure she likes the system. As you begin your research, you find out two pieces of crucial information. One is that a command like ECHO ATDT 911 > COM1 will dial the phone. The ATDT tells the modem to dial, 911 is the phone num-ber, and >COM1 pipes everything to the port to which the modem is connected. The second piece of information is that, once the modem has finished dialing and the user has picked up the receiver, the command ECHO ATH > COM1 will cause the mo-dem to remove itself from the circuit without severing the connection.

Note that these commands won't work on all modems. A few modems are designed without an IRQ setting and won't respond to commands piped to the COM port. You can test your modem by issuing the command:

```
ECHO ATDT phone number > COM1
```

at the command line, where phone number represents an actual number to dial. If the modem doesn't dial the phone, you modem is incompatible with this approach and you can't complete this problem.

Problem 11

A friend of yours recently bought his son a computer for his high school graduation. His son will use the computer in college to write term papers and do his homework. Your friend doesn't expect his son to create a lot of important data, so he isn't worried about performing backups too often. Just to be sure, though, he has asked you to write a batch file that will list the files that need to be backed up so his son can decide if it's time to perform a backup.

Problem 12

Your boss recently purchased a laptop computer. He likes the computer and keyboard, but has trouble changing subdirectories because the backslash key is located in an awkward position. You have decided to try to win favor with the boss by writing a batch file to make it easier for him to change subdirectories, without using the backslash key.

You're looking for a system that will work with any subdirectory, mainly because you don't know how your boss has his hard disk structured. That leaves out a system where your boss runs the batch file with a nickname for the most common subdirectories.

Problem 13

You've started trying to learn to use piping. As you experiment, you find a lot of zero-length files appearing on your hard disk, so you decide to write a batch file to automatically delete all the zero-length files in the current subdirectory.

31

Writing DOS and
Windows Batch File Utilities

One of the things you've seen quite clearly in this book is that batch files need help. While the batch language is useful, there are many necessary things, like counting, that it simply can't do. When your needs exceed the abilities of the batch language, then a possible solution is to write your own batch file utility.

Wait, don't turn the page! While it sounds like you need to be an experienced programmer, batch file utilities are some of the easiest programs you can write. They're so easy because most batch file utilities perform just one thing. Look at the CHOICE.COM program that Microsoft added to MS-DOS 6. All it does is display a prompt, get a single character from the user, and place it in the errorlevel. Batch file utilities are as simple as that.

What Is a Batch File Utility?

What is a batch file utility? One answer to this question is any program that runs within a batch file. Yet, that isn't a very good answer because it would make your word-processing, database, and spreadsheet programs batch file utilities! So I'll say that a batch file utility is any program designed to take information from a batch file or provide information to a batch file in order to enhance its operation. In order to do this, a batch file utility must be able to interface with the batch file.

As part of this chapter, you'll see how to interface three languages—QuickBASIC, Builder or Builder Lite, and Pascal—with the batch language. You'll also develop two useful batch utilities in each language. As you'll see, the process is fairly painless. All three of these languages run under DOS. In the next chapter, you'll see how to use REXX to easily and dramatically expand the power of batch files under OS/2.

What It Needs

In order to write a batch utility, you need two things: a way to get information from the batch file to the utility and a way to get information from the utility to the batch file. In between getting the information into the batch utility and getting it out, the program works exactly like any other program you might write in that language.

There are four ways to get information into a batch file utility:

From the command line. A DOS command line is limited to 127 characters and must contain the name of the utility program to run, so this restricts the amount of information that can be passed this way. Unless you need to pass a lot of information to the utility, this is generally the best way, however, because you don't have to worry about having enough environmental space or deleting the variables after you use them.

From the environment. Placing information into the environment avoids the command-line length limitation, but requires that the user have an adequate environment. It also means you have to worry about cleaning up the environment after you're done.

Asking users. This doesn't take information from the batch file, but rather asks the user a question. This works the same regardless if you're writing a batch file utility or general program, so it isn't discussed here. However, remember that this option is always available to you.

Polling the equipment. This also doesn't take information from the batch file and works the same in a standard program as it does in a batch file utility. For that reason, it isn't covered here.

Of course, not all batch file utilities require input information. For example, a password protection program might have the password compiled into the program, so all that's required is to run it. A menu program where the menu options are hard-wired into the code would also require no inputs.

There are four ways to get information out of a batch file utility and back into the batch file:

Store a number in the errorlevel. The errorlevel is one byte of information that can contain a number, from 0 to 255. It was specifically designed for utilities to pass information back to a batch file. All batch files and programs access the same errorlevel. The password protection program might pass back a 1 if the password is correct and a 0 if it's wrong, or the menu program might pass back the option selected as an errorlevel.

Store the results in the master copy of the environment. Since the errorlevel has room for only one byte of information, it isn't useful for utilities that need to pass back a lot of information. For example, a utility to multiply two numbers together couldn't use the errorlevel unless its results were restricted to integers from 0 to 255. One way to avoid this is to pass back the information in the environment. However, batch file utilities get a copy of the environment and that copy is erased when they terminate, so they can't use their copy of the environment for this. As you'll see, some languages can search through memory, find the master copy of the environment, and make their changes there, thus making sure the environmental variables they create remain available after they terminate.

Write a batch file to store the results in the master copy of the environment. Not all languages can find the master copy of the environment in memory and make their changes there. However, almost every language, including the batch language, can create disk files. These languages can store information in the environment by creating a temporary batch file with a single line like SET ANSWER=2234. The batch file that runs the utility can call this temporary batch file after running the utility in order to place the results into the environment. As you'll see, QuickBASIC must do this to pass back information that won't fit in the errorlevel.

Print the results to the screen or printer. Since this doesn't make the information available to the batch file and works the same for a batch file utility or general program, it's not covered in detail here. Nevertheless, you might want your batch file utilities to simply perform fancy screen formatting or otherwise produce output for the screen, so keep this option in mind.

The method you select for getting output from your batch file utility will depend on the purpose of your utility and the limitations of the language you select to write the utility.

QuickBASIC

You'll look at two QuickBASIC batch file utilities since BASIC is the closest thing available to a "universal" language. These techniques will work in a very similar fashion under GWBasic and most other versions of BASIC. The QuickBASIC compiler isn't able to access the errorlevel nor the master copy of the environment, so all of its output must be passed back to the batch file with a temporary batch file.

The first batch file utility takes the number passed to it on the command line, adds 1 to it, and passes the results back to the batch file. The second utility takes two numbers passed to it via the environment and multiplies them together. The numbers can be whole or decimal numbers. Even if QuickBASIC could access the errorlevel, this value wouldn't be passed back via the errorlevel.

Adding 1 to the command-line number

The command to read in the command line in QuickBASIC is:

```
Line$ = COMMAND$
```

This command works only in the QuickBASIC compiler and not the QBasic interpretative version that comes with MS-DOS. The command line is read in as a single line without the name of the program, so the command:

```
UTILITY/? 123
```

would cause Line$ to have a value of /? 123. Note that Line$ is a variable name and can be any legal string you choose. Once you have the command line, you need to check to make sure the user actually entered something. The code to do that is:

```
Length = LEN(line$)

IF Length = 0 THEN
    PRINT "Invalid Syntax, Enter 'ADD /?' For Help"
    BEEP
    END
END IF
```

Because the COMMAND$ function doesn't include the name of the program in the command line, the length of the command line will be zero if the user doesn't enter something on the command line. That represents an error because the utility expects a number to add to, so it displays an error message and exits.

Next you have to loop through the command line looking for just the first piece of information. If the user starts the ADD.EXE utility with the command:

```
ADD 123 UP 456
```

then only the first replaceable parameter has any meaning. Compute the length of the Line$ string and then loop through it one character at a time. Once you find a space, comma, Tab or semicolon, then you've found the end of the first input. At that point, you can jump out of the loop. The length was computed earlier; the code to do the rest is:

```
FOR I = 1 TO Length
    Char$ = MID$(Line$, I, 1)
    IF (Char$ <> " " AND Char$ <> CHR$(9) AND Char$ <> ",") THEN
        IF First = 0 THEN Build$ = Build$ + Char$
    ELSE
        First = 1
    END IF
NEXT I
```

The variable First starts off with a value of zero. It functions as a flag. Its value is zero while the first input is being processed, so each character is appended onto the end of a holding variable, Build$. As soon as the first space, Tab, or comma is found, the value of First is changed to a 1 and the remaining characters are ignored. That way, Build$ contains only the first input.

As you'll see with the next utility, you could just swap and begin appending characters onto another variable if you needed to pass the utility more than one input. You can use this option if you want the utility to add two numbers together or if you want the user to be able to enter the name of the output environmental variable rather than just using Answer.

Much of the rest of the code involves straight QuickBASIC programming to perform error checking and the addition. This is not a QuickBASIC programming book so I'm not going to cover it in detail, but I will go through it quickly.

Now that you have the first input, you can check to see if the user is requesting help with the command:

```
IF Build$ = "/?" OR Build$ = "?" THEN
```

If so, print the help messages and then exit the utility without performing any addition with the following commands:

```
IF Build$ = "/?" OR Build$ = "?" THEN
   PRINT "Adds One To Number Passed ";
   PRINT "To It On The Command Line"
   PRINT "And Creates JUNK.BAT With ";
   PRINT "The Command:"
   PRINT
   PRINT "SET ANSWER=#"
   PRINT
   PRINT "Where # Represents The Answer. ";
   PRINT "That Way, A Batch File Can ";
   PRINT "Easily Get The Answer Into ";
   PRINT "The Environment"
   END
END IF
```

Notice that the END command on the next-to-last line causes ADD.EXE to immediately terminate and return control to DOS or the batch file that called it.

Now that you know the user did not request help, you can convert the string variable Build$ that contains the input value, add 1 to it, and move on to the output stage. You could do this in just a couple of lines, but I don't recommend it. The utility needs several layers of error checking to make sure the user doesn't try to misuse the utility.

The first step is to convert the string to a number with the command Number = VAL(Build$). If the user enters a number, this conversion will work as you'd expect. If the user enters anything other than a number, say ADD One, then Number has a value of zero. If the user enters a mixture of numbers and letters, say ADD 123ABC, then Number has a value equal to all the numbers up to the first letter, or 123 in this example. You want to perform error checking to prevent nonnumeric data like One, but not mixed data like 123ABC since this is just an example. If you're constructing utilities to be used by inexperienced people, consider all possible inputs when validating values. The code to perform the error checking and the addition follows:

```
IF Number = 0 THEN
      IF ASC(Build$) = 48 THEN
          Number = 1
      ELSE
          PRINT "Invalid Input"
          PRINT "Enter ADD /? For Help"
          BEEP
          END
      END IF
ELSE
    Number = Number + 1
END IF
```

If Number has a value of zero, then it checks to see if the first character of the string variable is a 0 with the command IF ASC(Build$) = 48. If so, it stores 0 to Number since it's a valid input, and 0 + 1 = 1. If Number was 0 and the first character wasn't 0, then the user entered a nonnumeric first character. The utility prints out an error message, beeps the speaker, and exits without creating the output batch file. If Number wasn't 0, then it adds 1 to its value. Note that this addition doesn't require a whole number, so ADD.EXE will work with noninteger numbers.

You're almost ready to create the output file, but a quirk in QuickBASIC is going to cause you to do some extra work first. Anytime you need to output a numeric answer, you'll have the same problem with QuickBASIC. QuickBASIC adds a leading space when printing nonnegative numbers, so 47 is preceded by a space. The command SET ANSWER=47 therefore becomes SET ANSWER= 47, which is clearly not what you want. Part of the solution is to convert Number to a string, but even that doesn't clear up the problem entirely because QuickBASIC pads this string with leading spaces. You must strip off the leading spaces. The code to do all this is:

```
Answer$ = STR$(Number)
Answer$ = LTRIM$(Answer$)
```

Now you're ready to create your output file. I've used the name JUNK.BAT for the file, and the utility doesn't perform any error checking to keep from overwriting JUNK.BAT. (Note: the commands I've used to create JUNK.BAT will overwrite any existing file rather than appending to it.) This error checking could be performed in either the QuickBASIC program or the batch file. I've skipped it since on my system I assume that files named JUNK*.* are subject to be overwritten, and I never use them for anything permanent. Again, when using this approach to write utilities for inexperienced users, you'd be well advised to check to make sure the file exists and ask the user about overwriting it. The code to create the file follows:

```
OPEN "JUNK.BAT" FOR OUTPUT AS #1
    PRINT #1, "SET ANSWER="; Answer$
CLOSE
```

As you can see, the process of creating ADD.EXE is mostly QuickBASIC programming with a little extra thrown in to facilitate communication with the batch file. To illustrate ADD.EXE in action, SHOWADD.BAT uses it to loop through 20 loops. The operational code for SHOWADD.BAT is:

```
@ECHO OFF
ECHO Will Loop Through Loop 20 Times
SET Answer=0
:TOP
ADD %Answer%
CALL JUNK.BAT
DEL Junk.BAT
ECHO Loop Number %ANSWER%
IF NOT %ANSWER%==20 GOTO TOP
```

```
ECHO Loops Done
SET ANSWER=
```

The files ADD.BAS, ADD.EXE, and SHOWADD.BAT are all on the disk in the sub-directory \UTILITY\DOS\YOU-MAKE\QB-ADD. That version of SHOWADD.BAT has documentation and offers command-line help.

Multiplying two numbers together

This utility takes two numbers from the environment and multiplies them together. You could, of course, take these two numbers from the command line since it's un-likely they'll cause the command line to exceed 127 characters.

Even though MULTIPLY.EXE takes its usual inputs from the environment, it has to start out reading the command line. It does this to check if the user typed /? or ? to request help. If so, it displays a help message and exits. It must do this first because the routines that follow display error messages if the required environmental vari-ables don't exist, and you wouldn't want that to happen to a user who's requesting help. Other than the help message, this code is identical to the code in ADD.BAS, so it's not shown here.

Next, the program reads the two environmental variables NUMBER1 and NUM-BER2 with the commands:

```
Input1$ = ENVIRON$("NUMBER1")
Input2$ = ENVIRON$("NUMBER2")
```

If either of the environmental variables is missing, these commands won't cause a problem. The associated string variable isn't created, so, if NUMBER1 doesn't exist, then Input1$ isn't created. This is a violation of the way the utility is supposed to work and will create problems later on, so the utility must check for this condition. The code to check Input1$ is:

```
IF Input1$ = "" THEN
    PRINT "NUMBER1 Environmental Variable Missing"
    BEEP
    END
END IF
```

The code for Input2$ is identical except that, of course, Input1$ is changed to In-put2$ and the error message specifies NUMBER2. Like ADD.BAS, MULTIPLY.BAS must check to make sure that numbers and not letters are entered. The code is very close to the code in ADD.BAS and is shown here for Input1$:

```
IF Number1 = 0 THEN
        IF ASC(Input1$) <> 48 THEN
            PRINT "Invalid Input For NUMBER1 ";
            PRINT "Environmental Variable"
            PRINT "Enter MULTIPLY /? For Help"
            BEEP
            END
```

```
        END IF
END IF
```

Number2 is handled in a similar fashion. Next, the two numbers are multiplied together and converted to a space-free string with the commands:

```
Answer$ = STR$(Number1 * Number2)
Answer$ = LTRIM$(Answer$)
```

and finally the output batch file is created with code identical to ADD.BAS. The batch file SHOWTIME.BAT uses Batcmd to prompt the user for two numbers, which it stores in the environment by calling SAYERROR.BAT. It uses MULTIPLY.EXE to multiply them together and finally shows the results. The operational code follows:

```
BATCMD GN Enter First Number To Multiply
CTTY NUL
CALL SAYERROR
CTTY CON
SET NUMBER1=%ERROR%

BATCMD GN Enter Second Number To Multiply
CTTY NUL
CALL SAYERROR
CTTY CON
SET NUMBER2=%ERROR%

MULTIPLY

CALL JUNK.BAT
DEL JUNK.BAT

ECHO %NUMBER1% X %NUMBER2% = %ANSWER%

SET NUMBER1=
SET NUMBER2=
SET ANSWER=
SET ERROR=
GOTO END
```

Notice the use of CTTY NUL and CTTY CON to keep SAYERROR.BAT from displaying its message to the screen. MULTIPLY.BAS, MULTIPLY.EXE, and SHOWTIME.BAT are all on the disk in the subdirectory \UTILITY\DOS\YOU-MAKE\QB-TIMES. That version of SHOWTIME.BAT has documentation and offers command-line help. For SHOWTIME.BAT to work, both BATCMD.EXE and SAYERROR.BAT must be in the current subdirectory or the path.

Builder and Builder Lite

Builder and Builder Lite are the perfect illustration for writing batch file utilities because they can set the errorlevel and write to the master copy of the environment. You'll write these utilities under Builder Lite, which ensures that they'll work under both Builder Lite and Builder. You'll use the same two batch file utilities you used for QuickBASIC.

The CD-ROM includes a fully functional copy of Builder Lite in the \BLDLITE sub-directory. It's not crippled in any way. This means that you can experiment with these programs and recompile them. To get the full documentation for Builder Lite, order my *Builder Lite: Developing Dynamic Batch Files* book. This book has a coupon in the back for it.

Adding 1 to the command-line number

Unlike QuickBASIC, Builder Lite requires that you declare your variables before using them. Declaring the variables tells Builder Lite what type they are and reserves a memory slot for them. The commands to declare variables are:

```
STRING  Str1, Str2
INTEGER Number, StrLong, Num1, Num2
```

Builder Lite doesn't work with noninteger numbers; variables declared as integers automatically ignore the decimal portion of a number. As a result, Builder Lite automatically restricts answers to integers (whole numbers).

Next, we need to read in the first input value. Builder Lite makes that very easy; the command Str1 := "%1" does this without the looping required under Quick-BASIC. Now you can test to see if help was requested with the following commands:

```
IF Str1 == "/?"
    SAY "Reads A Number From The Command Line"
    SAY "Adds One To It And Sets Errorlevel Equal To Answer"
    EXIT 0
END

IF Str1 == "?"
    SAY "Reads A Number From The Command Line"
    SAY "Adds One To It And Sets Errorlevel Equal To Answer"
    EXIT 0
END
```

The EXIT 0 command causes Builder Lite to exit the program and set the error-level to zero. The SAY command is very similar to the PRINT command in QuickBA-SIC. The next error check is to see if the user forgot to enter the number to add 1 to. The code to do that follows:

```
IF Str1 == ""
    SAY "No Number Entered On Command Line"
    BEEP
    EXIT 255
END
```

Since this is an error, the program beeps the speaker with the BEEP command and exits with the errorlevel set to 255. Setting the errorlevel to 255 for an error makes testing for errors in a batch file much easier. Since the IF ERRORLEVEL test is a greater-than-or-equal test, you have to use dual IF tests to test for a single errorlevel value. However, since the errorlevel cannot exceed 255, the single IF ERROR LEVEL 255 test can test for this value.

The next error check is to loop through the string variable Str1 and make sure it contains only numbers. The code to do this is:

```
Num1 := 0
REPEAT StrLong
    Num1 := Num1 + 1
    Str2 := MidStr Str1, Num1, 1
    Num2 := StrToNum Str2
    IF Num2 == 0
        IF Str2 <> "0"
            SAY "Nonnumeric Data Entered"
            BEEP
            EXIT 255
        END
    END
END
```

The Repeat loops through the string, while the MidStr function grabs one character at a time. That single character is converted to a number. If the number is 0, then the single character is checked to see if it's a 0. If not, the user entered a nonnumeric character, and the program exits with an error message, sets the errorlevel to 255, and beeps the speaker.

This is a more detailed test than that in QuickBASIC because every character is examined in detail. As a general rule, this is the level of detail you want for your batch file utilities in order to completely isolate the utility and make sure no errors reach it.

Next, the program performs the actual mathematics with the following commands:

```
Number := StrToNum Str1
Number := Number + 1
```

Since the value is to be passed back to the batch file via the errorlevel, the program checks to make sure the value isn't too high for the errorlevel with the following code:

```
IF Number > 255
    SAY "Answer Exceeds 255 And ";
    SAY "Errorlevel Will Not Handle This"
    BEEP
    EXIT 255
END
```

Since a negative number won't get past the routine that checks for nonnumeric data, the program doesn't need to check for a negative answer. In MULTIPLY.BLD, this filter is modified to allow negative numbers to pass. Finally, it exits and stores the answer in the errorlevel with the command EXIT Number.

SHOWADD.BAT has been slightly modified to work with this new version of ADD.EXE. Since the answer is passed back via the errorlevel, SHOWADD.BAT now calls on SAYERROR.BAT to convert the errorlevel to an environmental variable named ERROR. Everything is stored on the CD-ROM in the \UTILITY\DOS\YOU-MAKE\BLD-ADD subdirectory.

Multiplying two numbers together

Like ADD.BLD, MULTIPLY.BLD must declare variables and check the command line for a help request. Other than using more variables than ADD.BLD, these are performed in an identical fashion. Next, the two environmental variables NUMBER1 and NUMBER2 must be read into the program. The commands to do this are:

```
Str1 := "%NUMBER1%"
Str2 := "%NUMBER2%"
```

It checks to make sure that NUMBER1 exists by making sure that Str1 has a value. The code that does this is:

```
IF Str1 == ""
   SAY "No Number Entered In NUMBER1 In Environment"
   BEEP
   EXIT 255
END
```

Str2 is checked in an identical fashion. Now, each of the two string variables must be checked to see if they contain any nonnumeric characters. The code to do that on Str1 is:

```
StrLong := Length Str1

Num1 := 0
REPEAT StrLong
   Num1 := Num1 + 1
   Str3 := MidStr Str1, Num1, 1
   Num2 := StrToNum Str3
   IF Num2 == 0
      Flag := 1
      IF Str3 == "0" Then Flag := 0
      IF Str3 == "-" Then Flag := 0
      IF Str3 == "." Then Flag := 0
      IF Flag == 1
         SAY "Non-Numeric Data In NUMBER1 In Environment"
         BEEP
         EXIT 255
      END
   END
END
```

This code loops through all the characters in Str1. It first sets the variable Flag equal to 1. Then it pulls off the next character, stores it in the variable Str3, then converts Str3 to the number Num2. If this number is a 0, then error checking is required to make sure it's a valid number. Otherwise, it's a number and no additional error checking is required for this character.

When Num2 equals 0, the code checks to see if the string Str3 is a 0, negative sign, or period. If it is, it's a valid character and the Flag variable is changed to 0. Next, the

Flag variable is checked to see if it still equals 1. If so, it displays an error message, beeps the speaker, and exits the program because a nonvalid character was found. Next, the other input is checked in the same way.

After this, you know you have two valid numbers stored in the string variables. They're converted to numbers and multiplied together, and the answer is converted back to a string with the following code:

```
Number1 := StrToNum Str1
Number2 := StrToNum Str2
Answer := Number1 * Number2
Str1 := IntToStr Answer
```

While the period was allowed as a valid character in the error checking, this is for illustration. Builder Lite (and Builder) works only with integers, so the process of converting the string to a number will strip off the period and any numbers that follow it so the final answer is an integer. It actually strips off the decimal portion rather than rounding, so both 12.001 and 12.999 becomes 12 when stored to a numeric variable.

The answer is converted back to a string because the output routine requires a string. Finally, the answer is written to the master copy of the environment with the command SET "Answer" = Str1.

The batch file SHOWTIME.BAT illustrates MULTIPLY.EXE by prompting the user for two single digits with Batcmd, storing these digits in the environment with SAY-ERROR.BAT, and then using MULTIPLY.EXE to compute the answer. The operational code is:

```
BATCMD GN Enter First Number To Multiply
CTTY NUL
CALL SAYERROR
CTTY CON
SET NUMBER1=%ERROR%

BATCMD GN Enter Second Number To Multiply
CTTY NUL
CALL SAYERROR
CTTY CON
SET NUMBER2=%ERROR%

MULTIPLY

ECHO %NUMBER1% X %NUMBER2% = %ANSWER%

SET NUMBER1=
SET NUMBER2=
SET ANSWER=
SET ERROR=
```

The files MULTIPLY.BLD, MULTIPLY.EXE, and SHOWTIME.BAT are all on the CD-ROM in the subdirectory \UTILITY\DOS\YOU-MAKE\BLD-TIME. That version of SHOWTIME.BAT has documentation and offers command-line help.

Turbo Pascal

Many programming languages, such as Turbo Pascal, Turbo C, and QuickBASIC, include libraries of routines that enable you to recall the contents of environment variables. By contrast, these same languages lack routines to write to new or existing environment variables in the master and/or current environment.

The reason for these missing routines is probably due to the complicated process of writing to environmental variables. In order to write to a new or existing environmental variable, you need to manage the list of environmental variables maintained by DOS. Therefore, you must first locate it in the computer's memory, a not-too-easy task to begin with. Once you locate the list, you need to perform the following general steps:

1. Determine whether or not the targeted environment variable already exists.

2. If the environment variable exists, you must first remove it from the list.

3. Insert the name of the targeted environment variable and its contents in the list.

This process uses dynamic lists and employs pointers to alter rather crucial data in memory, not a programming job for just anyone.

The EnvLib Library Unit

Rather than reinventing the wheel, let me present a library unit developed by Sunny Hill Software, which is currently sold by TurboPower Software as part of their Turbo Professional package. These routines are contained on the CD-ROM in the file ENVLIB.PAS. I'm providing the source code, with the permission of TurboPower Software. This file gives you (and any colleagues who program in Turbo Pascal) the opportunity to study how to write routines in order to manipulate the environmental variables of the master and current environment.

Instead of going through the complicated tasks of the various library routines, let me focus on the following few components: the record type EnvRec, procedure MasterEnv, procedure CurrentEnv, function GetEnvStr, and function SetEnvStr.

The EnvRec record type is a structure that stores the segment address location, size, and pointer to the master or current environment. The Master and CurrentEnv procedures return information via the parameter Env (which has the type EnvRec). The data in the parameter contains the handle of the targeted environment. The code is:

```
procedure MasterEnv(var Env : EnvRec);
procedure CurrentEnv(var Env : EnvRec);
```

The function GetEnvStr returns the contents of an environment variable. If the targeted environment variable doesn't exist, the function returns an empty string. The first parameter has the EnvRec record type and is a handle to the targeted environment. The second parameter is a string that represents the name of the accessed environment variable. The code follows:

```
function GetEnvStr(Env : EnvRec; Search : string)
                 : string;
```

The function SetEnvStr is perhaps the most valuable library function for your purpose. This function allows Turbo Pascal utilities to write a string to new or existing environmental variables. The function returns the logical true value if it's successful (that is, if you didn't run out of environment space). Otherwise, the function yields false. The first parameter has the EnvRec record type and acts as a handle to the targeted environment. The second parameter is a string that represents the name of the targeted environmental variable. The third parameter represents the new value of the targeted environmental variable. The code is:

```
function SetEnvStr(Env : EnvRec; Search, Value : string)
                   : Boolean;
```

Adding 1 to the command-line number

Now let's look at a few examples that use the EnvLib library units to write Turbo Pascal batch file utilities and test batch files. This batch file utility performs the same tasks as the ADD.BAS batch file utility I presented earlier in this chapter. The ADD.PAS utility follows the same general program logic in its QuickBASIC counterpart. As you might expect, the differences between the QuickBASIC and Turbo Pascal languages affect the exact program statements in ADD.BAS and ADD.PAS.

ADD.PAS uses the {$X+} compiler directive to allow the program to discard the result of functions. I use this directive specifically to discard the results of function SetEnvStr. It also contains the clause Uses EnvLib;, which enable it to import various routines from the EnvLib library unit.

The ADD.PAS program declares a number of variables that store and manipulate data using the following code. I'll cover these variables as I discuss the different blocks of statements in ADD.PAS.

```
VAR Answer, Build : STRING;
    ErrorCode : INTEGER;
    Number : LONGINT;
    E : EnvRec;
```

The first program statement invokes the procedure MasterEnv, which is exported by the EnvLib library unit. The argument for MasterEnv is the record variable E. This statement obtains vital information related to the location and size of the master environment. The code is:

```
{ Get Information on Master Environment }
MasterEnv(E);
```

The following statement enables the program to retrieve the first command-line argument, using the predefined Turbo Pascal function ParamStr:

```
{ Get The First Command, Build Argument }
Build := ParamStr(1);
```

The argument of 1 selects the first command-line argument by number. If there are no command-line arguments, ParamStr returns an empty string, which is assigned to the string variable Build. Next, the program checks for a help request using an IF THEN statement. This statement displays on-line help and ends the program when the variable Build contains either an empty string or strings /? and ?. The code for this is:

```
{ Now, Check For Help Request }
IF (Build = '/?') OR (Build = '?') OR (Build = '') THEN BEGIN
  WRITE('Adds 1 To Number Passed ');
  WRITELN('And Saves It To Variable ANSWER. ');
  WRITE('A Batch File Should Examine The ');
  WRITELN('The Environment Variable ANSWER.');
  HALT;
END;
```

If the program doesn't execute the statements in the THEN clause, it proceeds to convert the characters in variable Build into a number. That number is stored in the long integer variable Number. Because of the extended range of long integers, you can use the Turbo Pascal utility to add 1 to the ANSWER environmental variable when the latter already has values well above 32767, which is the upper limit in the QuickBASIC and Builder versions. This extended numeric range is one of the benefits of using a programming language like Turbo Pascal.

The conversion statement uses the predefined Turbo Pascal procedure VAL and employs the variable ErrorCode to report the conversion error status. The Error-Code is an integer variable that stores the index of the first offending character in the string of variable Build. If there's no error in the conversion, the variable ErrorCode contains 0. Unlike the QuickBASIC VAL function, the Turbo Pascal version either entirely succeeds or fails in its task—there are no results from partial conversion.

```
{ Now Convert Build To Number }
VAL(Build, Number, ErrorCode);
```

The program then checks the conversion error status by using an IF THEN ELSE statement, as shown in the following code. This statement determines if the variable ErrorCode contains a positive value. If the condition is true, there's a conversion error and the program executes the statements in the THEN clause. These statements display a warning message and end the program. Otherwise, the program executes the statement in the ELSE clause to increment the content of variable Number.

```
IF ErrorCode > 0 THEN BEGIN
  WRITELN('Invalid Input');
  WRITELN('Enter ADD /? For Help');
  WRITE(^G); { Beep }
  HALT;
END
  ELSE
    Number := Number + 1;
```

Following a successful addition, the program converts the value in the Number variable to a string and stores it in the Answer variable. The program uses the predefined Turbo Pascal procedure STR to perform this task, as shown here:

```
{ Convert Number To String To
  Avoid Space In Batch File }
STR(Number, Answer);
```

The last statement saves the value of string Answer in the environmental variable ANSWER. This statement uses the SetEnvStr procedure, which is exported by the Env-Lib library unit. Notice that the first argument in the following code for the SetEnvStr procedure is the record variable E. The second argument is the string ANSWER, which specifies the name of the environmental variable. The third argument is the variable Answer, which supplies the value written to the environmental variable ANSWER.

```
{ Assign String to Environment Variable ANSWER }
SetEnvStr(E, 'ANSWER', Answer);
```

The Pascal version of SHOWADD.BAT is very similar to its QuickBASIC counterpart, and executes a batch file loop 20 times. The main difference between the two is the loop that invokes the ADD.EXE utility. The operational code is as follows:

```
:TOP
   ADD %Answer%
   ECHO Loop Number %ANSWER%
   IF NOT %ANSWER%==20 GOTO TOP
   ECHO Loops Done
GOTO END
```

Notice that, after the loop calls the ADD.EXE utility, there's no call to a temporary batch file. Since ADD.EXE writes directly to the environmental variable ANSWER, there's no need for such a batch file. Consequently, the Turbo Pascal version of SHOWADD.BAT runs faster than the QuickBASIC version because it bypasses the invocation of other batch files.

The files ADD.PAS, ADD.EXE, and SHOWADD.BAT are all on the CD-ROM in the subdirectory \UTILITY\DOS\YOU-MAKE\PAS-ADD. That version of SHOWADD.BAT has documentation and offers command-line help.

Adding 1 and letting users pick the environmental variable

The ADD.PAS batch file utility systematically stores the result of the addition in the environmental variable ANSWER. You can modify the utility to store the result in an environmental variable that the user specifies. You can also make the new version use the environmental variable ANSWER if the user doesn't enter a name.

The PLUS.PAS batch file utility will be the enhanced version of ADD.PAS. The new utility uses the variable EVarName to store the name of the custom environmental variable. After assigning the first command-line argument to the Build variable, the program assigns the second command-line argument to the EVarName variable. This argument represents the name of the targeted environmental variable, shown here:

```
{ Get The Second Command, Build Argument }
EVarName := ParamStr(2);
```

The program then uses an IF statement to assign the string ANSWER to the variable EVarName if there's no second command-line argument. The IF statement compares the variable EVarName with an empty string to test whether or not the condition is true, using the following code:

```
{ Use The Name ANSWER If User Does Not
    Specify The Name Of An Environment Variable }
IF EVarName = " THEN
    EVarName := 'ANSWER';
```

The call to the SetEnvStr uses a different second argument, and PLUS.PAS passes the variable EVarName to the SetEnvStr procedure to supply it the name of the targeted environmental variable. The rest of the lines in PLUS.PAS are the same as the ones in ADD.PAS, except for the last statement:

```
{ Assign String to Environment Variable
    Specified By The Pascal Variable EVarName }
SetEnvStr(E, EVarName, Answer);
```

The files PLUS.PAS, PLUS.EXE, and SHOWPLUS.BAT are all on the CD-ROM in the subdirectory \UTILITY\DOS\YOU-MAKE\PAS-PLUS. SHOWPLUS.BAT is identical to SHOWADD.BAT except that the environmental variable sum is specified on the command line to replace answer, and the PLUS command is used instead of ADD.

Multiplying two numbers together

Let's look at another Turbo Pascal batch file utility. This one presents the Pascal version of the MULTIPLY.BAS utility I presented earlier. The utility carries out the following tasks:

- Reads the contents of two environmental variables, NUMBER1 and NUMBER2.
- Converts the contents of NUMBER1 and NUMBER2 into numbers.
- Multiplies the converted numbers.
- Writes the result in the environmental variable ANSWER.

Like ADD.PAS, MULTIPLY.PAS imports the routines it needs to manipulate the environmental variables from the EnvLib library, using the command Uses EnvLib;. The MULTIPLY.PAS utility also declares a set of variables to store and manipulate data with the commands:

```
VAR Answer, Build, Input1, Input2 : STRING;
    ErrorCode1, ErrorCode2 : INTEGER;
```

```
Number1, Number2 : LONGINT;
E : EnvRec;
```

The first program statement invokes the procedure MasterEnv (exported by the EnvLib library unit) to store the data for the master environment in the record variable E, using the commands:

```
{ Get Information on Master Environment }
MasterEnv(E);
```

Next, the program assigns the first command-line argument to the variable Build. This command line argument serves to invoke the on-line help. Otherwise, the MULTIPLY.PAS utility needs no command-line arguments, since it handles its input and output data through the environmental variables NUMBER1, NUMBER2, and ANSWER. That code is:

```
{ Get The First Command, Build Argument }
Build := ParamStr(1);
```

The program then checks if the utility is invoked with a help request. The program performs this task using the following IF THEN statement. Notice that the statement examines the condition where the variable Build stores either string /? or ?. The condition doesn't compare the Build variable with an empty string, since the utility works without command-line arguments. This code is as follows:

```
{ Now, Check For Help Request }
IF (Build = '/?') OR (Build = '?') THEN BEGIN
   WRITE('Multiplies Two Numbers Together ');
   WRITELN('Passed To It Via The Environment');
   WRITE('Using The Names NUMBER1 And NUMBER2.');
   WRITELN('Assigns Result To ANSWER.');
   WRITE('A Batch File Should Examine The ');
   WRITELN('The Environment Variable ANSWER.');
   HALT;
END;
```

In the next step, the program copies the contents of environmental variables NUMBER1 and NUMBER2 to the string variables Input1 and Input2, respectively. This step involves the GetEnvStr function, which is exported by the EnvLib library unit. The first argument for the GetEnvStr function is the record variable E. The second argument is the name of the accessed environmental variable. The GetEnvStr function yields the contents of the specified environmental variable, or an empty string if the variable is undefined. That code is:

```
{ Now Get The Numbers From The Environment }
Input1 := GetEnvStr(E, 'NUMBER1');
Input2 := GetEnvStr(E, 'NUMBER2');
```

It's possible that either NUMBER1 or NUMBER2, or both, are undefined. The program detects the existence of the environmental variables NUMBER1 and NUM-

BER2 by examining the contents of variables Input1 and Input2. The utility uses two similar IF THEN statements to determine if variable Input1 or Input2 stores an empty string. If so, the program displays a warning message and then exits. The code for Input1 is:

```
IF Input1 = " THEN BEGIN
   WRITELN('NUMBER1 Environmental Variable Missing');
   WRITE(^G); { Beep }
   HALT
END;
```

While not shown, the code for Input2 is identical except for the variable names. Once the program determines that the environmental variables NUMBER1 and NUMBER2 exist, it proceeds to convert the contents of the variables Input1 and Input2 into numbers. The program uses the predefined VAL procedure to store the converted numbers in the long integer variables Number1 and Number2. The VAL procedure uses the variables ErrorCode1 and ErrorCode2 to store the error status of the conversions. That code is as follows:

```
{ Now Convert Strings To Number }
VAL(Input1, Number1, ErrorCode1);
VAL(Input2, Number2, ErrorCode2);
```

Next, the program determines whether or not both of the conversions went smoothly. The program uses two similar IF THEN statements to display error messages and exit if the value in either ErrorCode1 or ErrorCode2 is positive. The code for ErrorCode1 is:

```
{ Now Check To Make Sure That
  There Is No Conversion Error }

IF ErrorCode1 > 0 THEN BEGIN
   WRITE('Invalid Input For NUMBER1 ');
   WRITELN('Environmental Variable');
   WRITELN('Enter MULTIPLY /? For Help');
   WRITE(^G);
   HALT;
END;
```

While not shown, the code for NUMBER2 is identical except for the variable names. After the previous set of verifications, the program proceeds to multiply the numbers in variables Number1 and Number2 and store the string image of the result in the variable Answer. The program performs these two tasks in a single call to procedure STR, shown here:

```
{ Convert Number To String To Avoid
  Space In Batch File }
STR(Number1 * Number2, Answer);
```

The last statement saves the value of string Answer in the environmental variable ANSWER. This statement uses the SetEnvStr procedure, which is exported by the

EnvLib library unit. The statement is similar to the last one in the ADD.PAS utility:

```
{ Assign String to Environment Variable ANSWER }
SetEnvStr(E, 'ANSWER', Answer);
```

The files MULTIPLY.PAS, MULTIPLY.EXE, and SHOWTIME.BAT are all on the CD-ROM in the subdirectory \UTILITY\DOS\YOU-MAKE\PAS-TIME. The code for SHOWTIME.BAT is identical to the code for the QuickBASIC batch file.

Windows 3.1

Windows 3.1 allows you to shell out to DOS by running another copy of COMMAND.COM. It does the same thing if you run a batch file. The Builder Lite and Pascal batch file utilities that write directly to the master copy of the environment behave differently under Windows. When either utility runs, there are four different environments being used by DOS:

- The master copy of the environment created by DOS when the computer booted.

- The copy of the environment passed by DOS to Windows.

- The second master copy of the environment created by COMMAND.COM when Windows ran it to give you a DOS prompt or run a batch file.

- The copy of this second master copy of the environment passed to either the Builder Lite or the Pascal routine.

Just keeping up with all these copies of the environment is difficult! When Builder Lite reads from or writes to the master copy of the environment, it uses the third environment listed, the second copy of the master environment created when COMMAND.COM runs Windows. That way, the changes it makes are available to the batch file while it's running. Most of the time, this is what you want the utility to do.

When a Pascal program reads from or writes to the master copy of the environment, it uses the true master copy of the environment, or the first environment listed. That means if the environmental variables NUMBER1 and NUMBER2 don't exist prior to loading Windows, then MULTIPLY.EXE will report an error—even if the batch file that runs it under Windows creates them, since that batch file creates them in the COMMAND.COM environment running under Windows (the third environment listed). It also means that when MULTIPLY.EXE writes the results to ANSWER while running under Windows, that value isn't available to a batch file because the batch file reads the environment from the version of COMMAND.COM that Windows runs and not the master copy of the environment modified by MULTIPLY.EXE.

In other words, you can't use these Pascal utilities while running under Windows, but you can use the Builder Lite utilities. As a result, it's very important to test your utilities under Windows and understand how they interact with Windows if you ever intend to use them with Windows.

Summary

A batch file utility is any program designed to take information from a batch file or provide information to a batch file in order to enhance its operation. Because they generally perform only one specific task, batch file utilities tend to be some of the simplest programs you can write in any language. In order to program a batch file utility, you need a way to get information into the program and a way to get information out of the program.

- There are four ways to get information into a batch file utility: the command line, the environment, asking the user, and polling the equipment.

- There are four ways to get information out of a batch file utility and back into the batch file: the errorlevel, the master copy of the environment, an on-the-fly batch file, and printing to the screen or printer.

- The QuickBASIC compiler lacks the ability to write to the master copy of the environment and to set the errorlevel when a program exits.

- The COMMAND$ function lets QuickBASIC read the command line, minus the name of the program.

- Once you obtain the command line in QuickBASIC with the COMMAND$ function, you have to manually separate it into its component parts in order to access the different replaceable parameters.

- In QuickBASIC, the END command causes the program to immediately terminate and return control to DOS. After displaying help, this is an excellent way for help routines to terminate.

- In QuickBASIC, numeric results have to be converted to strings and trimmed to avoid placing spaces in the environment.

- In QuickBASIC, the only viable output method for a batch file utility is writing a temporary batch file for the main batch file to CALL in order to place the results into the environment.

- Batch file utilities need extensive error checking to make sure the user enters exactly the information that the utility expects to receive.

- Even when a batch file is taking its usual input from the environment or user, or by polling the equipment, it must still check the command line to see if the user requested help.

- In QuickBASIC, the ENVIRON$ function reads in environmental variables. All environmental variables come in as string variables even if they're numbers.

- Builder and Builder Lite can read from the command line and environment, set the errorlevel, and write to the master copy of the environment. This makes these languages excellent tools for writing batch file utilities.

- Builder Lite uses %1 to represent the first replaceable parameter, %2 to represent the second, and so on, so it's very easy to read replaceable parameters into a Builder Lite program.

- The EXIT *number* command causes a Builder Lite program to immediately exit to DOS and set the errorlevel to the number specified after the command.

- Setting the errorlevel to 255 for an error makes testing for errors in a batch file much easier.

- Builder Lite can read in environmental variables by surrounding their name with percent signs and double quotes, so the command Str1 := "%NUMBER1%" would read the environmental variable NUMBER into the variable Str1.

- Builder Lite can write to the master copy of the environment with a command like SET "Answer" = Str1.

- The Turbo Professional package, developed by Sunny Hill Software and marketed by TurboPower Software, allows Turbo Pascal programs to read from and write to the master copy of the environment.

- The function SetEnvStr in the Turbo Professional package is used by a Turbo Pascal program to write a string to a new or existing environmental variable.

- When storing results in an environmental variable, sometimes it's useful to let the user specify the name of the environmental variable to use.

- When a Builder Lite program alters the master copy of the environment under Windows, it alters the COMMAND.COM copy of the environment for that DOS session rather than the true master copy of the environment.

- When a Pascal program alters the master copy of the environment under Windows, it alters the true master copy of the environment. This can cause batch files running under Windows to bomb if they depend on a Pascal utility.

Chapter 32

Writing OS/2 Batch File Utilities

REXX programs can do anything a batch file can do, generally with far fewer lines of code, and writing OS/2 batch files requires no knowledge of REXX. Additionally, running the REXX utilities later in this chapter and even changing their prompts requires no knowledge of REXX.

REXX Programming

Covering REXX in detail would require an entire book, so this chapter is naturally an introduction to REXX. If you're interested in learning more about REXX, check out the on-line documentation that comes with OS/2 or my *Writing OS/2 REXX Programs* book, also from McGraw-Hill.

REXX is short for *restructured extended executor*. REXX was developed as a mainframe language by Mike Cowlishaw of IBM, and became so popular that it was selected as the standard command language for the IBM systems application architecture, or SAA.

With many computer languages, the program's author must take care of a great many details. For example, variables must be declared as either strings or numbers, often in advance. These details help ensure that the resulting program is structured properly. REXX was designed to let you get your programming job done quickly with a minimum of up-front fussing with the program structure. This makes it easier and quicker to use REXX, but working on larger programs can be more difficult.

Both batch files and REXX programs are stored in files with a .CMD extension. The only way OS/2 has to tell them apart is to look at the file itself and see which type it is. In order to facilitate this, OS/2 requires that the first two characters in a REXX program be /*. If the file begins with /*, then OS/2 knows it's a REXX program; otherwise, it assumes it's a batch file.

The selection of the /* characters isn't as arbitrary as it seems. REXX comments must begin with a /* and end with a */, so OS/2 is simply requiring that REXX programs begin with a comment. Anything placed between a /* and a */ is a comment and has no impact on program operations.

Like batch files, REXX programs are ASCII files. Additionally, they're ready to run as written and don't need to be compiled. So as soon as you make a modification to one of the utilities in this chapter, it's ready to test. Of course, you should always keep a backup copy in case your modifications don't work as you expect.

REXX uses the SAY command instead of the ECHO command to display information on the screen. If the information isn't inside quotation marks, it's converted to all uppercase, so you'll want to surround your messages with quotation marks—as they appear in all the utilities in the next chapter. For the most part, it's the messages you'll want to customize, changing them to request specific information. A simple REXX program using comments and the SAY command would be:

```
/* NAME:    REXX-1.CMD */
/* PURPOSE: Demonstration REXX Program */
/* VERSION: 1.00 */
/* DATE:    June 11, 1993 */

SAY Hello Reader
Say I Am A New REXX Program
```

Since neither line is surrounded by quotation marks, both lines will be displayed in all uppercase. All of these files can be found in the \REXINTRO subdirectory of the CD-ROM.

Variables and Branching

In a batch file, the only variables you have access to are environmental variables. REXX can create its own variables by assigning a value to a variable name. From then on, that variable name is replaced with the contents of the variable. The following example will make that clearer:

```
/* NAME:    REXX-2.CMD */
/* PURPOSE: Demonstration REXX Program */
/* VERSION: 1.00 */
/* DATE:    June 11, 1993 */

READER="Ronny"
SAY Hello Reader
Say I Am A New REXX Program
```

In this program, READER is now a variable name, so the first line it displays is HELLO Ronny. (Since "Ronny" is in quotation marks when created, it isn't converted to uppercase.)

REXX variables aren't limited to strings; they can also contain numbers. Unlike many languages, there's no difference in REXX between a string and a numeric variable. REXX can perform the normal mathematical operations of addition, subtraction, multiplication, and division with numeric variables. The results can be either stored to a variable or printed with the SAY command. The following example illustrates that:

```
/* NAME:    REXX-3.CMD */
/* PURPOSE: Demonstration REXX Program */
/* VERSION: 1.00 */
/* DATE:    June 11, 1993 */

First=12
Second=14
SAY "Sum Is" First + Second
Times=First*Second
Say "Product Is" Times
```

Like a batch file, REXX programs generally flow from top to bottom in a straight line. REXX programs have two commands to alter program flow, EXIT and SIGNAL. The EXIT command causes a REXX program to immediately terminate and return control to the operating system.

With a batch file, you specify a label with a colon and a name, e.g., :TOP, and you can jump to that label with a GOTO TOP command. In REXX, you mark a label with a name and a colon (TOP:), and you can jump to that label with a SIGNAL command, like SIGNAL TOP. You must be very careful when using a SIGNAL command in REXX, however, because it closes all loops. In REXX, SIGNAL also has many other uses.

One way to get input from the user is with the PULL command, which takes everything the user enters until pressing Return and stores it in a variable. The following program illustrates that:

```
/* NAME:    REXX-4.CMD */
/* PURPOSE: Demonstration REXX Program */
/* VERSION: 1.00 */
/* DATE:    June 11, 1993 */

SAY "Enter Your First Name"
PULL First
SAY "Enter Your Last Name"
PULL Last
Say "Hello" First Last
```

The PULL command can easily handle more than one variable, so this program could be shortened to the following:

```
/* NAME:    REXX-5.CMD */
/* PURPOSE: Demonstration REXX Program */
/* VERSION: 1.00 */
/* DATE:    June 11, 1993 */

SAY "Enter Your Name"
PULL First Last
Say "Hello" First Last
```

Each variable after the PULL command is assigned one word of the response. If the number of words exceeds the number of variables, all the extra words are assigned to the last variable. If there aren't enough words for all the variables, those extra variables aren't created.

Logic Testing and Looping

REXX supports logic testing with both IF THEN and IF THEN ELSE statements, as illustrated by the following program:

```
/* NAME:    REXX-6.CMD */
/* PURPOSE: Demonstration REXX Program */
/* VERSION: 1.00 */
/* DATE:    June 11, 1993 */

SAY "Enter Two Numbers"
PULL One Two
Total=One+Two
IF Total > 20 THEN SAY "Total Over 20"
   ELSE SAY "Total Less Than Or Equal To 20"
```

This program prompts the user for two numbers. Once it has the two numbers, it totals them and prints a different message if the total is over 20 or less than or equal to 20.

REXX uses DO WHILE and DO UNTIL to loop until specific conditions are met. They work very similarly, only the DO WHILE loop requires the condition to exist first and DO UNTIL doesn't. For example, the following program is an arithmetic test that prompts the user for two numbers and then keeps prompting for the sum until the right number is entered:

```
/* NAME:    REXX-7.CMD */
/* PURPOSE: Demonstration REXX Program */
/* VERSION: 1.00 */
/* DATE:    June 11, 1993 */

SAY "Enter Two Numbers"
PULL First Second
Answer=First+Second
Respond=0
DO UNTIL Respond = Answer
   SAY "What Is" First "+" Second
   PULL Respond
END
```

The DO UNTIL Respond = Answer line could be replaced with DO WHILE Respond <> Answer since Respond has a value before the loop begins. There's also a LEAVE command that causes REXX to immediately exit a loop. You could rewrite this test as follows to provide the user an option to "give up":

```
/* NAME:    REXX-8.CMD */
/* PURPOSE: Demonstration REXX Program */
/* VERSION: 1.00 */
/* DATE:    June 11, 1993 */

SAY "Enter Two Numbers"
PULL First Second
```

```
Answer=First+Second
Respond=0
DO UNTIL Respond = Answer
   SAY "What Is" First "+" Second
   PULL Respond
   IF Respond=STOP THEN LEAVE
END
```

Since the PULL command converts the response to uppercase, no conversion is needed before performing the IF test on the response variable. If you need to loop through a command or series of commands a specific number of times, a DO command followed by a number does just that, as the following program illustrates:

```
/* NAME:    REXX-9.CMD */
/* PURPOSE: Demonstration REXX Program */
/* VERSION: 1.00 */
/* DATE:    June 11, 1993 */

DO 100
  SAY "Counting To 100"
END
```

If you need to know the line number, then you can modify the DO loop to include a variable to contain the loop number, as shown here:

```
/* NAME:    REXX-10.CMD */
/* PURPOSE: Demonstration REXX Program */
/* VERSION: 1.00 */
/* DATE:    June 11, 1993 */

DO I = 1 TO 100
  SAY "Counting To 100. On Line" I
END
```

Subroutines

Like a batch file, a REXX subroutine is a small section of code designed to be reused. With REXX, the subroutine must be stored as part of the main file. It starts with the subroutine name followed by a colon (just like a line name) and ends with a RETURN command. So a subroutine acts as a special type of GOTO command. The following program illustrates this:

```
/* NAME:    REXX-7.CMD */
/* PURPOSE: Demonstration REXX Program */
/* VERSION: 1.00 */
/* DATE:    June 11, 1993 */

CALL Setup
CALL Problem
EXIT

SETUP:
   SAY "Enter Two Numbers"
   PULL First Second
   Answer=First+Second
```

```
       Respond=0
RETURN

PROBLEM:
   DO UNTIL Respond = Answer
      SAY "What Is" First "+" Second
      PULL Respond
   END
RETURN
```

Notice the EXIT command before the beginning of the subroutines. Since REXX processes files from beginning to end unless told to do otherwise, after it finished running the programs it would run the subroutines again because they're at the bottom—unless you tell it to quit before reaching them.

You can place parameters to a subroutine by placing them after the subroutine name, and you must separate multiple parameters with commas. The following program illustrates that:

```
/* NAME:    REXX-12.CMD */
/* PURPOSE: Demonstration REXX Program */
/* VERSION: 1.00 */
/* DATE:    June 11, 1993 */

CALL Count 50, "Ronny"
EXIT

COUNT:
   Count = Arg(1)
   Name  = Arg(2)
   SAY "Hello" Name "Counting To" Count
   DO I = 1 To Count
     SAY "Line Number" I "Of" Count
   END
RETURN
```

The Arg function (short for argument) is used to transfer the information passed to the subroutine to variables.

This is just a sample of the power of the REXX language. If you're at all interested in programming, you'll find that REXX is a worthwhile language to study.

Batch File Utilities in REXX

The REXX utilities in this section will allow you to write even more powerful REXX utilities. You don't need any knowledge of REXX to run and modify these batch file utilities, other than knowing you must run the programs with the CALL command.

Getting information from the user

OS/2 retains many of the limitations of the DOS batch language, which is to say it's very limited in its ability to get information from the user. The only native abilities OS/2 batch files have of getting information from users are allowing them to enter replaceable parameters on the command line or press Ctrl–Break to stop a batch file. That's a fairly limited set of tools.

Fortunately, REXX lets you fill in the missing gaps of the OS/2 batch language. Plus, since every version of OS/2 comes with REXX, you can easily modify these programs, something you usually can't always do with a batch file utility.

Getting words from the user

One of the things you will want your batch files to do is ask users for information, such as their name or the name of a file to erase, copy, or run. For this task, you need a utility that can accept full words rather than a single character. GET.CMD, shown here, does just that:

```
/* Name:     GET.CMD */
/* PURPOSE: A REXX Program To Get Information From The User */
/* VERSION: 1.00 */
/* DATE:     May 27, 1993 */
/* Copyright (c) 1993 McGraw-Hill */

SAY "Enter A Single Word"
PARSE PULL Word .
ENV = 'OS2ENVIRONMENT'
LastRC = VALUE('Return',Word,Env)
```

The PARSE PULL Word . line waits for the user to enter a line of text and press return; then it strips off everything except the first word. The next two lines write that word to the environment.

The most likely change for you to make is the Enter A Single Word prompt on the first operational line of the program, after all the comments. You can use any message you want inside quotation marks. Unlike batch files, REXX programs don't have a problem with piping symbols inside messages, as long as those messages are inside quotation marks. You can even drop the quotation marks. If you do that, however, the prompt will be converted to all uppercase and you must avoid piping symbols.

If you're going to convert the user's response to uppercase anyway, as you might do if you needed to test on it, then it's easy to have this program do that automatically. Just drop the PARSE command on the second operational line, leave the command as PULL Word, and the user's response will be converted to uppercase. If you want to store the response in the environment under a different name, change the Return on the last line to the environmental variable name you want to use.

Additionally, it's not necessary to have just one version of each utility. You might take a copy of GET.CMD, which gets a word from the user, and create GET-BIG.CMD to get uppercase responses, GET-FILE.CMD with a different prompt to get filenames, and GET-NAME.CMD with yet a different prompt to get the user's name to include it in messages.

Converting to uppercase

When the information you receive via replaceable parameters must be tested, capitalization can become a problem. If the user is supposed to enter one of several flags, like Daily, then you have to test for daily, Daily, and DAILY just to catch the common capitalizations. This requires a lot of logic testing and can still miss unusual capitalization. An easier approach is just to force it to be all uppercase. CAPITAL.CMD does just that.

Call CAPITAL.CMD, pass it a word as a replaceable parameter, and it will convert that word to all uppercase and store it in the environment:

```
/* Name:    CAPITAL.CMD */
/* PURPOSE: Convert A Word To All Uppercase */
/* VERSION: 1.00 */
/* DATE:    May 30, 1993 */
/* Copyright (c) 1993 McGraw-Hill */

Word = ARG(1)
PARSE UPPER VAR Word OutWord Word
/* Delete This Line And The Next Two Lines */
/* If You Do Not Want The Word Echoed */
SAY OutWord
ENV = 'OS2ENVIRONMENT'
LastRC = VALUE('Return',OutWord,Env)
```

The `Word = ARG(1)` line reads in the command line passed to the program. The next line strips off all but the first word. The next two lines are comments. The next line prints the capitalized word to the screen, and the last two lines write it to the environment.

CAPITAL.CMD doesn't have a prompt since it runs without user intervention. As the comments in the program indicate, you can delete the two preceding comments and the `SAY OutWord` line if you don't want the uppercase word echoed to the screen.

The second operational line strips off all but the first word if more than one is passed to the utility. Since it stores the results in the environment, storing multiple words under a single environmental variable wouldn't normally be very useful. However, if you need this capability, just remove the last `Word` from this line so it becomes `PARSE UPPER VAR Word OutWord`, and it will convert everything it's passed to uppercase and store the entire string in the environment under an environmental variable name. Like GET.CMD, you can change the Return on the last line to another name if you want to alter the environmental variable name it uses.

Getting any character from the user

Many times, all you need is a single character from users, who are picking from a list or answering Y or N to a prompt. GET-ONE.CMD handles this problem when you want to accept any character. The next three utilities work similarly but take more restricted lists of characters. GET-ONE.CMD is as follows:

```
/* Name:    GET-ONE.CMD */
/* PURPOSE: REXX Program To Get A Single
            Character From User */
/* VERSION: 1.00 */
/* DATE:    May 30, 1993 */
/* Copyright (c) 1993 McGraw-Hill */

CALL RxFuncAdd 'SysGetKey', 'RexxUtil', 'SysGetKey'
SAY "Enter A Single Character"
Character = SysGetKey(echo)
```

```
ASCII = C2D(Character)
Exit ASCII
```

As the PURPOSE comment shows, REXX comments can span more than one line. Once REXX sees a /*, it treats everything it sees as comments until it encounters a */. As written, GET-ONE.CMD echoes the key that's pressed to the screen. To prevent that, replace the echo on the third operational line with noecho. Of course, you'll want to change the prompt on the second operational line.

The line starting with CALL loads an extended REXX function that's used to get a single keystroke from the user. The next line displays a prompt, and the line that follows the prompt actually reads the single character and stores it to the variable named Character. The next line converts it to an ASCII code and stores it to the variable named ASCII, and the last line exits and sets the errorlevel to the ASCII value of the character the user entered.

GET-ONE.CMD stores its results in the errorlevel. Some of the utilities that follow will show you how to test and modify that value. You might want to review them for ideas.

Getting a letter

Testing on all 256 possible ASCII values is a lot of testing for most of the questions you'll want to ask. GETA2Z.CMD reduces the testing by restricting the user to entering just a letter:

```
/* Name:     GETA2Z.CMD */
/* PURPOSE: This Is A REXX Program To Get A Single
            Character From The User */
/* Copyright (c) 1993 McGraw-Hill */
/* PURPOSE: Returning A As 1, B As 2, And So On */
/* VERSION: 1.00 */
/* DATE:     May 30, 1993 */

CALL RxFuncAdd 'SysGetKey', 'RexxUtil', 'SysGetKey'
TOP:
ASCII = 0
SAY "Enter A Single Character A-Z"
AnyCharacter = SysGetKey(echo)
PARSE UPPER VAR AnyCharacter Character
IF Character = "A" then ASCII = 1
IF Character = "B" then ASCII = 2

/* C-X Handled In A Similar Fashion */

IF Character = "Y" then ASCII = 25
IF Character = "Z" then ASCII = 26
SAY
IF ASCII = 0 then SAY "ERROR 1: Enter A-Z ^G"
IF ASCII = 0 THEN SIGNAL TOP
Exit ASCII
```

The AnyCharacter = SysGetKey(echo) line obtains a single character from the user just as it did before, only this time the AnyCharacter variable name is used instead of Character. Since logic testing will be performed on this variable, the PARSE

UPPER VAR AnyCharacter Character line converts the character to uppercase and stores it under the variable name Character.

After that, a series of 26 tests are performed on the Character variable to see if it's a letter. For example, IF Character = "A" then ASCII = 1 tests to see if the character is an A; if it is, it stores a number representing its position in the alphabet to the ASCII variable. After these tests are finished, the program checks the value of the ASCII variable. If it's still zero, then the user entered something other than a letter. The utility displays an error message and goes through the loop again with the SIGNAL command. You can alter this error message if you like. In addition to displaying the error message, the prompt has a ^G in it, so it beeps the speaker as part of the error message.

When the user enters a letter, the program exits and sets the errorlevel to the value of the ASCII variable. You might recall that the ASCII variable stores the letter's position in the alphabet. Like other utilities, you'll probably want to change the prompt at the top of the utility. Additionally, you might want to change the error message at the bottom of the utility. You can change it just like any other message.

If you like, you can reduce the number of letter choices available. To do that, just delete the entire IF Character line for those letters you don't want the program to accept. Or even better, just comment out those lines by starting them with a /* and ending them with a */. That way, you can easily add them back later if you need them. If you do delete letters, make sure to tell the users so they don't get frustrated trying to enter a letter the program won't accept.

Getting a number

If you want the user to pick from just a few single-character options, a number works better than a letter because there are only ten of them (0 through 9). GET-0-9.CMD is as follows:

```
/* Name:     GET-0-9.CMD */
/* PURPOSE: This Is A REXX Program To Get
   A Single Number From The User */
/* PURPOSE: Returning 0 As 0, 1 As 1, And So On */
/* VERSION: 1.00 */
/* DATE:     May 30, 1993 */
/* Copyright (c) 1993 McGraw-Hill */

CALL RxFuncAdd 'SysGetKey', 'RexxUtil', 'SysGetKey'
TOP:
ASCII = 999
SAY "Enter A Single Character 0-9"
Character = SysGetKey(echo)
IF Character = "0" then ASCII = 0
IF Character = "1" then ASCII = 1
IF Character = "2" then ASCII = 2
IF Character = "3" then ASCII = 3
IF Character = "4" then ASCII = 4
IF Character = "5" then ASCII = 5
IF Character = "6" then ASCII = 6
IF Character = "7" then ASCII = 7
IF Character = "8" then ASCII = 8
IF Character = "9" then ASCII = 9
```

```
SAY
IF ASCII = 999 then SAY "ERROR 1: Enter 0 - 9 ^G"
IF ASCII = 999 THEN SIGNAL TOP
Exit ASCII
```

GET-0-9.CMD works much like GETA2Z.CMD. Its differences involve the input section. Since numbers cannot be upper- or lowercase, it accepts the user's input directly into the Character variable and doesn't perform a conversion to it. Also, since a 0 entry would result in ASCII having a value of zero, ASCII is first set to 999 instead of 0, and the program knows it got a value response when ASCII is no longer 999. Otherwise, it works the same as GETA2Z.CMD.

Like GETA2Z.CMD, you can change the prompt and error message and reduce the number of choices available to the user. The process is identical to altering GETA2Z.CMD.

Yes or no

Sometimes, you just want to ask users "Do you really want to do this?" When all you need is a Y or N response, YESORNO.CMD is the best choice. It sets the errorlevel to zero for a Y and one for an N:

```
/* Name:     YESORNO.CMD */
/* PURPOSE: This Is A REXX Program To Get Yes
            Or No From The User */
/* PURPOSE: Returning Yes As 0, No As 1 */
/* VERSION: 1.00 */
/* DATE:     May 30, 1993 */
/* Copyright (c) 1993 McGraw-Hill */

CALL RxFuncAdd 'SysGetKey', 'RexxUtil', 'SysGetKey'
TOP:
ASCII = 999
SAY "Enter A Single Character Y)es or N)o"
Character = SysGetKey(echo)
IF Character = "Y" then ASCII = 0
IF Character = "y" then ASCII = 0
IF Character = "N" then ASCII = 1
IF Character = "n" then ASCII = 1
SAY
IF ASCII = 999 then SAY "ERROR 1: Enter Y)es or N)o ^G"
IF ASCII = 999 THEN SIGNAL TOP
Exit ASCII
```

YESORNO.CMD is a modified version of GET-0-9.CMD. Rather than converting the letter to uppercase as GETA2Z.CMD does, it just tests for the upper- and lowercase versions of both letters. Other than testing for two letters rather than ten digits, it's identical to GET-0-9.CMD. You might want to modify the prompt, error message, or errorlevel values it returns for a yes or no.

Did the user request help?

Like DOS, OS/2 has problems with the /? switch when users enter it after the name of the batch file, but without a space between them. Like the DOS NEEDHELP.EXE program, NEEDHELP.CMD tests the command line to see if users request help and sets the errorlevel accordingly. NEEDHELP.CMD is as follows:

```
/* Name:    NEEDHELP.CMD*/
/* PURPOSE: Checks To See If A User
            Requested Help And Sets Errorlevel */
/* VERSION: 1.00 */
/* DATE:    July 15, 1994 */
/* Copyright (c) 1993 McGraw-Hill */

Input = ARG(1)
IF Input = "" THEN EXIT 255

Kount = Length(Input)
DO I = 1 TO Kount
  ToTest = SubStr(Input,I,2)
 IF ToTest = "/?" THEN EXIT 1
END
EXIT 0
```

The Input = ARG(1) line reads the command line, and the next line sets the errorlevel and exits if the program isn't passed a command-line parameter. The next line stores the length of the command-line parameter to a variable, and the next line starts a loop through all the characters. The next line stores the next two characters to a variable. The next line checks to see if those two characters are /? and, if so, sets the errorlevel to 1 and exits. The End line closes the loop. The program reaches the EXIT 0 line only if the command-line parameter doesn't contain a /?, and it sets the errorlevel to zero and exits the program. To use NEEDHELP.CMD, call it from another batch file with the command:

```
:CALL NEEDHELP %0 %1
```

and then use an IF ERRORLEVEL test to jump to a special section if the user requested help. Typically, NEEDHELP.CMD doesn't need any modifications.

Batch File Utilities in VX-REXX

REXX is a command-line language. That means it doesn't normally have a graphical interface. While OS/2 includes some minor Presentation Manager tools for REXX, they're fairly limited. VX-REXX is an extension of Watcom International's REXX. It's a very powerful visual interface, and adds object-orientated programming to REXX. To learn more about VX-REXX, consult my *Writing OS/2 VX-REXX Programs* book, also from McGraw-Hill.

BATHELP.EXE and SCAN.ERX

BATHELP.EXE is a VX-REXX program that searches your current hard disk for all your OS/2 batch files and REXX programs (.CMD). For each program, it searches the file for a PURPOSE: comment line. It then displays the name of each file, the full path to each file, and the purpose line in a visual display that you can scroll around.

SCAN.ERX is a macro for the OS/2 Enhanced Editor. It scans the file you're currently editing and displays a dialog box listing every REXX label it finds. Double-click on the label name to jump to that point in the file. To run the macro, select Command Dialog from the menu and enter RX SCAN. If you're writing REXX batch file utilities, you'll find this macro useful.

BATHELP.EXE is located in the \UTILITY\OS2\BATHELP subdirectory of the included CD-ROM, and SCAN.ERX is in the \UTILITY\OS2\REXX\SCAN subdirectory. In order for both the VX-REXX program and macro to work, the included VROBJ.DLL file must either be in the current subdirectory or in a subdirectory in your path.

Other REXX utilities

I wrote all these REXX utilities. The utilities that follow were all written by Gary Murphy:

BACKCONF.CMD. Under OS/2, your CONFIG.SYS file does double duty, taking care of all the functions of both the CONFIG.SYS and AUTOEXEC.BAT files under DOS. BACKCONF.CMD will make a backup copy of this important file if the archive bit is turned on.

CHKCONF.CMD. This REXX program verifies the syntax of your CONFIG.SYS file.

MDCMD.CMD. This REXX program constructs a batch file for you. You supply it with the file specification, command to put before the filename, and command to put after the filename. It searches the current subdirectory and makes a list of each file that matches your file specification, appends the commands, and writes them to a batch file.

PATHLIST.CMD. The REXX program lists all the subdirectories in an environmental variable, like the path.

RXSUMRY.CMD. The REXX program summarizes the PURPOSE entries of all the REXX and batch files in the current subdirectory. It's similar to the BatHelp program discussed previously, only it works in the current subdirectory.

SPACE.CMD. This REXX program reports the space used by a subdirectory.

Each of these REXX programs are contained in a subdirectory branching off \UTILITY\OS2\REXX. The subdirectory will have the same name as the REXX program, only without the extension.

Summary

- One of the advantages of the REXX programming language is its ability to yield powerful programs while remaining user-modifiable.
- The SAY command is to REXX what the ECHO command is to a batch file.

- You can create a variable with REXX just by assigning a value to a variable name with an equal sign.

- The EXIT command immediately terminates a REXX program. Its most common use is to separate the body of a REXX program from subroutines.

- You mark lines and subroutines in REXX by placing a name followed by a colon on a line by itself.

- The SIGNAL command jumps to a named line.

- The PULL command gets information from users.

- REXX supports logic testing with IF THEN and IF THEN ELSE statements.

- DO WHILE and DO UNTIL loops repeat a series of statements until some condition is met.

- REXX subroutines must be stored as part of the main program.

- Subroutines are executed with the CALL command.

- GET.CMD is a REXX program that lets the batch file get names and filenames from the user.

- CAPITAL.CMD takes a single word and converts it to all uppercase for easy IF testing.

- GET-ONE.CMD gets a single character from the user and returns its ASCII value via the errorlevel.

- GETA2Z.CMD gets a single letter from the user and returns an errorlevel of 1 for A, 2 for B, and so on. It's not case-sensitive.

- GET-0-9.CMD gets a single number from the user and returns an errorlevel of 0 for zero, 1 for one, and so on.

- YESORNO.CMD gets a Y or N from the user and returns an errorlevel of 0 for yes and 1 for no.

- NEEDHELP.CMD tests to see if the user requested command-line help and sets the errorlevel accordingly. It must be called from a batch file and expects %0 and %1 as input parameters.

33

Modifying DOS with DOSKEY and Batch Files

If you've upgraded to MS-DOS 5 or later, then you have a copy of DOSKEY. DOSKEY is a memory-resident program that allows you to change the operation of any of the DOS commands. Novell DOS 7 and PC DOS 6.2 also come with a version of DOSKEY.

I'll begin by showing you just how powerful DOSKEY is. If you haven't loaded DOSKEY, change to your DOS subdirectory and enter DOSKEY at the command line. Then change to your batch subdirectory and create this simple batch file:

```
@ECHO OFF
FOR %%J IN (%1) DO ECHO %%J...To Be Deleted
BATCMD YN Do You Want To Delete These Files?
IF NOT ERRORLEVEL 1 GOTO END
DEL %1
:END
```

Give the batch file the name of KEYDEL.BAT. Since it uses Batcmd, you'll need to store the file in a subdirectory in the path.

Now create a temporary subdirectory and create some temporary files, called JUNK.1 through JUNK.9. While in that temporary subdirectory, enter the command DOSKEY DEL=KEYDEL $1 at the command line. Then enter the command DEL JUNK.?. As you can see, DOS will run your macro rather than using its internal DEL command.

If you look at KEYDEL.BAT, you'll see that it uses the DEL command to perform the actual deletion, but DOSKEY is supposed to replace the DEL command with KEY-DEL.BAT. That's the real advantage of DOSKEY. When you change a command with DOSKEY, it changes only for the command line, so your batch files continue to behave normally. When you enter the DEL command from the command line, DOSKEY maps it onto KEYDEL.BAT; when a batch file uses the DEL command, including KEY-DEL.BAT, it's not mapped, so it accesses the actual DOS internal command.

Before continuing, you need to know about one problem. There's a bug in some versions of DOSKEY that prevents the /P switch from working when you alias a command. Even if it's built into the batch file or passed to it as a parameter, the batch file will abort the first time the user answers Yes to the prompt, and the file won't be erased.

Later on in this chapter, you'll see how to get around that with a clever batch file.

DOSKEY Basics

Since you're this far in this book, it's a safe bet you're pretty familiar with batch files. A DOSKEY macro is very much like a batch file, but some of the symbols you use are different:

$1–$9. In a batch file, the replaceable parameters are represented by %0 through %9, where %0 is the name of the batch file and %1 through %9 are the first nine replaceable parameters entered on the command line after the name of the batch file. In a DOSKEY macro, the name of the macro isn't available and the replaceable parameters are represented by $1 through $9 rather than %1 through %9, but they work the same.

$*. This stands for the entire command line after the macro name, making it easy to pass long command lines through DOSKEY. This isn't supported by Novell DOS 7.

Piping. You can't include piping or redirection symbols in a DOSKEY command directly because DOS processes the pipe before it gets to DOSKEY. To overcome that, DOSKEY allows you to replace the pipes with symbols not processed by DOS. The greater-than pipe (>) becomes $G, the less-than pipe (<) becomes %L, and the vertical bar pipe (¦) becomes $B. However, some versions of DOSKEY still have problems with pipes, so sometimes a properly written macro containing pipes will execute, but the pipe won't work.

You make a DOSKEY assignment with a command like:

```
DOSKEY command=replacement parameters
```

where *command* is the item you type on the command line, *replacement* is what you want DOSKEY to replace it with, and *parameters* are any parameters you want DOSKEY to pass from the command line to the replacement command.

What You Can Do with DOSKEY

DOSKEY has three different functions: command shortening, command name changing, and function changing. Let's take a look at how each of these works.

Command shortening

This is actually the easiest way to use DOSKEY. You simply define the "shorthand" you plan to use on the command line. For example, if you were cleaning up your hard disk and planned to repeatedly enter a directory command, you might use the following DOSKEY command:

```
DOSKEY D=DIR $1 /P /OE
```

That way, if you entered D on the command line by itself, you'd get a directory of all the files in the current subdirectory. Entering D *.TXT would give you just the text files.

Command name changing

This allows you to change the names of internal commands or programs to something you're more likely to remember. For example, you might use the following to make a system more friendly:

```
DOSKEY KILL=DEL $* /P
DOSKEY GONE=DEL $* /P
DOSKEY DESTROY=DEL $* /P
```

This allows you to use commands that are easier to remember to perform common tasks. It also illustrates that the term *command name changing* is a little misleading. While it does allow you to access the command under a new name, or even several new names as shown here, the old name also works.

Function changing

You've already seen this one in action with KEYDEL.BAT. Here, you write a batch file (or even a .EXE or .COM program) to perform a task in place of a DOS internal command, and then use DOSKEY to map the DOS internal command onto the batch file.

This function changing is an excellent way to protect your system against running dangerous commands with Windows. You wouldn't want to run the ASSIGN, CHKDSK, JOIN, or SUBST commands under Windows. To avoid this, you can start Windows with the following batch file (only the operational code is shown):

```
@ECHO OFF
DOSKEY ASSIGN=ECHO ASSIGN Command Not Allowed Under Windows
DOSKEY CHKDSK=ECHO CHKDSK Command Not Allowed Under Windows
DOSKEY JOIN=ECHO JOIN Command Not Allowed Under Windows
DOSKEY SUBST=ECHO SUBST Command Not Allowed Under Windows

WIN %1 %2 %3 %4 %5 %6 %7 %8 %9

DOSKEY ASSIGN=
DOSKEY CHKDSK=
DOSKEY JOIN=
DOSKEY SUBST=
```

This batch file can be found on the CD-ROM that comes with this book, under the name WINSAFE.BAT.

What if you remapped a command using DOSKEY, but want to access the original command? Say you remapped the DEL command to execute a batch file. Just enter a space on the command line before the command. Spaces before commands don't affect DOS, but they fool DOSKEY's remapping, so the command works without being remapped.

Putting It Together

If you loaded DOSKEY as described previously, it loaded with a default storage area of 512 bytes. While this is large enough to demonstrate the power of DOSKEY, it's too small to be really useful. To increase the size of the DOSKEY storage space, load it with a command like this:

```
DOSKEY /BUFSIZE=2000
```

Thus 2,000 is the size (in bytes) that DOSKEY allocates for storage. This space is used both to store macros and old command lines. I use 2,000 on my system and I rarely run out of space.

If you've been following along with this chapter on your computer, then you've already loaded DOSKEY with the default buffer size. That's too small for what you'll be doing next. DOSKEY lacks an unload command, so you must reboot to remove it from memory. However, you can load a second copy and give that second copy a larger storage space. To do that, enter the following command:

```
DOSKEY /REINSTALL BUFSIZE=2000
```

To show you the power of DOSKEY, run KEYASSGN.BAT in Figure 33.1. This batch file creates a number of new commands and modifies the way several commands operate. Table 33.1 summarizes these new commands. Several of them run one of two batch files: KEYERASE.BAT in Figure 33.2 and MOVEIT.BAT in Figure 33.3. The commands that rely on KEYERASE.BAT just change the way existing commands work, while the commands that rely on MOVEIT.BAT create entirely new commands. Note how KEYERASE.BAT avoids the problem associated with using the /P switch in a DOSKEY macro.

Batch File Line	Explanation
@ECHO OFF	Turn command-echoing off.
REM NAME: KEYASSGN.BAT REM PURPOSE: Make DOSKEY Assignments REM VERSION: 1.00 REM DATE: December 25, 1991 REM Batch Assignment	Documentation remarks.
NEEDHELP %0 %1 IF ERRORLEVEL 1 GOTO HELP	Use the NeedHelp utility program to check and see if the user requested help.
REM Batch Files REM ==========	Documentation remarks.

Figure 33.1 KEYASSGN.BAT creates a number of useful DOSKEY commands.

Batch File Line	Explanation
ECHO Attaching Batch Files ECHO Please Wait	This batch file takes several seconds to run with nothing showing on the screen, so tell the user it's running.
DOSKEY DEL=KEYERASE $* DOSKEY ERASE=KEYERASE $*	Remap the DEL and ERASE commands to KEYERASE.BAT.
DOSKEY NUKE=KEYERASE $* DOSKEY GONE=KEYERASE $* DOSKEY KILL=KEYERASE $* DOSKEY ZAP=KEYERASE $*	Remap four new keywords to KEY-ERASE.BAT. Since they are remapped to the same batch file, these new commands will function identically to the DEL and ERASE commands.
DOSKEY MOVE=MOVEIT $* DOSKEY RELOCATE=MOVEIT $* DOSKEY NEWDIR=MOVEIT $*	Create three new commands by mapping them onto a batch file. If only one command accessed this batch file, it would have been easier just to give the batch file the name of the new command and include it in a subdirectory in the path. Since these three names access the same batch file, they will function identically.
REM Commands REM ========	Documentation remarks.
BATCMD SL ECHO Renaming Commands ECHO Please Wait	Skip a line and let the user know the batch file is still running.
DOSKEY CHECK=CHKDSK $*	Remap the CHECK command to run CHKDSK. You could write a batch file called CHECK.BAT to do the same, but this approach uses no disk space.
DOSKEY MACROS=DOSKEY /MACROS DOSKEY MACRO=DOSKEY /MACROS	Remap these two commands onto the DOSKEY command to show the macros that have been defined.
DOSKEY DIR=DIR $1 /P	Alter the way the DIR command operates by forcing it to include a /P switch.
DOSKEY FILES=DIR $1 /P	Add a new command that operates by running DIR.
DOSKEY FF1=ECHO ^L $G LPT1 DOSKEY FF2=ECHO ^L $G LPT2 DOSKEY FORMFEED1=ECHO ^L $G LPT1 DOSKEY FORMFEED2=ECHO ^L $G LPT2	Create several formfeed commands that pipe a ^L (formfeed) character to the printer.
DOSKEY HIDE=ATTRIB +H $1	Replace the hard-to-understand ATTRIB +H command with an easy-to-understand replacement.
DOSKEY UNHIDE=ATTRIB -H $1 DOSKEY READONLY=ATTRIB +R $1 DOSKEY RO=ATTRIB +R $1 DOSKEY UNREADONLY=ATTRIB -R $1 DOSKEY UNRO=ATTRIB -R $1	Replace several other ATTRIB commands with easy-to-understand and easy-to-remember replacements.
DOSKEY LINES25=MODE CON: LINES=25 DOSKEY LINES43=MODE CON: LINES=43 DOSKEY LINES50=MODE CON: LINES=50	Add commands to change the display type. These commands require that you load ANSI.SYS in your CONFIG.SYS file.
DOSKEY LIST=FOR %%J IN ($1) DO TYPE %%J $b MORE	Create a command to display text files using DOS commands.
DOSKEY FILEFIND=ATTRIB \$1 /S	Create a command to locate files anywhere on the current drive using DOS commands.

Batch File Line	Explanation
BATCMD SL ECHO Finished GOTO END	Tell the user the batch file is finished and exit the batch file.

:HELP
   ECHO This Batch File Uses DOS 5.0's
   ECHO DOSKEY To Make A Number Of
   ECHO Useful Command Changes
	First part of section that displays help when the user starts the batch file with a /? or a ? as the first replaceable parameter.

IF NOT EXIST KEYASSGN.BAT GOTO END
   ECHO Press Any Key To See The
   ECHO Assignments
   PAUSE
   TYPE KEYASSGN.BAT | FIND "DOSKEY "| FIND "="
| FIND "TYPE KEYASSGN.BAT"/V | MORE
GOTO END
	This section types the file to display the commands, as long as the file is in the current subdirectory.

:END	Label marking the end of the batch file.

Figure 33.1 Continued.

TABLE 33.1 DOSKEY Macro Summary

New or modified command	Function
DEL	Runs KEYERASE.BAT instead of functioning as an internal command.
ERASE	Runs KEYERASE.BAT instead of functioning as an internal command.
GONE	A new command to erase files.
KILL	A new command to erase files.
MOVE	Moves files to a new location by copying them to the new location and then deleting them from the original location. It has extensive error-checking.
NUKE	A new command to erase files.
ZAP	A new command to erase files.
RELOCATE	Moves files to a new location by copying them to the new location and then deleting them from the original location. It has extensive error-checking.
NEWDIR	Moves files to a new location by copying them to the new location and then deleting them from the original location. It has extensive error-checking.
CHECK	Runs CHKDSK.
MACROS	Displays the currently assigned DOSKEY macros.
MACRO	Displays the currently assigned DOSKEY macros.
DIR	Automatically includes the /P switch.
FILES	Displays a list of files.
FF1	Sends a formfeed to LPT1.
FF2	Sends a formfeed to LPT2.
FORMFEED1	Sends a formfeed to LPT1.
FORMFEED2	Sends a formfeed to LPT2.
HIDE	Changes a file's attribute to hidden.
UNHIDE	Turns off a file's hidden attribute.

TABLE 33.1 Continued

New or modified command	Function
READONLY	Turns on a file's read-only attribute.
RO	Turns on a file's read-only attribute.
UNREADONLY	Turns off a file's read-only attribute.
UNRO	Turns off a file's read-only attribute.
LINES25	Sets the text mode of the screen to display 25 lines. Requires loading ANSI.SYS in the CONFIG.SYS file.
LINES43	Sets the text mode of the screen to display 43 lines. Requires loading ANSI.SYS in the CONFIG.SYS file. Also requires an EGA screen.
LINES50	Sets the text mode of the screen to display 50 lines. Requires loading ANSI.SYS in the CONFIG.SYS file. Also requires a VGA screen.
LIST	Types files to the screen and pipes the output through the MORE filter.
FILEFIND	Locate files on the current drive only.

Batch File Line	Explanation
`@ECHO OFF`	Turn command-echoing off.

`REM NAME:     KEYERASE.BAT`
`REM PURPOSE: DOSKEY Erase Replacement`
`REM VERSION: 1.00`
`REM DATE:    December 25, 1991`
	Documentation remarks.

`NEEDHELP %0 %1` `IF ERRORLEVEL 1 GOTO HELP`	Use the NeedHelp utility program to check and see if the user requested help.
`IF (%1)==(XYZ123ABC) GOTO PROMPT`	When the batch file calls itself as a subroutine, jump to a section to handle that.
`IF (%1)==() GOTO NOTHING`	If the user fails to enter the name of any files to delete, jump to an error-handling section.
`:TOP`	Label marking the top of the main portion of the batch file.
`FOR %%J IN (%1) DO ECHO %%J....To Be Erased!`	List the files to be deleted.
`BATCMD YN Do You Want To Erase These Files?`	Ask the user about deleting these files.
`IF NOT ERRORLEVEL 1 GOTO END`	If the user says no, exit the batch file.
`BATCMD YN Do You Wish To Be Ask` `Individually?`	Ask the user about prompting for each file individually.
`IF NOT ERRORLEVEL 1 DEL %1` `IF NOT ERRORLEVEL 1 GOTO NEXT`	If the user does not want individual prompting, delete the files and jump to a section called NEXT.
`:TOPLOOP`	Label marking the top of a section to individually delete the files. The user reaches this point only by answering yes to the above prompt asking about individual deletion.
`FOR %%J IN (%1) DO CALL KEYERASE XYZ123ABC %%J`	Loop through all the files to be deleted. For each file, call this batch file as a subroutine, pass it a subroutine flag, and the name of the batch file to delete.

Figure 33.2 KEYERASE.BAT replaces the DEL and ERASE commands once you have run KEYASSGN.BAT.

Batch File Line	Explanation
GOTO NEXT	Go to the NEXT section to continue looping.

:NEXT
   SHIFT
   IF NOT (%1)==() GOTO TOP
GOTO END
	Section to check to see if the user specified another set of files to delete. If so, jump back to the processing section of the batch file.

:NOTHING ECHO Did Not Specify Files To Erase! ECHO The Format For The Command Is: BATCMD SL ECHO ERASE *.BAK ECHO DEL *.TXT BATCMD SL ECHO Where You Replace *.BAK or *.TXT ECHO With The File You Wish To Erase GOTO END	Section to handle the problem when the user fails to specify any files to erase.

:PROMPT
   BATCMD YN Delete %2?
   IF ERRORLEVEL 1 DEL %2
GOTO END
	Subroutine section that handles asking about deleting a single file. Note the use of %2, because %1 is the subroutine flag.

:HELP ECHO This Batch File Is An Intelligent ECHO Replacement For The DEL And ERASE ECHO Commands Designed To Be Mapped To ECHO Those Commands Using DOSKEY ECHO OK To Run From Command Line GOTO END	Section that displays help when the user starts the batch file with a /? or a ? as the first replaceable parameter.
:END	Label marking the end of the batch file.

Figure 33.2 Continued.

Batch File Line	Explanation
@ECHO OFF	Turn command-echoing off.
REM NAME: MOVEIT.BAT REM PURPOSE: DOSKEY Move Command REM VERSION: 1.00 REM DATE: January 12, 1992	Documentation remarks.
NEEDHELP %0 %1 IF ERRORLEVEL 1 GOTO HELP	Use the NeedHelp utility program to check and see if the user requested help.
IF (%1)==() GOTO NOSOURCE	If the user did not enter the name of a file to move, jump to an error-handling routine.
IF (%2)==() GOTO NOTARGET	If the user did not enter the name of a subdirectory to move the files to, jump to an error-handling routine.
IF NOT EXIST %1 GOTO NOFILES	If the files the user wants to move do not exist, jump to an error-handling routine.
IF NOT EXIST %2\NUL GOTO DIRGONE	If the target subdirectory does not exist, jump to an error-handling routine.

Figure 33.3 MOVEIT.BAT adds several new commands to DOS, including a MOVE command.

Batch File Line	Explanation
`IF EXIST %2\%1 GOTO ALREADY`	If the files already exist in the target sub-directory, jump to an error-handling routine.
`XCOPY %1 %2\*.*`	Copy the files.
`IF ERRORLEVEL 1 GOTO OOPS`	If there is a copy error, jump to an error-handling routine.
`DEL %1`	Delete the original files.
`GOTO END`	Exit the batch file.

`:OOPS`
`BATCMD BE 5`
`ECHO A Copy Error Has Occurred`
`ECHO Source Files *NOT* Erased`
`GOTO END`
	When XCOPY reports an error, display an error message and exit the batch file.

`:ALREADY`
`ECHO Files Named %2\%1 Already Exist`
`ECHO This Routine Will *NOT*`
`ECHO Overwrite Files`
`ECHO You Must Delete The %2\%1 Files`
`ECHO In Order To Use This Routine`
`GOTO END`
	When the files already exist in the target subdirectory, display an error message and exit the batch file.

`:DIRGONE`
`ECHO You Specified Moving The %1`
`ECHO Files Into The %2 Subdirectory`
`ECHO However The %2 Subdirectory`
`ECHO Does Not Exist`
`ECHO (Must Be Entered As C:\BAT`
`ECHO *NOT* C:\BAT\)`
`BATCMD SL`
`GOTO SYNTAX`
	When the specified target subdirectory does not exist, display an error message and jump to a routine to display the proper syntax before exiting the batch file.

`:NOFILES`
`ECHO You Specified Moving The`
`ECHO %1 Files But None Of`
`ECHO These Files Exist`
`GOTO SYNTAX`
	When the source files do not exist, display an error message and jump to a routine to display the proper syntax before exiting the batch file.

`:NOSOURCE`
`ECHO Source Files Not Specified`
`GOTO SYNTAX`
	When the user does not specify the source files to move, display an error message and jump to a routine to display the proper syntax before exiting the batch file.

`:SYNTAX`
`ECHO Enter MOVEIT {Source} {Target}`
`ECHO Where {Source} Are The Files`
`ECHO To Move And {Target} Is The`
`ECHO Location To Move Them To`
`BATCMD SL`
`ECHO DOSKEY Users May Enter The`
`ECHO Command As MOVE {Source} {Target}`
`ECHO Although The MOVEIT Command`
`ECHO Will Also Work`
`GOTO END`
	This section displays the proper syntax for the command and then exits the batch file. It is called by several other error sections.

Batch File Line	Explanation
:NOTARGET ECHO Target Subdirectory Not Specified GOTO SYNTAX	When the user specifies a target subdirectory that does not exist, display an error message and jump to a routine to display the proper syntax before exiting the batch file.
:HELP ECHO MOVEIT.BAT Moves Files From One ECHO Location To Another With ECHO Extensive Error Checking BATCMD SL ECHO Designed To Work With DOSKEY ECHO However It Can Also Be Run ECHO As A Stand-Alone Batch File GOTO END	Section that displays help when the user starts the batch file with a /? or a ? as the first replaceable parameter.
:END	Label marking the end of the batch file.

Figure 33.3 Continued.

Command-Line Recall

(The Novell DOS 7 version of DOSKEY doesn't support command-line recall, so Novell DOS 7 users can ignore the discussion that follows.)

The MS-DOS and PC DOS versions of DOSKEY also store your command lines so you can reuse them. Just press the up arrow to scroll back through your commands one at a time. When you get to one you want to reuse, just press Return to run it.

If you remember the beginning of the command, just type in the first few letters and press F8. That will take you back to the last command that started with the letters you entered. If it's not the command you want, press F8 again to go to the command before that starting with the letters you entered.

If you want to review all the commands you've entered, just press F7. It will list all your commands with line numbers to the left. If there's more than will fit on one screen, it will show them one screen at a time and wait for you to press a key before showing the next screen. You can use the numbers to select a command by pressing F9 and entering the number. That brings the command to the command line so you can make sure you want to run it. If you do, just press Return.

Purging Command Lines and Macros

It's easy to purge the command-line storage and macros from DOSKEY. Pressing Alt–F7 will purge all the command lines and pressing Alt–F10 will purge the macros. You can purge a single DOSKEY macro with the command:

```
DOSKEY macro=
```

where *macro* is the name of the macro to purge and nothing follows the equal sign.

Summary

- DOSKEY allows you to have DOS automatically translate commands entered on the command line into different commands before running them.

- You can also map commands onto batch files and pass the contents of the command line to that batch file.

- Using DOSKEY to map a command onto a batch file can cause that command to behave far differently than its normal DOS operation.

- DOSKEY allows you to easily recall old command lines. This isn't supported by the Novell DOS version of DOSKEY.

- You can easily purge DOSKEY macros and command lines from memory.

- Once you see how powerful DOSKEY is, I'm sure it'll be one of the programs you load in your AUTOEXEC.BAT file.

34

Getting Input from Users in DOS

Communication with a batch file is mostly in one direction; the batch file "talks" to the user via ECHO statements. Prior to MS-DOS 6, the only way you could communicate with a batch file was by using replaceable parameters when starting the batch file. Once the batch file was running, you had no control over it other than by using Ctrl–Break.

MS-DOS 6 added a utility to DOS called CHOOSE. Basically, CHOOSE allows you to ask the user a question requiring a single-character response and store that response in the errorlevel. The batch file can then test that response with one or more IF ERRORLEVEL statements and branch accordingly. While CHOOSE was new to MS-DOS, however, many utilities had already been written to provide this same service to batch files.

All the utilities in this chapter allow a batch file to ask the user a question. Most accept a single keystroke and place a value to represent that keystroke in the errorlevel for testing. For that reason, I call these programs "errorlevel askers."

A few utilities manage to be more than just errorlevel askers. Generally, they accept a multiple-character response and store it under an environmental variable. While an errorlevel asker is adequate for most applications, these advanced programs allow you to develop more complex applications.

Unluckily, DOS is very inhospitable to programs that query users. A program gets a copy of the environment to work with, but when the program terminates, its copy of the environment is erased. As a result, these types of programs can't easily use the environment to transfer information back to the calling batch file. To combat this, a querying program could search through memory for the original copy of the environment and modify it.

Please note that many of the utility sets in Chapter 38 perform all of the functions of the programs in this chapter. Before deciding to use one of these programs, you might want to review Chapter 38 to see if one of those utility sets would be a better choice for you.

Answer

Version. 1.0

Price. Free

Category. Public domain

Author. Frank Schweiger

CD-ROM directory. \UTILITY\DOS\ANSWER
To use Answer, enter a command like:

```
ANSWER prompt
```

Answer displays the prompt and then has the user enter information directly after it. For better appearance, include a couple of trailing spaces in the prompt.

Answer stores users' responses in the master environment under the environmental variable ANSWER. Even though Answer was written in early 1986, it still works perfectly under MS-DOS 6.2. If you want to ask users more than one question, you should ensure that the contents of ANSWER are transferred to another variable after each question.

AskIt

Version. 2.2

Price. Free

Category. Copyrighted

Author. David MacLean; his address is as follows:
408 Cape Mudge Road
Quathiaski BC V0P 1N0
Canada

CD-ROM directory. \UTILITY\DOS\ASKIT
AskIt is a user-configurable errorlevel asker. Its syntax is:

```
ASKIT "prompt" keystroke code
```

where *keystroke* is an acceptable keystroke and *code* is the errorlevel value to return for that code. AskIt accepts ENTER for the Return key, ESCAPE for Escape, and F1 through F12 for the function keys. So the command line:

```
ASKIT "Make A Selection" a 1 A 1 b 2 B 2 c 3 C 3 ESCAPE 99
```

would return a 1 if users press A, 1 if they press B, 3 if they press C, and 99 if they press the Escape key. Notice that both upper- and lowercase letters must be specified. Keystrokes not listed on the command line are ignored by AskIt.

BatKit

Version. 5.5

Price. $15

Category. Shareware

Author. Ken Hipple, at the following address:
311 Summer Oak Trail
Madison, MS 39110

CD-ROM directory. \UTILITY\DOS\BATKIT55

BatKit is a very advanced utility for getting information from the user. Naturally, it can display a prompt. This prompt can be plain and come from the command line, or it can be highly formatted and come from a disk file. BatKit even has a utility to capture an ASCII screen and turn it into a screen that can be quickly displayed by BatKit.

BatKit can accept single-character responses and set the errorlevel accordingly, which is its default mode of operation. It can also accept multiple-character responses and store the response in the environment. If BatKit is run under Windows or a secondary command processor, it has switches to control which environment gets modified. BatKit provides for extensive input validation so a batch file can make sure only acceptable responses are entered. There are also switches to control how long BatKit will wait for a response.

Of all the programs designed to get a response from the user and report that response back to the batch file, BatKit is the most powerful one available.

Capital

Version. 1.0

Price. Free

Category. Written for this book

Author. Ronny Richardson

CD-ROM directory. \UTILITY\DOS\CAPITAL

CAPITAL.EXE doesn't query the user. Rather, it's used to process information provided by the user. You pass it a single word and it converts that word to uppercase and stores the results in the environment under the environmental variable RONNY. Additionally, it has built-in documentation, offers command-line help if you start it with a /? or ?, and performs extensive error checking to make sure it was passed exactly one word to convert to uppercase.

I wrote Capital in Builder Lite, a subset of the Builder language. The source code is included on the CD-ROM in case you want to modify its operation. The CD-ROM also includes a fully functional copy of Builder Lite in the \BLDLITE subdirectory. This means you can experiment with these programs and recompile them. To get the full documentation for Builder Lite, you can buy my *Builder Lite: Developing Dynamic Batch Files*. This book has a coupon in the back for that purpose.

The major use for Capital is converting replaceable parameters to uppercase before performing logic testing on them. This is the major reason for limiting it to handling one word at a time; by their nature, replaceable parameters are always one word. To test to see if the first replaceable parameter is Daily, for example, you'd use the following code in your batch file:

```
CAPITAL %1
IF %RONNY%==DAILY GOTO Daily
```

Hold

Price. $10

Category. Shareware

Author. The Unique Solutions Center, at:
496 Parklane Rd.
Oakville Ontario L6G 4J8
Canada

CD-ROM directory. \UTILITY\DOS\HOLD

You start Hold with a command like Hold 8, and it will pause the batch file for the specified number of seconds. You can abort the pause by pressing any key. The pressed keystroke is not returned to the batch file.

GetKey

Version. 1.23A

Price. Free

Category. Copyrighted

Author. Pinnacle Software, at the following address:
P.O. Box 714, Airport Rd.
Swanton, VT 05488

CD-ROM directory. \UTILITY\DOS\SEE

GetKey is an errorlevel asker that's included with the See package. The syntax is:

```
GETKEY prompt characters
```

where *characters* are the acceptable keystrokes. The first character returns an errorlevel of 1, the second 2, and so on. If one of the characters is preceded by an at sign (@), then that character is used as the default if the user presses Return or the spacebar. Only characters listed on the command line are accepted by GetKey and capitalization is ignored, making GetKey very easy to use.

Getkey

Version. 2.0

Price. $10

Category. Shareware

Author. Matthew G. Moody, at:
206 Waterwood Dr.
Goose Creek, SC 29445-4838

CD-ROM directory. \UTILITY\DOS\GETKEY20

Getkey is an advanced errorlevel asker that can take the options from either the command line or an ASCII file. It can display a prompt and accept characters like the MS-DOS's CHOOSE. It can also display a menu and return the errorlevel of the selected item. It can be either case-sensitive or case-insensitive, and it has a timer that can default to an assigned value. It also has on-line, pop-up help either that you can request from the command line or that pops up if you enter an invalid parameter. The package comes with a number of sample batch files.

GetSet

Version. 1.2

Price. $10

Category. Shareware

Author. Bob Lafleur, at the following address:
45 Ionia Street
Springfield, MA 01109

CD-ROM directory. \UTILITY\DOS\GETSET12

To use GetSet, first create an environmental variable containing the default text. For example, in prompting the user for a filename, you might create the environmental variable:

```
SET name=*.*
```

and then give the user the option of modifying this with GetSet. The user-edited contents can be longer or shorter than the original. You can even place special symbols into the environmental variable that GetSet will replace with system information before passing on to the user to edit. This allows you to preload the name of the current drive and subdirectory into the environmental variable that's used to get a filename from the user. You can also use GetSet to place information about the date and time, such as the day of the week, into the environment.

GetSet doesn't alter the environment itself. Rather, it writes out a batch file to make the change. Your batch file can then call this batch file to make the changes and then delete it. This is a safe approach that will work under any version of DOS as well as under Windows, all without any trouble.

IsItWin

Version. 1.00

Price. Free

Category. Written for this book

Author. Ronny Richardson

CD-ROM directory. \UTILITY\DOS\ISITWIN

Occasionally, it would be nice for your batch files to know if they're running under Windows. For example, while the CHKDSK command is safe under Windows, the CHKDSK/f command can destroy your hard disk. Without knowing if Windows is running, your only choice is to not allow CHKDSK/f in your batch files.

Windows always creates an environmental variable called windir when it's running, and this variable points to the subdirectory where Windows is located. However, Windows is very tricky about this variable. DOS leaves the contents of your environmental variable alone, but it always converts environmental variable names to all uppercase. However, Windows bypasses DOS and creates the windir environmental variable name in lowercase. This keeps you from being able to alter the windir environmental variable yourself, either in a batch file or from the command line. As a result, the normal batch IF tests to see if the windir environmental variable that exists won't work.

To get around this problem, I wrote a small program in Builder Lite called ISITWIN.EXE; it's included on the CD-ROM that comes with this book. IsItWin sets the errorlevel to 1 if it's running while you're shelled out of Windows, and it sets the errorlevel to 0 if it's run from the command line without Windows loaded in memory. That way, you can build Windows-checking into those batch files that need it. IsItWin works by testing on windir, bypassing DOS so it can test on a lowercase environmental variable.

NeedHelp

Version. 1.00

Price. Free

Category. Written for this book

Author. Ronny Richardson

CD-ROM directory. \UTILITY\DOS\NEEDHELP

There are basically two ways a user can run a batch file and request help: BATCH/? and BATCH /?. If you're running DR DOS 5 or 6 exclusively, then you won't have a problem because they automatically split the batch file name from the switch, so %0 is BATCH and %1 is /?, no matter which way the user enters the information. However, MS-DOS doesn't do this. If you run BATCH/? under any version of MS-DOS, then %0 is BATCH/? and %1 is empty.

So running a batch file called BATCH.BAT under MS-DOS and checking for a /? switch requires testing for the most likely capitalizations:

```
IF (%1)==(/?) GOTO HELP
IF %0==BATCH/? GOTO HELP
IF %0==batch/? GOTO HELP
IF %0==Batch/? GOTO HELP
```

And even this won't catch unusual capitalizations. Note that I didn't use parentheses around %0. I omitted them because %0 always has a value.

To avoid this problem, I wrote the program NEEDHELP.EXE. To use NeedHelp, just pass it your %0 and %1 variables with a space between them. It checks to see if the %1 variable or the last two characters of %0 are /?. If so, it sets the errorlevel to 1; otherwise, it sets it to 0. In other words, an errorlevel of 1 indicates the user requested help while an errorlevel of 0 indicates the user didn't request help.

If you don't pass NeedHelp a parameter, it sets the errorlevel to 255. It does this because %0 always exists, so not receiving a parameter means you made an error. It doesn't object to only one parameter because %1 might not have a value.

To use NeedHelp, place these following lines near the top of your batch file:

```
NEEDHELP %0 %1
IF ERRORLEVEL 1 GOTO HELP
```

Now your batch files will work the same under MS-DOS as they do under DR DOS, without you having to worry about how the specific operating system handles command-line switches. You also no longer have to worry about capitalization. I wrote NeedHelp in Builder Lite, and the source code is included on the CD-ROM that comes with this book.

Opal Batch Organizer and Extender

Version. 1.2

Price. $15

Category. Shareware

Author. Opal Computing, at the following address:
244-53 90th Ave.
Bellerose, NY 11426

CD-ROM directory. \UTILITY\DOS\OBOE12

Opal Batch Organizer and Extender has three functions. You can use it to get information from the user, beep the speaker (it can control the frequency and duration), and position the cursor at any location on the screen.

When using it to get information from the user, you specify the prompt, keys that are considered valid, default keystroke if the program times out, and the number of seconds to wait if the user doesn't enter a keystroke. Keystrokes are case-insensitive and the first valid keystroke is returned as an errorlevel of 1, the second as an errorlevel of 2, and so on.

Y_or_N

Version. 1.5

Price. Free

Category. Copyrighted

Author. Joseph R. Ellis, at:
228 Field Circle, SE
Hickory, NC 28602-5414

CD-ROM directory. \UTILITY\DOS\Y-OR-N

Y_or_N asks the user a question and waits for a response. It sets the errorlevel to 1 for a Y, 2 for an N, and 3 for a time-out or the user pressing Return. Y_or_N is case-insensitive and will accept only a Y, N, or Return. It has very nice prompting, timing, and sound facilities, and comes with a demonstration program to display all its features. If you need to ask users yes/no questions, Y_or_N is as nice a program as you'll find.

Chapter

35

Communicating with Users in DOS

DOS offers only the very bland TYPE and ECHO commands for batch files to communicate with users. These are, as my daughter would say, "booooooring." If you use ANSI.SYS (and very few of you do), then you can change the color of the text and background, but only through complex escape sequences that are difficult to understand and use. You can't even use ANSI.SYS when writing batch files for others because you never know if they use it.

The utilities in this chapter all improve on batch file communications. They range from a very simple program that skips a line to programs that let you control almost every aspect of the screen. Among them, you'll find many different ways to avoid using boring screens.

Many of the utility sets in Chapter 38 perform all the functions of programs in this chapter. You might want to review this chapter to see if one of those utility sets would be a better choice for you.

AnsiHere

Version. 1.0

Price Free

Category *PC Magazine*; this program is *not* included on the CD-ROM. All *PC Magazine* programs are available from their area on CompuServe. See any issue of the magazine for details.

If ANSI.SYS is loaded, you can design nice colorful screens by echoing the proper escape sequences, but if you echo those same escape sequences without ANSI.SYS loaded the screen becomes a real mess. Your batch file needs a way to determine if ANSI.SYS is loaded so it can use a colorful screen if it is and a plain one if it's not.

While DOS offers no method to test for ANSI.SYS, AnsiHere does. Running Ansi-Here without any parameters displays a message on the screen indicating whether or not ANSI.SYS is loaded. Even better for your batch file, AnisHere will set the error-level to 0 if ANSI.SYS is missing and to 1 if it's present. That way, your batch file can jump to different screen-handling sections depending on the status of ANSI.SYS.

ASCII.EXE

Version. 1.0

Price. Free

Category. Written for this book

Author. Ronny Richardson

CD-ROM directory. \UTILITY\DOS\ASCII

If you're trying to draw a box on the screen using high-order ASCII characters or are trying to use high-order ASCII characters for other purposes and you forget the code you need, just run ASCII.EXE and it will display all the printable codes for you in one neat screen. I often program in Windows or OS/2, and I run ASCII.EXE in one session while programming in another session so I can easily refer back to it. ASCII.EXE is a DOS program, but it runs fine in a DOS session under OS/2.

BatScreen

Version. 1.0

Price. Free

Category. Written for this book

Author. Doug Amaral

CD-ROM directory. \UTILITY\DOS\BATSCREN

BatScreen takes an ASCII text file and converts it to a small .COM file. When you enter the name of the .COM file at the command-line prompt or in a batch file, the file will flash up on the screen almost instantly.

To run BatScreen to compile a screen, first create the screen with any ASCII editor. Arrange the text in the file the way you want it to appear on the screen. Feel free to use high-order ASCII characters. Once the screen is ready, change to the subdirectory containing the ASCII file and enter BS at the command-line prompt. BatScreen will present a screen showing all the nonblinking color choices, with a box around the currently selected color combination. Use the cursor to select the color combination you want. If you want the text to blink, press PgDn and select from a screen of blinking color choices.

Next, BatScreen prompts you for the name of the ASCII file. To completely fill the screen, the ASCII file should contain 80 columns and 24 rows. If the file is larger, BatScreen will ignore the extra information. Finally, BatScreen asks you if you want to clear the screen when the program displays. Answer Yes and the .COM file will clear the entire screen, set it to the colors you selected, and display the contents of the ASCII file. Answer No and the .COM file will clear off only enough lines to display the message. Blinking text and not clearing the screen is perfect for error messages and other occasions when you want to grab the user's attention. A solid-color full screen is great for menus and general-purpose text.

The original ASCII file isn't modified and doesn't need to be present for the .COM file to operate, so you can modify and recompile it if you ever need to change the screen. Additionally, once you've created the .COM file, you don't need BatScreen to display the screen.

Cleave

Version. 1.57

Price. $6

Category. Shareware

Author. Samuel Kaplin, at the following address:
3520 W. 32nd Street #214
Minneapolis, MN 55416

CD-ROM directory. \UTILITY\DOS\CLEAV157

Cleave is a unique replacement for the CLS command. It divides the screen into four vertical strips and then clears the screen by "sliding" the sections off the screen in alternating directions.

EQO

Version. 1.0a

Price. An unspecified donation is requested.

Category. Shareware

Author. Jeremy Sawicki, at:
523 Kapity Dr.
Mogadore, OH 44260-9534

CD-ROM directory. \UTILITY\DOS\EQO10A

The ECHO command is fairly limited in what it can do. Basically, it can display text, a blank line, and the status of command echoing. EQO is an advanced replacement for the ECHO command that does much more. It has special symbols to display pipes and redirection symbols and an easy way to display control characters, high-order ASCII characters, and an Escape for use in sending ANSI control characters. In addition, it has special characters to display commonly used information such as the time, date, path, current drive, and DOS version. You can enter multiple lines of text on one line, and spread a single line of text over several EQO commands.

EQO is one of the best replacements for the ECHO command I've seen. The program subdirectory includes a sample batch file I wrote called EQO-DEMO.BAT that illustrates many of the abilities of EQO.

GetColor

Version. 2.2

Price. Free

Category. Copyrighted

Author. Richard B. Simpson, at:
14933 McKnew Rd.
Burtonsville, MD 20866-1340

CD-ROM directory. \UTILITY\DOS\GETCOLOR
If your batch file is going to use ANSI to change screen colors, you need to know two things: whether ANSI is loaded and how to reset the screen colors when the batch file is finished. GetColor does both. When you run GetColor, it sets the error-level to indicate if ANSI is loaded. It also writes a small batch file to the C:\ subdirectory that issues the ANSI commands to reset the screen colors to their current values. When the batch file is finished, it calls this secondary batch file to return the screen colors to their original value.

Press Any Key

Version. 3.0

Price. Free

Category. Copyrighted

Author. David Smith, at the following:
1104 Mason Dr.
Hurst, TX 76053

CD-ROM directory. \UTILITY\DOS\PRESKEY3
Press Any Key gives you 30 different replacements for the DOS PAUSE command, all from one program, using a command-line parameter. These replacement com-

mands clear or cover the screen, so you don't want to use them if the user is expected to read anything on the screen.

Text Font

Version. 2.4

Price. $19

Category. Shareware

Author. Rob W. Smetana, at:
Pro-Formance
132 Alpine Terrace
San Francisco, CA 94117

CD-ROM directory. \UTILITY\DOS\TEXTFT24
Text Font is a database of 12 different and unusual screen fonts you can use in text to make your batch file screens stand out from the ordinary. To select a different font, enter TF #, where # is a number from 1 to 12. The entire screen is converted to that font, even the text that has already been displayed, so only one font can be displayed at once. The command TF 0 returns the screen to normal. The fonts have no effect in graphics mode, and running a graphics program will reset the screen display when the program quits.

The fonts are different enough from DOS that they'll really make your screens stand out. Registered users receive a much larger database of fonts (about 50) to use in their programs. They also receive a small memory-resident program to restore the selected screen font when a program running in graphics mode resets the screen.

TurboTXT

Version. 3.23

Price. Free with TurboBAT

Category. Shareware

Author. Foley Hi-Tech Systems, at:
185 Berry St., Suite 4807
San Francisco, CA 94107
(415) 882-1730

CD-ROM directory. \TURBOBAT
If you want to compile a single screen for use in a batch file or as a menu, BatScreen is your best approach. However, if you have a larger ASCII file that you want users to be able to browse without owning any other utility, TurboTXT is an ex-

cellent tool. TurboTXT takes your ASCII file and turns it into a compiled .EXE file with full support for paging through the file, searching for specific text, and printing the text. If you use a screen size other than 80×24, the compiled program will detect this and adjust itself automatically.

If you're looking for a convenient way to distribute short manuals or other types of information for the reader to view, TurboTXT gives you an excellent way to do that without depending on the user having a file viewing program like LIST.COM. The VIEWCONT.EXE program in the \TURBOBAT subdirectory of the CD-ROM is a compiled version of COUNT.TB. You can run this program to see all the features of a compiled TurboTXT file.

VGA Clear Screen

Version. 2.1

Price. $20

Category. Shareware

Author. David Smith, at the following address:
1104 Mason Dr.
Hurst, TX 76053

CD-ROM directory. \UTILITY\DOS\VLS

VGA Clear Screen clears the screen in 31 interesting patterns, and each pattern is selected by a command-line switch. Its registration price might seem high, but you can register all the utilities for only $5 more, and the complete collection is well worth it.

DOS Menu Programs

I discussed menus back in Chapter 26, but managing all the batch files necessary to work with even a moderate number of programs can be a daunting task for an inexperienced user. That's where these batch file-based menu programs come in. I've chosen not to cover menu programs in depth since OS/2 and Windows supersede menu programs by letting you select programs to run in a graphical environment. I'll discuss a few of the more interesting menu programs in this chapter for those of you who need a menu system under DOS and don't want to develop the batch file-based system already discussed.

AMenu

Price. Free

Category. Copyrighted

Author. Rene Bollinger

CD-ROM directory. \UTILITY\DOS\AMENU

AMenu reads the file MENU.DAT and uses it to display a menu. It treats each line as a separate menu item, and it can handle up to 16 items. If there are more than nine entries, it uses letters for the remaining options. Once the user makes a selection, that selection is reported back to the batch file in the errorlevel.

Choose

Version. 3.0

Price. $20

Category. Shareware

Author. HFK Software, at the following address:
68 Wells Rd.
Lincoln, MA 01773-3702

CD-ROM directory. \UTILITY\DOS\CHOOSE30
Choose displays a menu on the screen and allows the user to make a selection using the up and down arrow keys, or an optional hotkey for each menu item. The user's selection is reported back to the batch file via the errorlevel.

Unlike some menu programs that require complex construction, Choose is fairly simple to use. If you like, you can simply list menu options on the command line. For example, the following command line would give the user two choices, Yes or No:

```
choose {WCB}Yes Or No Selection^{Y}es^{N}o
```

Five to seven longer menu options could easily be entered on a command line. For more complex menus, the data for the menu can be read from an ASCII file. Each menu option can be assigned a unique highlighted hotkey, and other formatting is supported.

Choose excels at presenting shorter menus. It's also good for presenting the user with a limited number of choices, where you might otherwise use one of the error-level askers from Chapter 34.

DRMenu

Version. 3.0

Price. Free

Category. Freeware (copyrighted but no registration fee)

Author. T. D. Roper, at:
201 Winding Brook Dr.
Garner, NC 27529

CD-ROM directory. \UTILITY\DOS\DRMENU30
DRMenu takes all your batch files and automatically constructs the shell of a very nice menu program. You then edit the configuration file to finish out your menu. The menu system you end up with is very nice and extremely easy to use.

Since DRMenu automatically builds a menu system around all your batch files, the easiest way to start is to copy just those batch files you want in the menu system to a temporary subdirectory. You can then run the DRMENU installation program on this subdirectory. Later, if you like, you can copy everything back to your common batch file subdirectory.

DRMenu displays a moving lightbar menu that initially has a generic title at the top and uses the names of the batch files as menu options. You can easily edit the configuration file to change this to a meaningful title and longer, more meaningful descriptions of the batch files. DRMenu runs your batch files for each menu selection and leaves the batch files unaltered so you can continue to use them outside of DR-Menu. When it runs your batch file, it keeps a tiny bit of code in memory to regain control, but it uses almost no memory. Given its price (free), this is an excellent menu system.

Menu_Man

Version. 2.00

Price. $20

Category. Shareware

Author. MicroMetric, at:
98 Dade Ave.
Sarasota, FL 34232-1609

CD-ROM directory. \UTILITY\DOS\MENU-MAN

Menu_Man is a batch file menu program. It can place its menus anywhere on the screen and control their color. In addition, it has numerous options for how they look (shadowed and the like) and how they're displayed (exploding, slowly expanding, etc.). The menus can stay on the screen until the user makes a selection or they can time-out after a specified length of time, with the time remaining shown as part of the menu.

Menu_Man stores its data in an unusual format. It's typical to create an ASCII file containing the menu data since most menus are too complex to be constructed on the command line. Rather than using a separate file, Menu_Man has you store the menu data as remarks in a batch file directly below the Menu_Man command. I think this works better because you don't have to worry about an extra file when you distribute your batch files, plus it makes the menu data more accessible for modification. Menu_Man is a well-thought-out and very powerful menu program.

EnviMenu

Price. Free

Category. Copyrighted

Author. Nombas, at:
P.O. Box 875
Medford, MA 02155-0007

CD-ROM directory. \UTILITY\DOS\CENVIDOS

EnviMenu demonstrates some of the functions of the CEnvi program, discussed in Chapter 40. The program presents a menu on the screen and, as you highlight each option, a longer help line is displayed. The EnviMenu commands, menu options, and batch commands to run them are all stored in one file. This makes transporting the menu structure easy, but it can make longer menus fairly complex.

Hard Disk Menu System

Version. 2.11

Price. $24

Category. Shareware

Author. MicroFox Company, at:
P.O. Box 447
Richfield, OH 44286-0447

CD-ROM directory. \UTILITY\DOS\HDM464

The Hard Disk Menu System (HDMS) is an excellent multipage menu system. It starts up with a list of pages on the left and menu options for that page on the right. The different pages allow you to group similar options together. By putting both the page name and menu options on the same screen, you can rapidly switch between various pages. You select pages and menu options with letters, or you can use a mouse to make selections. If you have ten or fewer pages, you can configure the program so you can select options with different function keys.

HDMS uses no memory while running your programs. For each menu option, it can issue a command or run a batch file that issues as many commands as you like. The syntax is a little cryptic, but you'll quickly get used to it. You configure HDMS while it's running using the Lotus-like slash key to bring up the configuration menu. You can set colors, titles, help screens, and more.

HDMS supports most networks, including Novell, 3COM, Token Ring, and others. It supports the use of individual IDs and passwords. There's a screen blanker and it can even dial your phone for you. This is a very handy menu program.

Sparkle & Menu Magic

Version. 3.5

Price. $29

Category. Shareware

Author. Rob W. Smetana, at the following address:
Pro-Formance
132 Alpine Terrace
San Francisco, CA 94117

CD-ROM directory. \UTILITY\DOS\SPARKL35

You begin menu construction with Menu Magic by filling out a screen that has room for a title and up to eight menu options. Once this is finished, you use the cursor to pick colors and border options. Finally, you supply a filename and Menu Magic writes out the skeleton of a batch file for you to work with and a .COM file containing your actual menu. Optionally, you can skip the .COM file and have it write a batch file that calls on Sparkle to draw the menu.

The generation of the .COM file is a nice touch. It gives you a program you can distribute to other users who don't have Sparkle, and the menus it generates are very nice looking. They support pressing the first letter to jump to a menu option and using a mouse to select an option. The selected option is reported back to the batch file via the errorlevel. If you want more than eight menu options, you can have it read in an ASCII file and convert it to a menu.

Sparkle also has the ability to generate a number of custom sounds, display text in large letters, pause a batch file for a specified period of time, prompt the user for a single character and report it back via the errorlevel, report on the monitor type, draw boxes on the screen, including some very fancy "exploding" boxes, and print text on the screen at a specified location.

Sparkle-2

Version. 2.4

Price. $29 (included as part of registration for Sparkle & Menu Magic)

Category. Shareware

Author. Rob W. Smetana, at:
Pro-Formance
132 Alpine Terrace
San Francisco, CA 94117

CD-ROM directory. \UTILITY\DOS\SPKL2-24

Sparkle-2 was designed as an extension to Sparkle & Menu Magic, and is included in the registration fee for the original program. It adds the following abilities:

- Painting the screen.
- Reversing colors.
- Getting a multicharacter response from the user and placing it in the environment.
- Three different types of "Press any key . . ." messages.
- Viewing any ASCII file.
- Reporting the major DOS version number.

37

Dealing with Files, Disks, and Subdirectories in DOS

Batch files can use only standard DOS commands for dealing with files. For example, they can't find out how much free space a disk has or the date of a file. A number of batch file utilities, however, will help you overcome these limitations.

Many of the utility sets in Chapter 38 perform all the functions of programs in this chapter, so you might want to review Chapter 38 before reading this chapter.

CFGCNTRL

Version. 1.1

Price. $29

Category. Crippleware

Author. Tessler's Nifty Tools, at:
P.O. Box 1791
San Ramon, CA 94583

CD-ROM directory. \UTILITY\DOS\TNT\CFGCNTRL

Windows stores information about how it appears and operates in several .INI files, including WIN.INI. In order to start Windows under a different configuration, you must modify one or more of these files. CFGCNTRL gives you that ability in a batch file. Its tools allow you to add and remove sections from an ASCII file from within a batch file. CFGCNTRL can test to see if sections of a file exist, and it can append sections to the file from either the command line or another ASCII file.

If you're going to modify Windows configuration files, doing so from a batch file is much safer than doing so interactively because you know the batch file will perform the same action each time without worrying about a mistake. Nevertheless, figuring out which actions to take can be complex, so it's best left to advanced users. Once you do figure out what actions to do, it's fairly easy to configure CFGCNTRL to perform those actions. It also works in Lan Manager as well as your AUTOEXEC.BAT and CONFIG.SYS files.

CHKPARM

Version. 1.0

Price. $19

Category. Crippleware

Author. Tessler's Nifty Tools, at:
P.O. Box 1791
San Ramon, CA 94583

CD-ROM directory. \UTILITY\DOS\TNT\CHKPARM
CHKPARM takes the parameter passed to it and figures out if it's a program, file, or subdirectory and if it's located on a local or remote (network) drive. Then it sets the errorlevel accordingly. This can make your batch files much more intelligent when they must operate in a network environment.

DelEx

Version. 1.29

Price. $6

Category. Shareware

Author. Samuel Kaplin, at the following address:
3520 W. 32nd St., #214
Minneapolis, MN 55416

CD-ROM directory. \UTILITY\DOS\DELEX129
DelEx deletes all the files except the ones you specify. For example, the command:

```
DELEX *.BAT
```

is the same as DEL *.*, only the *.BAT files are *not* erased.

DIR2BAT

Version. 1.6

Price. $19

Category. Crippleware

Author. Tessler's Nifty Tools, at:
P.O. Box 1791
San Ramon, CA 94583

CD-ROM directory. \UTILITY\DOS\TNT\DIR2BAT

DIR2BAT searches through your hard disk to find the files that match the specifications given on the command line. It then writes a batch file listing those files one at a time, with any commands you supply. You can then append the commands to the filenames and issue more than one command for each filename. This is a quick way to process a lot of files.

ForAge

Version. 1.00A

Price. Free

Category. Copyrighted

Author. Pinnacle Software, at:
P.O. Box 714, Airport Rd.
Swanton, VT 05488

CD-ROM directory. \UTILITY\DOS\FORAGE

ForAge returns the name of the oldest or newest file in a group of files. It can pass that name on to a command or add text before and/or after the name in a fashion that's useful for piping to a temporary batch file. For example, the command:

```
FORAGE N *.BAT EDIT @@
```

would start the MS-DOS 6 editor with the newest batch file already loaded. You can also use this to make a backup or print the newest report.

IsItZero

Version. 1.0

Price. Free

Category. Written for this book

Author. Ronny Richardson

CD-ROM directory. \UTILITY\DOS\ISITZERO

It's often useful to know if a file is a zero-length file. Usually, you pipe some information through the FIND filter and then pipe it to a file. Since FIND doesn't support the errorlevel, your only way to find out if FIND found the information you asked for is to see if the resulting file contains any information. If FIND was unsuccessful, it will be a zero-length file, and MS-DOS won't copy zero-length files.

Unfortunately, DR DOS copies them, so you can't write batch files that use this technique that will run under both operating systems. Plus, it's time-consuming to have the batch file copy a file to another name, test to see if the copy exists, and then delete both copies. ISITZERO.EXE overcomes this. The command ISITZERO *file* sets the errorlevel to 4 if *file* is a zero-length file, and to 3 if it contains data. Since IsItZero works under all versions of DOS, it makes writing a common batch file for both systems easy, and it's quicker and neater than copying files.

I wrote IsItZero in Builder Lite, and both the program and source code are included on the CD-ROM that comes with this book. The CD-ROM also includes a fully functional copy of Builder Lite in the \BLDLITE subdirectory.

PocketD Plus

Version. 5.1

Price. $39 (private and educational use), $58 (commercial)

Category. Shareware

Author. Jeff Rollason, at:
Pocketware
Box 2369, Hendon
London NW4 1NR
England

CD-ROM directory. \UTILITY\DOS\POCKET41

PocketD Plus is a difficult program to categorize. You can use it to display a menu and get a selection from the user, accept input from the user, and construct custom batch files. All of these make it a useful batch file utility. However, its primary purpose is as a DOS command-line file management tool, completely unrelated to its batch file abilities.

PocketD Plus constructs its menus from the command line, so a simple menu would be constructed with the following (continued on the page for readability):

```
D /Y1234 /'//@t1. Lotus/@t2. WordPerfect/@t3. dBASE/@t4.
  Windows/@tESC Exit//@t?'
```

The D is the name of the program file, D.EXE. The /Y is the user input command. It figures out from the commands that follow that it needs to display the menu. The 1234 are the valid keystrokes. Each /@t specifies a menu option, and the /@ESC specifies the action to take, exiting in this case, if the user presses the Esc key. Menu commands like this can be entered directly from the batch file, or the command sequence can be stored in the environment under the variable names AA to AZ. If this sequence were stored under AU, the menu could be executed with the command D /AU.

You can use any single keystrokes you like, so the following would be an equally valid command (again, continued for readability):

```
D /Y2468 /'//@t2. Lotus/@t4. WordPerfect/@t6. dBASE/@t8.
  Windows/@tESC Exit//@t?'
```

Once a menu is displayed, PocketD Plus knows it needs to wait for a response. Only the characters entered after the /Y and Escape are accepted; any others are ignored. The returned errorlevels represent the position of the response in the menu, so selecting WordPerfect would return an errorlevel of 2.

PocketD Plus can also get a keystroke from the user, with or without a prompt. The command to do this would look like the following:

```
D /Y_ny '//&R Yes or no?'
```

Again, D.EXE is the name of the program and /Y is the user input command. It figures out from the &R that follows that it's to display a prompt. The _ny stands for the valid keystrokes, with the _ being the space and Return. If the batch file had already displayed a prompt, the command D /Y_ny would be enough to get input from the user. Again, the errorlevel equals the position in the string of valid keystrokes that matches the user's input.

PocketD Plus is primarily a command-line file management tool. It's a fairly small utility; D.EXE is only 32K. But don't let its small size fool you. PocketD Plus is the single most powerful file management tool I've seen running from the command line. It has over 200 options and suboptions. It can search based on filenames, strings in a file, or location inside an archived file. It has 23 copying options alone! You can construct filename templates to control which files it acts on, view files inside archives, view a file from a directory listing, see full-size bar charts, use advanced wildcard options, and much, much more.

PocketD Plus has so many command-line options that it's possible for you to have problems with the DOS 127-character command-line limit while using PocketD Plus. I suggest that you load DOSKEY while using PocketD Plus so you don't have to retype entire commands while experimenting with the program.

As you might expect, with so many command-line options and switches, PocketD Plus can be intimidating and even (dare I say it) difficult to learn to use well. That's where a second program from the same package comes in, MenuD. MenuD has 60 menus and over 400 options that allow you to construct PocketD Plus commands by working through a menu. Once you've finished constructing your command, MenuD writes it to a batch file.

While it will take some time and practice to learn to use PocketD Plus, if you're a command-line junky this is the file manager for you. If you're simply looking for a menu program or errorlevel asker program, then consult Chapters 36 or 34, respectively, for a program that's simpler to learn to use.

QIC-BAT for CMS

Version. 1.2

Price. $23

Category. Shareware

Author. Douglas East, at the following address:
Command Line Software
3431 Florida Dr.
Loveland, CO 80538

CD-ROM directory. \UTILITY\DOS\QICBAT12

QIC-BAT for CMS is an intelligent batch file generation program for Colorado tape drives. You use it to select the files in your hard disk that you want to back up, and it generates a batch file to control the CMS DOS software (up to version 4.03) to actually perform the backup. Without QIC-BAT for CMS, you must work through the CMS menus every time you perform a backup. With QIC-BAT for CMS, you work through the menus once and then the resulting batch file quickly and easily performs the backup every time after that.

The QIC-BAT for CMS menus are very clearly written and easy to use. QIC-BAT for CMS knows the rules of the CMS software and won't let you make invalid selections, such as trying to erase the tape on the second hard drive you back up to a tape. The resulting batch file is fairly complex, but QIC-BAT for CMS will let you view a comprehensible explanation of what the batch file is doing.

If you use CMS software to perform backups, QIC-BAT for CMS is a well-thought-out program that will make your backups faster and simpler.

StripX

Version. 1.6

Price. Free

Category. Copyrighted

Author. Joseph R. Ellis, at:
228 Field Circle, SE
Hickory, NC 28602-5414

CD-ROM directory.   \UTILITY\DOS\STRIPX

StripX is designed to strip off the extension or path from a filename and pass it to a batch file. You run StripX by giving it the name of the file to strip and the name of a batch file to run. It passes the stripped name to the batch file as %1 and the full name as %2. Its default is to just strip the extension, but a switch lets you strip off the path to the file. Of course, if you're entering the filename yourself it would be easier to enter it without the extension. StripX was designed to be used in a batch file when you're processing multiple files or the filename is coming from another source.

38

DOS Batch File Utilities

Several people weren't content to produce just a couple of batch utilities; instead, they've produced entire sets of utilities. This chapter covers those sets.

Basically, you can produce a set of batch utilities in one of two ways. You can write a separate program for each function, but you end up with a lot of small utilities cluttering up your hard disk. Alternatively, you can build one massive program that does everything and use keywords to tell the program which task to perform.

I strongly prefer the second approach because, under most conditions, using one program saves disk space, often quite a bit of it.

A Batch View

Version. 2.00

Price. $15

Category. Shareware

Author. Robin R. Latham, at the following address:
2607 Betty Lane
Arlington, TX 76006

CD-ROM directory. \UTILITY\DOS\ABATVW

A Batch View is a utility set designed to allow you to create personal or graphical interface for your batch files. It will also add a great deal of power to them by providing you with several other utilities. A Batch View is made up of several different programs:

ABATINFO. This provides a variety of system information. It can set the errorlevel so a batch file can respond accordingly.

ABATJOB. This is a screen drawing program to design unique displays.

ABATMENU. ABATMENU creates pop-up menus and allows configuration of the video screen. Menus are centered and have 3-D shadowing, and the program returns an errorlevel to the batch file. Up to 48 menu items are allowed and a mouse is supported. Menu items can come from the command line or a file.

ACLS. This clears the screen in several different ways and sets screen colors.

AECHO. AECHO displays text on the screen, and controls placement and color. It can also display text from an ASCII file in a similar manner.

AMSCROLL. This provides scrolling messages and frames.

AMSG. This creates pop-up messages and prompts for batch. It can display information about the system, and allows the user to input information to be stored in an environmental variable.

As you can see, this inexpensive shareware set offers a lot of power for the money. Its features are compared to other utility programs in this chapter in Table 38.1. While all the utilities run fine under DOS, several of the programs will lock up when running in a DOS session under Windows.

Batch Environment

Price. $200 per server (not per PC)

Category. Commercial

Author. Transvision Software, at:
Klovsteinen 143
5033 Bergen
Norway

This is a commercial program that must be ordered from the authors. Batch Environment is a utility aimed squarely at the network administrator. Even its pricing reflects this, with a per-server rather than a per-PC price. Batch Environment is designed to create environmental variables describing the particular machine on which it's installed. The network batch files can then use this information to run differently for different configurations. In addition to the environmental variables containing program-related information, the program also generates the following:

Date variables. These return the number of days and seconds between two dates, the current day of the week, the current date, and the current time.

Disk variables. These return the boot drive, current subdirectory, current drive, available disk space, total disk space, volume label, whether a disk is ready and whether it's formatted, the disk serial number, disk type, and more.

File variables. These return the archive bit for a file, wildcards in a file specification, file date comparisons, the date of a file, whether a file is in the path, and the time of a file.

Memory variables. These check for available and total expanded, extended, and conventional memory, and the expanded memory management version.

Resident program variables. These check whether or not the following programs are loaded: ANSI, APPEND, ASSIGN, DOSKEY, DR DOS, DRIVER.SYS, HIMEM.SYS, NLSFUNC, PRINT.COM, SHARE, XMS, and a mouse driver.

Screen variables. These check for the screen type, video mode, size of the video adapter, and video adapter address.

System variables. These return the code page, CPU type, Break status, country the computer is configured for, multitasking support, DOS version, DeskView status, free environmental space, total environmental space, PC type, whether a math co-processor is installed and a printer is on-line, number of serial and parallel ports, ROM version, and more.

All of this information can make configuring your network scripts to fit individual workstations much easier.

BatchMan

Price. Free

Category. Copyrighted

Author. Michael Mefford

All *PC Magazine* files are available from their area on CompuServe. See any issue of *PC Magazine* for details. BatchMan is a tiny 6,359-byte file that gives you 48 commands, many of which are useful in batch files. Many of its functions are compared to those of other utility sets in this chapter in Table 38.1. You can download the full source code for BatchMan along with the program and share it, as long as it's not in a commercial setting.

Since BatchMan is contained in a single .COM file, the command to execute it is specified on the command line. For example:

```
BATCHMAN CLS
```

will clear the screen. When a command needs additional options, those too are specified on the command line.

Batcmd 1.1

Version. 1.1

Price. Free

Category. Written for this book

Author. Doug Amaral

CD-ROM directory. \UTILITY\DOS\BATCMD
Doug Amaral of hyperkinetix, the maker of Builder and Builder Lite, wrote Batcmd 1.0 especially for this book. I added a couple of commands and made some minor modifications to the help system to produce the version 1.1 that's included in this book. Batcmd is designed to be run from inside a batch file. The general format of the command is:

```
BATCMD keyword [prompt]
```

where *keyword* is a two-letter command abbreviation that tells Batcmd what to do and *prompt* is an optional message to tell the user what information to enter. The prompt can contain multiple words and shouldn't be enclosed in quotation marks because they would end up showing in the final prompt.

Asking the user a question is Batcmd's strong suit, so we'll look at that first. There are two major types of questions: those that require a single character in response and those that require more than one character. This is a major distinction because, when a question requires only a single character, the program can accept that character without requiring the user to press Return, while a multiple-character response always requires the user to press Return.

Single-character responses

Batcmd offers several different ways to ask the user a question, depending on what type of information you need.

YN (yes or no). This command accepts only an N or Y keystroke in either upper- or lowercase. For an N in either case, Batcmd YN sets the errorlevel to 0; for a Y in either case, it sets it to 1. This is probably the Batcmd option you'll use the most. Many of the questions you'll want to ask the user are things like "Do you really want to erase all these files? (Y/N)" or "This takes six hours, do you want to continue? (Y/N)." Using the YN option is much nicer than using a Pause command and telling the user to press Ctrl–Break to stop the batch file.

GN (get number). This command accepts any single-digit number from the user and exits with the errorlevel set to that number. If any other keystroke is entered, Batcmd beeps and continues waiting for a number. This command can display an optional prompt if it's included after the command. When you want the user to select between just a few options, this might be the best approach. If you need fewer than ten options, just start at 0 and go back through the prompting loop if the user enters a number that's too high. You can do this with just one IF test. For example, if your last option is number 6, then loop back through the options whenever the errorlevel is 7 or higher.

GL (get letter). This command accepts any letter from the user and exits with the errorlevel set to 1 for an A, 2 for a B, and so on. If any other keystroke is entered, Batcmd beeps and continues waiting for a letter. This command can display an optional prompt if it's included after the command. If you're designing a menu system where you want the user to be able to make a selection using any letter, this option is the best way to implement it. It's also the best approach when you have a lot of options you're willing to letter sequentially. Because the errorlevels run from A on up, if they stop at N (an errorlevel of 14), then you can test for an invalid response with a single IF test that tests for an errorlevel of 15 or higher. However, if you want the user to select from only a few of the letters or if you want to pick and choose certain letters to use, then using the GF (get from list) option is a better approach.

GU (get uppercase letter). This command accepts only uppercase letters from the user. If the user enters a lowercase letter or any nonletter keystroke, Batcmd beeps and continues waiting for an uppercase letter. The errorlevel is set to the ASCII value of the uppercase letter, so A is reported as 65, B is reported as 66, and so on. This command can display an optional prompt if it's included after the command. This is a specialized version of the GL (get letter) option. For most applications, GL is more useful.

GF (get from list). This command accepts a keystroke from the user only when it's on the list of acceptable keystrokes. The format of the command is BATCMD GF *list prompt*, where *list* is a listing of all valid keystrokes without spaces between them and *prompt* is the user message to display. The list of keystrokes is case-sensitive, so in order to accept only A through C from the user in either case the command would have to be entered as BATCMD GF AaBbCc *prompt*.

 If the user enters an invalid keystroke, Batcmd beeps and continues waiting for a valid keystroke. Once the user enters a valid keystroke, Batcmd sets the errorlevel to that keystroke's position in the list. For the example in the last paragraph, if the user entered B, the errorlevel would be set to 3 because a capital B is the third character in the list. Batcmd checks the list from right to left. That is an issue only if you use duplicates in the list. If your list was Ronny, then n would be reported via an errorlevel of 4 and not 3 because the n in the fourth position is the first lowercase n encountered moving right to left.

 This approach is designed for those occasions when you have a number of different selections from which the user can pick. If you have fewer selections, then having the user pick a number would be a better choice. At first glance, you might think that treating upper- and lowercase letters separately would double the number of IF tests in the batch file, but this isn't the case. If you issue BATCMD GF AaBbCc *prompt*, shown earlier, you know the errorlevel will be 1 to 6 and you want to treat upper- and lowercase letters the same. The following batch file segment does that:

```
BATCMD GF AaBbCc
IF ERRORLEVEL 5 GOTO C
IF ERRORLEVEL 3 GOTO B
IF ERRORLEVEL 1 GOTO A
```

You want to jump to the C section when the errorlevel is 5 to 6. Because the IF ERRORLEVEL 5 statement is a greater-than-or-equal test and no values exceed 6, it handles both cases automatically. Once 5 and 6 have been eliminated, the IF ERROR LEVEL 3 statement tests for 3 and 4, which is B. The last statement could be replaced with just a GOTO A because everything else has been eliminated; I used an IF test just for consistency's sake.

GK (get key).   This command accepts any keystroke from the user and exits with the errorlevel set to the ASCII value of that keystroke. This command can display an optional prompt if it's included after the GK command. Only very rarely will you need this tool. When you need to restrict entries, the GF option works better. The GF option also works better if you have less than 26 options because you can easily list all the letters. At 26 options, GL is better because it handles getting just letters automatically. About the only time you'll need this option is when you're doing something where you need to accept absolutely any keystroke from the user.

Multiple-character responses

Occasionally, you want to ask the user a question that requires a multicharacter response, for example asking for a name to customize the prompt or a specific filename. Multicharacter responses cannot be stored in the errorlevel because that variable has room for only one byte of information. Batcmd has a way around this. The GE option asks the user a question and stores the results in the master copy of the environment under the name Batcmd. This command will display a prompt if you enter GE 1 on the command line.

Before using Batcmd, you might want to check the environment to see how much free space you have; Batcmd has a CE option that does this for you. It sets the errorlevel to the number of free bytes in the environment, up to 255. If more than 255 bytes are free, it sets the errorlevel to 255. You can enter up to 65 bytes of information in response to the GE prompt, and you also need room for the environmental variable name and some internal markers for DOS. Thus, to be absolutely certain of not running out of space, check for a value of around 73. Most users enter far less than 65 characters, so I usually tailor my tests to the type of information I'm asking for.

Which of these many Batcmd options you use really depends on the type of information you're asking for. To give you a better understanding of each option, SHOWGETS.BAT in Figure 38.1 uses all the options in a functioning batch file. Most of the examples perform logic testing on the user's response. SHOWGETS.BAT requires the Batcmd program and the SAYERROR.BAT batch file to either be in the current subdirectory or in the path when it runs.

Batch File Line	Explanation
`@ECHO OFF`	Turn command-echoing off.

`REM NAME:    SHOWGETS.BAT`
`REM PURPOSE: Show Using Batcmd In Bat`
`REM VERSION: 1.00`
`REM DATE:    May 18, 1992`
	Documentation remarks.

`NEEDHELP %0 %1` `IF ERRORLEVEL 1 GOTO HELP`	Use the NeedHelp utility program to check and see if the user requested help.
`CLS`	Clear the screen.
`ECHO This Demonstration Takes About` `ECHO Ten Minutes To Run`	Explain what is happening to the user.
`BATCMD SL`	Use Batcmd to skip a line.
`BATCMD YN Do You Want To Continue? (Y/N)`	Use the yes/no option of Batcmd to ask the user a question.
`IF NOT ERRORLEVEL 1 GOTO END`	If the user did not answer yes, jump to the end of the batch file.
`ECHO I'm Glad You Decided To Stay`	Acknowledge that the user answered yes.
`BATCMD CE`	Use Batcmd to check and see how much environmental space is free.
`IF NOT ERRORLEVEL 25 GOTO ERROR`	If there are not 25 bytes of free environmental space, jump to an error-handling section.
`BATCMD SL`	Use Batcmd to skip a line.
`BATCMD GE Please Enter Your Name:`	Use Batcmd to ask the user's name. This is stored in the environment under the name Batcmd.
`CLS`	Clear the screen.
`GOTO TOP1`	Jump to the next section of the batch file.

`:ERROR`
`ECHO Your Environment Does Not Have Enough Free`
`ECHO Space For The Entire Demonstration So I`
`ECHO Am Skipping Asking Your Name`
`ECHO In The Prompts, You Will See A Blank`
`ECHO Where You Should See A Name`
`PAUSE`
`CLS`
`GOTO TOP1`
	Section to explain the problem of inadequate free environmental space to the user.

`:TOP1`	Label marking the top of the first loop.
`    BATCMD SL`	Use Batcmd to skip a line.
`    ECHO %BATCMD%:`	Display the user's name if it was stored in the environment.

Figure 38.1 SHOWGETS.BAT illustrates how to use Batcmd to get information from the user in a variety of formats.

Batch File Line	Explanation
ECHO For The Next Question, Only A ECHO Number Will Be Acceptable, But ECHO You Might Want To Try Other ECHO Things First To See What Happens ECHO This Will Be Repeated Until ECHO You Answer With A 0	Tell the user what will happen next.
BATCMD GN Enter A Number 0-9	Ask the user to enter a number 0-9 using Batcmd.
IF ERRORLEVEL 9 ECHO 9 Entered IF ERRORLEVEL 8 IF NOT ERRORLEVEL 9 ECHO 8 Entered IF ERRORLEVEL 7 IF NOT ERRORLEVEL 8 ECHO 7 Entered IF ERRORLEVEL 6 IF NOT ERRORLEVEL 7 ECHO 6 Entered IF ERRORLEVEL 5 IF NOT ERRORLEVEL 6 ECHO 5 Entered IF ERRORLEVEL 4 IF NOT ERRORLEVEL 5 ECHO 4 Entered IF ERRORLEVEL 3 IF NOT ERRORLEVEL 4 ECHO 3 Entered IF ERRORLEVEL 2 IF NOT ERRORLEVEL 3 ECHO 2 Entered IF ERRORLEVEL 1 IF NOT ERRORLEVEL 2 ECHO 1 Entered IF ERRORLEVEL 8 IF NOT ERRORLEVEL 1 ECHO 0 Entered	Test the errorlevels in order to tell the user what number was selected.
IF ERRORLEVEL 1 GOTO TOP1	If the user entered anything other than zero, continue looping.
CLS	Clear the screen.
:TOP2	Label marking the top of the second loop.
ECHO %BATCMD%:	Display the user's name if it was stored in the environment.
ECHO For The Next Demonstration Only ECHO A Letter Will Be Accepted ECHO You Might Want To Try Other Things First ECHO The Demonstration Will Continue Until ECHO You Enter An A	Tell the user what will happen next.
BATCMD SL	Use Batcmd to skip a line.
BATCMD GL Enter Any Letter	Use Batcmd to ask the user a question and accept any letter in response.

Figure 38.1 Continued.

Batch File Line	Explanation

`IF ERRORLEVEL  1 IF NOT ERRORLEVEL  2 ECHO A Entered`
`IF ERRORLEVEL  2 IF NOT ERRORLEVEL  3 ECHO B Entered`
`IF ERRORLEVEL  3 IF NOT ERRORLEVEL  4 ECHO C Entered`
`IF ERRORLEVEL  4 IF NOT ERRORLEVEL  5 ECHO D Entered`
`IF ERRORLEVEL  5 IF NOT ERRORLEVEL  6 ECHO E Entered`
`IF ERRORLEVEL  6 IF NOT ERRORLEVEL  7 ECHO F Entered`
`IF ERRORLEVEL  7 IF NOT ERRORLEVEL  8 ECHO G Entered`
`IF ERRORLEVEL  8 IF NOT ERRORLEVEL  9 ECHO H Entered`
`IF ERRORLEVEL  9 IF NOT ERRORLEVEL 10 ECHO I Entered`
`IF ERRORLEVEL 10 IF NOT ERRORLEVEL 11 ECHO J Entered`
`IF ERRORLEVEL 11 IF NOT ERRORLEVEL 12 ECHO K Entered`
`IF ERRORLEVEL 12 IF NOT ERRORLEVEL 13 ECHO L Entered`
`IF ERRORLEVEL 13 IF NOT ERRORLEVEL 14 ECHO M Entered`
`IF ERRORLEVEL 14 IF NOT ERRORLEVEL 15 ECHO N Entered`
`IF ERRORLEVEL 15 IF NOT ERRORLEVEL 16 ECHO O Entered`
`IF ERRORLEVEL 16 IF NOT ERRORLEVEL 17 ECHO P Entered`
`IF ERRORLEVEL 17 IF NOT ERRORLEVEL 18 ECHO Q Entered`
`IF ERRORLEVEL 18 IF NOT ERRORLEVEL 19 ECHO R Entered`
`IF ERRORLEVEL 19 IF NOT ERRORLEVEL 20 ECHO S Entered`
`IF ERRORLEVEL 20 IF NOT ERRORLEVEL 21 ECHO T Entered`
`IF ERRORLEVEL 21 IF NOT ERRORLEVEL 22 ECHO U Entered`
`IF ERRORLEVEL 22 IF NOT ERRORLEVEL 23 ECHO V Entered`
`IF ERRORLEVEL 23 IF NOT ERRORLEVEL 24 ECHO W Entered`
`IF ERRORLEVEL 24 IF NOT ERRORLEVEL 25 ECHO X Entered`
`IF ERRORLEVEL 25 IF NOT ERRORLEVEL 26 ECHO Y Entered`
`IF ERRORLEVEL 26 IF NOT ERRORLEVEL 27 ECHO Z Entered`
	Test the errorlevels in order to tell the user what letter was selected.

`IF ERRORLEVEL 2 GOTO TOP2`	If the user entered anything other than the letter A, continue looping.
`CLS`	Clear the screen.
`:TOP3`	Label marking the top of the third loop.
`    ECHO %BATCMD%:`	Display the user's name if it was stored in the environment.

`    ECHO For The Next Demonstration Only`
`    ECHO An Uppercase Letter Will Be Accepted`
`    ECHO You Might Want To Try Other Things First`
`    ECHO The Demonstration Will Continue Until`
`    ECHO You Enter An A`
	Tell the user what will happen next.

`    BATCMD SL`	Use Batcmd to skip a line.
`    BATCMD GU Enter Any UPPERCASE Letter`	Use Batcmd to ask the user a question and accept any uppercase letter in response.

Batch File Line	Explanation
| ```
IF ERRORLEVEL 65 IF NOT ERRORLEVEL 66 ECHO A Entered
IF ERRORLEVEL 66 IF NOT ERRORLEVEL 67 ECHO B Entered
IF ERRORLEVEL 67 IF NOT ERRORLEVEL 68 ECHO C Entered
IF ERRORLEVEL 68 IF NOT ERRORLEVEL 69 ECHO D Entered
IF ERRORLEVEL 69 IF NOT ERRORLEVEL 70 ECHO E Entered
IF ERRORLEVEL 70 IF NOT ERRORLEVEL 71 ECHO F Entered
IF ERRORLEVEL 71 IF NOT ERRORLEVEL 72 ECHO G Entered
IF ERRORLEVEL 72 IF NOT ERRORLEVEL 73 ECHO H Entered
IF ERRORLEVEL 73 IF NOT ERRORLEVEL 74 ECHO I Entered
IF ERRORLEVEL 74 IF NOT ERRORLEVEL 75 ECHO J Entered
IF ERRORLEVEL 75 IF NOT ERRORLEVEL 76 ECHO K Entered
IF ERRORLEVEL 76 IF NOT ERRORLEVEL 77 ECHO L Entered
IF ERRORLEVEL 77 IF NOT ERRORLEVEL 78 ECHO M Entered
IF ERRORLEVEL 78 IF NOT ERRORLEVEL 79 ECHO N Entered
IF ERRORLEVEL 79 IF NOT ERRORLEVEL 80 ECHO O Entered
IF ERRORLEVEL 80 IF NOT ERRORLEVEL 81 ECHO P Entered
IF ERRORLEVEL 81 IF NOT ERRORLEVEL 82 ECHO Q Entered
IF ERRORLEVEL 82 IF NOT ERRORLEVEL 83 ECHO R Entered
IF ERRORLEVEL 83 IF NOT ERRORLEVEL 84 ECHO S Entered
IF ERRORLEVEL 84 IF NOT ERRORLEVEL 85 ECHO T Entered
IF ERRORLEVEL 85 IF NOT ERRORLEVEL 86 ECHO U Entered
IF ERRORLEVEL 86 IF NOT ERRORLEVEL 87 ECHO V Entered
IF ERRORLEVEL 87 IF NOT ERRORLEVEL 88 ECHO W Entered
IF ERRORLEVEL 88 IF NOT ERRORLEVEL 89 ECHO X Entered
IF ERRORLEVEL 89 IF NOT ERRORLEVEL 90 ECHO Y Entered
IF ERRORLEVEL 90 IF NOT ERRORLEVEL 91 ECHO Z Entered
``` | Test the errorlevels in order to tell the user what letter was selected. |
`IF ERRORLEVEL 66 GOTO TOP3`	If the user entered anything other than the letter A, continue looping.
`CLS`	Clear the screen.
`:TOP4`	Label marking the top of the fourth loop.
`ECHO %BATCMD%:`	Display the user's name if it was stored in the environment.
| ```
ECHO For This Next Demonstration
ECHO Only The Letters "Ronny" Will Be Accepted
ECHO And The Capitalization Must Match Exactly
ECHO You Might Want To Try Other Entries First
``` | Tell the user what will happen next. |
| `BATCMD SL` | Use Batcmd to skip a line. |
| `BATCMD GF Ronny Select From The Letters "Ronny"` | Use Batcmd to ask the user a question and accept only letters in the list. |
| ```
IF ERRORLEVEL 1 IF NOT ERRORLEVEL 2 ECHO R Entered
IF ERRORLEVEL 2 IF NOT ERRORLEVEL 3 ECHO o Entered
IF ERRORLEVEL 4 IF NOT ERRORLEVEL 5 ECHO n Entered
IF ERRORLEVEL 5 IF NOT ERRORLEVEL 6 ECHO y Entered
``` | Test the errorlevels in order to tell the user what letter was selected. |
| `IF ERRORLEVEL 2 GOTO TOP4` | If the user entered anything other than the letter R, continue looping. |
| `CLS` | Clear the screen. |

Figure 38.1 Continued.
```

Batch File Line	Explanation
ECHO %BATCMD%:	Display the user's name if it was stored in the environment.
ECHO For This Next Demonstration Any Character ECHO Will Be Accepted And Its Errorlevel Shown	Tell the user what will happen next.
BATCMD GK Enter Any Keystroke	Use Batcmd to ask the user a question and accept any key-stroke.
CALL SAYERROR	Run the SAYERROR.BAT batch file to display the errorlevel.
:END	Label marking the end of the batch file.

AD (add 1 to MATH).   This command adds one to the contents of the MATH environmental variable. If the MATH environmental variable doesn't exist, Batcmd will display an error message and do nothing. If MATH exists but contains something other than a number, its contents will be treated as though they were a 0. As a result, its value is replaced with a 1 (0 + 1).

The AD command isn't included in Batcmd to give batch files mathematical power. In fact, it's difficult to perform anything other than the simplest math via the AD command. Rather, AD allows your batch files to go through loops a specific number of times. For example, you might ask the user for a password with GE and then use AD to make sure the user gets only three attempts at the password.

BE (beep the speaker).   This command beeps the speaker. If the command is entered as BATCMD BE, then it beeps the speaker once. If it's entered as BATCMD BE n, then it will beep the speaker n times. Once started, you can't stop this beeping without re-booting, so Batcmd limits n to 99 or less. If you need to beep the speaker more than 99 times, you can repeatedly run BATCMD or include it in a FOR loop.

BS (blank the screen).   This command clears the screen, identically to the DOS CLS command. However, if you enter colors after the command, it clears the screen to those colors. The command format is BATCMD BS *foreground background*. Table 25.1 shows the color numbers you can use with the BS command. All 16 can be used for the foreground color, but only the first eight can be used for the background color.

CC (check conventional memory).   This command checks to see how much conventional memory is available, and returns the number of 32K blocks through the error-level; a value of 10 would indicate that 320K is free. Use this command to make sure enough memory is available if a program being run by a batch file is particularly sensitive to available memory. Keep in mind that using Batcmd slightly reduces the amount of available memory that's listed.

CE (check environmental memory).   This command checks to see how much environmental space is free, and returns the number of free bytes through the errorlevel.

Because the errorlevel is limited to an integer from 0 to 255, this command returns 255 for any environment where the free space exceeds 255 bytes. This is a good way for batch files that depend on the environment to check to make sure space is available. In particular, you might want to use the CE command before the GE command if it's storing crucial information in the environment.

CH (check number of hard drives).   This checks to see how many hard drives are installed. It returns a 0 if there are no hard drives; otherwise, it sets the errorlevel equal to the number of hard drives. It checks the number of physical hard drives, not the number of partitions. Thus, a 100MB drive that's partitioned into three 32MB partitions and a fourth 4MB partition still counts as one physical drive to Batcmd. It doesn't include any CD-ROM drives or other nonstandard drives.

CL (check LIM memory).   This command checks to see how much LIM memory is free and returns with an errorlevel equal to the number of 32K blocks of expanded memory. This is useful as a check prior to running a program that requires a minimum amount of LIM memory. (LIM is an acronym for the Lotus-Intel-Microsoft specification for expanded memory.)

CM (check mouse).   This sets the errorlevel to 1 if it finds a mouse and to a 0 otherwise. Some older programs need a special command-line switch in order to use a mouse; this command lets the batch file check for the presence of a mouse when it runs rather than forcing it to behave in a certain fashion.

CS (check space).   This command checks to see how much free space is available on a drive, and returns the number of 32K blocks of free space in the errorlevel. When the free space exceeds 8160K, it returns 255. If the command is entered as BATCMD CS, it uses the default drive. If the command is entered as BATCMD CS *drive*, then it checks the amount of free space on the specified drive. This command is especially useful before running a database program where you're working with large files, because many database programs create a lot of working files on disk.

EX (exit).   Enter this as BATCMD EX *n*, where *n* is a number from 0 to 255. Batcmd sets the errorlevel to the number specified and exits. If no number is specified, Batcmd sets the errorlevel to 0. If a fractional number is specified, Batcmd uses only the integer portion of the number, so BATCMD EX 33.3 would result in an errorlevel value of 33. If a number over 255 is specified, 256 is repeatedly subtracted from the specified number until the resulting number falls between 0 and 255, the only valid values for the errorlevel. If a negative number is specified, 256 is repeatedly added to the specified number until the resulting number is between 0 and 255.

One use for this command is to give your batch files the ability to report their results via the errorlevel, just as programs do. Another use is to reset the errorlevel to 0. Sometimes, when working with subroutines, it's useful to put errorlevel testing at the top of a loop, as COPYTHIS.BAT (the solution to problem 7 in Chapter 24) does. However, this can cause problems if a program run before the batch file has set the errorlevel because, the first time through the loop, COPYTHIS.BAT hasn't yet run XCOPY and thus the errorlevel still contains the value from the last program. Adding a BATCMD EX 0 to the top of any batch file using errorlevel testing avoids this problem.

PC (position cursor). This command positions the cursor at specified coordinates on the screen. The format of the command is BATCMD PC *row column*, where *row* is the row number to move the cursor to (1 to 24) and *column* is the column number to move the cursor to (1 to 80). If a noninteger row or column number is used, the fractional portion of the number is ignored. If a 0, negative number, or number outside the acceptable boundaries is used, Batcmd aborts with an error message and sets the errorlevel to 1.

   This command replicates ANSI's ability to position the cursor. Being able to position the cursor can make it easier to draw complex screens and can help keep the screen uncluttered.

RB (reboot the computer). This command performs a warm reboot of the computer, which can be useful if you're writing a batch file to change the configuration of the computer or if you want to be able to abort a password batch file after a specific number of attempts.

SD (store day). This stores the day of the month in the errorlevel. If the date is March 21, BATCMD SD will set the errorlevel to 21. This command, and the date and time commands that follow, are useful for performing specific tasks on a specific day. For example, you might perform an incremental backup every Friday and a full backup on the first of every month.

SH (store hour). This command stores the hour of the day, in 24-hour format, in the errorlevel. If the time is 6:30 P.M., BATCMD SH sets the errorlevel to 18.

SL (skip line). This command causes a batch file to skip a single line on the screen, just like echoing an Alt–255.

SM (store minute). This command stores the minute of the hour in the errorlevel. If the time is 6:30 P.M., BATCMD SM sets the errorlevel to 30.

SO (store month). This command stores the month of the year in the errorlevel. If the date is March 21, BATCMD SO would set the errorlevel to 3.

SS (store second). This command stores the second in the errorlevel. Of course, this information changes rapidly, but the errorlevel is updated only each time the command is run. If the time is 6:30:15, BATCMD SS sets the errorlevel to 15.

SU (subtract 1 from MATH). This command subtracts 1 from the contents of the MATH environmental variable. If MATH doesn't exist, Batcmd displays an error message and does nothing. If MATH exists but contains something other than a number, its contents are treated as though they were a zero. Like the AD command discussed previously, SU is designed for looping and not really for adding mathematical power to batch files.

SY (store year). This command stores the last two digits of the year in the errorlevel, so 1992 is stored as 92 and 2000 is stored as 0.

VO (volume label). This command stores the volume label of the specified drive in the environment under the BATCMD environmental variable.

BatUtil 4.0

Version. 1.0

Price. $49.00 (Included as part of STACKEY)

Category. Shareware

Author. CTRLALT Associates; register with:
Advanced Support Group
11900 Grant Place
Des Peres, MO 63131
(800) 788-0787 or (314) 965-5630
(314) 966-1833 fax

CD-ROM directory. \UTILITY\DOS\BATUTIL\BATUTIL
BatUtil is far more than just a batch utility; it's really a batch language disguised as a batch utility. Table 38.1 compares its features to the features of other utilities covered in this chapter. To use BatUtil, you enter a command like:

```
BATUTIL [HOUR]
```

on the command line. When you enclose the command in square brackets, [ ], Bat-Util returns the results in the errorlevel. If you enclose the command in curly braces, {}, BatUtil also returns the results as an environmental variable. BatUtil needs only the first two characters of the command and ignores capitalization, so [HOUR], [Ho], [HoUr] and [ho] all mean the same thing.

BatUtil can discover as much if not more information about the environment than any other package described in this book, including files, the console, memory, the computer itself, time, and date information. It can discover if a file exists in the current subdirectory or along the path, if a file has today's date, if a path exists, the number of files matching one or more file specifications, and which of two files is older. It can report on all types of memory and can even tell you which operating system is in use.

BatUtil has numerous commands to obtain time and date information, including the date, hour, minute, month, day of week, and year. It has powerful tools for working with the environment. It can add directories to and delete directories from your path. It can even modify environmental variables interactively.

If finding information about the system and environment was all BatUtil did, it would still be a very powerful package, but BatUtil can do much more. It especially excels at screen handling. It supports all the DOS prompt metastrings along with some of its own to display the date and time.

BatUtil also offers menus. What makes them particularly nice is how little work you must do to use them. You can construct a simple working menu with the command:

```
BATUTIL {MENU Lotus Word dBASE Graphics Games Quit}
```

That simple command will clear the screen and display a colored menu in the screen's center, with the six options listed after the MENU command. The user can select one by either pressing the first uppercase letter on each line, moving the lightbar cursor to an option and pressing Return, or by double-clicking on an option with the mouse. The first menu option gets an errorlevel value of 1, the second a value of 2, and so on.

BatUtil figures out the options by dividing them by spaces. If you really need a space in a menu option, you can replace it with a $S metastring character to make BatUtil display the space properly. Thus, the first part of the previous menu line could easily become:

```
BATUTIL {MENU Lotus$S1-2-3 Microsoft$SWord dBASE$SIII+
```

and the $S metastring characters would be replaced by spaces. If you want to add a title to the menu, you can do so with the HEADER command. Again, the first part of the command with a title in it would look like this:

```
BATUTIL {HEADER Sample Menu}{MENU Lotus$S1-2-3 Microsoft$SWord dBASE$SIII+
```

You can have the menu pop onto the screen, display a shadow behind it, and even use the function keys to make the menu selection.

While fitting all the BatUtil commands for the menu onto one line isn't difficult, you can avoid this by storing the menu text in a file. This also allows for some added features. You can include multiple menus in the same file by adding a batch file label (a colon followed by a name) at the top of each set of text. You can also add help text to the file. When the user highlights a menu option, the menu program will show the associated help text at the bottom of the screen, much like when Lotus displays a line of help text below the menu depending on which option is highlighted.

BatUtil does have one drawback: the manual is hard to read. As I worked through the manual, however, I began to see the underlying structure of BatUtil and found that reading and following the manual became less difficult.

BatUtil is possibly the single most useful batch utility in this book. Instead of trying to put together a batch file toolkit with five or ten other utilities, you can just use BatUtil. I can't think of a single thing you might want to do with a batch file that you can't do with BatUtil! Spend a day or two with it; you'll come away with one powerful toolkit.

CFG

Version. 2.4

Price. $25

Category. Shareware

Author. Mark Treadwell, at the following address:
4 Mumford Ave., #1
Newport, RI 02840-1719

CD-ROM directory. \UTILITY\DOS\CFG24

CFG is a very powerful batch file utility, and many of its commands are designed to run in your CONFIG.SYS file. None of the other utilities discussed in this chapter offer that much functionality. CFG also offers commands and functions not found in any other batch file utility. All this combines to make CFG the perfect choice for real power users.

When you run CFG from the command line or in a batch file, you use it in the usual fashion, with CFG followed by a keyword and perhaps some switches. When you run CFG in the CONFIG.SYS file, however, you load it as a device driver. For example, the following would determine if ANSI were loaded from within a CONFIG.SYS file:

```
DEVICE=C:\DRIVERS\CFG.COM ANSI
```

When used in the CONFIG.SYS file, once the command action is completed CFG unloads itself from memory. The following switches are of particular interest:

/E. This places the results of a command into the errorlevel for easy testing in a batch file. There's a subswitch to place the errorlevel into an environmental variable as well.

/D. When a result is likely to be too large to report via the errorlevel (which is limited to numbers from 0 to 255), this switch lets you specify a divisor to use before storing the number in the errorlevel. For example, with hard disk space, you might divide the value reported by the DriveSpace keyword by 1,000 before storing it in the errorlevel.

/@. This places the results of a command into the environment.

/2. When you run CFG under Windows or in any other situation where it isn't loaded directly from the main copy of COMMAND.COM, you have to decide which environment you want to change. By default, CFG changes the master copy, so you won't see the changes if you're running CFG under Windows. The /2 switch causes the changes to be made in the secondary command processor, thus allowing the changes to be seen under Windows.

Table 38.1 compares the features of CFG with those of other utility sets. I won't go into these features in detail, but a few of them do deserve special mention.

CFG offers a good mathematical toolkit. Equations are performed with 64-bit, unsigned integers and returned as a 32-bit result. This means it can work with numbers from 0 to $2^{32} - 1$. In addition to the usual addition, subtraction, multiplication, and division, it can perform bitwise AND, OR, and XOR.

CFG can find out information about your system that many other utilities miss. For example, it can find out which country code and code page you're using and if Break is on. It can tell if ANSI, DOSKEY, and SHARE are loaded. It can find out how many rows and columns are currently being displayed, and it can check another drive to see if there's room to copy a file.

CFG can also do some things you might not expect. It can swap the addresses for your COM ports or hide them if you want. It can hide and unhide your printer ports and swap two printer ports. It can even find out if Stacker is running and if you're running a task-switching program.

CFG can find out if a particular device driver is loaded into memory, it can stuff keystrokes into the keyboard buffer, and it can write information to and read information from the 16-byte DOS interapplication communication area (IACA). Using IACA, it can facilitate communication between the CONFIG.SYS and AUTOEXEC.BAT files on pre-MS-DOS 6 systems.

While CFG lacks things like menus that you'll find in BatUtil, it makes up for them with all the many special tasks it performs. Every power user's toolkit needs to have a copy of CFG in it.

DOS Tool Box

Price. $25 ($35 with printed manual)

Category. Shareware

Author. Solid Oak Software, at:
P.O. Box 6826
Santa Barbara, CA 93160

CD-ROM directory. \UTILITY\DOS\DOSTB

DOS Tool Box is a collection of 82 small programs, and Table 38.1 compares their capabilities to those of the other utility sets in this chapter. Each program performs just one task. A couple are of particular interest. Everyday lets you divide commands into those you want to run each time the computer boots and those to run daily, weekly, and monthly, and it makes sure that the proper commands are executed at the proper time—all without a memory-resident component. One of a pair of programs saves the name of the current subdirectory while the other quickly returns to this saved subdirectory. There are also programs for hiding and unhiding files and subdirectories. Combined with its utilities to simulate hardware and network faults and lock up the computer, you can assemble a fairly good security system.

Many of these 82 utilities are unique enough that they aren't represented in Table 38.1, which lists only the most common features. Nevertheless, they're interesting and useful and worth checking out.

Solid Oak Software is also the author of the commercial program Disk Historian, which tracks your file usage so you can figure out which files on your hard disk aren't being used and move them to floppy disks or tape to free up valuable hard disk space.

Scanion Enterprises Batch File Utilities

Version. 2.2

Category. Freeware

Author. Paul Scanion

CD-ROM directory. \UTILITY\DOS\SEBFU

Scanion Enterprises' Batch File Utilities (SEBFU) is a collection of over 100 batch file utilities. Each command in SEBFU is a separate .COM file. As a result, your disk can end up cluttered with quite a number of small program files. You might consider erasing the programs you aren't likely to use. The programs included with SEBFU are as follows:

8BALL.COM. This program computes a random number that's an integer from 0 to 2.

ACOLOR.COM. This program sets the screen colors via ANSI.

BEEP.COM. This program sounds the speaker.

BIGLTR.COM. This program displays a large 10-character message on the screen. It doesn't work with a VGA system.

BOX.COM. This program draws a box on the screen.

CALCYR.COM. This program calculates the difference between two years to see if they're the same.

CBLNKOFF.COM. This program turns cursor blinking off.

CBLNKON.COM. This program turns cursor blinking on.

CDCK.COM. This program checks to see if a CD-ROM drive is attached and then sets the errorlevel accordingly. If you have a CD-ROM drive, you could use this in program-loading batch files to access the drive and ensure that you've turned it on. Some CD-ROM software locks up if the drive isn't turned on.

CDD.COM. This program moves down toward the root directory a specified number of levels.

CGABORDR.COM. This program changes the color of the border on a CGA display.

CHGC.COM. This program changes the color of the screen in a specific range, useful for printing a window in a color different from the rest of the screen.

CHGLOCK.COM. This program toggles the status of the Caps Lock, Num Lock, and Scroll Lock keys.

CHKDRVR.COM. This program checks for a number of device drivers and sets the errorlevel accordingly.

CHKSUM.COM. This program computes a checksum for a specified file and tests the results against a specified value. A batch file can use this to perform a quick-and-dirty test to see if a crucial file had been specified by a virus.

CLRIGHT.COM. This program clears the screen in an unusual fashion.

CLRKEY.COM. This program clears the type-ahead buffer. A batch file might use this before asking an important question to force the user to think twice about the answer.

CLRLEFT.COM. This program clears the screen in an unusual fashion.

COINTOSS.COM. This program randomly generates an errorlevel of 0 or 1.

CR.COM. This program pauses the batch file until the Enter key is pressed. It ignores other keystrokes, although it beeps for invalid ones. Pressing Esc will exit the program. CR.COM really functions as a specialized PAUSE command.

CURSOR.COM. This program controls cursor attributes.

DETANSI.COM. This program checks to see if ANSI.SYS was installed in the CONFIG.SYS file and then sets the errorlevel accordingly. This is a good way for the batch file to decide between plain screens and ANSI-formatted screens.

DFREE.COM. This program measures the amount of free space on the specified drive and sets either the errorlevel or an environmental variable to report its results. A batch file could run DFREE prior to running a program requiring a lot of disk space.

DFREE2.COM. Displays the amount of free space on the specified drive in a slightly different format than DFREE.COM.

DLST.COM. This program displays a list of all the files in the current subdirectory.

DLST2.COM. This program displays a list of all the files in the current subdirectory.

DRVCK.COM. This program checks to see if a drive exists and sets the errorlevel accordingly. It can perform this task without triggering the DOS "Abort, Ignore, or Fail" error message.

DRVLST.COM. This program stores a list of logical drives in an environmental variable called VAR.

DSKRDY.COM. This program checks to see if a drive is ready to receive data and then sets the errorlevel accordingly. It can perform this task without triggering the DOS "Abort, Ignore, or Fail" error message.

DSKRDY2.COM. This program checks to see if there's a disk in a floppy drive.

EL.COM. This program lists the available computer equipment, and can set the errorlevel accordingly.

ENVSIZE.COM. This program checks to see how much free environmental space is available and then sets the errorlevel accordingly. This is useful for batch files that use a number of environmental variables, as it allows them to make sure enough free space exists before running.

EXECDEC.COM. This program randomly generates an errorlevel of 1 or 0.

FLST.COM. This program is for listing ASCII files.

FNDHID.COM. This program displays hidden files and subdirectories.

FSIZE.COM. This program checks to see how large a file is and then sets the errorlevel accordingly.

FSIZE2.COM. This program checks to see how large a file is and then sets the errorlevel accordingly.

FUNKEY.COM. This program waits for the user to press a key, F1 through F10, and then sets the errorlevel accordingly. It ignores other keystrokes, although it beeps for invalid ones. Pressing Esc will exit the program. Unfortunately, FUNKEY doesn't recognize the F11 to F15 keys found on newer keyboards. Still, with more programs making use of function keys, this is an especially nice way to get input from the user.

GALF.COM. This program waits for the user to press a letter key, which is then converted to uppercase. The errorlevel is set accordingly, with A equal to 1, B equal to 2, and so on, rather than using the ASCII values. This makes it easy to get an alphabetic response from the user.

GALF2.COM. This program waits for the user to press a letter key, which is then converted to uppercase. The errorlevel is set accordingly, with A equal to 1, B equal to 2, and so on, rather than using the ASCII values. This makes it easy to get an alphabetic response from the user and allows you to specify which letters will be accepted.

GCURS.COM. This program finds the coordinates of the cursor and returns either the row or column as an errorlevel value or both as environmental variables. This is useful for finding the position of the cursor after the user has entered some information.

GDIR.COM. This program sets the environmental variable DIR equal to the current path, which is useful for writing batch files that return to their starting directory when finished.

GDRIVE.COM. This program sets the errorlevel to indicate the current drive, useful for writing batch files that return to their starting drive when finished.

GETCOLR.COM. This program returns an errorlevel to indicate the current screen color, which is useful for restoring the screen to the appropriate color after a batch file has finished.

GETMCB.COM. This program displays a list of the current memory usage.

GETNUM.COM. This program waits for the user to press a number and sets the errorlevel accordingly. It ignores other keystrokes, although it beeps for invalid ones. Pressing Esc will exit you from the program. Because it accepts only numbers, GET-NUM is an excellent way for the user to select a menu option.

GETVER.COM. This program sets the errorlevel to indicate the major version of DOS in use.

GEXT.COM. This program retrieves an extended keystroke.

GMEM.COM. This program returns the amount of free memory available as the errorlevel or in an environmental variable.

GMEM2.COM. This program is an expanded version of GMEM.COM that also checks extended and expanded memory.

GSMODE.COM. This program sets the video mode.

HDTYPE.COM. This program displays the hard disk types supported by your system.

INKEY.COM. This program accepts a single keystroke from the user and sets the errorlevel to its ASCII value (thus, a typical errorlevel-asking type program).

INKEY2.COM. This is a small utility to get input from the user and return it to the batch file via the errorlevel.

INSTR.COM. This program searches an environmental variable and places a specified portion of that environmental variable into another environmental variable.

INVERT.COM. This program swaps the foreground and background colors, useful for developing eye-catching warning screens.

KBTEST.COM. This program tests your system to see if it supports a 101-key keyboard.

KEYSTAT.COM. This program sets the errorlevel to indicate the status of the Caps Lock, Num Lock, or Scroll Lock keys.

KILL0.COM. This program erases zero-byte files.

KILL02.COM. This program erases zero-byte files.

KSTAT.COM. This program checks to see if a keystroke is waiting in the keyboard buffer.

LCASE.COM. This program converts an environmental variable into lowercase.

LEN.COM. This program returns the length of a specified environmental variable.

LIMCK.COM. This program checks to see if an LIM (expanded memory) driver is attached and sets the errorlevel accordingly.

LINE.COM. This program draws a line on the screen using the user-supplied coordinates.

LNCNT.COM. This program displays the number of lines in an ASCII file.

LOCATE.COM. This program positions the cursor at a specific location on the screen.

LOG.COM. This program maintains a system log for tracking computer usage.

LWRITE.COM. This is a text editor.

MAKE0.COM. This program creates empty files.

MATH.COM. This program adds and subtracts with environmental variables.

MID.COM. This program places a portion of one environmental variable into another environmental variable.

MOUSECK.COM. This program checks to see if a mouse is attached and sets the errorlevel accordingly.

MOVCUR.COM. This program moves the cursor by a specified amount.

MUSIC.COM. This program plays music from a batch file.

ONEDICE.COM. This program generates a random number, from 1 to 6, and returns it via the errorlevel.

PAGE.COM. This program changes the video page.

PATHCK.COM. This program checks to see if the specified subdirectory exists in the path, which is useful for checking if a program's subdirectory is in the path before trying to run that program.

PFF.COM. This sends a form feed to the printer.

PRDY.COM. This checks to see if the printer is ready and sets the errorlevel accordingly.

PRINT.COM. This sends a character string to the printer.

PRINTC.COM. This program prints the ASCII character or characters that correspond to the numbers entered on the command line.

PRNSET.COM. This program performs a hardware reset of the printer.

PSTRING.COM. This program sends a string of characters to the printer port.

PWRD.COM. This program is designed to add simple passwords to batch files.

RESP.COM. This program accepts a multicharacter response from the user and stores it under the environmental variable specified on the command line. This surpasses other programs because you can specify the environmental variable name to use. Use this approach only when a single character response isn't enough, for example, when asking for the name of the user, a program to run, or a data file.

ROWS.COM. This program sets the errorlevel to the current video rows.

SAFEFMT.COM. This program formats only floppy disks.

SAVEKEY.COM. This program places the specified key in the type-ahead buffer.

SCRLMSG.COM. This program displays a moving message at the bottom of the screen.

SDATE.COM. This program sets the date.

SETERR.COM. This program sets the errorlevel to the numeric value specified on the command line.

SOUND.COM. This sounds the speaker.

STIME.COM. This sets the time.

STRING.COM. This program repeats a string a specified number of times.

SV28.COM. This program sets EGA/VGA systems to 28-line mode.

SWIDTH.COM. This program sets the errorlevel to indicate the width of the display.

SWPCOM.COM. This swaps the COM ports.

SWPRN.COM. This swaps the printer ports.

TC.COM. This toggles the cursor.

TD.COM. This program displays the date and time at the specified location.

TRIM.COM. This program removes leading and trailing spaces from environmental variables.

TWODICE.COM. This program generates two random numbers, from 1 to 6.

UCASE.COM. This program converts environmental variables to all uppercase.

V12.COM. This program sets the number of video display lines to 12.

V35.COM. This program sets the number of video display lines to 35.

V43.COM. This program sets the number of video display lines to 43.

V50.COM. This program sets the number of video display lines to 50.

VBLNKOFF.COM. This turns video blinking off.

VBLNKON.COM. This turns video blinking on.

VMATH.COM. This program performs addition, subtraction, multiplication, and division and displays the results on the screen.

VTYPE.COM. This program sets the errorlevel to indicate the current video type.

WAIT.COM. This program pauses the batch file a specified number of seconds.

WDATE.COM. This program returns portions of the current date as an errorlevel.

WINDOW.COM. This program clears a portion of the screen.

WRITE.COM. This program displays a message on the screen.

WRITE2.COM. This program is a more powerful version of WRITE.COM that can control color and text position.

WRITEC.COM. This program displays characters on the screen and sends commands to ANSI.

WRITEF.COM. This program writes a small file to the screen, which is useful for displaying a menu or help text quickly.

WTIME.COM. This program returns portions of the current time as an errorlevel.

XMSCK.COM. This program checks to see if extended memory is installed and sets the errorlevel accordingly.

YN.COM. This program waits for the user to press either the Y or N key and sets the errorlevel accordingly. It ignores other keystrokes, although it beeps for invalid ones. Pressing Esc will exit the program. Thus, YN is perfect for questions like "Do you want to delete these files?" or "This takes three hours. Do you want to continue?"

At one time, these utilities were distributed as shareware with only a modest registration requirement, but the author failed to gather many registrations. He therefore dropped the shareware requirement and now distributes them as freeware. Although he no longer supports them as he did when they were shareware, some of these utilities would be a very useful addition to your batch file utility collection.

Steenburgh's Stuff

Version. 3.01

Price. $19.95 (basic registration), $29.95 (deluxe registration). Basic registration includes the current version on disk, and deluxe registration includes the disk plus a printed manual.

Category. Shareware

Author. Tay-Jee Software, at:
P.O. Box 835
Lexington, VA 24450-0835

CD-ROM directory. \UTILITY\DOS\SSTUFF30

Steenburgh's Stuff is a collection of 21 useful batch utilities. Each utility is a separate stand-alone program:

Batbox. This is a menu program that can handle up to ten menu items. It reads the menu from an ASCII file. Menu items can be selected via a hotkey or number, or by moving the cursor to the desired item and pressing Return. The selection is reported via the errorlevel or optionally by placing the menu text in the environment.

Box. This program draws nine different boxes on the screen, providing control over placement, size, and color. You can then use other Steenburgh's Stuff tools to place text in these boxes so they look like dialog boxes.

Chkdrv. This either returns a list of all valid drives or checks to see if the specified drive letter is valid. If it's valid, it returns the drive type.

Chkprn. This program checks on the status of a printer connected to ports LPT1 through LPT3 and returns that information via the errorlevel.

Chksys. This program checks to see if any of the following are loaded: ANSI, AP-PEND, ASSIGN, DOSKEY, EMM386, GRAFTABLE, HIMEM, KEYB, NLSFUNC, PRINT, SHARE, or Windows. It can also check on the FILES= setting.

Clk. This displays the time and date in a variety of formats.

Cursor. This changes the cursor shape back and forth between an underline and a block.

Dosver. This returns the DOS version and can compare the DOS version to a given string.

Input. This is an advanced utility for getting input from the user. It can accept either single-character or multicharacter responses. Single-character responses can be either unlimited or restricted to specific values. There's a yes/no option that accepts only a Y or N, a drive option that lists the available drives and accepts only their letters as input, and a timed input that will default to a specified value after a given interval. Multicharacter responses can be either variable or fixed-length, and the program will either store the response in the environment or execute it as a command.

Kls. This program clears the screen and sets the color without ANSI. It can also detect the video display mode and amount of video memory, and set the errorlevel accordingly.

Launcher. This presents you with a list of data files to select from and then starts the associated program with the selected data file as input.

Music. This plays songs from music data files. The files are fairly easy to build if you're musically inclined. Being musically impaired, I didn't attempt it.

Rand. This generates a random number in the range specified by the user.

Sift. This is a superset of the DOS FIND filter that gives you a number of different ways to manipulate your data files. For example, it can strip out all the numbers or convert it to all uppercase.

Skip. This utility skips the specified number of blank lines.

Sounder. This is an advanced noise-making program that lets you control the pitch, frequency, duration, and much more.

Space. This reports the free and total space on a disk, the amount of space required by a group of files, and if there's enough space to copy the files.

Waitfor. This pauses the batch file for the specified number of seconds.

Whenisit. This allows a batch file to determine the second, minute, hour, day, month, and year and use this information to make intelligent decisions. It can also run programs only once a day.

Write. This program writes text to the screen at the location you specify using the colors you specify. The text can come from the batch file or from an ASCII file.

XD. This changes to the specified drive and subdirectory, creating the subdirectory if it doesn't already exist.

Steenburgh's Stuff is a very powerful and useful collection of utilities at a very reasonable price.

Ultra ToolBox

Version. 6.2

Price. $20, $25 for all the author's utilities

Category. Shareware

Author. David Smith, at the following address:
1104 Mason Dr.
Hurst, TX 76053

CD-ROM directory. \UTILITY\DOS\ULTRA

Ultra ToolBox is a large collection of batch files and command-line utilities, so large that the author split the functions into two separate .EXE files. The division is logical enough that it's unlikely to cause any confusion.

Ultra ToolBox uses command-line parameters. For example, the command ULT /DOSVER reports the major DOS version via the errorlevel, and ULT /PRSCR performs a screen print. The available functions range from very useful, like reporting on hardware via the errorlevel, to plain strange, like computing wind chill and playing a practical joke.

Ultra ToolBox is more like a combination of DOS utilities and batch utilities. Many of its available functions, like getting a map of your hard disk, make more sense when run from the command line than from a batch file.

The shareware version displays a reminder to register and pauses briefly before executing each command. If you don't want to have to deal with a large (100K) utility, the utility has an option to write out tiny .COM files for its most common functions.

Ultra ToolBox contains 250 functions and does just about anything you might want a batch file utility to do, and many of its functions are also useful from the command line. Its features are summarized in Table 38.1, which compares many of the utility collections discussed in this chapter. The interface is clean, easy to learn, and easy to use. Additionally, its price is low: $20 for the utility and $25 if you want all the author's other nice utilities. All future upgrades are free. The power, ease of use, and low price make this one of your best shareware bargains—one I highly recommend.

Utility_Belt

Version. 1.1b

Price. $27

Category. Shareware

Author. Herne Data Systems Limited, at:
P.O. Box 250
Tiverton Ontario N0G 2T0
Canada
(519) 366-2732 for voice or fax

CD-ROM directory. \UTILITY\DOS\UTILITYB
Utility_Belt is a collection of 18 different, stand-alone batch utilities:

Beep. This beeps the speaker. You can control the sound and thus use it to play tunes.

Confirm. This lets you get input from the user when you want only a yes or no response.

Getkey. This waits for the user to press any key then returns its ASCII value as an errorlevel.

Hang. This utility locks the computer so it must be rebooted. It's useful as part of a security system.

Reboot. This utility reboots the computer. It's useful either in a security system or when a batch file needs to change the configuration.

Select. This lets the user select from a list of options. It's typically used to construct simple menus.

Sleep. This pauses the batch file for a specified period of time.

TimeCheck. This returns an errorlevel based on the time of the day or day of the week. You might use this in your AUTOEXEC.BAT to run a program on only a certain day or at only a certain time.

Vpat. This program displays text at a specified location on the screen.

Vpbh. This clears the current video page to a specified color with a "black hole" effect.

Vpbox. This draws a box on the screen. You control the size and location.

Vpcls. This utility clears a specified video page to a specified color.

Vpcopy. This copies a video page to another page, which allows you to save and later recall screens.

Vpflip. This switches instantly between video pages.

Vpset. This program sets the current video display page for text modes. Other utilities in the set can use different video pages for faster display switching.

Vpstripe. This program clears the screen and then displays stripes.

Vptnt. This clears the current video page to a specified color with an explosive special effect.

Wait. This gives the user the option of continuing or quitting, and sets the errorlevel accordingly. You might use this to have the user insert a disk or turn on a printer before continuing.

All of the Utility_Belt programs were written in assembler, so they're compact and fast. Each of the programs is self-documenting. If you run the programs without any command-line options, you'll get a summary of the syntax and available options. Its features are compared to the features of other utility sets in Table 38.1.

TABLE 38.1 Batch File Utility Set Comparison

	A Batch View	ANSI.SYS	Batchman	BatUtil	CFG	DOS	DOS Tool Box	Ultra ToolBox	Utility_Belt
Disk space									
Disk free space	■			■	■		■	■	
Total disk space	■			■	■				
Display									
Display a menu	■			■					
Tell if ANSI loaded			■	■	■		■	■	
Environment									
Determine if DOSKEY loaded					■				
Determine the country code setting					■				
Determine the current system code page table					■				
Free space	■			■	■			■	
Read from environment	■			■	■	■		■	
Read from and write to the interapplication communication area					■				
Total space	■			■	■			■	
Write to environment	■			■	■	■		■	
File information									
Determine if there is room to copy a file to a drive			■		■				
File date	■			■				■	
File time	■			■				■	
Split filename into components					■				
Getting input from user									
Compare two strings			■						
Get a keystroke	■		■	■	■			■	■
Get a number			■	■	■				
Get a string	■			■	■			■	
Input from file				■					
Menus	■			■					■
Validate numbers			■	■					
Hardware descriptions									
Alternative command processors				■	■		■	■	
Control toggles (ScrollLock, NumLock, CapsLock)	■		■	■				■	
CPU type				■	■		■		
Determine drive type					■				
Determine if drive is ready					■				
Determine if specified device driver in memory					■				
Enhanced keyboard				■					
Math coprocessor present				■	■		■	■	
Mouse present	■			■	■		■	■	
Number of COM ports				■			■		
Number of floppy drives				■			■	■	
Number of game ports				■				■	
Number of monitors				■					
Number of printer ports				■			■		

TABLE 38.1   Continued

	A Batch View	ANSI.SYS	Batchman	BatUtil	CFG	DOS	DOS Tool Box	Ultra ToolBox	Utility_Belt
Printer status				■				■	
Video mode in use	■		■	■	■		■	■	
Mathematics									
Addition				■	■			■	
Division				■	■			■	
Multiplication				■	■			■	
Subtraction				■	■			■	
Memory									
Free DOS memory	■		■	■	■			■	
Free EMS memory	■		■	■	■			■	
Free extended memory	■		■	■	■			■	
HiMem loaded	■			■	■				
Total DOS memory	■			■	■			■	
Total EMS memory	■			■	■			■	
Total extended memory	■			■	■			■	
Other									
Convert case of character string in environment					■				
Lock up computer					■		■	■	■
Looping			■						
Reboot computer			■		■		■	■	■
Set errorlevel to specified value				■	■			■	
Path									
Display path				■		■			
Interactive edit				■					
Long (greater than 122 characters) path				■		■			
Save/restore path			■						
Pausing									
Pause batch file			■	■	■	■			
Timed pause			■	■	■		■	■	■
Returning information to user									
Current drive	■			■	■		■	■	
Return date	■			■	■	■	■	■	
Return day	■			■	■		■	■	
Return month	■			■	■		■		
Return time	■			■	■	■		■	
Return year	■			■	■			■	
Sending output to user									
Beep speaker			■	■	■	■	■	■	■
Clear the screen	■		■	■		■		■	■
Clear the screen with colors	■	■	■	■	■			■	■
Control cursor shape			■		■				
Control video page					■				■
Determine number of columns being displayed			■		■				
Determine number of rows being displayed			■		■				

TABLE 38.1   Continued

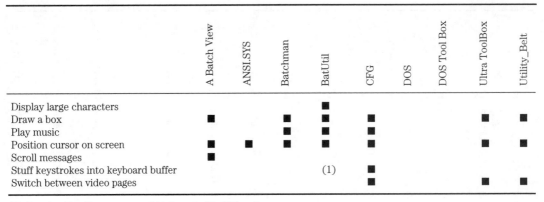

	A Batch View	ANSI.SYS	Batchman	BatUtil	CFG	DOS	DOS Tool Box	Ultra ToolBox	Utility_Belt
Display large characters				■					
Draw a box	■		■	■	■			■	■
Play music			■	■	■				
Position cursor on screen	■	■	■	■	■			■	■
Scroll messages	■								
Stuff keystrokes into keyboard buffer				(1)	■				
Switch between video pages					■			■	■

(1) Requires StacKey program, which is part of BatUtil package

XSet

Version. 4.02

Price. 600 BEF (About $18 U.S.)

Category. Shareware

Author. Marc Stern, at the following address:
Au. de Louisiana Basilique 376 bte 19
1080 Bruxelles
Belgium

CD-ROM directory. \UTILITY\DOS\XSET40

XSET is an extremely powerful program for manipulating DOS environmental variables. In the process, it adds a great deal of power and flexibility to your batch files. XSET has seven major functions:

- Capturing the output of other programs and placing it in the environment. In order for this to work, the program must report its results without bypassing DOS.

- Manipulation of strings coming from the command line or other programs.

- Mathematical calculations.

- Creating environmental variables larger than the DOS limit of 127 characters. This allows you to create a very long path. (MS-DOS 6 allows the same thing as long as the SET command is placed in the CONFIG.SYS file.)

- Accessing system information, such as the date, and placing it into the environment.

- Clearing the current environment and restoring a saved environment.

- Providing access to a high-level user interface.

All together, XSET provides more than 60 commands to perform these functions. There are four different ways to use XSET. You can use it like you would the DOS SET command. For example:

```
XSET Name="Ronny"
```

You'd normally use this to store information from an XSET keyword in a variable, but you can also use it to get input from the user:

```
XSET YourName
```

You can use DOS redirection to capture the results of another program, like this:

```
DIR C:\COMMAND.COM | XSET command
```

And finally, you can use it to store the results of an XSET command into a variable. For example:

```
XSET variable TIME
```

Of course, the method you use depends on what you're asking XSET to do. The second and fourth methods are the ones you'll use a lot. The second method basically allows you to prompt users for information and then place that information into the environment. While the users are entering their response, they can move around the response and edit it, making it easier to correct mistakes than with some similar utilities. You can also place a time limit and go to a default response if the user fails to respond. You want to precede this command with a prompt by using the /PROMPT option. You can also control the color of the prompt and draw a box around it. Finally, you can hide the characters while they're being entered in case you're accepting a password.

There's also a keyword to get a single keystroke from the user and place it in the environment, much like the errorlevel askers from Chapter 34, only you have the powerful string manipulation abilities of XSET to alter this string. You can use the command to limit the input to specified characters. Note that having the keystroke in the environment rather than in the errorlevel makes testing it much easier.

The fourth method really shows the power of XSET. Here, you use keywords to get information from the computer and place it in the environment. The keywords are as follows:

Date and time commands. There are commands to get the date in several formats—the day, month, year, day of the week, time, hour, minute, and second—and to return the number of days between two dates.

Disk and file commands. There are commands to return the full path to a file, the drive of a filename, the drive and directory of a filename, the extension of a filename, the name of a file without the extension, the name and extension of a file without the path, the "true name" of a file after resolving all SUBST and similar commands, the size of a file, the date of a file, the time of a file, the current subdirectory of a drive, the volume label of a drive, the free bytes on a drive, the density (360K, 720K, etc.) of a diskette, and the status (readable, removable, not ready, etc.) of a drive.

Other commands. There are commands to return the minimum and maximum in a series of numbers, the CPU type, a random number, and the errorlevel, copy environmental variables longer than 127 characters (DOS can't do this), clear the environment of all variables, show the environment (including environmental variables longer than 127 characters), display a single variable in a format suitable for redirection, load an environment from disk, and display the size of the environment.

The only drawback to using XSET is that it's picky about the order in which switches are entered. For example, the command XSET /PROMPT "Enter Your Name" UserName works, but the command XSET UserName /PROMPT "Enter Your Name" doesn't. The only difference is the second has the environmental variable name before the switch, while the first has it after. The trick is to experiment on the command line before writing your batch file and always try several arrangements of the parameters before assuming the command doesn't work.

Other than the minor problem of switch arrangement, XSET is a very powerful program for manipulating the environment and will be a welcome enhancement to your batch file toolkit. While you might think that registering a program from Belgium is difficult, the author includes a disk file explaining the process, so if you like XSET don't let his location stop you from registering!

39

Other DOS Batch File Utilities

This chapter discusses batch file utilities that didn't fit into any other category.

CapStat

Version. 1.1

Price. $19

Category. Shareware

Author. Tessler's Nifty Tools, at:
P.O. Box 1791
San Ramon, CA 94583

CD-ROM directory. \UTILITY\DOS\TNT\CAPSTAT

CapStat sets the errorlevel to indicate if local printing is being captured by Netware to go to a network printer. This can be useful to configure programs locally.

ControlP

Version. 1.2

Price. $19

Category. Crippleware

Author. Tessler's Nifty Tools, at the same address as the previous utility.

CD-ROM directory. \UTILITY\DOS\TNT\CONTROLP

The only way to print with batch files is to pipe ECHO commands or the output of specific programs to the printer. ControlP improves on that by allowing a batch file to toggle screen printing on and off. While screen printing is on, everything printed to the screen also goes to the printer.

CronTab

Version. 2.21

Price. Free, but a charity donation is requested. Commercial users must pay for the program.

Category. Copyrighted/shareware

Author. Thomas Harold, at the following address:
P.O. Box 368
Camp Hill, PA 17001

CD-ROM directory. \UTILITY\DOS\CRONTAB

CronTab is designed to be executed by your AUTOEXEC.BAT file. It then runs programs on the schedule you've selected. CRONTAB.DAT contains a list of programs to run and a schedule to run them by. For example, you might run some programs every time you boot, other programs once a day, and still other programs twice a week. You have the option of running the programs only at the specified time or "catching up" the next time you boot if you skipped using the computer on a day a program would have otherwise run.

CronTab is easy to configure; you simply use its brief scripting language to create CRONTAB.DAT. It's also very easy to use. There's a version of OS/2 as well.

DaysLeft

Version. 1.1

Price. $5

Category. Shareware

Author. Bob Lafleur, at the following address:
45 Ionia St.
Springfield, MA 01109

CD-ROM directory. \UTILITY\DOS\DAYSLEFT

DaysLeft displays the number of days left until a specified date. With redirection, you can create a temporary batch file that places this information in the environment.

Do-For

Version. 2.4

Price. Free

Category. Copyright

Author. Glenn Snow

CD-ROM directory. \UTILITY\DOS\DO-FOR24
Do-For is an advanced replacement for the batch FOR command. Its syntax is:

```
DO-FOR [@date] [flags] filemask command
```

You can modify the normal FOR filemask with flags to include or exclude subdirectories and files with or without specified attributes (archive, system, read-only, or hidden) as well as files before or after a given date. This is a very imaginative program that's more useful the more you use it.

Do-Once

Version. 2.3

Price. Free

Category. Copyright

Author. Glenn Snow

CD-ROM directory. \UTILITY\DOS\DO-ONC23
Do-Once is designed to be executed from your AUTOEXEC.BAT file (although it will work in any batch file) and control how other programs or batch files are executed. You can run, for example, an incremental backup the first time you boot every day, a full backup every Friday, and your hard disk testing program the first time you boot each month. You can use it to schedule as many different programs as you like.

DVRun

Version. 1.1

Price. $19

Category. Crippleware

Author. Tessler's Nifty Tools, at:
P.O. Box 1791
San Ramon, CA 94583

CD-ROM directory. \UTILITY\DOS\TNT\DVRUN
Some batch files need to run differently when DeskView is running. DVRun checks and sets the errorlevel accordingly.

Envi_Man

Version. 1.10

Price. $20

Category. Shareware

Author. MicroMetric, at:
98 Dade Ave.
Sarasota, FL 34232-1609

CD-ROM directory. \UTILITY\DOS\ENVI-MAN
Envi_Man is primarily a command-line utility for displaying the contents of the environment and the space required for each entry, with options to increase the amount of space. It's also useful in batch files since it has an option to set the errorlevel to the amount of free environmental space. Batch files that require a lot of space can use this to check first to make sure they have enough space to run.

Everyday

Price. Free

Category. Copyrighted

Author. David Smith, at the following address:
1104 Mason Dr.
Hurst, TX 76053

CD-ROM directory. \UTILITY\DOS\EVERYDAY
Everyday is designed to be placed in your AUTOEXEC.BAT file to run one or more programs once a day when you first boot. It gives you the option of running or not running each program.

FDate

Version. 8.4b

Price. Free

Category. Copyrighted

Author. Stephen Ferg

CD-ROM directory. \UTILITY\DOS\FDATE84B

FDate is a very powerful program for working with dates in a batch file. It can perform all sorts of date arithmetic, such as figuring out the number of days until Christmas and finding all the holidays in any year. You can display the results or store them in the environment. FDate also has functions to get both a single keystroke and multiple keystrokes from the user.

The program comes with two sample batch files; one displays all the holidays for the year of your choice and the other displays the federal holidays for the year of your choice. It also comes with one of the most comprehensive manuals I've seen for a batch file utility. If you need to manipulate dates in your batch file, FDate is the most powerful utility you'll find.

FreeFile

Version. 1.0

Price. Free

Category. Copyrighted

Author. Mark Treadwell, at:
4 Mumford Ave., #1
Newport, RI 02840-1719

CD-ROM directory. \UTILITY\DOS\FREEFILE

FreeFile examines the system file table (SFT) that DOS uses to track the state of open files. It displays the location of each SFT block, the file entries it contains, and the status of those entries. It closes file handles orphaned by resident programs, freeing the SFT entry. It then searches memory to locate the program that originally orphaned the SFT entry and updates its job file table for the changes to the SFT. Additional options include displaying previously open files, detailed information about each entry, and various display options.

Get

Version. 2.61

Price. $15

Category. Shareware

Author. Bob Stephan, at the following address:

Moby Disk
1021 San Carlos Rd.
Pebble Beach, CA 93953

CD-ROM directory. \UTILITY\DOS\GET261

Get is designed primarily to get requested information regarding the computer and its environment, and place the results in either the environment or the error-level. For example, GET D returns the major DOS version and GET E returns the amount of free environmental space. Get knows when it's running in an OS/2 DOS session and, since some of its commands must work differently under an OS/2 DOS session, it responds accordingly. Get divides its functions into four broad categories:

Disk and file commands. There are commands to check the amount of free space on the disk, total amount of space on the disk, volume label, size of a file, and current subdirectory.

Memory and system commands. There are commands to get and change the BREAK setting, get the DOS version, and check for a printer, the amount of free conventional and environmental memory, a math coprocessor, 4DOS and Windows.

Screen I/O. There are commands to clear the screen with control over the colors, set the video mode, control video borders, and echo text with or without a Return at the end of the line.

String handling. There are commands to get a single character, yes/no response, and character string from the user, display a scrolling 4,000-character prompt, convert a string to lower- or uppercase, check to see if a keystroke is pending in the keyboard buffer, stuff keystrokes into the keyboard buffer, and toggle the NumLock, CapsLock, and ScrollLock keys. In fact, Get is as good or better than the user-querying programs in Chapter 34 that do nothing else.

There are a number of switches to control how Get operates. The documentation is dense, with a lot of information packed into a few words. GET.EXE is a small program, 7,375 bytes for the unregistered version, but it packs a lot of power into that small space.

Go

Version. 2.30A

Price. $19

Category. Shareware

Author. Pinnacle Software, at:
P.O. Box 714, Airport Rd.
Swanton, VT 05488

CD-ROM directory. \UTILITY\DOS\GO

A common reason for writing batch files is to perform software installation, especially less expensive and shareware packages where writing a custom installation program is overkill. Go eliminates the need to do this. It reads all the compressed files on the floppy disk and presents them in a menu, so users can select which one to install. Then it prompts for a subdirectory to install to and handles everything else automatically. It can also display information before installation and start the program after installation.

As is, Go displays an advertisement for Pinnacle Software and uses only zipped files. When you register, the company removes the advertising, modifies the program to display any text you like, and gives you the option of using some other compression program, such as the royalty-free LHA. While not strictly a batch file utility, Go is a good way to avoid having to write an installation batch file.

Go includes a program called Seterr that you can use to set the errorlevel to any value. Its syntax is:

```
SETERR n
```

where n is a number from 0 to 255 to set the errorlevel to. This can be useful for debugging batch files that test the errorlevel.

HoldOn

Version. 2.14

Price. $6

Category. Shareware

Author. Samuel Kaplin, at the following address:
3520 W. 32nd St., #214
Minneapolis, MN 55416

CD-ROM directory. \UTILITY\DOS\HOLDN214

HoldOn is a small batch file utility that pauses the batch file for a specified period of time. Time can be specified in milliseconds, eighteenths of a second, seconds, minutes, or hours. It's very useful when you need to pause a batch file for a period of time. You might, for example, have your AUTOEXEC.BAT file pause for 30 seconds to give your network time to respond.

Interval

Version. 1.97

Price. $10

Category. Shareware

Author. Samuel Kaplin, at the previous address.

CD-ROM directory. \UTILITY\DOS\INTUL197
Interval is designed to be executed from your AUTOEXEC.BAT file (although it will work in any batch file) and control how other programs or batch files are executed. Intervals are set up in days, so you can set up a backup program to run every seven days, for example. Interval can control as many different programs as you like and, for each program it controls, it keeps a log of each time the program is run.

KBStuff

Version. Prerelease version 0

Price. $10

Category. Shareware

Author. David MacLean, at:
408 Cape Mudge Rd.
Quathiaski B.C. V0P 1N0
Canada

CD-ROM directory. \UTILITY\DOS\KBSTUFF
KBStuff is designed to stuff keystrokes into the keyboard buffer. You begin by creating a script file that contains the name of the program to run, the subdirectory to run it from, and the keystrokes to stuff into the buffer. The first time KBStuff runs this script, it compiles it into a data file it can load faster. Then afterwards it runs it from the compiled version. The scripting language is simple and easy to learn, but fairly effective. You can easily automate routine activities with your batch files and KBStuff.

KeyToggle

Version. 1.27

Price. $6

Category. Shareware

Author. Samuel Kaplin, at:
3520 W. 32nd St., #214
Minneapolis, MN 55416

CD-ROM directory. \UTILITY\DOS\KEYTG127

KeyToggle is a program for setting the status of your ScrollLock, CapsLock, NumLock, and Insert keys. You'd typically run it once from your AUTOEXEC.BAT file.

MakeName

Version. 1.01A

Price. $6

Category. Shareware

Author. Pinnacle Software, at:
P.O. Box 714, Airport Rd.
Swanton, VT 05488

CD-ROM directory. \UTILITY\DOS\MAKENAME

MakeName generates a filename based on the date and time. It uses a slick encoding scheme (explained in the manual) to include both the date and time in an eight-character filename. This encoding scheme means you can easily determine when the filename was created, plus it allows a unique name to be generated every two seconds.

MakeName requires one parameter: the name of an environmental variable to use. Rather than searching through memory to find the master copy of the environment, MakeName creates a brief batch file that assigns the name to the environmental variable. The batch file that calls MakeName then calls this batch file to place the name into the environment.

MakeName has two uses. You can use it to create a report name, for example, to create a daily accounting report while keeping prior reports for historical purposes. The ability of MakeName to supply date-based unique names makes that easy. You can also use MakeName to generate unique temporary processing files when a batch file needs to create a working file.

Multi-Print

Version. 3.8

Price. $39

Category. Shareware

Author. Rob W. Smetana, at:
Pro-Formance
132 Alpine Terrace
San Francisco, CA 94117

CD-ROM directory. \UTILITY\DOS\MP38

You're probably going to want to register and use several of the shareware programs on the CD-ROM that comes with this book. For each of these, you'll likely want to print the manual for easier reference, but that can take up a lot of paper. Multi-Print reduces the paper requirements by printing ASCII files in smaller fonts on Epson, DeskJet, and LaserJet printers. While the printing is smaller, it's still very readable. If you print on both sides of the paper, you can get between two and nine pages worth of information on a single sheet of paper.

Unlike similar programs, Multi-Print is completely menu-driven and very easy to use. I was able to use it immediately without even looking at the manual.

OneADay

Version. 1.10

Price. $15

Category. Shareware

Author. Gray Software Development, at:
2704 Elva Dr.
Kokomo, IN 46902

CD-ROM directory. \UTILITY\DOS\1ADAY11

There are some jobs you want to perform only occasionally, like a full backup or optimizing your hard disk. One way is to try to remember to do them yourself. A better way is to put the commands in your AUTOEXEC.BAT file (or another batch file you frequently run) and use OneADay to run the programs at the appropriate time. It can run a program once a day, once a week, once a month, on certain days, or every time it runs. You can configure it to present you with options and let you override them. In short, it does an excellent job of controlling when your programs execute.

Path Master

Version. 3.5

Price. $25

Category. Shareware

Author. David Smith, at the following address:
1104 Mason Dr.
Hurst, TX 76053

CD-ROM directory. \UTILITY\DOS\PM36

Some of the more common reasons for writing batch files is to switch between different paths and to add or delete a subdirectory from your path. As you add more and more programs to your hard drive, it becomes very difficult to live with the 122 characters DOS gives you for a path. A DOS command line can be 127 characters, but the PATH= part of the statement takes five of them, leaving 122 for the path itself. (MS-DOS 6.*x* lets you have a longer path if you create it in your CONFIG.SYS file, but you can't alter it with a batch file.)

Path Master solves this problem. It makes it easy to switch between multiple paths and to modify your existing path. It also includes tools to find files anywhere along your path and save your current environment to a batch file so it can easily be recreated. If you need to use more than one path, Path Master is the easiest method you'll find for doing so.

Path_Man

Version. 1.15

Price. $15

Category. Shareware

Author. MicroMetric, at:
98 Dade Ave.
Sarasota, FL 34232-1609

CD-ROM directory. \UTILITY\DOS\PATH-MAN

Path_Man searches the path to see if it finds the specified file. The results are reported via the errorlevel to allow a batch file to make an intelligent decision about trying to run a program or load a data file. Optionally, it can display the location of the file. Wildcards are supported.

QTOD

Version. 1.21

Price. Free, but a charity donation is requested. Commercial users must pay for the program.

Category. Copyrighted/shareware

Author. Thomas Harold, at the following address:
P.O. Box 368
Camp Hill, PA 17001

CD-ROM directory. \UTILITY\DOS\QTOD121

QTOD displays the date and time on the command line in a format suitable for redirecting to another file, such as a backup log or computer usage log. This nifty installation program gives you a great deal of flexibility over how the date and time are displayed. There's also an OS/2 version.

Ram-Man

Version. 2.5

Price. $20

Category. Shareware

Author. Rob W. Smetana, at:
Pro-Formance
132 Alpine Terrace
San Francisco, CA 94117

CD-ROM directory. \UTILITY\DOS\RAMMAN25

As you read about all the great batch file utilities in this book, you're naturally going to want to experiment with some of them. One difficulty you might have is having to look at documentation while working with a utility. You could print the manuals, but that can take up a lot of paper, especially if you aren't sure you want to keep using the program.

Ram-Man is a good solution. It's a 30K memory-resident program that you pop up to look at an ASCII file. You can read the manual till you find something you want to try and then quickly go to DOS to work with the program. When you later go back to Ram-Man, it remembers where you were in the document. Ram-Man keeps the document on disk and reads only one screen of it into memory at a time, so its memory requirements are fairly minor.

With the unregistered version, you must enter a long, randomly generated number to load the program into memory. This is the author's encouragement for you to register the program.

Scan

Price. $5.00

Category. Shareware

Author. EZ Software, at:
1222 144th St., SE
Mill Creek, WA 98012

CD-ROM directory. \UTILITY\DOS\SCAN

The CD-ROM that comes with this book has a lot of ASCII manuals. If you want to look at them online without printing them, you need an ASCII file viewer. Scan is just such a viewer, but it does much more. Scan allows you to move around the disk, listing all the files in each subdirectory. Then you can pick the ones you want to view. Scan also allows you to delete files, but, of course, this won't work on the CD-ROM. Given its low price and excellent features, Scan is a very good file viewer.

Please note that Scan won't run from the CD-ROM because it needs to create temporary files. Before running Scan, you must install it to your hard disk.

See

Version. 3.0

Price. Free

Category. Copyrighted

Author. Pinnacle Software, at:
P.O. Box 714, Airport Rd.
Swanton, VT 05488

CD-ROM directory. \UTILITY\DOS\SEE

See lets you quickly view and print ASCII files. This makes it handy to quickly view your batch files. For example, the command:

```
SEE *.BAT
```

would present a menu of all the batch files in the current subdirectory and let you pick one to view. See isn't an editor so you can't change any of the files you view. Still, it's a nice way to review your batch files (and other ASCII files) when you need to take a quick look at something or find a particular file.

See is free, but includes advertisement for other products from Pinnacle Software. For a $12 fee, you can obtain the executive version without the advertising. The See package includes GetKey, a nice errorlevel asker. It too is free and is discussed in Chapter 34.

SetEr

Version. 1.48

Price. $6

Category. Shareware

Author. Samuel Kaplin, at the following address:
3520 W. 32nd St., #214
Minneapolis, MN 55416

CD-ROM directory. \UTILITY\DOS\SETER148

SetEr sets the DOS errorlevel to the value specified on the command line. This is useful for testing batch files that depend on the errorlevel.

Sound Effects

Version. 6.1

Price. $15

Category. Shareware

Author. David Smith, at:
1104 Mason Dr.
Hurst, TX 76053

CD-ROM directory. \UTILITY\DOS\SFX61
Sound Effects is a collection of sound effects that can be played from your batch files. Each sound is in a separate .EXE file, and the program allows you to control several aspects of how the sounds are played. This is a good way to draw attention to your batch files.

StacKey

Version. 3.0

Price. $49.00 (Includes BatUtil)

Category. Shareware

Author. CTRLALT Associates

Register with. Advanced Support Group, at:
11900 Grant Place
Des Peres, MO 63131
(800) 788-0787 or (314) 965-5630
(314) 966-1833 fax

CD-ROM directory. \UTILITY\DOS\BATUTIL\STACKEY
You just can't do some things with batch files. For example, you can't load a file into Lotus 1-2-3; even if you somehow got the keystrokes into the buffer using DOS, Lotus would flush the buffer while loading. StacKey is a powerful tool for putting keystrokes into the keyboard buffer while working around all sorts of problems (like Lotus). StacKey itself is a 2K memory-resident program. To run StacKey in its simplest form, issue a command like:

```
STACKEY "DIR"CR
```

which tells StacKey to issue a DIR command and then press Return. For this example, you might tell StacKey to issue the commands "/FRMYFILE"CR to load a file.

StacKey has commands to delay issuing the command until after Lotus flushes the buffer. You can actually perform some fairly complex tasks using StacKey. Practically anything you can do typing from the keyboard you can do with StacKey.

StacKey has keywords and switches that allow it to perform tasks beyond managing the type-ahead buffer. It can:

- Delay a batch file until a specific time is reached or for a specified period of time. Of course, BatUtil (included with StacKey) does this as well.
- Switch monitors and ports.
- Change display modes.
- Modify the cursor. BatUtil also performs this.
- Beep the speaker. BatUtil also performs this.
- Print a screen dump.
- Reboot the computer. BatUtil can perform this as well.
- Immediately halt a batch file. If necessary, it can turn BREAK on before issuing a Ctrl–Break command.
- Get a single keystroke from the user—a task BatUtil performs exceptionally well.
- Wait for the user to press Enter, Y, or N.

After reading the StacKey manual, I felt that it was written by the same person who wrote the BatUtil manual (see Chapter 38). While complete, the StacKey manual is difficult to read and hard to follow.

If you need a program to manage the type-ahead buffer or to place keystrokes in the type-ahead buffer for a program to read, StacKey is an excellent choice.

Summit

Price. Free

Category. Copyrighted

Author. Summit Memory Systems

CD-ROM directory. \UTILITY\DOS\SUMMIT

Summit is a collection of the following seven utilities, most of which are useful to batch file authors:

Checksum. This processes a disk and computes a checksum. If anything on the disk changes, the checksum changes. It's useful for verification after copying.

Dir2Bat. This processes a group of files matching a given file specification and within a given date range, and constructs a batch file of those matching both criteria. Text can be specified to go before and/or after each filename.

FileGen. This program creates a file of a specified size and pattern. The resulting file is useful for certain types of testing, such as comparing backup methods.

IsLater. This program tests two files to see if one was created after the other, and sets the errorlevel accordingly. This can be very useful for a batch file that's designed to update specific files.

IsRoom. This program tests a given disk to see if there's room to copy a specified file, and then sets the errorlevel accordingly. It's very useful for installation programs.

TimeStam. This program echoes the date and time in a format that's perfect for piping.

YesNo. This program displays the prompt passed to it on the command line, waits for the user to press Y or N, and sets the errorlevel to 0 for N and 1 for Y. Case is ignored as are all other keystrokes.

Video FX

Version. 2.0

Price. $20

Category. Shareware

Author. David Smith, at the following address:
1104 Mason Dr.
Hurst, TX 76053

CD-ROM directory. \UTILITY\DOS\VID-FX2
   Video FX is a program for producing video special effects in your batch files. The effects are selected with a single program command-line parameter. Most of the effects are graphical screen clearings, but it can also change video modes and display large messages on the screen.

40

Alternative DOS Batch Languages

The programs in this chapter either completely replace the DOS batch language with their own languages or greatly enhance it. Although I evaluate each program individually, I'm not going to try and draw conclusions regarding which of these programs is "best." I'm involved with one of the companies enough that my judgments would probably be biased. One of the programs discussed in this chapter is called Builder, a batch file compiler that also adds a lot of new commands to the language. It was developed and is marketed by a company called hyperkinetix. One of the programmers for hyperkinetix, Doug Amaral, wrote the BatScreen screen compiler and Batcmd utility set I mention in this book and cover extensively in my *MS-DOS Batch File Programming*. Another hyperkinetix programmer, William Richardson (no relation), wrote the Bat Editor program I describe in this book and a program used to navigate the CD-ROM that comes with this book.

In addition, hyperkinetix has a "lite" version of Builder called Builder Lite. I wrote a book about this called, naturally, *Builder Lite*, that includes a full version of the Builder Lite program. While not as powerful as Builder, Builder Lite has enough features that many people use it as their primary batch utility.

Given all these connections between hyperkinetix and myself, I feel it would be inappropriate for me to try and judge their and their competitors' products. Therefore, I'll provide the facts about each product as well as I can, but it's up to you to draw your own conclusions. Table 40.1 compares the features of all the batch file languages discussed in this chapter.

Bat2Exec

Price. Free

Category. Copyrighted

TABLE 40.1 Batch File Language Comparison

	Bat2Exec	Builder	Builder Lite	PB Plus+	Personal REXX	PowerBatch
Altering program flow						
Define a label in programs	■	■	■	■	■	■
Go to command in programs	■	■	■	■	■	■
If/Then/Else		■	■		■	
Support external subroutines		■	■		■	
Support internal subroutines		■	■		■	
Getting information from user						
Get a character string from the user		■	■	■		■
Get a character string from the user with timeout				■		■
Get a yes/no keystroke from the user		■	■	■		■
Get a yes/no keystroke from the user with timeout				■		■
Get any keystroke from the user		■	■	■	■	■
Get any keystroke from the user with timeout				■		■
Logical operations						
Compare two values to see if they are equal	■	■	■	■	■	■
Compare two numbers to see if one is larger/ smaller than the other		■	■	■	■	■
Mathematical manipulations						
Generate a random number		■	■	■	■	■
Integer addition		■	■	■	■	■
Integer division		■	■	■	■	■
Integer multiplication		■	■	■	■	■
Integer subtraction		■	■	■	■	■
Real addition				■	■	■
Real division				■	■	■
Real multiplication				■	■	■
Real subtraction				■	■	■
Other						
Beep the speaker	■	■	■	■	■	■
Change environmental variable		■	■	■	■	■
Change path		■	■	■	■	■
Change subdirectories		■	■	■	■	■
Change prompt		■	■	■	■	■
Flush the keyboard buffer				■	■	■
Pause program for specified time		■	■	■	■	■
Pause program until a key is pressed	■	■	■		■	
Reboot the computer		■	■	■		■
Set errorlevel when exiting		■	■	■		■
Support variable arrays				■	■	
Swap program out of active memory to run another program		■	■	■	■	
Turn break on/off	■			■	■	■
Providing system information						
Check for a valid drive		■	■	■		■
Does a file exist	■	■	■	■	■	■
Does a subdirectory exist	■	■	■	■	■	■
Is a subdirectory in the path		■	■	■	■	■
Retrieve current time		■	■	■	■	■

TABLE 40.1 Continued

	Bat2Exec	Builder	Builder Lite	PB Plus+	Personal REXX	PowerBatch
Retrieve file size		■	■	■	■	■
Retrieve current date		■	■	■	■	■
Retrieve current drive		■	■	■		■
Retrieve current subdirectory		■	■	■		■
Retrieve environmental string	■	■	■	■	■	■
Retrieve total disk space		■	■	■		■
Retrieve volume label		■	■	■		■
Reading and writing text						
Close a file		■		■	■	
Create a new ASCII file		■		■	■	
Read an ASCII file		■		■	■	
Write to an ASCII file		■		■	■	
Screen writing						
Automatically center text on screen		■	■	■		■
Cause text written to screen to blink		■	■	■		■
Change screen background color		■	■	■		■
Change screen foreground color		■	■	■		■
Change the screen to 43 lines in text mode		■	■	■		■
Change the shape of the cursor		■	■	■	■	■
Clear a single line on the screen		■	■	■		■
Clear the contents of a box on the screen		■	■	■	■	■
Clear the screen	■	■	■	■	■	■
Create a "virtual" screen so screen writing limited to specified area				■		■
Draw a box on the screen		■	■	■	■	■
Position cursor on the screen		■	■	■	■	■
Print the screen				■		■
Read current screen colors		■	■	■		■
Save/restore screen contents		■	■	■		■
String manipulation						
Concatenate (combine) two strings		■	■	■	■	■
Convert a string to all lowercase		■	■	■	■	■
Convert a string to all uppercase		■	■	■	■	■
Extract a portion of a string		■	■	■	■	■
Find the length of a string		■	■	■	■	■

Author. Doug Boling

PC Magazine introduced their Bat2Exec batch file compiler in the August 1990 issue (volume 9, number 14) in the Utilities column. Bat2Exec is strictly a batch file compiler. It will compile existing DOS batch files, but it adds no new features to the language. Thus, you get additional speed and security without the overhead of learning new commands and working with a new environment. You can completely write and debug your batch files in DOS and then compile them. Like all *PC Magazine* programs, this is available from their area on CompuServe. See any issue of *PC Magazine* for details.

Compiling a batch file

To compile a batch file, enter:

```
BAT2EXEC file
```

at the DOS prompt. You must include the .BAT extension even though Bat2Exec compiles only .BAT files. Once you've compiled a batch file, the resulting .COM file generally operates just like the original batch file, only faster. Make sure to keep the original batch file in case you need to modify it.

The increase in speed is due to the difference in the way DOS handles .COM programs and batch files. As mentioned before, DOS loads an entire .COM program into memory and generally doesn't need to access the disk again to execute the program. DOS, however, reads a batch file from the disk one line at a time, thus reading the disk many times for a large batch file. Because the disk is generally the slowest component in a system, batch files run much more slowly.

You shouldn't compile any batch files that loads a memory-resident program. When a program loads a memory-resident program, DOS can't reclaim the memory used by the original program (the compiled batch file), resulting in the memory-resident program taking up much more room. In addition, the AUTOEXEC.BAT file should never be compiled, as DOS will run it only as a batch file. Finally, pressing Ctrl–Break while running a batch file displays a DOS "Terminate batch job? (Y/N)" message, while pressing Ctrl–Break during a compiled program run simply terminates the program.

Because Bat2Exec doesn't add any new features to DOS, the best candidates for compilation are batch files that take a long time to run. Bat2Exec-compiled batch files don't respond properly to the errorlevel if it's set prior to running the compiled program because DOS resets the errorlevel for each program it runs. Bat2Exec also resets the errorlevel to 0 when it exits or calls an external batch file.

Problems

Early versions of the program were buggy. One didn't work unless the last line of the file was an end-of-file marker, and other versions didn't handle the FOR command properly. Still another version ignored the CLS command. These problems seem to have all been resolved. If you tried an early version and gave up, you might want to take another look.

Builder

Version. 2.04

Price. $49.95 using the coupon in the back of this book (normally $149)

Category. Commercial

Author. Hyperkinetix Incorporated, at the following address:
18001 Irvine Boulevard, Suite H
Tustin, CA 92680
(714) 573-2260

Calling Builder a batch file compiler is like calling a 486/66 computer running Word for Windows 6 a fancy typewriter. Builder can take an existing batch file and compile it into a .EXE file, but this hardly begins to describe its functions. Builder includes over 200 extensions to the batch language, can write custom multidisk installation programs including file compression, and can produce very fancy menus.

Operation

Builder has two modes of operation: interactive and batch. In the interactive mode, Builder combines the compiler with a simple editor. If you load an existing batch file, Builder does a good job of converting it into a Builder file, automatically making the necessary changes.

When you finish writing the code, enter press F9, or press Alt-C and then choose Compile. If Builder finds errors while trying to compile the program, it will open a smaller window below the main window. In that window, it will give the line number for each line with an error and a brief error message. Often, the error message is simply "syntax error." If too many errors exist to fit on the screen, you can use the menu to switch to that window and scroll around. Once you've corrected all the errors, Builder will compile, link, and write the disk file automatically when you press F9.

While compiled batch files run faster than regular batch files, you'll want to use Builder mainly because it offers a wealth of enhancements. It can do almost anything that any other program listed in this book can do. To compile a batch file in batch mode, enter:

```
BLD file
```

on the command line. If the specified file is a batch file, Builder will automatically convert it into a Builder file and then try to compile it. If it's successful, it will create the program file automatically. If not, it will create a file containing all the error messages, print a brief error message to the screen, and then exit to DOS.

Command extensions

Builder adds over two hundred extensions to the batch language. While that's too many to explain in detail, the major enhancements are as follows, by category:

Control and logic commands. Builder adds true subroutines, case statements, an ELSE command, REPEAT and WHILE commands for looping, and an EXIT command.

Date and time operations. Builder can return the day of the week, system date and time, and time and date of a file.

Disk operations. Builder can tell if a subdirectory exists, the amount of total and free space on a disk, and if a disk is ready to be written to. It also has commands that duplicate the DOS commands to change subdirectories, create a subdirectory, list the current subdirectory, find the drive letter, and rename a subdirectory. Since these are Builder commands, you can store the results to variables that Builder can then manipulate.

File operations. Builder can create compressed files that span multiple disks for installation program, so it has commands to add files to, extract files from, and delete files in compressed files. There are commands for reading from and writing to an ASCII file, controlling the position within an ASCII file, and closing and saving an ASCII file. It has commands to pick a file from a list of available files, return the size of a file, list the extension of a file, and find out if a specified file exists on the DOS path. It also duplicates the DOS commands to copy, delete, change the attributes of, and move a file. Since these are Builder commands, you can store the results to variables that Builder can then manipulate.

Help. All Builder batch files can have context-sensitive help that pops up when you press F1.

Keyboard handling. Builder has commands to control the status of all the toggle keys, flush the keyboard, get information from the user, and stuff keystrokes into the keyboard buffer.

Logical operators. Builder supports all the expected logical operators, such as greater than and less than or equal to. It also supports AND, NOT, and OR and can test to see if one string is contained inside another string.

Mathematics. Builder supports integer addition, subtraction, multiplication, and division.

Menu operations. Builder has three types of menus: drop-down, moving lightbar (like Lotus), and pop-up. In addition to controlling the items in these menus, Builder allows you to control almost every aspect of their appearance. All three menus support a mouse, and menus can be nested in Builder. (Builder Lite, which is discussed later, doesn't support nested menus.)

Other. Builder can beep the speaker, set the errorlevel, encrypt and decrypt the contents of its program files (useful when passwords are stored there), reboot the computer, run any DOS command or program, suspend operation for a specified time, and suspend operation until a specified time is reached.

Screen handling.   Builder has commands to draw a box, erase all or a portion of the screen, set the screen colors, position the cursor, fill an area of the screen with characters or colors, save and restore the contents of the screen, and display text. It has commands to find out what type of adapter is being used, the maximum number of rows and columns DOS will allow it to display, if a mouse is installed, what the current video mode is, and where the cursor is currently positioned.

String handling.   String handling is a glaring weakness with DOS, but Builder corrects the problem. A string can be converted to all upper- or lowercase, the spaces can be trimmed from either or both sides, any portion of the string can be copied to another string, and the length of a string can be determined.

System information.   Builder can determine the type of CPU that's installed and if it has a math coprocessor, the amount of conventional, environmental, extended, and expanded memory that's installed and available, the number of the EMS driver, the DOS version, the number of drives, and if the printer is ready.

Using the compiler

As a test, I decided to write a program that would display the amount of free space on a floppy disk in the A drive. I call the program A-SIZE.BLD. The Builder source code and the resulting program can be found in the \UTILITY\DOS\A-FREE subdirectory.

I first added a few comments to the program. Builder uses a single quotation mark followed by a space to add comments to a program, as shown here:

```
''PURPOSE: Display Free Space On A Drive
'VERSION: 1.00
'DATE:     September 9, 1994
```

Builder requires that you declare your variables before you use them. The code to create all the variables used in the program is as follows:

```
LongInt Size
String Drive, Str1
```

I wanted Builder to display the size with commas. In Builder, the number doesn't need any special formatting to display commas; you just issue the Builder command:

```
USE COMMAS
```

which is the next command in the file. If you want to display numbers both with and without commas, use this command to turn the commas on, and DONT USE COMMAS to turn them back off. I wanted Builder to have command-line help, so the next lines are devoted to that:

```
Str1 := "%1"
Drive := "A:"

IF Str1 == "/?"
  SAY "Display Free Space On A Drive"
  EXIT 0
END

IF Str1 == "?"
  SAY "Display Free Space On A Drive"
  EXIT 0
END
```

The first line reads in the first replaceable parameter. Builder works properly whether or not a space is used before the first parameter. The next four lines display help and exit if the user enters /?, which is the normal way to request help, while the next four lines display help if the user enters the older DR DOS 5 question mark on the command line. The next step is to get the amount of free space on the A drive; the command to do that is:

```
Size := DiskFree Drive
```

Finally, the program writes the information to the screen. That code is:

```
SAY Size; "  Bytes Free On A Drive"
```

As you can see, even though this program was written in a language you aren't familiar with, the functions are understandable with just a little explanation. As a rule, most of the commands in Builder are easy to learn and use. Hyperkinetix also offers a number of extensions to the Builder language:

BuilderTools

This $69.95 collection is actually composed of stand-alone .EXE programs designed to be used with Builder-created programs. You can pass and return values to these powerful tools to take your applications to new heights, all without paying distribution royalties!

PowerTools. Ever need to locate a file or directory that you know is somewhere on your hard drive (even if it's hidden)? Now you can even remove a hidden file or directory. Have you ever wished it were possible to change a file's original time and date stamp?

AdvancedTools. Need to perform advanced mathematical calculations that involve trigonometric functions or evaluate floating-point formulas? Need to restrict output from an external program to a user-defined DOS box? Need PKZip-compatible archives or archives that span disks, but don't have access to PKZip's distribution license? You can do all this and more with BuilderTools.

Workbench for Builder

Workbench is the integrated development platform that allows you to compile and link complex Builder applications (multiple .OBJs and outside .LIBs) quickly and easily. That means you can get more done in less time, with less stress. And it's yours for only $39.95.

Workbench for Builder was created by Builder user and author of BuilderTools William Richardson both as a project management IDE for Builder and to generally enhance the development of large projects while using Builder.

Unlike the add-on libraries that have been developed for Builder, Workbench for Builder works with any version of the language. It provides a user-friendly, fully mouseable interface to your compiler, linker, editor, and source files.

Workbench for Builder is designed to allow you to develop Builder applications that require external libraries and multiple .OBJ files, or both, without constantly exiting to the command line. It's menu-driven and fully mouseable, and the main menu provides access to all functions, the Builder help system, current system vital statistics, and all Builder support programs.

By simply changing a few values in the Workbench for Builder configuration, you can tailor it to work not only with Builder, but also with Clipper, Force, and any other command-line-driven compiler/linker. This means you can create a consistent multilingual development environment to save you from constantly relearning different programs.

Workbench for Builder comes with its own text editor, but you aren't required to use it. You can configure it to work with any ASCII editor. The developer wanted to allow you to use your own editor and also provide an alternative if you didn't already have one. Its editor is fully featured, but limited to text files of no greater than 32K in size.

The package includes the full Builder source code of Workbench for Builder. This means that you can create a custom version of Workbench for Builder that works just the way you want it to.

SuperBuilder

SuperBuilder is the new advanced function library and training guide for Builder. SuperBuilder brings you over 45 new advanced functions (all written in Builder) including source code, along with programming tips, how-tos, and sample code. The price is $69.95.

SuperKnowledge SuperKnowledge is 60 pages of Builder tips. Specific topics dissected include arrays, subroutines, loops, and reusable code.

SuperFunctions. Over 40 advanced functions make up the SuperBuilder library. Some of these functions allow you to record and call on a history of user input during program operations; tag files in a pick-list created dynamically at runtime and return them in a string array; control and edit user input; prompt users for action based on dialog boxes; format input as phone numbers, social security numbers, dates and times; and create screen boxes that give your program a Windows look and feel.

You get the source code for each of these functions; they're all written in 100% native Builder code. That means you can change their operation and customize the functions for your specific needs.

MoreBuilder library

MoreBuilder is a super function library for use with Builder. Written by one of Builder's original code masters, Douglas J. Amaral, MoreBuilder functions enhance system diagnosis, screen handling, string handling, mouse support, and printer support. It costs $69.95.

MoreBuilder gives you 102 new functions and keywords to use in your Builder coding. The best part is that these new abilities are easy to add to existing code, and don't require any compiler changes. The real benefit is that you're up and running with 102 new commands in just minutes.

WipeOut! library

WipeOut! is a collection of amazing sound and video effects that can be used in any Builder application, and it's only $39.95. WipeOUT! gives you 33 new functions and keywords to use in your Builder coding. It also brings true sound to Builder for the first time.

Builder Lite

Version. 1.00

Price. $29.95 or $32.95

Category. Commercial

Author. Hyperkinetix Incorporated, at the same address as the previous program.

Builder Lite is a reduced-function version of Builder. Builder Lite has many of the features of Builder, but it doesn't support nested menus, reading from or writing to files, or creating installing programs. A full, working copy of Builder Lite is included on the CD-ROM in the \BLDLITE subdirectory. This version has no restrictions or limitations on it.

My book *Builder Lite*, also available from McGraw-Hill, retails for $32.95. There's a coupon at the back of this book you can use to order Builder Lite. Builder Lite is an excellent program, but since hyperkinetix has a coupon in this book that offers the full version of Builder for only $49.95, you'd probably be better off purchasing the full version.

CEnvi

Version. 1.009

Price. $38

Category. Shareware

Author. Nombas, at the following address:
P.O. Box 875
Medford, MA 02155-0007

CD-ROM directory. \UTILITY\DOS\CENVIDOS

C is an extremely powerful programming language, so powerful in fact that many developers write commercial programs using it. But C can be difficult to learn, and you need a compiler before you can use your programs.

Wouldn't it be nice if you could write powerful C-like programs without the complexity and the compiler, and be able to issue commands to the operating system like a batch file? Well, CEnvi does just that.

The author of CEnvi explains that he loves to program in C and wanted to bring the power of C to more users. He obviously needed to make C easier to learn, so he took out the pointers and variable type declarations, two of the most difficult parts of C. By making the language interactive, he also eliminated the need for a compiler. Since advanced versions of C are called C++, he decided to call this new language Cmm for C minus minus (C--).

CEnvi is his command-line implementation of the Cmm language. The *envi* portion of CEnvi refers to the way CEnvi uses environmental variables as if they were program variables. In addition to the DOS version, there are versions for OS/2, Windows, and Windows NT.

If a CEnvi program is fairly short, it can be entered on the command line. Or a batch file can call CEnvi as though it were a batch file utility. For example, COUNT.BAT is as follows, without remarks:

```
@echo off
SET COUNT=0
:TOP_OF_LOOP
   CEnvi COUNT = COUNT + 1
   ECHO %COUNT%
   IF NOT %COUNT%==%1 GOTO TOP_OF_LOOP
```

COUNT.BAT runs as a normal batch file except for the fourth line, which calls on CEnvi. Here, CEnvi reads the COUNT environmental variable and increases its value by one.

When the commands are longer or more complex, you'll need to create a CEnvi source-code file. By convention, these have a .CMM extension. When a batch file calls CEnvi and passes it a source-code filename, CEnvi searches both the current subdirectory and the full path to find the file. To avoid having to use a separate file for your CEnvi source code, you can place the code in a batch file between the GOTO CENVI_EXIT command and the :CENVI_EXIT label. DOS will ignore all this because of the GOTO command, but CEnvi will use it as source code.

CEnvi commands can be very simple, like the previous COUNT.BAT example, or they can be more complex and C-like, as this still fairly short TEE.CMM source code file illustrates:

```
//*********************************************
//*** Tee.cmm - Send lines to screen and ***
//*** ver.1      to output file           ***
//*********************************************

main(argc,argv)
{
  if ( 2 != argc )
     Instructions();
  else {
     // open output file
     if ( NULL == (fp=fopen(argv[1],"w")) )
        printf("Could not open file \"%s\" for writing.\a\n",argv[1])
     else {
        // read in each line, and send to file and screen
        while ( NULL != (line=gets()) ) {
           printf("%s\n",line)
           fprintf(fp,"%s\n",line)
        }
        fclose(fp)
     }
  }
}

Instructions()
{
 printf("Tee.cmm - Pipe output to screen AND to a file\n");
 printf("USAGE: Tee.cmm <FileSpec>\n");
 printf("Where: FileSpec = Name of file to create and write text to\n");
 printf("Example: To see output of a dir listing, but also save it
   in a file:\n");
 printf("dir ¦ cenvi tee.cmm dir.txt\n");
}
```

The documentation that comes with CEnvi does a good job of teaching the language, so I won't try to duplicate it here. CEnvi also comes with a number of sample batch files and source-code files.

While CEnvi is primarily an alternative language rather than a compiler, it does have an option to bind the source code and CEnvi program together into an executable stand-alone file. This file can be distributed royalty-free.

CEnvi is not for the faint of heart. If you don't already know a little C it can be difficult to learn, and if you don't have some programming experience the underlying logic can be hard to follow. However, if you have some programming experience and are longing for more power than most batch alternatives offer, CEnvi is just the thing for you. In addition to the DOS version, there are versions for OS/2 and Windows. All three are included on the CD-ROM.

PowerBatch and PB Plus+

Version. 2.2

Price. $30 for the shareware PowerBatch; $45 for the commercial program, PB Plus+

Category. Shareware and commercial

Author. Computing Systems Design Incorporated, at:
4437 Ormond Trace
Marietta, GA 30066

CD-ROM directory. \POWERBAT

There are actually three different versions of this program: the commercial PB Plus+ and the registered and unregistered versions of PowerBatch. They share a common interface and many common commands, but there are several differences. The unregistered version of PowerBatch displays a reminder to register, and programs compiled with the unregistered version display a similar reminder when they terminate. You can see this by running any of the precompiled demo programs in the \POWERBAT\PBDEMO subdirectory. The registered version of PowerBatch doesn't display these messages. You can see this by running the demo programs in the \POWERBAT\PLUSDEMO subdirectory.

PB Plus+ is available only from Computing Systems Design, and has the following features, not available in either the registered or unregistered version of PowerBatch:

- Variable array support

- Mouse support

- Reading and writing ASCII files

- Saving areas of the screen for instant restoration

- Swapping the compiled code out of memory while running other programs

Other than these differences, the three programs are the same, so I'll discuss them together. When referring to PowerBatch, I'm talking about all three versions—unless otherwise specified.

Installation

Keep one thing in mind before you experiment with the version of PowerBatch included on the CD-ROM. The first time you run the unregistered version of Power-Batch, it modifies its .EXE file to reflect the date you started your evaluation. Since a CD-ROM cannot be modified, this operation will fail, so before using PowerBatch copy it to a subdirectory on your hard disk. If your hard disk space is tight, the only two files that have to be copied to the hard disk in order to use PowerBatch are POWERMAK.EXE and SMLMODEL.MDL. You have three installation options:

- Copy the PowerBatch files to a subdirectory in your path. This allows you to compile your programs regardless of where they're stored.

- Copy the PowerBatch files to a subdirectory not in your path, and write and compile your programs in that subdirectory.

- Copy the PowerBatch files to a subdirectory not in your path, then specify the full path to the compiler when you want to compile a program. For example, if it were stored in the C:\POWERBAT subdirectory and that isn't in your path, you could still compile a program from any subdirectory with the command:

```
C:\POWERBAT\POWERMAK program
```

You can, of course, write a batch file or DOSKEY macro to automate this.

Getting started

Calling PowerBatch a *batch file compiler* isn't exactly accurate. Unlike Bat2Exe, it doesn't compile existing batch files into stand-alone programs without any modifications. However, that isn't a particularly significant limitation. PowerBatch offers so many enhancements that you'll want to scrap your existing batch files and batch file languages and rewrite the batch files in native PowerBatch code. Besides, the modifications required to get most batch files to run under PowerBatch are fairly minor. As a simple example, I created EXAMPLE.BAT:

```
@echo off
dir
mem
pause
```

This batch file, the PowerBatch source code, and the resulting PowerBatch program can be found in the \POWERBAT\MYDEMO subdirectory of the CD-ROM. When I ran this on my machine, DOS reported that the largest program I could run was 572K. Then I renamed it to EXAMPLE.PWR and tried to compile it with Power-Batch. It correctly identified lines 2 through 4 as DOS commands, but objected to the first command.

Since a compiled program would never echo commands, that line was redundant, so I removed it. PowerBatch compiled this version fine. Under the shareware program, DOS reported that the largest program I could run was 492K, and under the commercial PB Plus+ it reported that my largest program was 486K. Neither is a large size penalty, and PB Plus+ does have the option of swapping out almost all of the code.

I tried a number of other batch files and, while none of them ran unmodified under PowerBatch, without exception the modifications were fairly minor and easily accomplished. Of course, you're going to want to immediately move on to writing programs under PowerBatch that aren't possible using DOS.

Using the compiler

PowerBatch is a very high-level language, so it generally takes fewer PowerBatch commands to perform a particular operation than it takes in a lower-level language like C or Pascal. PowerBatch commands also tend to be easy to learn and use. I wrote several very useful applications after just one afternoon of studying the program. PB Plus+ has about 100 commands. Since PowerBatch supports fewer operations, it naturally has fewer commands.

As a test, I decided to write a program that would display the amount of free space on a floppy disk in the A drive. I call the program A-SIZE.PWR. The PowerBatch source code and the resulting PB Plus+ program can be found in the \POWER-

BAT\MYDEMO subdirectory of the CD-ROM. I first added a few comments to the program. PowerBatch uses a semicolon followed by a space to add comments to a program, as follows:

```
; ; PURPOSE: Find The Amount Of Free Space On A Drive
; VERSION: 1.00
; DATE:    July 27, 1994
```

PowerBatch always returns the cursor to the top left of the screen when the program terminates, so I decided to have the program clear the screen and position the cursor at the top left of the screen before running. The code to do that is:

```
CLEAR
GOTOXY 1,1
```

Notice that most of these commands make sense even if you aren't a PowerBatch user. That's one beauty of the language; commands make sense when you read them.

PowerBatch requires that you declare your variables before you use them. When you declare a variable, you must give PowerBatch its name and the maximum number of characters it will contain. The code to create all the variables used in the program is as follows:

```
VARIABLE First,      3
VARIABLE Second,     3
VARIABLE Third,      3
VARIABLE HowLong,    2
VARIABLE TotalSpace, 20
VARIABLE FreeSpace,  20
VARIABLE OutSpace,   20
VARIABLE Drive,       1, "A"
VARIABLE MyMessage,  80, "Free Space On A Drive Is..."
```

Notice that the last variable, MyMessage, is assigned a size and then has text following it. This is how to assign an initial value to a variable in PowerBatch.

First, Second, and Third store pieces of the size. Since a size isn't reported with commas, these are used by the routine that adds the commas. First stores the right three numbers, so if the size was 1,400,128 they'd store the 128. Second stores the 400 and Third stores the 1. HowLong stores the length of the size variable for comparison. TotalSpace stores the total space on the A drive and FreeSpace stores the amount of free space. Only FreeSpace is used, but both are reported by the Power-Batch function. OutSpace stores the free space after the commas are added, Drive stores A to report on the A drive, and MyMessage stores text.

The next step is to get the amount of free space on the A drive. The command to do that is as follows:

```
?DiskSpace Drive, TotalSpace, FreeSpace
```

The ?DiskSpace function must be passed the drive to test, and only the first letter is significant. In the example, the Drive variable contains A, but you could change this to another drive. Note that the formatting routine is currently designed to work with only seven digits, so 9,999,999 is the largest number it could handle.

Next, the program computes the length of the FreeSpace variable using the Length function. Note that this returns the length of the contents of that variable and not the space allocated for the variable. Once that's stored to the HowLong variable, that variable is tested and the program jumps to different locations depending on the length of the variable. This code is as follows:

```
LENGTH HowLong, FreeSpace
COMPARE HowLong, 3, , Three, Three
COMPARE HowLong, 4, , , Four
COMPARE HowLong, 5, , , Five
COMPARE HowLong, 6, , , Six
COMPARE HowLong, 7, , , Seven
```

The Compare command tests the first two items that are passed to it, the How-Long variable and 3 on the second line. If the first value is greater than the second, the program jumps to the first label, which is missing in all these tests. If the first value is less than the second, the program jumps to the second label, which is used only in the first test. If they're equal, the program jumps to the third label.

In this example, the program jumps to the Three label for a length of between 1 and 3, the Four label for a length of 4, the Five label for a length of 5, the Six label for a length of 6, and the Seven label for a length of 7. There's always more than one way to tackle a programming problem, and there's most probably an approach that doesn't require separate sections for each length. I was looking for code that was easy to explain, not necessarily the shortest.

Section Three moves the contents of the FreeSpace variable into the OutSpace output variable because no commas need to be added when there are three or fewer numbers. The Four section splits off the last three numbers using the MIDSTRING function and stores them to one variable. The thousands number is stored to another variable, and then the CONCAT function recombines them into the output variable with a comma added. The code for these two sections is:

```
LABEL Three
   CONCAT OutSpace, FreeSpace
GOTO End

LABEL Four
  MIDSTRING First, FreeSpace, 2,3
  MIDSTRING Second, FreeSpace, 0,1
  CONCAT OutSpace, Second, ",", First
GOTO END
```

The code for sections Five, Six, and Seven is very similar. Finally, the program writes the information to the screen. That code is as follows:

```
LABEL End
CONCAT MyMessage, OutSpace
WRITELINE MyMessage
```

For more examples, check out the \POWERBAT\PBDEMO subdirectory of the included CD-ROM, which contains demo programs compiled with PowerBatch, and the \POWERBAT\PLUSDEMO subdirectory, which contains programs compiled with PB Plus+. Both subdirectories contain the source code and compiled versions.

Drawbacks

The drawbacks to PowerBatch and PB Plus+ are fairly minor. You have to declare the variables in advance, but I found it cumbersome to have to declare their sizes as well. If you allocate too little space to an array variable, PB Plus+ (PowerBatch doesn't support arrays) will dynamically add more space, but with regular variables both PowerBatch and PB Plus+ simply cut off part of the contents of the variable without generating a warning message. If they're going to force you to declare a size, they should either warn you when you exceed it or deal with the problem, as PB Plus+ does with arrays.

Neither PowerBatch nor PB Plus+ includes an editor, so you must edit with your own editor, exit it and run PowerBatch to compile, then go back if there are problems. An integrated environment would be easier to work in. I got around this by editing in one Windows session and compiling in another. At least that way I didn't have to leave my editor to compile. Finally, neither program would reposition the cursor, which is a drawback if you're writing small utilities that simply display information on the screen and then exit, like my example A-SIZE program.

Personal REXX

Version. 3.00

Category. Commercial

Author. Quercus Systems, at:
P.O. Box 2157
Saratoga, CA 95070
(408) 867-REXX

CD-ROM directory. \UTILITY\DOS\PERSONAL(demo version)

Chapter 32 provides an introduction to REXX under OS/2, so I won't repeat that information here. While REXX is an excellent programming language, IBM won't port the language to non-IBM operating systems, so the only PC platforms IBM offers REXX for are OS/2 and PC DOS 7. This oversight is corrected in very fine fashion by Quercus Systems' Personal REXX package for DOS, Windows, Windows NT, and OS/2.

Personal REXX is an implementation of IBM REXX version 4.0. It also includes the instructions and functions used in REXX for CMS, OS/2, and SAA. There are some differences between Personal REXX and IBM OS/2 REXX, most of which are fairly minor:

- IBM OS/2 REXX expects a .CMD extension on a REXX program, while Personal REXX expects a .REX. In order to successfully run the same program under both

IBM OS/2 REXX and Personal REXX, you must either keep two copies of the program or rename the one copy as you change platforms. Given the ability of OS/2 to dually boot into either OS/2 or DOS and its ability to run a DOS session, this can be an annoying problem.

- Personal REXX scans the program for syntax errors while loading it into memory, and IBM OS/2 REXX waits until it's executing the program.

- IBM OS/2 REXX maintains the same pointer for reading and writing with CHARIN, CHAROUT, LINEIN, and LINEOUT, while Personal REXX properly maintains separate pointers.

- By default, IBM OS/2 REXX displays commands passed to the operating system, while Personal REXX doesn't.

- IBM OS/2 REXX requires that you use the CALL command to run another REXX program, and Personal REXX doesn't.

Under Personal REXX, there are three different ways to execute a REXX program. You can enter RX *program*. Starting a REXX program with the RX command requires that a tiny memory-resident program be loaded first. This program is required only if you use the stack, global variables, or certain utilities. You can enter REXX *program*. This is the normal way to execute a REXX program; it loads the REXX.EXE processor first. Or you can start a REXX program just like a batch file by entering its name on the command line. However, this method requires that the memory-resident REXX Batch Manager program be loaded first to modify the way COMMAND.COM operates to also search for *.REX files.

Personal REXX includes a package of functions that adds a window interface to your REXX programs. You can use these windows to make a selection from a menu or to enter data into one or more data fields.

REXX is an excellent and very powerful replacement for the batch language. The availability of Personal REXX under OS/2, Windows NT, Windows, and DOS means that you can use it as your batch language on all these platforms, something no other language offers. Not only is REXX an excellent batch language, it's a powerful programming language.

TurboBat

Version. 3.23

Price. $19.95

Category. Shareware

Author. Foley Hi-Tech Systems, at the following address:
185 Berry St., Suite 4807
San Francisco, CA 94107
(415) 882-1730

CD-ROM directory. \TURBOBAT

TurboBat is specifically designed to compile batch files. It adds fewer commands to the batch language than the other compilers, but the commands it adds are tightly focused on the actions typically performed by a batch file. The result is a language that's fairly simple to use, yet very powerful. TurboBat includes commands to perform the following:

- IF THEN ELSE logic testing
- Other advanced logic testing, including tests such as less than or greater than
- Advanced looping with REPEAT UNTIL and WHILE WEND commands
- Getting a keystroke from the user
- Getting a string from the user and placing it in the environment
- Controlling the color of the screen
- Controlling how messages are displayed

It also supports true subroutines and much more. To make debugging easier, you can compile programs with TurboBAT so the resulting .COM file steps through the code, line by line.

Perhaps the best way to see how easy it is to write a TurboBat program is to go ahead and write a program. The following program counts from 0 to 99,999 and displays the results on the screen. First it checks to see if the user requested command-line help and then continues with the NeedHelp program.

```
NEEDHELP %0 %1
SET Errorlevel=%?
IF (%Errorlevel%)==(1) GOTO HELP

IF ERRORLEVEL 1 GOTO HELP
```

The first line runs NeedHelp. The second line is a TurboBat command to store the current errorlevel to the environmental variable Errorlevel. The third line checks this environmental variable to see if the user requested help and, if so, jumps to the help section.

The next line is a standard batch file check to see if the user requested help. I left it in both because this file began as a standard batch file and also to show that TurboBat has no trouble with standard batch commands. Once I started adding TurboBat commands that wouldn't run under DOS, I renamed COUNT.BAT to COUNT.TB to prevent it being run from the command line. Since TurboBat expects a .BAT extension, I then had to specify the full name to the compiler. Strangely, the manual never suggests doing this, but I think it's an excellent precaution to prevent users from trying to run a TurboBat script containing nonbatch commands.

Next, the program loops through all the digits. The single line to do this is:

```
FOR %%H IN (0 1 2 3 4 5 6 7 8 9) FOR %%I IN (0 1 2 3 4 5 6 7 8 9)
FOR %%J IN (0 1 2 3 4 5 6 7 8 9) FOR %%K IN (0 1 2 3 4 5 6 7 8 9)
FOR %%L IN (0 1 2 3 4 5 6 7 8 9) GOSUB DISPLAY
```

While this line wraps in the book, it's a single line in the code. It violates three DOS rules for batch files. The FOR command is nested, it uses a GOSUB command, and the line is longer than 127 characters. While none of this is supported by DOS, TurboBat handles it fine. It supports nesting the FOR command and long lines, and GOSUB is a TurboBat command.

A subroutine must begin with a label that matches the name of the subroutine, :DISPLAY in this case. It must also end with a RETURN command. The GOSUB command causes the program to jump to the label, just like a GOTO command. The RETURN command causes control to return to the line following the GOSUB command. The Display subroutine is as follows:

```
:DISPLAY
    REM Subroutine To Display Count
    IF (%H%)==(0) IF (%I%)==(0) SCREEN 12 38 %J%%K%%L%
    IF (%H%)==(0) IF NOT (%I%)==(0) SCREEN 12 36 %I%,%J%%K%%L%
    IF NOT (%H%)==(0) SCREEN 12 35 %H%%I%,%J%%K%%L%
RETURN
```

It performs a series of logic tests to decide if the program displays a number that's three, four, or five digits long. It doesn't check for one or two digits because the program runs so fast that they won't stay on the screen long enough to really be visible.

Notice that the FOR variables are tested outside the FOR loop as environmental variables. This ability to jump to a subroutine to perform multiple actions on items that match in the FOR loop is a terrific advantage when using TurboBat scripts to process files. The SCREEN command positions the cursor and displays the text.

The resulting program is very fast. Originally, I had the program loop from 0 to 999 and it went so fast that I inserted a DELAY command after the line to display the text to make sure it displayed each number. I thought I had made a logic error that was causing it to skip numbers, but it ran perfectly. I ended up increasing the count to 99,999 so the program would run long enough so you could see it running.

41

Windows Batch File Utilities

The utilities presented in this chapter are designed to enhance a DOS batch file running under Windows. The next chapter covers utilities that replace the DOS batch language with a language designed specifically for Windows.

%COMSPEC% isn't really a utility, but it's a nice addition to many Windows batch files. What if you want to run a batch file under Windows to configure your DOS session for a particular configuration? Say, for example, you want the session to have a particular path or certain memory-resident packages loaded. If you install the batch file to the desktop, however, when you run it the DOS session closes as soon as Windows finishes running the batch file! This forces you to load a standard DOS session and run the configuration batch file before starting to work.

There's a better way. If you make the last command in your configuration batch file %COMSPEC%, the batch file will configure the DOS session and then leave you at a DOS prompt to do your work. As always, the EXIT command takes you back to Windows. The trick is that the COMSPEC environmental variable contains the full path to COMMAND.COM, so using it as a command runs another DOS session. This keeps Windows from shutting the session down after the batch file terminates.

IsItWin

Version. 1.0

Price. Free

Category. Written for this book

Author. Ronny Richardson

CD-ROM directory. \UTILITY\DOS\ISITWIN

IsItWin checks to see if Windows is currently running and sets the errorlevel accordingly. This can be very useful when a batch file needs to run a program like CHKDSK/F that shouldn't be run under Windows.

IsItWin was written in Builder Lite, a subset of the Builder language. The source code is included in the subdirectory in case you want to modify its operation. The CD-ROM includes a fully functional copy of Builder Lite in the \BLDLITE subdirectory. This means you can experiment with these programs and recompile them. To get the full documentation for Builder Lite, order my *Builder Lite: Developing Dynamic Batch Files* from McGraw-Hill, and make sure to use the coupon in the back of this book.

SmilerShell

Version. 2.1b

Price. $23.45

Category. Shareware

Author. Bandon Data Systems, at:
1023 Key Route Boulevard
Albany, CA 94706
(800) 242-4775 or (510) 526-8470

CD-ROM directory. \UTILITY\DOS\SMISHL21

Starting a DOS session just to run a DOS command or short batch file can be time-consuming, especially when you don't run the batch file often enough to install it on your desktop. SmilerShell makes it easy to access the DOS command line and DOS commands from inside Windows.

SmilerShell displays a command line in a graphical box. Like the DOS command line running DOSKEY, the SmilerShell command line has command recall and command macros. Like the DOS command line, it can run internal and external DOS commands, batch files, and DOS programs. It also supports pipes and redirections, just like DOS. Unlike DOS, SmilerShell can run Windows programs and can be configured to always be visible. It has a speedy subdirectory-changing program similar to Norton NCD, supports cutting and pasting just like other Windows programs, and can display available system resources.

If you need to access the command line occasionally from within Windows but don't want the overhead of starting a "real" DOS session, SmilerShell is the best alternative I've seen. An even more powerful commercial version is available for $32.45 directly from Bandon Data Systems.

WinEdit

Version. 3.0

Price. $29.95 (Lite version), $59.95 (Standard version), and $89.95 (Professional version). This book contains a coupon for a free Lite license.

Category. Shareware

Author. Wilson WindowWare, at:
2701 California Ave. SW, Suite 212
Seattle, WA 98116
(800) 762-8383

CD-ROM directory. \UTILITY\WINDOWS\WINEDIT

Windows and all three types of DOS come with an ASCII editor, so you might be wondering why you'd want to spend money on yet another editor. The answer is that WinEdit's abilities far exceed those of any of these editors. While not as powerful as Brief, the favorite of many programmers, WinEdit is less expensive and has the power you need for writing all but the most complex programs. WinEdit comes in three flavors: Lite, Standard, and Professional. Let's look at all three:

Lite. This version can open as many files as you like, up to a total of 16 megabytes. The program is fast, even with a number of large files loaded into memory. Multiple pages can be tiled or cascaded. In printing, it supports headers, footers, and page numbers, and can compress two pages onto a single page. It supports up to 2,000 undo and redo operations. While entering code, it supports automatic indenting. You can record and play back keystrokes, and it has online help. An unregistered version of WinEdit is included on the CD-ROM, and the book includes a coupon for a free license of the Lite version.

Standard. This version supports all the features of WinEdit Lite, plus it can work with many popular compilers to compile, make, execute, debug, and rebuild files. It can save different configuration files if you work with multiple compilers and it can be linked to popular Help libraries.

Professional. This version supports all the features of WinEdit Standard, and it supports a 280-function advanced macro language. This macro language offers such features as file management, string manipulations, cursor movement, and even some network support.

For writing batch files, WinBatch files, or batch file compiler scripts, you'll probably find the Lite version to be an excellent choice that's far superior to the editors included with DOS or Windows. If you have more advanced needs, consider the Standard or Professional versions.

42

Windows Alternative
Batch File Languages

CEnvi

Version. 1.009

Price. $38

Category. Shareware

Author. Nombas, at:
P.O. Box 875
Medford, MA 02155-0007

CD-ROM directory. \UTILITY\WINDOWS\CENVIWIN

CEnvi is a C-like replacement for the batch language. I discussed the DOS version in more detail back in Chapter 40, so I won't duplicate that information here. I will, however, highlight a few of the differences between the DOS and Windows versions.

Under Windows, you can associate the .CMM files with the CEnvi program so you can run a source-code file by simply clicking on it in the File Manager. Once this association has been created, you can also install the .CMM files to the desktop and run them simply by double-clicking on their icons. The Windows version of CEnvi also includes functions to create, work with, and remove dialog boxes and Windows.

Personal REXX

Version. 3.00

Category. Commercial

Author. Quercus Systems, at the following address:
P.O. Box 2157
Saratoga, CA 95070
(408) 867-REXX

Personal REXX for DOS was described in Chapter 40 and REXX was described in Chapter 32. REXX is designed to work in a text-based environment, just like a batch file. Personal REXX simulates this environment under Windows by displaying a text window for REXX programs that either show output or request input from the user.

REXX excels at sending commands to the operating system, be it DOS, Windows, or OS/2. Personal REXX for Windows is no different. While a DOS batch file running under Windows is able to start only DOS programs, Personal REXX programs can start both DOS and Windows programs.

Personal REXX for Windows provides some features specifically designed to work with Windows. Using Personal REXX, you can:

- Start a Windows program.

- Perform asynchronous program execution. Normally, when REXX starts a program, it waits for that program to terminate before moving on to the next line, just like a batch file. Personal REXX is able to start a program and then continue executing the REXX program while the program runs.

- Access Windows .INI initialization files.

- Display a message box. This is a graphical box containing a custom message and an OK button you must press to continue.

- Display a question box. This is similar to a message box, but has Yes and No buttons, and the program can tell which button has been clicked.

- Display a cancel box. This is similar to a question box, but a Cancel button is also included.

- Display a prompt box. This is a graphical box that prompts the user for a long string of information. In addition to an area to enter the information, there are OK and Cancel buttons to click in order to tell the program you're finished entering information.

- Display a choice box. This is a graphical box containing a number of choices to pick from. It's similar to the list of files you get when you open a document using a Windows word processor. There are OK and Cancel buttons to click in order to tell the program you're finished entering information.

- Play .WAV files.

Other than these extra Windows-specific features, the Windows version of Personal REXX is almost identical to the DOS version. As a result, many REXX programs will run under either version without modification.

REXX is an excellent and very powerful replacement for the batch language. The availability of Personal REXX under OS/2, Windows NT, Windows, and DOS means that you can use it as your batch language on all these platforms, something no other language offers. Not only is REXX an excellent batch language, it's also a powerful programming language.

WinBatch

Version. 5.0

Price. $69.95

Category. Shareware

Author. Wilson WindowWare, at:
2701 California Ave. SW, Suite 212
Seattle, WA 98116
(800) 762-8383

CD-ROM directory. \UTILITY\WINDOWS\WINBATCH

While DOS batch files will run under Windows, they're able to run only DOS programs. So you couldn't start a Windows program like Solitaire using a DOS batch file. WinBatch is a specialized Windows batch language designed especially to work in the Windows environment and allow you to control Windows programs.

A simple example

Before I discuss WinBatch in any detail, let's look at a fairly simple example called WINMINE.WBT. It's designed to prompt you for the number of minutes you want to play the Minesweeper game that comes with Windows. This program is based on the SOL.WBT sample that comes with WinBatch, only it has been highly modified. This was the first batch file I wrote under WinBatch, and the entire writing and debugging process took less than two hours—which is an indication of how easy WinBatch is to use.

The first thing the batch file has to do is to find out how long you want to play. The code to do that follows. It's shown without comments, but the actual code has extensive comments. This prompt requires an integer and version 4, which I was using when I wrote this. (Version 5 adds an Int function that could be used to convert the MinutesToPlay variable to an integer.)

```
Title = "How Long Do You Want To Play Minesweeper?"
Question = "Please Enter An Integer"
MinutesToPlay = AskLine(Title, Question, "1")
```

Once the batch file has the length of time, it has to figure out if the Minesweeper program is already running. If it is, the next line jumps to a section to activate that window. Otherwise, it runs the program and then jumps to a section that's run once the program is running.

```
If WinExist("Minesweeper") == @TRUE Then Goto Activate
RunZoom("WinMine.exe", "")
Goto Loaded
```

The Activate section activates the Minesweeper program and zooms it out in case it was minimized. It then jumps to the Loaded section to recombine the two paths (Minesweeper not loaded or already loaded).

```
:Activate
WinActivate("Minesweeper")
WinZoom("Minesweeper")
Goto Loaded
```

Once Minesweeper has either been loaded from disk if not running or made active if running, the batch file runs the Loaded section, which initializes the SecondsTo-Play and SecondsAlreadyPlayed variables and changes the title of the Minesweeper window to Minesweeper (. Later, a time and closing parenthesis will be added.

```
:Loaded
WinTitle("Minesweeper", "Minesweeper (")
SecondsToPlay = MinutesToPlay * 60
SecondsAlreadyPlayed = 0
Goto TimeIt
```

After running the Loaded section, the batch file runs the TimeIt section. This section functions as a large loop that performs the actual timing. The first line is a label. The second line updates the variables. The third line makes sure the window still exists. (It won't if the user quit the game.) If the window no longer exists, the batch file exits. The fourth line appends the time that remains onto the window title, along with a closing parenthesis. The fifth line delays the batch file for ten seconds. This keeps the batch file from running continually and updating the window continually. During this delay, the user can still play the game or perform other functions due to Windows' multitasking. The sixth line updates the timer variable by ten seconds. The seventh line checks to see if you have more time; if so, it continues in the loop. The last line is reached only when you run out of time. This line beeps the speaker and then runs the next section.

```
:TimeIt
SecondsRemaining = SecondsToPlay - SecondsAlreadyPlayed
If WinExist("Minesweeper (") == @FALSE Then Exit
WinTitle("Minesweeper (", "Minesweeper (%SecondsRemaining% seconds left)")
Delay(10)
SecondsAlreadyPlayed = SecondsAlreadyPlayed + 10
If SecondsAlreadyPlayed < SecondsToPlay Then Goto TimeIt
Beep
```

Since no one likes to stop a winning game, the next section lets you continue to play for one more minute. Each time you run out of time, you can continue to play for another minute, continuing in this fashion indefinitely (but clicking on OK once a minute would certainly get tiring).

The first line is a label and the second line hides the Minesweeper game. If the batch file didn't do this, you could ignore the prompt and continue playing the game indefinitely since it isn't closed until after the prompt is responded to. You can still ignore the prompt, but you can't continue to play the game. The third line asks you if you want one more minute. The next line redisplays the Minesweeper window that was just hidden. If you answer no to the prompt, the fifth line jumps to a section to close the line. If you answer yes, the sixth line jumps to a section to give you one more minute.

```
:MoreTime
WinHide("Minesweeper")
GetMoreTime = AskYesNo("More Time?","Would You Like One More Minute?")
WinShow("Minesweeper")
IF GetMoreTime == @NO Then Goto ShutDown
IF GetMoreTime == @YES Then Goto Increment
```

The increment section simply adds 60 seconds to the SecondsToPlay variable and jumps back into the timing loop:

```
:Increment
SecondsToPlay = SecondsToPlay + 60
Goto TimeIt
```

The ShutDown section closes the Minesweeper game down once time has expired. If you click on the Cancel button when given the option of continuing one more minute, the first two lines take over. Without the special :Cancel label, if you clicked on Cancel the batch file would immediately terminate. However, that leaves Minesweeper in memory and hidden. When there's a :Cancel label, the batch file automatically jumps there if you click on Cancel, and that shuts down the Minesweeper window. Since clicking on Cancel causes the batch file to skip the code where the window is redisplayed with the WinShow command, that command is issued after the :Cancel label since a hidden window can't be closed. The fourth line tries to close the window. If there's a problem, the fifth line causes the program to continue looping through this code until it successfully closes the window. The sixth line displays a prompt and the seventh line exits the batch file.

```
:Cancel
WinShow("Minesweeper")
:ShutDown
WinClose("Minesweeper (")
If WinExist("Minesweeper (") == @TRUE Then Goto ShutDown
Message("Minesweeper's Over", "Time Is Up!")
Exit
```

Both WINMINE.WBT and SOL.WBT, a modified version of this batch file to run Solitaire, can be found in the \UTILITY\WINDOWS\WINBATCH\MYSAMPLE subdirectory on the CD-ROM. This subdirectory also contains the compiled versions of these batch files, which were created with the WinBatch compiler, discussed later in this chapter.

The WinBatch language

WinBatch is hard to classify. It started out as a batch file language for Windows, but soon surpassed this modest goal and became a very powerful macro language able to control almost every aspect of Windows. With Version 5, it surpasses even that. It has now reached the point of being a true computer language.

WinBatch is an interpreter, which means you must write a script. This script must be an ASCII file and each line must be less that 255 characters. You can write the batch file with any ASCII editor, but if you use the WinEdit editor discussed in Chapter 41, WinEdit can help you with any WinBatch keyword if you put the cursor on that word and click with the right mouse button. Each WinBatch file must end with the .WBT extension.

The WinBatch language began as a very batch-like language, as the following line, from WINMINE.WBT, shows:

```
IF GetMoreTime == @NO Then Goto ShutDown
```

The IF, ==, and Goto components of this statement are straight out of a DOS batch file, and it's likely that any batch file author would understand this statement without any explanation. The language still maintains much of those roots and is very accessible to anyone with batch file experience.

Both the unique needs of the Windows environment and the natural expansion and evolution of WinBatch, however, have moved it well beyond your basic "batch files under Windows" language. It consists of the following major components:

Commands. WinBatch tends to use functions for most of its operations, with commands reserved for program flow, looping, and logic applications. While these tend to be fairly limited up through version 4, version 5 introduces a wealth of structured programming commands that have really expanded WinBatch into a true programming language.

Comments. These are nonexecuted statements you can add to your program to document it. Anything on a line after a semicolon is ignored as a comment. Comments can be on a line by themselves, or you can add a comment to the end of an operational line.

Functions. These are used to tell WinBatch, Windows, DOS, or a program to do something. For example, the function RUN("WINWORD.EXE","") would run Microsoft Word for Windows without any parameters. There are so many functions in WinBatch that it would take too long to list them all, but here are the various function categories:

- Clipboard handling
- DDE
- Directory management
- Disk drive management
- Information display
- File management
- Information input
- Mathematical/arithmetic
- Menu management
- Miscellaneous
- Multimedia
- Networking
- Process control
- Program management
- String handling
- System information
- Window management

No matter what you want to do with WinBatch, it's likely that there's a function to handle it.

Operators.   These perform an action on one or more variables. There are unary operators, such as two's complement; binary arithmetic operators, such as modulo and left shift; binary relational operators, such as greater-than and less-than; the assignment operator; and precedence and evaluation order operators, such as parenthetical grouping and shift operators.

Variables.   A variable is nothing more than a placeholder for data of interest. WinBatch works with both string and numeric data. Unlike DOS batch files, WinBatch has a number of ways to get data from the user and a wealth of functions to perform string and mathematical manipulations on that data. WinBatch comes with a number of predefined variables, called *constants*, that reflect information regarding the Windows environment. For example, @CANCEL contains information about how the program handles clicking on a Cancel button, and @SHIFT tells if the Shift key is being pressed.

Other components

WinBatch includes a companion program called WinMacro. WinMacro lets you create macro files and then attach them to the control menu of any Windows application.

You can then run the macro either from the control menu or by using a hotkey. This allows WinBatch to serve as a universal macro language so you can avoid learning different macro languages for different packages.

WinBatch also includes two utilities, Dialog Editor and WinInfo. Dialog Editor lets you create and modify dialog boxes by manipulating elements on the screen. While it sounds complex, it's really quite easy to use. WinInfo will read the size and position of a window for you and automatically generate the appropriate WinBatch code to size and position that window for you. This code is placed in the Clipboard for easy pasting into a program. This makes it a little easier to write your code.

WinBatch conclusion

With WinBatch, you can quickly learn enough to write Windows batch files to automate almost any aspect of Windows. After using the product for less than a day, I had written batch files to run my games for a limited amount of time, load multiple Windows programs at once so I could open all the programs I normally use for writing with one click, and perform routine file management, such as backing up changed files incrementally and deleting certain working files. If these are the sorts of tasks you want to perform, WinBatch is well worth its $69.95 shareware registration fee.

However, WinBatch doesn't stop there. It has evolved into a full programming language for Windows. You can use WinBatch to control your Windows programs to log onto online services at night to retrieve files and then perform a full backup to tape, or keep a notebook and desktop computer files synchronized. A network administrator might use WinBatch to write batch files to install software across the network, monitor network activity, or even limit access to server-based packages.

In fact, you can do almost anything with WinBatch that you could do with a version of BASIC that had full access to and control over the entire Windows environment, only with a much simpler and easier-to-use interface. WinBatch is that powerful! If you buy only one Windows batch utility, WinBatch is the one to buy.

In addition to this version, there are 32-bit WinBatch versions available for Windows 95, Windows NT, and several non-Intel platforms. Contact Wilson WindowWare for more information.

WinBatch Compiler

Version. 5.0

Price. $395.00

Category. Commercial

Author. Wilson WindowWare, at the following address:
2701 California Ave. SW, Suite 212
Seattle, WA 98116
(800) 762-8383

If you distribute your WinBatch batch files to other users, they must own a copy of WinBatch to run them. If these users are simply running your scripts, however, you can compile WinBatch batch files into royalty-free stand-alone programs that don't require WinBatch to operate. The WinBatch compiler adds no new functions; it simply lets someone who doesn't own WinBatch run WinBatch programs.

WinCMD

Price. Free

Category. Copyrighted

Author. Douglas Boling

WinCMD is a Windows batch language from *PC Magazine*. (All *PC Magazine* files are available from their area on CompuServe. See any issue of the magazine for details.) Unlike DOS running under Windows, WinCMD makes extensive use of the Windows environment. WinCMD batch files are ASCII files with a .WCM extension. WinCMD also offers extensive debugging facilities, including the ability to step through a batch file one line at a time.

WinCMD is very much like a simple programming language. It supports variables, and allows you to use these variables at any time in place of hardwired data. It has a number of mathematical, logical, and bitwise operators. WinCMD batch files can run both DOS and Windows programs. Unlike a batch file, WinCMD doesn't pause when it runs a program and wait until that program terminates. Rather, it continues executing the batch file, which makes more sense in the Windows environment. There are commands to perform the following:

- Conditional (WHILE) looping

- Displaying information for the user

- Functions

- IF THEN ELSE programming

- Subroutines

- Unconditional looping

and built-in functions to perform the following:
- Converting a string to uppercase

- Displaying a Windows dialog box requesting information from the user in an entry field

- Displaying a Windows message box

- Finding out how long Windows has been running

- Getting the name of the program that created a window

- Getting the name of the active program

- Pausing the batch file

- String manipulation
- Stuffing keystrokes into the Windows event queue

Since WinCMD was released, *PC Magazine* has published two extensions to the language. The first added four categories of functions: moving and resizing windows, reading and writing files, accessing the Clipboard, and controlling multimedia devices. The second extension added four new string functions, functions to access the Windows dialog box for loading and saving files, three new window control functions, and functions to get the system date and time.

WinCMD isn't nearly as powerful as WinBatch or Personal REXX for Windows, but WinCMD is all the Windows batch file language that many people need. Since WinCMD is available free from *PC Magazine*, you might want to try it first before moving on to some of the more powerful alternatives.

43

OS/2 Batch File Utilities

CEnvi

Version. 1.009

Price. $38

Category. Shareware

Author. Nombas, at the following address:
P.O. Box 875
Medford, MA 02155-0007

CD-ROM directory. \UTILITY\OS2\CENVIOS2

CEnvi is a C-like replacement for the batch language. The DOS version was discussed in more detail back in Chapter 40 and the Windows version in the last chapter.

Under OS/2, you can define a different external processor to process batch files if the first statement in them is EXTPROC. So you can easily write batch files that run under CEnvi, and still have others run under the OS/2 batch processor. You can also store your CEnvi source code in a REXX program, between the `SIGNAL CENVI_EXIT` command and `CENVI_EXIT:` label, much as you can under DOS and OS/2 batch files.

You can associate .CMM files with CEnvi by changing the notebook settings for CENVI.EXE, and then run a .CMM program by double-clicking on its icon. You can configure a .CMM program to support OS/2 dropping and dragging.

CRONTAB

Version. 2.21

Price. Free, but a charity donation is requested. Commercial users must pay for the program.

Category. Copyrighted/shareware

Author. Thomas Harold, at:
P.O. Box 368
Camp Hill, PA 17001

CD-ROM directory. \UTILITY\OS2\CRONTAB2

CRONTAB is designed to be executed by your CONFIG.SYS file. It then runs programs on the schedule you've selected. CRONTAB.DAT contains a list of programs to run and a schedule to run them by. For example, you might run some programs every time you boot, other programs once a day, and still other programs twice a week. You can run only the programs at their specified time, or "catch up" the next time you boot if you skip using the computer on a day a program would have otherwise run.

CRONTAB's brief scripting language makes it easy to configure, and it's very easy to use. There's a version of DOS as well (discussed in Chapter 39).

Personal REXX

Version. 3.00

Category. Commercial

Author. Quercus Systems, at:
P.O. Box 2157
Saratoga, CA 95070
(408) 867-REXX

Personal REXX provides support for the REXX language under OS/2. There are also Windows and DOS versions for true cross-platform support, and the OS/2 version is included with the DOS version at no additional charge. Personal REXX for DOS was described in Chapter 40 and REXX was described in Chapter 32.

The OS/2 version of Personal REXX is designed to be a complete replacement for the IBM version of REXX that ships with OS/2. Personal REXX is a superset of IBM OS/2 REXX, so any program that runs under the IBM OS/2 version should run fine under the Personal REXX version. Personal REXX adds a number of new features to the REXX language, including:

- Array manipulations, such as array copying, array sorting, merging two arrays, reading an array from disk, and writing an array to disk

- Computing the cyclical redundancy check number for a file
- Creating and accessing local and remote OS/2 named pipes
- Date arithmetic
- Date format conversion
- Evaluating transcendental math functions
- Listing all array "tails"
- Searches in strings, files, and compound variables

These enhancements mean that Personal REXX is a wise investment for OS/2 even though IBM ships OS/2 with a version of REXX included free of charge. The enhancements are also supported in the DOS and Windows versions.

REXX is an excellent and very powerful replacement for the batch language. The availability of Personal REXX under OS/2, Windows NT, Windows, and DOS means that you can use it as your batch language on all these platforms, something no other language offers.

QTOD

Version. 1.21

Price. Free, but a charity donation is requested. Commercial users must pay for the program.

Category. Copyrighted/shareware

Author. Thomas Harold, at the following address:
P.O. Box 368
Camp Hill, PA 17001

CD-ROM directory. \UTILITY\OS2\QTOD200

QTOD displays the date and time on the command line in a format suitable for redirecting to another file, such as a backup log or computer usage log. Naturally, it's designed to be run from the command line. This nifty installation program gives you a great deal of flexibility over how the date and time are displayed. There's also a DOS version.

REXXLIB for OS/2

Version. 3.00

Price. $20 for basic registration and $50 for full registration

Category. Shareware

Author. Quercus Systems, at:
P.O. Box 2157
Saratoga, CA 95070
(408) 867-REXX

CD-ROM directory. \UTILITY\OS2\REXXLB
The previous description for Personal REXX lists a number of features that Personal REXX adds to the REXX language. If you choose to stick with the IBM version of REXX, this set of functions duplicates all those nifty features. A basic registration of $20 gets you a manual and online technical support. A full registration of $50 gets you the manual, online technical support, phone and fax technical support, and a license to redistribute the functions as part of an application.

Wpsbkup

Version. 2.11

Price. $15

Category. Shareware

Author. New Freedom Data Center, at the following address:
P.O. Box 461
New Freedom, PA 17349

CD-ROM directory. \UTILITY\DOS\WPSBKUP
Under OS/2, it takes a lot of work to set up your desktop exactly the way you want it. Once you have all your batch files, programs, and folders configured the way you want it, Wpsbkup can create a backup of your desktop. If you've ever had to reinstall OS/2, you can use Wpsbkup to restore your desktop to its state at your last backup. It's interesting to note that Wpsbkup creates a series of OS/2 batch files that you can then run to perform the actual restoration of your desktop.

While not exactly crippleware, the version of Wpsbkup included on the CD-ROM is restricted. Once you install it, it will execute only 15 times. After that, you must register to continue using it. Since Wpsbkup performs the desktop backup, but simply creates batch files to do the restoration, there's no restriction on the number of restorations you can perform.

Solutions to Problems

Solution 1

FORMAT.BAT gives some general information on formatting a disk and then pauses before the actual formatting in case the user wants to press Ctrl–Break.

Batch File Line	Explanation
`@ECHO OFF`	Turn command-echoing off.

`REM NAME:    FORMAT.COM`
`REM PURPOSE: Format Diskette In A Drive`
`REM VERSION: 1.00`
`REM DATE:    May 12, 1992`
	Documentation remarks.

`NEEDHELP %0 %1` `IF ERRORLEVEL 1 GOTO HELP`	Use the NeedHelp utility program to check and see if the user requested help.
`CLS`	Clear the screen.

`ECHO PURPOSE`
`ECHO`
`ECHO    You Are About To Format A Disk.`
`ECHO This Prepares The Disk To Be Used`
`ECHO By The Computer But It Also Erases`
`ECHO Any Information Already On The Disk.`
`ECHO`
	Explain the purpose to the user. Note that the lines that appear to be an ECHO command by itself also contain the invisible Alt-255 character.

`ECHO What To Do`
`ECHO`
`ECHO    Place The Disk To Be Formatted`
`ECHO In The A Drive (The One On Top) And`
`ECHO Press Any Key. If You Are Not Sure`
`ECHO You Want To Erase This Disk, Press`
`ECHO Ctrl-Break And Answer Yes To Stop`
`ECHO This Batch File.`
`ECHO`
	Tell the user what to do.

Solution 1 Continued

Batch File Line	Explanation
ECHO Safety Check ECHO ECHO If You Break Out Of This Batch ECHO File, You Can Check The Disk To See ECHO If It Has Any Files With The DIR A: ECHO Command From The DR DOS Prompt. ECHO	Tell the user what to do if he encounters a problem.
PAUSE	Pause the batch file prior to running the formatting program to give the user a chance to read the screen and abort the process if desired.
XYZ A:	Perform the formatting using the renamed XYZ.COM.
GOTO END	Jump to the end of the batch file.

:HELP
   ECHO Formats A Floppy Disk
   Echo In The A Drive
GOTO END
	Display a help screen and exit the batch file when the user requests help.

:END	Label marking the end of the batch file.

Solution 2

AUTO-1.BAT is a sample AUTOEXEC.BAT file that performs the four tasks outlined in the book. In order for this file to work properly, you would have to rename it AUTOEXEC.BAT and store it in the root directory of the boot drive.

Batch File Line	Explanation
@ECHO OFF	Turn command-echoing off.
REM NAME: AUTO-1.BAT REM Of Course, To Run REM Properly, Would Need REM To Be Renamed To REM AUTOEXEC.BAT REM PURPOSE: Solution To Problem #2 REM VERSION: 1.00 REM DATE: May 12, 1992	Documentation remarks.
REM Delete These Tests After REM Renaming To AUTOEXEC.BAT IF NOT (%0)==() ECHO Do Not Run From Command Line IF NOT (%0)==() ECHO Sample AUTOEXEC.BAT File IF NOT (%0)==() GOTO END	Warning remarks in case the user runs from command line. Will display a warning and drop out to DOS.
REM Set Path REM ========	Documentation remarks for this section.
ECHO Creating Path	Tell the user what will happen next.

Batch File Line	Explanation
PATH=C:\;C:\DRDOS;C:\BAT;C:\NORTON;C:\123; C:\WP;C:\UTILITY;C:\MENU	Set the path using a DR DOS command. Of course, in the batch file this is all on one line.
REM Create Environmental Variables REM ==============================	Documentation remarks for this section.
ECHO Creating Environmental Variables	Tell the user what will happen next.
SET TEMP=C:\TEMP SET DOSONLY=YES SET LIB=D:\BLDLITE SET OBJ=D:\BLDLITE	Create four environmental variables and store values to them.
REM Turn Off Screen Prints REM =====================	Documentation remarks for this section.
ECHO Turning Off Screen Prints	Tell the user what will happen next.
NOPRTSCR	Run a utility program to turn off screen printing. Many such programs are available on networks such as CompuServe and PC-Link.
REM Starting Menu REM =============	Documentation remarks for this section.
ECHO Starting Menu	Tell the user what will happen next.
MENU	Run the menu program.
:END	Label marking the end of the batch file.

Solution 3

ACCTHELP.BAT explains how to use three accounting programs stored on the computer.

Batch File Line	Explanation
@ECHO OFF	Turn command-echoing off.
REM NAME: ACCTHELP.BAT REM PURPOSE: Provide Accounting Help REM VERSION: 1.00 REM DATE: May 12, 1992	Documentation remarks.
CLS	Clear the screen.
ECHO Introduction ECHO ECHO This Accounting System Uses Three ECHO Different Programs To Manage Customer ECHO Accounts. They Are: ECHO 1. DAILY.EXE ECHO 2. WEEKLY.EXE ECHO 3. ANNUAL.EXE ECHO	Display the first section of information. Note that the lines containing just an ECHO command are followed by an Alt-255 character to display a blank line.

Solution 3 Continued

Batch File Line	Explanation
ECHO Daily ECHO ECHO This Program Performs The Closing That ECHO Is Required Each Day. It Can Be Run By ECHO Any Clerk Using The General Clerical ECHO Password. Note That It Must Be Run ECHO After 4PM And Not Before. ECHO	Display the next section of information.
PAUSE	Pause the program until the user presses a key. This gives the user time to read the screen.
CLS	Once the user presses a key, clear the screen.
ECHO Weekly ECHO ECHO This Program Performs The Closing That ECHO Is Required Each Week. It Can Be ECHO Run Only By A Senior Clerk Or Above And ECHO Requires A Management-1 Password. It ECHO Must Be Run On The Last Working Day Of ECHO The Month And Must Be Run After ECHO Running The Daily Closing Program. ECHO	Display the next section of information.
ECHO Annual ECHO ECHO This Program Performs The Annual ECHO Closing Required At The End Of Each ECHO Year. It Can Be Run Only By A Branch ECHO Manager And Requires A Management-4 ECHO Password. It Must Be Run On The Last ECHO Day Of The Year After Running The Daily ECHO Closing Program. ECHO	Display the next section of information.
PAUSE	Pause the program until the user presses a key. This gives the user time to read the screen.
CLS	Once the user presses a key, clear the screen.
ECHO Backups ECHO ECHO Corporate Policy Requires Two Backups ECHO To Be Performed After A Weekly Closing. ECHO One Backup Must Be Sent To The IS ECHO Department At Headquarters (24/185) ECHO And The Other Retained Locally. ECHO Three Backups Are Required After An ECHO Annual Closing. In Addition To The IS ECHO And Local Copies, A Copy Is To Be ECHO Sent To The Legal Department (28/185). ECHO	Display the next section of information.

Batch File Line	Explanation
ECHO More Help ECHO ECHO If You Need More Help, Contact: ECHO ECHO Mark Williams ECHO 24/185 ECHO Extension 256 ECHO	Display the last section of information.
PAUSE	Pause the program until the user presses a key.

Solution 4

RUNCHECK.BAT continually runs a program called Check-It-Out and displays the results on the screen.

Batch File Line	Explanation
@ECHO OFF	Turn command-echoing off.
REM NAME: RUNCHECK.BAT REM PURPOSE: Run Check-It-Out Program REM And Report Errors REM Solution To Problem #4 REM VERSION: 1.00 REM DATE: May 17, 1992	Documentation remarks.
NEEDHELP %0 %1 IF ERRORLEVEL 1 GOTO HELP	Use the NeedHelp utility program to check and see if the user requested help.
CLS	Clear the screen.
:TOP	Label marking the top of a loop.
CHKITOUT	Run the Check-It-Out program.
IF ERRORLEVEL 1 ECHO CheckItOut Had Problems IF ERRORLEVEL 1 GOTO TOP	If it had a problem, display a message and continue looping.
ECHO Check-It-Out Ran Fine GOTO TOP	If it did not have a problem, it reaches this point so display a message and continue looping.
:HELP ECHO Continually Runs CHKITOUT GOTO END	Display a help screen and exit the batch file when the user requests help.
:END	Label marking the end of the batch file.

Solution 5

BOOT-4-D.BAT is called by the AUTOEXEC.BAT file and reboots the computer if the D drive is not working.

Batch File Line	Explanation
@ECHO OFF	Turn command-echoing off.
REM NAME: BOOT-4-D.BAT REM PURPOSE: Reboot Until D Drive Works REM Solution To Problem #5 REM VERSION: 1.00 REM DATE: May 17, 1992	Documentation remarks.
NEEDHELP %0 %1 IF ERRORLEVEL 1 GOTO HELP	Use the NeedHelp utility program to check and see if the user requested help.
IF EXIST D:*.* GOTO END	If any file on the D drive exists, then the batch file does not need to do anything so jump to the end.
IF NOT (%0)==() ECHO Do Not Run From Command Line IF NOT (%0)==() ECHO Rename To AUTOEXEC.BAT IF NOT (%0)==() GOTO END	Make sure the user does not run from command line—except to get help.
BOOT	Run a program to reboot the computer. Of course, this halts the execution of this batch file.

:HELP
   ECHO Reboots If D Drive
   ECHO Not Working
GOTO END
	Display a help screen and exit the batch file when the user requests help.

:END	Label marking the end of the batch file.

Solution 6

READFILE.BAT displays the files entered on the command line one at a time by typing them to the screen and using the MORE filter to display them one screen at a time.

Batch File Line	Explanation
@ECHO OFF	Turn command-echoing off.
REM NAME: READFILE.BAT REM PURPOSE: Display ASCII Files REM VERSION: 1.00 REM DATE: May 17, 1992	Documentation remarks.
NEEDHELP %0 %1 IF ERRORLEVEL 1 GOTO HELP	Use the NeedHelp utility program to check and see if the user requested help.
:TOP	Label marking the top of a loop.
CLS	Clear the screen.
IF (%1)==() GOTO END	If there are no more replaceable parameters, jump to the end of the batch file.
ECHO Displaying %1	Display the name of the next file to be displayed.

Batch File Line	Explanation
`TYPE %1 | MORE`	Type the file and use the More filter to display it one screen at a time.
`SHIFT`	Move all the replaceable parameters down one level and make another replaceable parameter available as %9.
`PAUSE`	Pause the program until the user presses a key.
`GOTO TOP`	Continue looping.

`:HELP`
`   ECHO Display ASCII Files`
`GOTO END`
	Display a help screen and exit the batch file when the user requests help.

`:END`	Label marking the end of the batch file.

Solution 7

COPYTHEM.BAT copies all the files specified on the command line to the A drive only if that file does not already exist on the A drive.

Batch File Line	Explanation
`@ECHO OFF`	Turn command-echoing off.

`REM NAME:     COPYTHEM.BAT`
`REM PURPOSE: Copy Files To A Drive`
`REM VERSION: 1.00`
`REM DATE:    May 26, 1992`
	Documentation remarks.

`NEEDHELP %0 %1` `IF ERRORLEVEL 1 GOTO HELP`	Use the NeedHelp utility program to check and see if the user started the batch file with a /? switch.
`IF (%1)==() GOTO ERROR`	If the user did not request help and did not specify files to copy, jump to an error-handling section. This must come after running the NeedHelp routine since COPYTHEM/? will not have a %1 under MS-DOS.
`IF (%1)==(XYZ123ABC) GOTO SUB`	If the batch file is running as a subroutine, jump to the subroutine section.
`:TOP`	Label marking the top of the main loop.
`   IF ERRORLEVEL 1 GOTO END`	If XCOPY reported an error via the errorlevel in the subroutine, exit the batch file.
`   IF (%1)==() GOTO END`	Once the batch file runs out of replaceable parameters, exit the batch file.
`   FOR %%J in (%1) DO CALL COPYTHEM XYZ123ABC %%J`	Loop through all the files matching the current %1 replaceable parameter and call this batch file as a subroutine for each one. This is required to handle files individually when the user specifies a wildcard.
`   SHIFT`	Move all the replaceable parameters down one level.

Solution 7 Continued

Batch File Line	Explanation
GOTO TOP	Continue looping.
:SUB	Label marking the top of the subroutine portion of the batch file.
IF EXIST A:%2 ECHO %2 Already On A Drive	If the file is already on the A drive, warn the user.
IF EXIST A:%2 GOTO END	If the file is already on the A drive, exit the subroutine without copying the file.
XCOPY %2 A:	If the subroutine reaches this point, the file does not exist on the A drive so copy it with XCOPY in order to use the errorlevel.
IF ERRORLEVEL 1 ECHO Problem Copying %2	If XCOPY reports an error via the errorlevel, display a warning message.
GOTO END	This is the end of the subroutine to exit the batch file so control will return to the calling version of this batch file.

:ERROR
   ECHO Must Speficy The Files To
   ECHO Copy On The Command Line
GOTO END
	Display an error message and exit when the user does not enter any replaceable parameters.

:HELP
   ECHO Copies The Files You Specify
   ECHO On The Command Line To The
   ECHO A Drive Without Writing
   ECHO Over Any Files
GOTO END
	Display help and exit when requested by the user.

:END	Label marking the end of the batch file.

Solution 8

When run with a command following its name, USEOVER.BAT stores that command to an environmental variable and then runs the command. When run alone, USE-OVER.BAT runs the command stored in the environment.

Batch File Line	Explanation
@ECHO OFF	Turn command-echoing off.
REM NAME: USEOVER.BAT REM PURPOSE: Use A Command Over And Over REM VERSION: 1.02 REM DATE: August 3, 1991	Documentation remarks.
NEEDHELP %0 %1 IF ERRORLEVEL 1 GOTO HELP	Use the NeedHelp utility program to check and see if the user started the batch file with a /? switch.
IF (%1)==() GOTO JUSTCMD	If the user did not enter a new command, rerun the one already in the environment.
REM Construct Command in REM Environmental Variable	Documentation remarks.

Batch File Line	Explanation
`SET COMMAND=`	If the batch file reaches this point, then the user has entered a new command so delete the old one. This command has no effect if an old value does not exist.
`:TOP`	Label marking the top of the loop to define the command.
`   SET COMMAND=%COMMAND% %1`	Replace the contents of the Command environmental variable with its current value plus %1 added to the end. Building the final variable in this fashion avoids having to limit the command to nine components.
`   SHIFT`	Move all the replaceable parameters down one level and make another replaceable parameter available as %9.
`   IF (%1)==() GOTO JUSTCMD`	If no more portions of the command exist, jump to a section to run the command.
`GOTO TOP`	If more portions of the command exist, loop through again and add them.
`:JUSTCMD`	Beginning of the section to run the command.
`   %COMMAND%`	Run the command.
`GOTO END`	Exit the batch file.

`:HELP`
`   ECHO JUSTCMD Runs Stored Command`
`   ECHO JUSTCMD Part1 Part2 ... PartN`
`   ECHO Stores And Runs The New Command`
`GOTO END`
	Display a help screen and exit the batch file when the user requests help.

`:END`	Label marking the end of the batch file.

Solution 9

COPYTHE2.BAT copies all the files specified on the command line to the A drive. Unlike COPYTHEM.BAT, COPYTHE2.BAT will ask the user what to do if there is already a version of the file on the A drive.

Batch File Line	Explanation
`@ECHO OFF`	Turn command-echoing off.

`REM NAME:      COPYTHE2.BAT`
`REM          Modified For Problem 9`
`REM          And Stored As COPYTHE2.BAT`
`REM PURPOSE: Copy Files To A Drive`
`REM VERSION: 2.00`
`REM DATE:    May 26, 1992`
	Documentation remarks.

`NEEDHELP %0 %1` `IF ERRORLEVEL 1 GOTO HELP`	Use the NeedHelp utility program to check and see if the user started the batch file with a /? switch.

Solution 9 Continued

Batch File Line	Explanation
`IF (%1)==() GOTO ERROR`	If the user did not request help and did not specify files to copy, jump to an error-handling section. This must come after running the NeedHelp routine since COPYTHEM/? will not have a %1 under MS-DOS.
`IF (%1)==(XYZ123ABC) GOTO SUB`	If the batch file is running as a subroutine, jump to the subroutine section.
`:TOP`	Label marking the top of the main loop.
`    IF ERRORLEVEL 1 GOTO END`	If XCOPY reported an error via the errorlevel in the subroutine, exit the batch file.
`    IF (%1)==() GOTO END`	Once the batch file runs out of replaceable parameters, exit the batch file.
`        FOR %%J in (%1) DO CALL COPYTHE2 XYZ123ABC %%J`	Loop through all the files matching the current %1 replaceable parameter and call this batch file as a subroutine for each one. This is required to handle files individually when the user specifies a wildcard.
`    SHIFT`	Move all the replaceable parameters down one level and make another replaceable parameter available as %9.
`GOTO TOP`	Continue looping.
`:SUB`	Label marking the top of the subroutine portion of the batch file.
`    IF EXIST A:%2 GOTO DUP`	If the file is already on the A drive, jump to the subroutine to handle this.
`    XCOPY %2 A:`	If the subroutine reaches this point, the file does not exist on the A drive so copy it with XCOPY in order to use the errorlevel.
`    IF ERRORLEVEL 1 ECHO Problem Copying %2`	If XCOPY reports an error via the errorlevel, display a warning message.
`GOTO END`	This is the end of the subroutine to exit the batch file so control will return to the calling version of this batch file.
`:DUP`	Beginning of the subroutine to deal with the file already existing on the A drive.
`    ECHO %2 Already Exists On A Drive`	Tell the user about the duplicate file.

`    ECHO A Drive`
`    ECHO -------`
`    DIR A:%2`
	Show the user the file on the A drive.

`    ECHO Current Drive`
`    ECHO ------------`
`    DIR %2`
	Show the user the file on the current drive.

`    BATCMD YN Overwrite %2 On A Drive (Y/N)?`	Ask the user if the batch file should overwrite the file on the A drive.

Batch File Line	Explanation
`    IF NOT ERRORLEVEL 1 GOTO END`	If the user answers no, exit the subroutine.
`    XCOPY %2 A:`	The subroutine only reaches this point if the user answers yes so copy the file.
`    IF ERRORLEVEL 1 ECHO Problem Copying %2`	If XCOPY reports an error via the errorlevel, display a warning message.
`GOTO END`	This is the end of the subroutine to exit the batch file so control will return to the calling version of this batch file.

`:ERROR`
`    ECHO Must Speficy The Files To`
`    ECHO Copy On The Command Line`
`GOTO END`
	Display an error message and exit when the user does not enter any replaceable parameters.

`:HELP`
`    ECHO Copies The Files You Specify`
`    ECHO On The Command Line To The`
`    ECHO A Drive Without Writing`
`    ECHO Over Any Files`
`GOTO END`
	Display help and exit when requested by the user.

`:END`	Label marking the end of the batch file.

Solution 10

PHONE.BAT dials the phone number for the nickname entered on the command line. You will have to enter your own nicknames and phone numbers before using PHONE.BAT.

PHONE1.BAT does everything PHONE.BAT does plus built-in error-checking. Before issuing a GOTO %1 command, it searches PHONE1.BAT to ensure that the specified batch file exists. While slower and more complex, this check prevents the batch file from aborting with the "Label not found" error message.

Batch File Line	Explanation
`@ECHO OFF`	Turn command-echoing off.

`REM NAME:    PHONE.BAT`
`REM PURPOSE: Telephone Database`
`REM VERSION: 1.00`
`REM DATE:    June 11, 1992`
	Documentation remarks.

`NEEDHELP %0 %1` `IF ERRORLEVEL 1 GOTO HELP`	Use the NeedHelp utility program to check and see if the user started the batch file with a /? switch.
`IF (%1)==() GOTO NONE`	If the user did not enter a nickname, jump to an error-handling section.
`GOTO %1`	Jump to the section for the nickname the user entered. If the nickname entered by the user does not exist as a label, the batch file will abort on this line.

Solution 10A Continued

Batch File Line	Explanation
REM ------------------------- REM The GOTO %1 Line Above Will REM Cause The Batch File To REM Abort If The Label Does REM Exist REM -------------------------	Documentation remarks.

:HELP
    ECHO Dials Phone
    ECHO The Syntax Is
    ECHO PHONE Nickname
 GOTO END
	Display a help screen and exit the batch file when the user requests help.

:NONE
    ECHO You Did Not Enter A
    ECHO Nickname To Dial
    ECHO The Syntax Is
    ECHO PHONE Nickname
 GOTO END
	Error section that handles the situation with the user does not enter a nickname.

:DIRECTORY
 :INFORMATION
    ECHO ATDT 411 > COM1
    ECHO Dial Information
    ECHO Press Any Key When Ringing
    PAUSE
    ECHO ATH > COM1
 GOTO END
	Section that handles dialing information. Notice the use of multiple labels. The echoing of ATDT and ATH is explained in the text.

:TAB
 :TABBOOKS
    ECHO ATDT 1 (800) 233-1128 > COM1
    ECHO Dialing McGraw-Hill
    ECHO Press Any Key When Ringing
    PAUSE
    ECHO ATH > COM1
 GOTO END
	Section that handles dialing McGraw-Hill.

:911
    ECHO ATDT 911 > COM1
    ECHO 911
    ECHO Press Any Key When Ringing
    PAUSE
    ECHO ATH > COM1
 GOTO END
	Section that handles dialing 911.

:END	Label marking the end of the batch file.

Solution 10B

Batch File Line	Explanation
@ECHO OFF	Turn command-echoing off.
REM NAME: PHONE1.BAT REM PURPOSE: Telephone Database REM Modified Version Of REM PHONE.BAT That Checks REM For Valid Label First REM VERSION: 1.00 REM DATE: June 11, 1992	Documentation remarks.
NEEDHELP %0 %1 IF ERRORLEVEL 1 GOTO HELP	Use the NeedHelp utility program to check and see if the user started the batch file with a /? switch.
IF (%1)==() GOTO NONE	If the user did not enter a nickname, jump to an error-handling section.
REM Type The Batch File And Search REM For A Valid Label	Documentation remarks.
TYPE C:\BAT\PHONE1.BAT|FIND ":%1">JUNK	Type the batch file and use the Find filter to search for the specified label. Notice that the full path to the batch file is specified. This is required since you never know from which subdirectory it will be run. Also note the colon before the %1. This makes sure the matching text is a label.
ISITZERO JUNK	Check to see if the resulting file is a zero-length file.
IF NOT ERRORLEVEL 4 GOTO %1	IsItZero sets the errorlevel to four for a zero-length file which indicates the label was not found. For any other errorlevel value, jump to the appropriate section.
GOTO MISSING	Jump to an error-handling section that handles the problem of the user entering an invalid label.

:MISSING
    ECHO The Label You Specified (%1)
    ECHO Does Not Exist As A Nickname
    ECHO PHONE1.BAT Aborting
GOTO END
	When the label is not found, explain the problem to the user and exit the batch file.

:HELP
    ECHO Dials Phone
    ECHO The Syntax Is
    ECHO PHONE Nickname
GOTO END
	Display a help screen and exit the batch file when the user requests help. From here on down, PHONE1.BAT is identical to PHONE.BAT.

:NONE
    ECHO You Did Not Enter A
    ECHO Nickname To Dial
    ECHO The Syntax Is
    ECHO PHONE Nickname
GOTO END
	Error section that handles the situation with the user does not enter a nickname.

Solution 10B Continued

Batch File Line	Explanation

:DIRECTORY
:INFORMATION
   ECHO ATDT 411 > COM1
   ECHO Dial Information
   ECHO Press Any Key When Ringing
   PAUSE
   ECHO ATH > COM1
GOTO END
	Section that handles dialing information. Notice the use of multiple labels. The echoing of ATDT and ATH is explained in the text.

:TAB
:TABBOOKS
   ECHO ATDT 1 (800) 233-1128 > COM1
   ECHO Dialing McGraw-Hill
   ECHO Press Any Key When Ringing
   PAUSE
   ECHO ATH > COM1
GOTO END
	Section that handles dialing McGraw-Hill.

:911
   ECHO ATDT 911 > COM1
   ECHO 911
   ECHO Press Any Key When Ringing
   PAUSE
   ECHO ATH > COM1
GOTO END
	Section that handles dialing 911.

:END	Label marking the end of the batch file.

Solution 11

SHOWBACK.BAT lists every file on the C drive that has been modified since the last backup.

Batch File Line	Explanation
@ECHO OFF	Turn command-echoing off.
REM NAME: SHOWBACK.BAT REM PURPOSE: Show Files Needing Backup REM VERSION: 1.00 REM DATE: June 11, 1992	Documentation remarks.
NEEDHELP %0 %1 IF ERRORLEVEL 1 GOTO HELP	Use the NeedHelp utility program to check and see if the user requested help.
ECHO ---WORKING--- ECHO ---This Takes Time---	Tell the user what is happening.
ATTRIB C:*.* /S | FIND " A " | MORE	Find the files needing backup and display them with the More filter.
GOTO END	Exit the batch file.
:HELP ECHO Shows Files Needing Backup GOTO END	Display a help screen and exit the batch file when the user requests help.
:END	Label marking the end of the batch file.

Solution 12

QCD.BAT allows the user to enter a drive and subdirectories after the batch file name without a colon or backslash, and it still changes to the proper subdirectory.

Batch File Line	Explanation
`@ECHO OFF`	Turn command-echoing off.

`REM NAME:      QCD.BAT`
`REM PURPOSE:   Speed Directory Changes`
`REM VERSION:   1.01`
`REM DATE:      December 20, 1991`
`REM REVISION:  1.01 Added Deleting`
`               NeedSpace So Program`
`               Would Work When Shelled`
`               Out`
	Documentation remarks.

`NEEDHELP %0 %1` `IF ERRORLEVEL 1 GOTO HELP`	Use the NeedHelp utility program to check and see if the user requested help.
`IF (%1)==() GOTO ERROR1`	The user did not specify a subdirectory so jump to an error section.

`IF (%1)==(\) CD\`
`IF (%1)==(\) SHIFT`
`IF (%1)==() GOTO END`
	If the user requested the root directory, change to there and exit.

`SET NEEDSPACE=`	Reset this environmental variable to make space in case QCD.BAT is run while shelled out of another program. On my system, Needspace contains a long string of Xs.
`SET DIR=NO`	Create a flag environmental variable.
`FOR %%J IN (a A b B c C d D) DO` `        IF (%1)==(%%J) SET DIR=YES`	Loop through all the drives to see if the user is changing drives. If so, change a flag.
`IF %DIR%==NO GOTO SKIP`	If the flag indicates no drive change, skip drive change code.
`%1:`	Change to the requested drive.
`SHIFT`	Remove the drive replaceable parameter.

`IF (%1)==(\) CD\`
`IF (%1)==(\) SHIFT`
`IF (%1)==() GOTO END`
	Check to see if the next replaceable parameter requests a change to the root directory and if so change there.

`:SKIP`	Label to skip drive change.
`SET DIR=`	Remove the drive change flag environmental variable.
`:TOPLOOP`	Top of loop to create environmental variable containing the subdirectory.
`    SET DIR=%DIR%\%1`	Add a subdirectory.
`    SHIFT`	Move all the replaceable parameters down one level.
`    IF NOT (%1)==() GOTO TOPLOOP`	If there are more replaceable parameters, continue looping.
`    CD %DIR%`	Change to the requested subdirectory.
`GOTO END`	Exit the batch file.

Solution 12 Continued

Batch File Line	Explanation

`:ERROR`
`    ECHO No Drive / Subdirectory Specified`
`    ECHO Use QCD Drive Sub1 Sub2 So On`
`    ECHO Without A Colon Or Backslash`
`GOTO END`
	Section to display an error message.

`:HELP`
`    ECHO QCD.BAT Will Change Drives And`
`    ECHO Subdirectories Without Entering`
`    ECHO The Colon After The Drive Or The`
`    ECHO Backslash Between The`
`    ECHO Subdirectories`
`    BATCMD SL`
`    ECHO Enter: QCD Drive Sub1 Sub2 So On`
`GOTO END`
	Display a help screen and exit the batch file when the user requests help.

`:END`	Label marking the end of the batch file.
`SET DIR=`	Reset the environmental variable used by the batch file.

`SET NEEDSPACE=XXXXXXXXXXXXXXXXXXXXXXXXXXXXXX`
`            XXXXXXXXXXXXXXXXXXXXXXXXXXXXXX`
`            XXXXXXXXXXXXXXXXXXXXXXXXXXXXXX`
`            XXXXXXXXXXXXXXXXXXXXXXXXX`
	Recreate the environmental variable that is used to free up environmental space when the batch file is run while shelled out.

Solution 13

KILLZERO.BAT will list the 0-length files on the screen and give you the option to delete them. If you select "Yes," it automatically deletes them all.

Batch File Line	Explanation
`@ECHO OFF`	Turn command-echoing off.

`REM NAME:    KILLZERO.BAT`
`REM PURPOSE: Erase Zero-Length Files`
`REM VERSION: 1.00`
`REM DATE:    June 11, 1992`
	Documentation remarks.

`IF (%1)==(ABC123XYZ) GOTO SUB1` `IF (%1)==(XYZ123ABC) GOTO SUB2`	If KILLZERO.BAT is being called as a subroutine, jump to the appropriate subroutine section.
`NEEDHELP %0 %1` `IF ERRORLEVEL 1 GOTO HELP`	Use the NeedHelp utility program to check and see if the user started the batch file with a /? switch.
`SET KILL=NO`	Create an environmental variable to act as a flag indicating if any zero-length files are found.
`FOR %%J IN (*.*) DO CALL KILLZERO ABC123XYZ %%J`	Loop through the files once and call KILLZERO.BAT as a subroutine to list the zero-length files.
`IF (%KILL%)==(NO) ECHO No Zero-Length Files To Erase` `IF (%KILL%)==(NO) GOTO END1`	If no zero-length files were found, display a message and jump to an exiting section.

Batch File Line	Explanation
BATCMD YN Erase These Files? (Y/N)	If the batch file reaches this point, zero-length files were found. Ask the user about deleting them.
IF NOT ERRORLEVEL 1 GOTO END1	If the user answers no, jump to an exiting section.
FOR %%J IN (*.*) DO CALL KILLZERO XYZ123ABC %%J	If the batch file reaches this point, the user elected to delete the 0-length files. Call KILLZERO.BAT as a subroutine to do that.
GOTO END1	Jump to an exiting section.
:SUB1	Label marking the beginning of the first subroutine.
ISITZERO %2	The filename is passed as the second replaceable parameter. Test it to see if it is a zero-length file.
IF ERRORLEVEL 4 ECHO %2 To Be Erased	If it is, display its name.
IF ERRORLEVEL 4 SET KILL=YES	If it is a zero-length file, set a flag.
GOTO END	Exit the subroutine.

:SUB2
   ISITZERO %2
   IF ERRORLEVEL 4 ECHO Killing %2
   IF ERRORLEVEL 4 ERASE %2
GOTO END
	Use the same procedures as the first subroutine to identify and delete the zero-length files. Be careful with this section. A mistake can cause all your files to be erased.

:HELP
   ECHO Automatically Erase
       Zero-Length Files
GOTO END
	Display a help screen and exit the batch file when the user requests help.

:END1 SET KILL= GOTO END	This exiting section is used to reset the environmental variable. This cannot be handled after the :END label since the subroutines use that label to exit and the value is still needed after the subroutines run.
:END	Label marking the end of the batch file.

B

Files on the CD-ROM

This appendix contains a description of all the files on the CD-ROM, broken down by subdirectory. Before looking at the files, let's take a moment to review the different types of programs discussed in this book.

Types of Programs

The main types of programs discussed in this book are as follows:

Commercial. These are programs you must buy in a computer store or order from the vendor or mail-order company. The CD-ROM contains demo versions of a few commercial programs. These are generally restricted in what they can perform. The back of the book contains some coupons for programs, so you can save money when you buy them.

Copyrighted. These are programs where the author retains the copyright, but doesn't require a registration fee. As a general rule, you can copy these programs to as many computers as you like and give copies to other users. Occasionally, the author will place a minor restriction on the program, such as not allowing it to be used at any military installation or not allowing the program to be included with any commercial product. Check the program documentation for any restrictions.

Shareware. These are try-it-before-you-buy-it programs. If you continue to use a shareware program beyond an initial evaluation period, you're expected to register it with the author and pay the registration fee. Complete registration instructions are included with the program. These programs are on the CD-ROM as a convenience to you, but the authors received no income from the sale of this book and CD-ROM. You must register and pay for these programs if you use them.

Crippleware. These are "sort of" shareware programs. They're limited in some way and the limitation won't prevent you from trying the program, but you won't receive the fully functional version until you register. For example, the DIR2BAT program can process only up to four files per subdirectory until you register and receive the full version. Most of the shareware programs on the CD-ROM are not crippleware.

PC Magazine. *PC Magazine* has published a number of batch file utilities. These are copyrighted, but are free to readers of *PC Magazine*. They can also be downloaded from the magazine's area on CompuServe. If you don't have a modem, you can write to *PC Magazine* to receive a free copy on disk by mail. *PC Magazine* doesn't allow their programs to be included with books not published by Ziff Davis, so these programs aren't included on the CD-ROM.

Public domain. This is a program the author makes no copyright claim to, so you're free to copy the program to any computer you use and give copies to other users. There's no fee for using these programs.

Written for this book. These are programs written either by me or someone else specifically for this book, and they're free when you buy this book. You may install a copy of each program on each machine you use, even if it's possible that more than one copy of a program will be run at once. You may not give away or sell copies of any of these programs and you may not upload any of them to a bulletin board system.

The Ultimate CD-ROM Manager

The root directory contains a file management program called The Ultimate CD-ROM Manager. The CD-ROM contains over 7,500 files and 250 subdirectories, so moving around and finding the files you want might be a little difficult, even with the complete listing in this appendix. However, The Ultimate CD-ROM Manager makes it easy. This program was written by William Richardson of hyperkinetix, the makers of the Builder batch file compiler.

To start The Ultimate CD-ROM Manager, just type ULT at the DOS prompt. This will create a split screen, with general information displayed on the right side and directory information on the left side. Along the bottom, you'll see the following options:

Copy. This lets you copy one or more files, which is very useful when you find the files you want to copy off the CD-ROM onto your hard disk.

Sort. This changes the order in which the files are listed.

Mask. This changes the files that are displayed. By default, *.* files are displayed.

Dir-L. This activates the left side of the screen to display a directory.

Dir-R. This activates the right side of the screen to display a directory. Having both sides activated is a handy way to copy files from one location to another, but it isn't required.

Format. This formats a floppy disk. This is handy if you're copying files from the CD-ROM to a floppy disk. You can't use it to format a hard disk.

View. This displays the highlighted ASCII file on the screen. This is a handy way to read documentation files.

Tree. This converts the entire screen to tree view. There will be a slight pause as it reads the CD-ROM drive. Once the tree is shown, you can highlight a subdirectory, press Return, and DOS will change to that subdirectory. While the tree is being displayed, you can highlight any subdirectory and press F1 to get a brief list of the contents of that subdirectory. This can be very useful when you're searching for a particular program.

Quit. This exits the program.

  This program is very handy for navigating the CD-ROM. If you use the Norton NCD program to navigate your hard disk, you'll find that the root directory of the CD-ROM contains the files needed to support NCD. To use it, just type NCD in any subdirectory on the CD-ROM to use NCD to navigate.

\BAT-FILE

This subdirectory contains no files. Rather, other subdirectories branch off it and these subdirectories contain the files. This branch of the CD-ROM stores the batch files (.BAT and .CMD) that are discussed in the book.

\BAT-FILE\DOS

This subdirectory, again, contains no files. This branch of the CD-ROM stores the DOS versions of the batch files (.BAT) discussed in the book.

\BAT-FILE\DOS\A\CHAP-01. This subdirectory contains the version of A.BAT discussed in Chapter 1.

\BAT-FILE\DOS\A\CHAP-05. This subdirectory contains the version of A.BAT discussed in Chapter 5.

\BAT-FILE\DOS\A\CHAP-10. This subdirectory contains the version of A.BAT discussed in Chapter 10.

\BAT-FILE\DOS\A\CHAP-16. This subdirectory contains the version of A.BAT discussed in Chapter 16.

\BAT-FILE\DOS\BAT. This subdirectory contains the DOS versions of the batch files discussed in the book.

\BAT-FILE\DOS\MENU1. Chapter 26 presents an in-depth discussion of DOS batch file menus. This subdirectory contains a complete nonresident nonnested menu system as a menu demonstration.

\BAT-FILE\DOS\MENU2. This subdirectory contains a complete hybrid resident nonnested menu system as a menu demonstration.

\BAT-FILE\DOS\MENU3. This subdirectory contains a complete stand-alone resident nonnested menu system as a menu demonstration.

\BAT-FILE\DOS\RONNYMD\CHAP-10. This subdirectory contains the version of RONNYMD.BAT discussed in Chapter 10.

\BAT-FILE\DOS\RONNYMD\CHAP-16. This subdirectory contains the version of RONNYMD.BAT discussed in Chapter 16.

\BAT-FILE\DOS\TOA\CHAP-10. This subdirectory contains the version of TOA.BAT discussed in Chapter 10.

\BAT-FILE\DOS\TOA\CHAP-11. This subdirectory contains the version of TOA.BAT discussed in Chapter 11.

\BAT-FILE\DOS\TOA\CHAP-12. This subdirectory contains the version of TOA.BAT discussed in Chapter 12.

\BAT-FILE\DOS\TOA\CHAP-16. This subdirectory contains the version of TOA.BAT discussed in Chapter 16.

\BAT-FILE\DOS\TOA\CHAP-22. This subdirectory contains the version of TOA.BAT discussed in Chapter 22.

\BAT-FILE\OS2

This subdirectory contains no files. Rather, other subdirectories branch off it and these subdirectories contain the files. This branch of the CD-ROM stores the OS/2 versions of the batch files (.CMD) that are discussed in the book.

\BAT-FILE\OS2\A\CHAP-01. This subdirectory contains the version of A.CMD discussed in Chapter 1.

\BAT-FILE\OS2\A\CHAP-05. This subdirectory contains the version of A.CMD discussed in Chapter 5.

\BAT-FILE\OS2\A\CHAP-10. This subdirectory contains the version of A.CMD discussed in Chapter 10.

\BAT-FILE\OS2\A\CHAP-16. This subdirectory contains the version of A.CMD discussed in Chapter 16.

\BAT-FILE\OS2\CMD. This subdirectory contains the OS/2 versions of the batch files discussed in the book. Many of them also have associated icon files with the same name and an .ICO extension.

\BAT-FILE\OS2\RONNYMD\CHAP-10. This subdirectory contains the version of RONNYMD.CMD discussed in Chapter 10.

\BAT-FILE\OS2\RONNYMD\CHAP-16. This subdirectory contains the version of RONNYMD.CMD discussed in Chapter 16.

\BAT-FILE\OS2\TOA\CHAP-10. This subdirectory contains the version of TOA.CMD discussed in Chapter 10.

\BAT-FILE\OS2\TOA\CHAP-11. This subdirectory contains the version of TOA.CMD discussed in Chapter 11.

\BAT-FILE\OS2\TOA\CHAP-12. This subdirectory contains the version of TOA.CMD discussed in Chapter 12.

\BAT-FILE\OS2\TOA\CHAP-16. This subdirectory contains the version of TOA.CMD discussed in Chapter 16.

\BAT-FILE\OS2\TOA\CHAP-22. This subdirectory contains the version of TOA.CMD discussed in Chapter 22.

\BATEDIT

This subdirectory contains the files for the BATedit editor, an ASCII file editor designed especially for editing DOS batch files. It was written by William Richardson of hyperkinetix, the makers of the Builder batch file compiler, especially for this book. I wrote two help files, one on the program itself and one on batch files.

\BLDLITE

This subdirectory contains the Builder Lite program, discussed in Chapter 40.

\BLDLITE\BTDEMO. This subdirectory contains a demo of the BuilderTools program, discussed in Chapter 40.

\BLDLITE\EXAMPLES. This subdirectory contains six example Builder programs.

\BLDLITE\MBDEMO. This subdirectory contains a demo of the MoreBuilder program, discussed in Chapter 40.

\BLDLITE\SBDEMO. This subdirectory contains a demo of the SuperBuilder program, discussed in Chapter 40.

\BLDLITE\WFBDEMO. This subdirectory contains a demo of the Workbench for Builder program, discussed in Chapter 40.

\BLDLITE\WODEMO. This subdirectory contains a demo of the WipeOut! for Builder program, discussed in Chapter 40.

\ICONS

This subdirectory contains no files. Rather, other subdirectories branch off it and these subdirectories contain the files. The CD-ROM contains numerous icons so you can make your batch files look impressive when you install them in the graphical environment of Windows or OS/2. This branch of the CD-ROM stores these icons.

\ICONS\OS2

Since there are so many icons on the CD-ROM, this subdirectory contains other subdirectories that contain the files. This branch of the CD-ROM stores the OS/2 icons.

\ICONS\OS2\ICONEASE. IconEase is an OS/2 icon management shareware program that makes it easy to look through a catalog of icons and assign one to the clipboard for a program or batch file. The program automatically arranges the icons alphabetically in a tabbed notebook. You click on a tab for the first letter of the icon name and then click on individual icon names to view them. Once you find one you want to use, clicking on a single button places it in the clipboard. After that, it's easy to assign the icon to a program or batch file using its Property Notebook.

I've compiled all 1,801 OS/2 icons into a single IconEase database so you can access all of them through IconEase. This database is also included in this subdirectory. If you like IconEase and have other OS/2 icons, New Freedom Data Center sells a database tool you can use to create your own icon data files for use with IconEase. It requires that you use an HPFS drive. Complete information can be found in the registration area of the IconEase help file.

It's impossible to use OS/2 a lot without an icon management tool like IconEase. Of all the OS/2 icon management tools I've seen, IconEase is the most intelligently designed. The icon database is compressed so you save space, but it's easy to view different icons and use them once you find one you like. If you agree with me and continue to use IconEase, please be sure to register your copy. I did.

\ICONS\OS2\1.OS2. This subdirectory contains all the OS/2 icon files (.ICO) whose names begin with the number 1.

\ICONS\OS2\3.OS2. This subdirectory contains all the OS/2 icon files (.ICO) whose names begin with the number 3.

\ICONS\OS2\4.OS2. This subdirectory contains all the OS/2 icon files (.ICO) whose names begin with the number 4.

\ICONS\OS2\5.OS2. This subdirectory contains all the OS/2 icon files (.ICO) whose names begin with the number 5.

\ICONS\OS2\6.OS2. This subdirectory contains all the OS/2 icon files (.ICO) whose names begin with the number 6.

\ICONS\OS2\7.OS2. This subdirectory contains all the OS/2 icon files (.ICO) whose names begin with the number 7.

\ICONS\OS2\8.OS2. This subdirectory contains all the OS/2 icon files (.ICO) whose names begin with the number 8.

\ICONS\OS2\A.OS2. This subdirectory contains all the OS/2 icon files (.ICO) whose names begin with the letter A.

\ICONS\OS2\B.OS2. This subdirectory contains all the OS/2 icon files (.ICO) whose names begin with the letter B.

\ICONS\OS2\C.OS2. This subdirectory contains all the OS/2 icon files (.ICO) whose names begin with the letter C.

\ICONS\OS2\D.OS2. This subdirectory contains all the OS/2 icon files (.ICO) whose names begin with the letter D.

\ICONS\OS2\E.OS2. This subdirectory contains all the OS/2 icon files (.ICO) whose names begin with the letter E.

\ICONS\OS2\F.OS2. This subdirectory contains all the OS/2 icon files (.ICO) whose names begin with the letter F.

\ICONS\OS2\G.OS2. This subdirectory contains all the OS/2 icon files (.ICO) whose names begin with the letter G.

\ICONS\OS2\H.OS2. This subdirectory contains all the OS/2 icon files (.ICO) whose names begin with the letter H.

\ICONS\OS2\I.OS2. This subdirectory contains all the OS/2 icon files (.ICO) whose names begin with the letter I.

\ICONS\OS2\J.OS2. This subdirectory contains all the OS/2 icon files (.ICO) whose names begin with the letter J.

\ICONS\OS2\K.OS2. This subdirectory contains all the OS/2 icon files (.ICO) whose names begin with the letter K.

\ICONS\OS2\L.OS2. This subdirectory contains all the OS/2 icon files (.ICO) whose names begin with the letter L.

\ICONS\OS2\M.OS2. This subdirectory contains all the OS/2 icon files (.ICO) whose names begin with the letter M.

\ICONS\OS2\N.OS2. This subdirectory contains all the OS/2 icon files (.ICO) whose names begin with the letter N.

\ICONS\OS2\O.OS2. This subdirectory contains all the OS/2 icon files (.ICO) whose names begin with the letter O.

\ICONS\OS2\P.OS2. This subdirectory contains all the OS/2 icon files (.ICO) whose names begin with the letter P.

\ICONS\OS2\Q.OS2. This subdirectory contains all the OS/2 icon files (.ICO) whose names begin with the letter Q.

\ICONS\OS2\R.OS2. This subdirectory contains all the OS/2 icon files (.ICO) whose names begin with the letter R.

\ICONS\OS2\S.OS2. This subdirectory contains all the OS/2 icon files (.ICO) whose names begin with the letter S.

\ICONS\OS2\T.OS2. This subdirectory contains all the OS/2 icon files (.ICO) whose names begin with the letter T.

\ICONS\OS2\U.OS2. This subdirectory contains all the OS/2 icon files (.ICO) whose names begin with the letter U.

\ICONS\OS2\V.OS2. This subdirectory contains all the OS/2 icon files (.ICO) whose names begin with the letter V.

\ICONS\OS2\W.OS2. This subdirectory contains all the OS/2 icon files (.ICO) whose names begin with the letter W.

\ICONS\OS2\X.OS2. This subdirectory contains all the OS/2 icon files (.ICO) whose names begin with the letter X.

\ICONS\OS2\Y.OS2. This subdirectory contains all the OS/2 icon files (.ICO) whose names begin with the letter Y.

\ICONS\OS2\Z.OS2. This subdirectory contains all the OS/2 icon files (.ICO) whose names begin with the letter Z.

\ICONS\WINDOWS

Other subdirectories branch off this subdirectory, and they contain Windows icons.

\ICONS\WINDOWS\DLLS.   When assigning an icon to a batch file or other program, if you don't know specifically which icon you want to use, working with individual icon files can be difficult. Windows allows you to group icons together into .DLL files and, when you use one of these .DLL files to select your icons, Windows lets you pick from all the icons in the .DLL. Since the number of icons in a .DLL file is limited, each letter and number is a separate .DLL file, so A.DLL contains all the icons starting with A, B.DLL contains all the icons starting with B, and so on. This subdirectory contains all these .DLL files.

\ICONS\WINDOWS\VBICONBR.   VB Icon Browser is a Windows icon management tool for preparing your icons for use with Windows. It's also shareware. When you start the program, it displays the hard disk directory tree on the left screen and the icons in its startup directory on the right side. It can display up to 36 icons at once. If there are more icons than that, you can use the scroll bar to view all of them.

Below the icons are three buttons you'll use to manage your icons: Delete, Copy, and Rename. VB Icon Browser is a drop-and-drag program, so these buttons are normally grayed out. When you click on an icon, you can hold the mouse button down and drag it to one of these buttons, which are then activated. With them, you can delete, copy, and rename icons; Copy and Rename will prompt you for a new name.

VB Icon Browser is one of the simplest to use Windows-based icon managers I've seen. It makes it easy to search through all your icons to find just the right one. It's also very easy to delete and rename icons because you can see what they look like while working on them.

\ICONS\WINDOWS\VBICONEX.   VB Icon Extractor extracts icons from Windows files. It's also a shareware program. Windows programs often store a number of icons inside their .EXE files. Windows itself can find and use these icons for any program, but it can be time-consuming to search through all your Windows files for icons. Not to worry; VB Icon Extractor does it for you. It displays the hard disk map on the left and files on the right. Once you've found a subdirectory containing Windows files, you can use VB Icon Extractor to automatically extract all the icons for you, name them, and place them in a holding subdirectory. It does all this without harming or modifying the original Windows program files.

No only can VB Icon Extractor extract the icons, it can process a subdirectory and remove all the duplicate icons. This alone is worth its price when you have a lot of icons to process. As an inducement to register your program, VB Icon Extractor skips about one third of the icons when extracting. It tells you this up front and even counts how many it skips. The registered version doesn't do this.

If you're hungry for more icons, this is a good way to find them. Using VB Icon Extractor, I found over 400 icons inside program files in my \WINDOWS subdirectory alone.

\ICONS\WINDOWS\0.WIN.   This subdirectory contains all the Windows icon files (.ICO) whose names begin with the number 0.

\ICONS\WINDOWS\1.WIN. This subdirectory contains all the Windows icon files (.ICO) whose names begin with the number 1.

\ICONS\WINDOWS\2.WIN. This subdirectory contains all the Windows icon files (.ICO) whose names begin with the number 2.

\ICONS\WINDOWS\3.WIN. This subdirectory contains all the Windows icon files (.ICO) whose names begin with the number 3.

\ICONS\WINDOWS\4.WIN. This subdirectory contains all the Windows icon files (.ICO) whose names begin with the number 4.

\ICONS\WINDOWS\5.WIN. This subdirectory contains all the Windows icon files (.ICO) whose names begin with the number 5.

\ICONS\WINDOWS\6.WIN. This subdirectory contains all the Windows icon files (.ICO) whose names begin with the number 6.

\ICONS\WINDOWS\A.WIN. This subdirectory contains all the Windows icon files (.ICO) whose names begin with the letter A.

\ICONS\WINDOWS\B.WIN. This subdirectory contains all the Windows icon files (.ICO) whose names begin with the letter B.

\ICONS\WINDOWS\C.WIN. This subdirectory contains all the Windows icon files (.ICO) whose names begin with the letter C.

\ICONS\WINDOWS\D.WIN. This subdirectory contains all the Windows icon files (.ICO) whose names begin with the letter D.

\ICONS\WINDOWS\E.WIN. This subdirectory contains all the Windows icon files (.ICO) whose names begin with the letter E.

\ICONS\WINDOWS\F.WIN. This subdirectory contains all the Windows icon files (.ICO) whose names begin with the letter F.

\ICONS\WINDOWS\G.WIN. This subdirectory contains all the Windows icon files (.ICO) whose names begin with the letter G.

\ICONS\WINDOWS\H.WIN. This subdirectory contains all the Windows icon files (.ICO) whose names begin with the letter H.

\ICONS\WINDOWS\I.WIN. This subdirectory contains all the Windows icon files (.ICO) whose names begin with the letter I.

\ICONS\WINDOWS\J.WIN. This subdirectory contains all the Windows icon files (.ICO) whose names begin with the letter J.

\ICONS\WINDOWS\K.WIN. This subdirectory contains all the Windows icon files (.ICO) whose names begin with the letter K.

\ICONS\WINDOWS\L.WIN. This subdirectory contains all the Windows icon files (.ICO) whose names begin with the letter L.

\ICONS\WINDOWS\M.WIN. This subdirectory contains all the Windows icon files (.ICO) whose names begin with the letter M.

\ICONS\WINDOWS\N.WIN. This subdirectory contains all the Windows icon files (.ICO) whose names begin with the letter N.

\ICONS\WINDOWS\O.WIN. This subdirectory contains all the Windows icon files (.ICO) whose names begin with the letter O.

\ICONS\WINDOWS\P.WIN. This subdirectory contains all the Windows icon files (.ICO) whose names begin with the letter P.

\ICONS\WINDOWS\Q.WIN. This subdirectory contains all the Windows icon files (.ICO) whose names begin with the letter Q.

\ICONS\WINDOWS\R.WIN. This subdirectory contains all the Windows icon files (.ICO) whose names begin with the letter R.

\ICONS\WINDOWS\S.WIN. This subdirectory contains all the Windows icon files (.ICO) whose names begin with the letter S.

\ICONS\WINDOWS\T.WIN. This subdirectory contains all the Windows icon files (.ICO) whose names begin with the letter T.

\ICONS\WINDOWS\U.WIN. This subdirectory contains all the Windows icon files (.ICO) whose names begin with the letter U.

\ICONS\WINDOWS\V.WIN. This subdirectory contains all the Windows icon files (.ICO) whose names begin with the letter V.

\ICONS\WINDOWS\W.WIN. This subdirectory contains all the Windows icon files (.ICO) whose names begin with the letter W.

\ICONS\WINDOWS\X.WIN. This subdirectory contains all the Windows icon files (.ICO) whose names begin with the letter X.

\ICONS\WINDOWS\Y.WIN. This subdirectory contains all the Windows icon files (.ICO) whose names begin with the letter Y.

\ICONS\WINDOWS\Z.WIN. This subdirectory contains all the Windows icon files (.ICO) whose names begin with the letter Z.

\OTHER

This branch of the CD-ROM stores shareware packages that aren't discussed in the book, but which are from vendors who provided packages that are discussed in the book.

\OTHER\ART. Complete Martial Artist is a copyrighted discussion of martial arts.

\OTHER\BAR. Bar Graph is a shareware program that displays a visual graph of hard disk usage.

\OTHER\BRING10. Copy It Over Here is a copyrighted program to copy files from multiple locations to the current subdirectory.

\OTHER\BYE. Quick Permanent File Deleter 1.1 is a copyrighted program from David Smith to permanently erase a file so nothing can recover it.

\OTHER\CLOCKIT. ClockIt is a copyrighted program to time multiple events, even if the computer is turned off.

\OTHER\CRUSH11. Crush is a shareware program designed to work in conjunction with PKZip or other archiver to improve compression rates.

\OTHER\DIGGER. Digger is a copyrighted program to compute the total size of files in a subdirectory.

\OTHER\DRIV-MAN. Driv_Man is a shareware program that displays space information on multiple drives on a single display.

\OTHER\DSPACE. Dspace is a shareware program that graphically displays the space usage of each subdirectory on your hard disk.

\OTHER\EXEMAS. EXE Master identifies the source for many .EXE files, including compiled batch files.

\OTHER\HIDIR128. HiDir is a shareware program that can hide subdirectories.

\OTHER\MASDIR54. MasDir is an excellent replacement for the DIR command. It gives you excellent control over how directory information is displayed and includes the ability to print directory listings. It's a shareware program.

\OTHER\MAXI18. Maxi18 is a shareware floppy disk formatting program that increases the number of sectors per track and the number of tracks per disk to increase disk capacity without data compression. For example, 1.4 megabytes of information will fit on a 1.2MB disk if you use Maxi18.

\OTHER\OPENTRAP. OpenTrap is a copyrighted program from Nombas that you run simultaneously with another program in order to see what files the second program opens.

\OTHER\PAR. Parse-O-Matic is a program for converting text in ASCII files to other formats. Its typical use is reformatting the output from one program into that of another program. Since Parse-O-Matic works with any ASCII file, you could pipe the output of a DIR command to a file and then use Parse-O-Matic to convert it to a batch file.

\OTHER\SEE. See is a shareware file viewer from MicroFox. It has full mouse support and can search for text.

\OTHER\SFXWIN. Sound Effects for Windows is a shareware program that has icons you install under Windows. When you click on them, they generate a sound effect.

\OTHER\SLOWDOS. SlowDOS is a copyrighted nonmemory-resident program from Nombas that you run simultaneously with another program in order to slow down the operation of the second program. It's perfect for use with games that run too fast.

\OTHER\TAD131. Tad is a shareware program for changing the time and date stamp of a file.

\OTHER\TMPSPACE. TmpSpace is a shareware program for displaying the amount of "recoverable" space on your hard disk, that is, space you can recover by erasing unwanted temporary files. You define which files are unwanted.

\OTHER\VASN129. VASN is a shareware program for changing the volume label and serial number of a disk.

\OTHER\WHTAPE21. WhTape is a tape-prompting program to remind you which tape to insert when you run your backup.

\POWERBAT

This subdirectory contains the shareware PowerBat program discussed in Chapter 40. Please see the note in Chapter 40 before trying to run this program as it will not run from the CD-ROM.

\POWERBAT\MYDEMO. This subdirectory contains the EXAMPLE.BAT and A-SIZE.PWR programs discussed in Chapter 40. It also contains compiled versions of the programs.

\POWERBAT\PBDEMO. This subdirectory contains the demo programs that come with PowerBat. Both the source code and compiled versions are included.

\POWERBAT\PLUSDEMO. This subdirectory contains the demo programs that come with the commercial PB Plus+ program. Both the source code and compiled versions are included.

\REXINTRO

REXX is an advanced command-line language that comes with OS/2, which makes REXX a nice replacement for OS/2 batch files when you need more power than a batch file offers. Chapter 32 contains a review of REXX.

\TURBOBAT

This subdirectory contains the TurboBat program. TurboBat is a shareware batch file compiler discussed in Chapter 40.

\UTILITY

This subdirectory contains no files. This branch of the CD-ROM stores the batch file utilities discussed in the book.

\UTILITY\DOS

This branch of the CD-ROM stores the DOS utilities discussed in the book.

\UTILITY\DOS\1ADAY11. OneADay lets you control how often other programs are executed by a batch file. It's a shareware program discussed in Chapter 39.

\UTILITY\DOS\A-FREE. This subdirectory contains the A-FREE.BLD Builder program discussed in Chapter 40 for displaying the free space on the A drive. It also contains the compiled version.

\UTILITY\DOS\ABATVW. A Batch View is a collection of programs that provide visual and general batch file utilities and programming aids. This shareware collection is discussed in Chapter 38.

\UTILITY\DOS\AMENU. AMenu is a simple but effective batch file menu system. It's a copyrighted program discussed in Chapter 36.

\UTILITY\DOS\ANSWER. Answer queries the user and places the multicharacter response in the environment. Answer is public-domain software discussed in Chapter 34.

\UTILITY\DOS\ASCII. This program displays an ASCII chart on the screen and leaves it there until you press any key. ASCII.EXE was written especially for this book and is discussed in Chapter 35.

\UTILITY\DOS\ASKIT.   AskIt is an errorlevel asker that lets you control the valid keystrokes. It's a copyrighted program discussed in Chapter 34.

\UTILITY\DOS\BATCMD.   BatCMD is an advanced batch file utility. It's discussed in detail in Chapter 38. BatCMD was written especially for this book.

\UTILITY\DOS\BATKIT55.   BatKit is a very advanced utility for getting information from the user. It's a shareware program discussed in Chapter 34.

\UTILITY\DOS\BATSCREN.   BatScreen is a screen compiler that will turn a 24-line, 80-column or smaller text file into a stand-alone .COM program. These files are useful for displaying colorful messages without using ANSI and for displaying menus. It's discussed in Chapter 35. BatScreen was written especially for this book.

\UTILITY\DOS\BATUTIL.   This subdirectory contains no files. Rather, two other subdirectories branch off it, and they contain the files. This branch of the CD-ROM stores the BATUTIL files.

\UTILITY\DOS\BATUTIL\BATUTIL.   This subdirectory contains the files for the Bat-Util program. BatUtil is an advanced batch file utility set, possibly the most powerful one included on this CD-ROM. It's a shareware program discussed in Chapter 38.

\UTILITY\DOS\BATUTIL\STACKEY.   This subdirectory contains the file for the StacKey program. StacKey places keystrokes into the keyboard buffer from a batch file. It's a shareware program discussed in Chapter 39.

\UTILITY\DOS\CAPITAL.   Capital takes a single word, converts it to all capital letters, and stores it in the environment under the variable name Ronny. It was written especially for this book, and is discussed in Chapter 34.

\UTILITY\DOS\CENVIDOS.   CEnvi is a shareware alternative batch language that's very much like the C language. There are versions for DOS, Windows, and OS/2. The DOS version is discussed in Chapter 40.

\UTILITY\DOS\CFG24.   CFG is a very powerful batch file utility set. It's a shareware program and is discussed in Chapter 38.

\UTILITY\DOS\CHOOSE30.   Choose is a simple-to-use menu program for batch files that can also be used to present the user with a limited number of choices. It's a shareware program and is discussed in Chapter 36.

\UTILITY\DOS\CLEAV157.   Cleave is a unique way to clear the screen in a batch file. It's a shareware program discussed in Chapter 35.

\UTILITY\DOS\CRONTAB.   CronTab is a program for running commands periodically. It's a copyrighted program discussed in Chapter 39. There's also an OS/2 version.

\UTILITY\DOS\DAYSLEFT. DaysLeft displays the number of days left until a given date. It's a shareware program discussed in Chapter 39.

\UTILITY\DOS\DELEX129. DelEx deletes all the files (*.*) except those specified on the command line. It's a shareware program and is discussed in Chapter 37.

\UTILITY\DOS\DMENU211. DMenu 2.11 is a shareware DOS menu from MicroFox that was received too late to include in the book. Unlike their other menu program, HDM, DMenu is designed more towards ease of use rather than raw power. Its menus are similar to those in Lotus 1-2-3. While designed for simplicity, it does support password protection, screen blanking, macros, and a mouse.

\UTILITY\DOS\DO-FOR24. Do-For is an advanced replacement for the batch FOR command. It's a copyrighted program discussed in Chapter 39.

\UTILITY\DOS\DO-ONC23. Do-Once is designed to run from your AUTOEXEC.BAT file and execute a program only at scheduled intervals. It's a copyrighted program discussed in Chapter 39.

\UTILITY\DOS\DOSTB. DOS Tool Box is a collection of 82 small .COM files that support many batch file operations. It's a shareware program and is discussed in Chapter 38.

\UTILITY\DOS\DRMENU30. DrMenu is a freeware batch file-based menu system. The version discussed in Chapter 36 is 2.1. After I wrote that chapter, the author released version 3.0, which is the one included on the CD-ROM.

\UTILITY\DOS\DRMENU30\INSTALL. This version of DRMENU has not been installed. Copy the files to your hard disk and run the installation program.

\UTILITY\DOS\ENVI-MAN. Envi_Man is a program for displaying the contents of the environment and supplying a batch file with the amount of free space. It's a shareware program and is discussed in Chapter 39.

\UTILITY\DOS\ENVIMENU. EnviMenu is a copyrighted menu program. It's discussed in Chapter 36.

\UTILITY\DOS\EQO10A. EQO is a replacement for the ECHO command, and contains many enhancements. It's a shareware program discussed in Chapter 35.

\UTILITY\DOS\EVERYDAY. Everyday is designed to run programs once a day from your AUTOEXEC.BAT. It's a copyrighted program discussed in Chapter 39.

\UTILITY\DOS\FDATE84B. FDate is designed to allow batch files to manipulate dates and get input from the user. It's a copyrighted program discussed in Chapter 39.

\UTILITY\DOS\FORAGE.   ForAge finds the newest or oldest file in a group of files and can pass the filename on to other programs. It's a copyrighted program discussed in Chapter 37.

\UTILITY\DOS\FREEFILE.   FreeFile is utility for controlling the DOS System File Table. It's a copyrighted program and is discussed in Chapter 39.

\UTILITY\DOS\GET261.   Get is a utility that gets information about the computer and places it in the environment or errorlevel. It's a shareware program discussed in Chapter 39.

\UTILITY\DOS\GETCOLOR.   GetColor is a utility to store the current screen colors for later restoration. It's a copyrighted program discussed in Chapter 35.

\UTILITY\DOS\GETKEY20.   Getkey is a utility to get a keystroke from the user. It's a shareware program discussed in Chapter 34.

\UTILITY\DOS\GETSET12.   GetSet is a utility to get information from users by allowing them to modify an environmental variable. It's a shareware program and is discussed in Chapter 34.

\UTILITY\DOS\GO.   Go is an installation program that processes compressed files automatically. It's a shareware program discussed in Chapter 39.

\UTILITY\DOS\HDM464.   HDM (short for hard disk menu) is an excellent shareware DOS menu program from MicroFox that was received too late to include in the book. In addition to menus, HDM provides security via passwords, macros, timed execution, tracking computer usage, mouse support, network support, phone dialer, a screen blanker, and customizable help text. If you're looking for a DOS menu program, this is one of the most powerful ones you'll find.

\UTILITY\DOS\HOLD.   Hold pauses the batch file for the specified number of seconds. It's discussed in Chapter 34.

\UTILITY\DOS\HOLDN214.   HoldOn pauses a batch file for a specified period of time. It's a shareware program discussed in Chapter 39.

\UTILITY\DOS\INTVL197.   Interval runs a command once during the specified interval. It's a shareware program discussed in Chapter 39.

\UTILITY\DOS\ISITWIN.   IsItWin sets the errorlevel to 1 if it's run from a DOS session under Windows and to 0 otherwise. It's discussed in Chapter 34. IsItWin was written especially for this book.

\UTILITY\DOS\ISITZERO.   IsItZero checks to see if the specified file is a zero-length file and sets the errorlevel accordingly. It's discussed in Chapter 37. IsItZero was written especially for this book.

\UTILITY\DOS\KBSTUFF. KBStuff stuffs keystrokes into the keyboard buffer. It's a shareware program and is discussed in Chapter 39.

\UTILITY\DOS\KEYTG127. KeyToggle sets the status of your Scroll Lock, Caps Lock, Num Lock, and Insert keys. It's a shareware program discussed in Chapter 39.

\UTILITY\DOS\MAKENAME. MakeName generates a unique filename based on the date and time. It's a shareware program discussed in Chapter 39.

\UTILITY\DOS\MENU-MAN. Menu_Man is a menu program for batch files. It's a shareware program discussed in Chapter 36.

\UTILITY\DOS\MP38. Multi-Print is a menu-driven program to print ASCII files using less paper. It's a shareware program discussed in Chapter 39.

\UTILITY\DOS\NEEDHELP. When NeedHelp is passed the %0 and %1 replaceable parameters of a batch file, it sets the errorlevel to indicate if the user requested command-line help. It's discussed in Chapter 34. NeedHelp was written especially for this book.

\UTILITY\DOS\OBOE12. Opal Batch Organizer and Extender is primarily designed to get information from the user. It's a shareware program and is discussed in Chapter 34.

\UTILITY\DOS\PATH-MAN. Path_Man searches the path to find a specified file. It's a shareware program discussed in Chapter 39.

\UTILITY\DOS\PERSONAL. This subdirectory contains a demo version of, QUERCUS SYSTEMS' Personal REXX for DOS, which is discussed in Chapter 40.

\UTILITY\DOS\PIZ. PIZ is a freeware program for processing a number of .ZIP files. It creates a subdirectory with the same name as each zipped file, extracts the files to that subdirectory, and then deletes the original .ZIP files. It was received too late to include in the book. PIZ includes a copy of the TMES 3.0 (short for the master environment set), from Tee Roper. TMES 3.0 is freeware to individual users, but companies are required to register the program. TMES is a gem of a program for working with the environment. You supply the program with the name of an environmental variable and a switch to indicate the information you want to store in that variable. For example, the command TMES Date /DOM would store the day of the month to the Date environmental variable. There are numerous date switches, mathematical switches, and path parsing switches, as well as a switch to get input from the user.

\UTILITY\DOS\PM36. Path Master is a utility program for managing your path. It's a shareware program discussed in Chapter 39.

\UTILITY\DOS\POCKET41. PocketD Plus is a powerful file management tool. It's a shareware program discussed in Chapter 37.

\UTILITY\DOS\PRESKEY3. Press Any Key 3.0 is a copyrighted utility that gives you 30 different ways to replace the PAUSE command. It's discussed in Chapter 35.

\UTILITY\DOS\QB216. QuickBatch is a complete batch file development environment. It's particularly useful if you use ANSI commands or color sequences in your batch files. It's a shareware program and is discussed in Chapter 39.

\UTILITY\DOS\QICBAT12. Qic-Bat for CMS interactively generates a batch file you can use with CMS to perform a backup. It's a shareware program discussed in Chapter 37.

\UTILITY\DOS\QTOD121. QTOD displays the date and time in a form suitable for redirecting to a file. It's a copyrighted program discussed in Chapter 39.

\UTILITY\DOS\RAMMAN25. Ram-Man is a memory-resident program for viewing ASCII files. It's a shareware program discussed in Chapter 39.

\UTILITY\DOS\SCAN. Scan is an ASCII file viewer that also lets you view subdirectories and manage your files. It's a shareware program and is discussed in Chapter 39.

\UTILITY\DOS\SEBFU. The Scanion Enterprises Batch File Utilities is a collection of freeware batch file utilities. It's discussed in Chapter 38.

\UTILITY\DOS\SEE. See is a program for viewing and printing ASCII files. The See package includes GetKey, an errorlevel-asking program. See and GetKey are copyrighted programs. See is discussed in Chapter 39 and GetKey is discussed in Chapter 34.

\UTILITY\DOS\SETER148. SetEr is a utility to set the errorlevel. It's a shareware program and is discussed in Chapter 39.

\UTILITY\DOS\SFX61. Sound Effects plays a number of sounds from DOS. It's a shareware program discussed in Chapter 39.

\UTILITY\DOS\SPARKL35. Sparkle & Menu Magic is a menu-construction program with extras. It's a shareware program and is discussed in Chapter 36.

\UTILITY\DOS\SPKL2-24. This subdirectory contains the Sparkle-2 program which is designed to work with Sparkle & Menu Magic. It's a shareware program and is discussed in Chapter 36.

\UTILITY\DOS\SSTUFF30. Steenburgh's Stuff is a collection of 21 very useful batch file utilities. It's a shareware program discussed in Chapter 38.

\UTILITY\DOS\STRIPX. StripX is a program to strip off the file extension. It's a copyrighted program discussed in Chapter 37.

\UTILITY\DOS\SUMMIT. Summit is a collection of seven copyrighted utilities from Summit Memory Systems. It's discussed in Chapter 39.

\UTILITY\DOS\TEXTFT24. Text Font is a collection of 12 different screen fonts. It's a shareware program discussed in Chapter 35.

\UTILITY\DOS\TNT. This subdirectory contains Tessler's Nifty Tools utility set. Some of the general files are contained in this subdirectory, while each program is in a different subdirectory branching off this subdirectory. You can register each program individually, but there's a substantial discount for registering all the programs at once. Most are crippleware. Once you register, you automatically receive the full version. Only those programs useful for writing batch files are discussed in the book.

\UTILITY\DOS\TNT\CAPSTAT. This contains the Tessler's Nifty Tools CapStat program for checking to see if printing is being Netware captured. It's a crippleware program, and is discussed in Chapter 39.

\UTILITY\DOS\TNT\CFGCNTRL. This contains the Tessler's Nifty Tools CFGCntrl program. It's a crippleware program, and is discussed in Chapter 37.

\UTILITY\DOS\TNT\CHEK2DUP. This contains the Tessler's Nifty Tools Chek2Dup program. It's a crippleware program.

\UTILITY\DOS\TNT\CHKPARM. This contains the Tessler's Nifty Tools ChkParm program for checking to see if a file is on local or remote drive. It's a crippleware program, and is discussed in Chapter 37.

\UTILITY\DOS\TNT\COMSPEED. This contains the Tessler's Nifty Tools ComSpeed program. It's a crippleware program.

\UTILITY\DOS\TNT\CONTROLP. This contains the Tessler's Nifty Tools ControlP program for toggling printing. It's a crippleware program and it's discussed in Chapter 39.

\UTILITY\DOS\TNT\COPYWA. This contains the Tessler's Nifty Tools CopyWa program. It's a crippleware program.

\UTILITY\DOS\TNT\CTRDUMP This contains the Tessler's Nifty Tools CtrDump program. It's a crippleware program.

\UTILITY\DOS\TNT\DELTREE. This contains the Tessler's Nifty Tools DelTree program. It's a crippleware program.

\UTILITY\DOS\TNT\DIR2BAT. This contains the Tessler's Nifty Tools Dir2Bat program for writing a custom batch file to act on every file. It's crippleware, and is discussed in Chapter 37.

\UTILITY\DOS\TNT\DVCPU. This contains the Tessler's Nifty Tools DVCPU program. It's a crippleware program.

\UTILITY\DOS\TNT\DVPROMPT. This contains the Tessler's Nifty Tools DVPrompt program. It's a crippleware program.

\UTILITY\DOS\TNT\DVRUN. This contains the Tessler's Nifty Tools DVRun program for checking to see if Deskview is running. It's crippleware, and is discussed in Chapter 39.

\UTILITY\DOS\TNT\EXPNDTAB. This contains the Tessler's Nifty Tools ExpndTab program. It's a crippleware program.

\UTILITY\DOS\TNT\FEEFIFO. This contains the Tessler's Nifty Tools FeeFiFo program. It's a crippleware program.

\UTILITY\DOS\TNT\GROWP. This contains the Tessler's Nifty Tools GrowP program. It's a crippleware program.

\UTILITY\DOS\TNT\GRP2INI. This contains the Tessler's Nifty Tools Grp2Ini program. It's a crippleware program.

\UTILITY\DOS\TNT\IFONSCRN. This contains the Tessler's Nifty Tools IfOnScrn program. It's a crippleware program.

\UTILITY\DOS\TNT\IFWAIT. This contains the Tessler's Nifty Tools IfWait program. It's a crippleware program.

\UTILITY\DOS\TNT\PARKHEAD. This contains the Tessler's Nifty Tools ParkHead program. It's a crippleware program.

\UTILITY\DOS\TNT\PDEL. This contains the Tessler's Nifty Tools PDel program. It's a crippleware program.

\UTILITY\DOS\TNT\PLAYER. This contains the Tessler's Nifty Tools Player program. It's a crippleware program.

\UTILITY\DOS\TNT\PRTSCRFF. This contains the Tessler's Nifty Tools PrtScrff program. It's a crippleware program.

\UTILITY\DOS\TNT\RLIST. This contains the Tessler's Nifty Tools RList program. It's a crippleware program.

\UTILITY\DOS\TNT\RWDIR. This contains the Tessler's Nifty Tools RWDir program. It's a crippleware program.

\UTILITY\DOS\TNT\SETBEEP. This contains the Tessler's Nifty Tools SetBeep program. It's a crippleware program.

\UTILITY\DOS\TNT\THOT4DAY. This contains the Tessler's Nifty Tools THot4Day program. It's a crippleware program.

\UTILITY\DOS\TNT\TUNE4DAY. This contains the Tessler's Nifty Tools Tune4Day program. It's a crippleware program.

\UTILITY\DOS\TNT\VDEL. This contains the Tessler's Nifty Tools VDel program. It's a crippleware program.

\UTILITY\DOS\TNT\VERS. This contains the Tessler's Nifty Tools Vers program. It's a crippleware program.

\UTILITY\DOS\TNT\ZDIR. This contains the Tessler's Nifty Tools ZDir program. It's a crippleware program.

\UTILITY\DOS\ULTRA. This contains the Ultra ToolBox program. This is an excellent shareware batch file utility set discussed in Chapter 38.

\UTILITY\DOS\UTILITYB. Utility_Belt is a shareware batch file utility set with 18 separate utilities designed to improve batch files. It's discussed in Chapter 38.

\UTILITY\DOS\VID-FX2. Video FX produces video special effects for your batch files. It's a shareware program and is discussed in Chapter 39.

\UTILITY\DOS\VLS. VGA Clear Screen is a screen clearing program. It's shareware program and is discussed in Chapter 35.

\UTILITY\DOS\XSET40. XSet is a powerful environmental variable manipulation program. It's a shareware program discussed in Chapter 38.

\UTILITY\DOS\Y-OR-NO. Y_or_N asks the user a question and sets the errorlevel according to the response. It's a copyrighted program discussed in Chapter 34.

\UTILITY\DOS\YOU-MAKE. This subdirectory contains no files. Rather, other subdirectories branch off it and these subdirectories contain the files. This branch of the CD-ROM stores the batch file utilities discussed in Chapter 31. This chapter describes how you can write your own batch file utilities for DOS batch files.

\UTILITY\DOS\YOU-MAKE\BLD-ADD. Add is a Builder Lite program that reads a number from the command line, adds one to it and sets the errorlevel to the answer. It is discussed in Chapter 31. This subdirectory contains the source code, compiled .EXE file, and a batch file to show the program in action. Add was written especially for this book.

\UTILITY\DOS\YOU-MAKE\BLD-TIME. Multiply is a Builder Lite program that reads two numbers from the environment using the environmental variables Number1 and Number2, multiplies those two numbers together, and stores the answer in the environment under the variable Answer. It's discussed in Chapter 31. This subdirectory contains the source code, compiled .EXE file, and two batch files to show the program in action. SHOWTIME.BAT is the program to run and SAYERROR.BAT is a program that SHOWTIME.BAT calls while running. Multiply was written especially for this book.

\UTILITY\DOS\YOU-MAKE\ENVLIB. The Envlib library unit was developed by Sunny Hill Software and is currently sold by TurboPower Software as part of their Turbo Professional package. I'm providing the source code with the permission of TurboPower Software. This file gives you (and any colleagues who program in Turbo Pascal) the opportunity to study how to write routines to manipulate the environmental variables of the master and current environment. They're discussed in Chapter 31.

\UTILITY\DOS\YOU-MAKE\PAS-ADD. This Add is a Pascal program that reads a number from the command line, adds 1 to it, and stores the answer to the environmental variable Answer. It's discussed in Chapter 31. This subdirectory contains the source code, compiled .EXE file, and a batch file to show the program in action. This example won't work in a DOS session under Windows. Add was written especially for this book.

\UTILITY\DOS\YOU-MAKE\PAS-PLUS. This version of Add is a Pascal program that reads a number from the command line, adds 1 to it, and stores the answer to the environmental variable Answer. If the user specifies the name of an environmental variable, that name is used instead. It's discussed in Chapter 31. This subdirectory contains the source code, compiled .EXE file, and a batch file to show the program in action. This example won't work in a DOS session under Windows. ADD.EXE was written especially for this book.

\UTILITY\DOS\YOU-MAKE\PAS-TIME. This Multiply is a Pascal program that reads two numbers from the environment using the environmental variables Number1 and Number2, multiplies those two numbers together, and stores the answer in the environment under the variable Answer. It's discussed in Chapter 31. This subdirectory contains the source code and compiled .EXE file. Multiply was written especially for this book.

\UTILITY\DOS\YOU-MAKE\QB-ADD. This version of Add is a QuickBASIC program that reads a number from the command line, adds 1 to it, and stores the answer to the environmental variable Answer. It's discussed in Chapter 31. This subdirectory contains the source code, compiled .EXE file, and a batch file to show the program in action. QuickBASIC can't write to an environmental variable directly, so it creates a temporary batch file that can be called to store the answer in the environment. Add was written especially for this book.

\UTILITY\DOS\YOU-MAKE\QB-TIMES. This version of Multiply is a QuickBASIC program that reads two numbers from the environment using the environmental variables Number1 and Number2, multiplies those two numbers together, and stores the answer in the environmental variable Answer. It's discussed in Chapter 31. This subdirectory contains the source code, compiled .EXE file, and two batch files to show the program in action. QuickBASIC can't write to an environmental variable directly, so it creates a temporary batch file that can be called to store the answer in the environment. Multiply was written especially for this book.

\UTILITY\OS2

This subdirectory contains no files. Instead, it contains subdirectories that store the OS/2 utilities discussed in the book.

\UTILITY\OS2\BATHELP. BatHelp is an OS/2 utility that searches for all REXX and OS/2 batch files (.CMD) and displays their help information when those files are constructed, as outlined in the book. It's discussed in Chapter 32. In order for BatHelp to work, the included VROBJ.DLL file must be either in the current subdirectory or in a subdirectory in your path. BatHelp was written especially for this book.

\UTILITY\OS2\CENVIOS2. CEnvi is a shareware alternative batch language that's very much like the C language. There are versions for DOS, Windows, Windows NT, and OS/2. The OS/2 version is discussed in Chapter 43.

\UTILITY\OS2\CRONTAB2.   CronTab runs commands periodically. It's a copyrighted program discussed in Chapter 43. There's also a DOS version.

\UTILITY\OS2\PMSLEEP.   PM Sleeper is used to either delay or time events. It's a shareware program and is discussed in Chapter 43.

\UTILITY\OS2\QTOD200.   QTOD displays the date and time in a form suitable for redirecting to a file. It's a copyrighted program and is discussed in Chapter 43.

\UTILITY\OS2\REXX.   This subdirectory contains no files. This branch of the CD-ROM stores the OS/2 REXX utilities discussed in the book.

\UTILITY\OS2\REXX\BACKCONF.   Under OS/2 your CONFIG.SYS file does double duty, taking care of all the functions of both the CONFIG.SYS and AUTOEXEC.BAT files. BackConf will make a backup copy of this important file if the archive bit is turned on. It's discussed in Chapter 32.

\UTILITY\OS2\REXX\CAPITAL.   CAPITAL.CMD takes a single word passed to it as an argument, converts it to uppercase, and stores the results in the environment under the variable Return. It's discussed in Chapter 32. Capital was written especially for this book.

\UTILITY\OS2\REXX\CHKCONF.   This REXX program will verify the syntax of your CONFIG.SYS file. It's discussed in Chapter 32.

\UTILITY\OS2\REXX\FF.   FF.CMD will find all the files below the current subdirectory that match the specification on the command line. While not a batch file utility, this REXX program does replace an OS/2 batch file that performs the same function. The REXX program, however, is much faster. It's discussed in Chapter 32, and was written especially for this book.

\UTILITY\OS2\REXX\GET.   GET.CMD gets a character string from the user and stores it in the environment under the Return variable. The character string can be any size as long as it doesn't exceed the OS/2 length limitation for the command line. It's discussed in Chapter 32. Get was written especially for this book.

\UTILITY\OS2\REXX\GET-0-9.   GET-0-9.CMD gets any single-digit number from the user and stores that number in the errorlevel. It's discussed in Chapter 32, and was written especially for this book.

\UTILITY\OS2\REXX\GET-ONE.   GET-ONE.CMD gets any single character from the user and stores its ASCII value in the errorlevel for testing by a batch file. It's discussed in Chapter 32. Get-One was written especially for this book.

\UTILITY\OS2\REXX\GETA2Z.   GETA2Z.CMD gets a letter from the user and returns a code representing that letter in the errorlevel. An A is returned as a 1, B as a 2, and so on. Capitalization is ignored. It's discussed in Chapter 32. GetA2Z was written especially for this book.

\UTILITY\OS2\REXX\ISITZERO. ISITZERO.CMD tests to see if the specified file is a zero-length file and returns the results in the errorlevel. It's discussed in Chapter 32, and was written especially for this book.

\UTILITY\OS2\REXX\MKCMD. This REXX program will construct a batch file for you. You supply it with the file specification, command to put before the filename, and command to put after the filename. It searches the current subdirectory and makes a list of each file that matches your file specification, appends the commands, and writes it out to a batch file. It's discussed in Chapter 32.

\UTILITY\OS2\REXX\NEEDHELP. When NEEDHELP.CMD is passed the %0 and %1 replaceable parameters of a batch file, it sets the errorlevel to indicate whether the user requested command-line help. It's discussed in Chapter 32, and was written especially for this book.

\UTILITY\OS2\REXX\PATHLIST. The REXX program lists all the subdirectories in an environmental variable like the path. It's discussed in Chapter 32.

\UTILITY\OS2\REXX\RXSUMRY. This REXX program summarizes the purpose entries of all the REXX programs and batch files in the current subdirectory. It's similar to the BatHelp program discussed previously, but it works only in the current subdirectory. It's discussed in Chapter 32.

\UTILITY\OS2\REXX\SCAN. SCAN.ERX is an Enhanced Editor macro that lists all the subroutines in a REXX program and allows you to easily jump to any one of them. It requires that VROBJ.DLL be in a subdirectory in your path, and it's discussed in Chapter 32. SCAN.ERX was written especially for this book.

\UTILITY\OS2\REXX\SETERROR. SETERROR.CMD is a REXX program that takes a number on the command line and sets the errorlevel equal to that number, which can make it easier to debug batch files. It's discussed in Chapter 32, and was written especially for this book.

\UTILITY\OS2\REXX\SPACE. This REXX program reports the space used by a subdirectory. It's discussed in Chapter 32.

\UTILITY\OS2\REXX\YESORNO. YESORNO.CMD is a REXX program that accepts only a Y or N response, in either upper- or lowercase, and sets the errorlevel accordingly. It's discussed in Chapter 32. YesOrNo was written especially for this book.

\UTILITY\OS2\REXXLB. REXXLB is a collection of over 150 functions designed to extend the capabilities of REXX in OS/2. It's a shareware program and is discussed in Chapter 43.

\UTILITY\OS2\WPSBKUP. WPSBkup is an OS/2 utility that makes a backup of your Workplace Shell. If you have to later reinstall OS/2 or if the Workplace Shell develops problems, you can use this to restore the last saved copy of your desktop. It's a shareware utility and is discussed in Chapter 43.

\UTILITY\WINDOWS

This subdirectory contains no files. It contains subdirectories that contain the Windows utilities discussed in the book.

\UTILITY\WINDOWS\CENVIWIN. CEnvi is a shareware alternative batch language that's very much like the C language. There are versions for DOS, Windows, and OS/2. The Windows version is discussed in Chapter 42.

\UTILITY\WINDOWS\SMISHL21. SmilerShell is a Windows-based DOS prompt that lets you quickly run batch files not installed to the desktop, and also run any DOS internal or external command, DOS program, or Windows program. SmilerShell is a shareware program. Note that, when you first start SmilerShell, it checks to see if it has an .INI initialization file. If it doesn't find one, it asks you about creating one. If you're running the program from the CD-ROM you must answer no, because it can't write a file to the CD-ROM.

\UTILITY\WINDOWS\WINBATCH. WinBatch is an excellent shareware batch language, made especially for Windows. It's discussed in Chapter 42.

\UTILITY\WINDOWS\WINBATCH\MYSAMPLE. This contains the SOL.WBT and WINMINE.WBT WinBatch batch files along with their compiled versions.

\UTILITY\WINDOWS\WINEDIT. WinEdit is an excellent shareware ASCII editor for Windows. It's discussed in Chapter 41.

\UTILITY\WINDOWS\WINEDIT\COMMON. This subdirectory contains files necessary to install WinEdit.

\UTILITY\WINDOWS\WINEDIT\WINEDIT. This subdirectory contains files necessary to install WinEdit.

\WINHELP

The files in this subdirectory are Windows help files. BAT-HELP.HLP will help you write better batch files and UTILITY.HLP will help you find just the batch file utility you're looking for.

Index

ABOUT THE AUTHOR

Ronny Richardson has written numerous articles for computer magazines, including *PC/Computing*, *Computer Shopper*, and *Atlanta Computer Currents*. He has written a number of books for McGraw-Hill on various batch-file-related topics.

Ronny has a Ph.D. in Business Administration from Georgia State University. When not writing computer books, he's an Associate Professor of Business at Quincy University in Quincy, Illinois, a liberal arts institution in the Franciscan tradition. You can reach him online via CompuServe at 70322,3100 and on the Internet at richaro@quincy.edu.

Other Titles from Ronny Richardson

Writing OS/2 REXX Programs

This book contains complete information on communicating with the user, including non-REXX commands, string handling, performing mathematics, logic testing and looping, built-in functions, subroutines, and user-defined functions. It shows you how to take full advantage of REXX, the powerful and flexible programming language that is included with OS/2.

ISBN 0-07-052372-X $39.95 Paperback/Disk

Builder Lite: Developing Dynamic Batch Files

With this book/disk package, even beginners will be building and testing powerful batch files in as little as ten minutes. The Builder Lite software makes it easy to manipulate displays, create menus, make complex calculations, customize system files, perform looping customize system files, perform looping operations, and more.

ISBN 0-8306-4175-0 $32.95 Paperback/Disk
ISBN 0-8306-4175-0 $44.95 Hardcover/Disk

Dr. Batch File's Ultimate Collection

Here's the prescriptions for total PC control—a new book/disk collection featuring Ronny "Dr. Batch File" Richardson's 120 favorite batch file programs for DOS. There are programs for creating and using keyboard macros, saving and reusing keyboard macros, saving and reusing command lines, tracking down viruses in COMMAND.COM, building Help screens and much more.

ISBN 0-8306-4113-0 $29.95 Paperback/Disk
ISBN 0-8306-4112-2 $39.95 Hardcover/Disk

In order to receive additional information on these or any other
McGraw-Hill titles, in the United States please call 1-800-822-8158.
In other countries, contact your local McGraw-Hill representative.

How to Order

Call 1-800-822-8158
24 hours a day,
7 days a week
in U.S. and Canada

Mail this coupon to:
McGraw-Hill, Inc.
P.O. Box 182067,
Columbus, OH 43218-2607

Fax your order to:
614-759-3644

EMAIL
70007.1531@COMPUSERVE.COM
COMPUSERVE: GO MH

Shipping and Handling Charges

Order Amount	Within U.S.	Outside U.S.
Less than $15	$3.50	$5.50
$15.00 - $24.99	$4.00	$6.00
$25.00 - $49.99	$5.00	$7.00
$50.00 - $74.49	$6.00	$8.00
$75.00 - and up	$7.00	$9.00

EASY ORDER FORM— SATISFACTION GUARANTEED

Ship to:
Name _____
Address _____
City/State/Zip _____
Daytime Telephone No. _____

Thank you for your order!

ITEM NO.	QUANTITY	AMT.

Method of Payment:
☐ Check or money order enclosed (payable to McGraw-Hill)

☐ VISA   ☐ DISCOVER

☐   ☐ MasterCard

Shipping & Handling charge from chart below	
Subtotal	
Please add applicable state & local sales tax	
TOTAL	

Account No. ▯▯▯▯▯▯▯▯▯▯▯▯▯

Signature _____ Exp. Date _____
Order invalid without signature

**In a hurry? Call 1-800-822-8158 anytime,
day or night, or visit your local bookstore.**

Code = BC15ZZA

BUILDER 2.0 ™

Get 100 more commands for less than 50 cents each!

Dear BUILDERLite Owner (It's on the CD ROM that came with this book),

We'd like to extend a special offer to you to upgrade to the latest version of BUILDER. If you're enjoying the added flexibility and strength of BUILDERLite than we're sure you'll love BUILDER.

What do you get with BUILDER? You'll receive almost 100 more keywords and commands including the ability to display a clock on screen, add a screen blanker to your program, swap your BUILDER application to EMS or disk when you call another program, full file I/O, and much more. You'll also get code generators to create custom installation scripts and menu programs, as well as a telecommunications interface that allows you to call directly into our bulletin board where you can meet and "talk" with other BUILDER enthusiasts.

If you need a fast, efficient way to write DOS systems level programs, then BUILDERLite is your answer. If you want even more power and ability, then you need BUILDER. **Normally $149.94 you get a special "upgrade offer" because you own BUILDERLite! Use this order form and get BUILDER for only $49.95!** (Plus $5.00 for shipping and handling.) BUILDER ships on 3.5" media and carries a 90 day money back guarantee.

Order BUILDER today and begin mastering DOS tomorrow!

Douglas J. Amaral
Douglas J. Amaral
BUILDER Developer

Name: _____

Address: _____

MC/VISA #: _____ Exp Date: _____

Phone: _____ COD (add $5.00): _____

Cardholder Signature: _____ (CA residents add 7.75%)

hyperkinetix, inc. 18001 Irvine Blvd, Suite H, Tustin, CA 92680 714/573-2260

Special Offer Coupon

○ Free WinEdit LIte License

○ 20 % Off WinBatch

○ 20 % Off WinEdit Std. and Pro

○ 20 % Off WinBatch Compiler

Just for purchasers of this book, we have a special offer—**20% off**—retail prices when you order any of our desktop automation products directly from us.

You can try WinEdit Lite from the CD ROM included with this book. If you like it, call or write us for a free license.

You can also evaluate the Standard and Professional versions. The coupon is worth 20% off of their prices from us.

An unlicensed single user version of WinBatch, our macro language that runs under Windows, comes with this book.

When you license your copy, you will get additional programming utilities, sample macros, manuals, and technical support.

To distribute your macros on LANs or to clients, we will want our WinBatch Compiler. It makes stand-alone, royalty-free Windows programs from your WinBatch macros.

Wilson WindowWare, Inc.
Suite 212, 2701 California Ave. SW
Seattle, WA 98116 U.S.A.

Tel: (206) 938-1740

Orders: (800) 762-8383

Fax: (206) 935-7129

Internet: wwwtech@halcyon.com
CIS: 76702, 1072 CIS Forum:
WINAPA, sec. 15

✂

Special Offer

14-36

○ WinEdit Lite—Reg. $29.95, Special: Free License from Wilson WindowWare.

○ WinBatch—Reg. $69.95, Special: $55.95

○ WinBatch Compiler—Reg. $395, Special: $316.00

○ WinEdit Standard—Reg. $59.95, Special: $47.95

○ WinEdit Pro—Reg. $89.95, Special: $71.95

Shipping is $5.00 in the US and Canada.
Others: $9.50

Wilson WindowWare, Inc.
Desktop Automation Tools

Special Offer
for readers of Ronny Richardson's

Ultimate Batch File Book

Register your copy of **Steenburgh's Stuff**, the premier batch file utility software, and receive absolutely free a copy of **6th Sense** -- **DOS 6 Utilities** with your order.

6th Sense is a pair of handy utilities for making sense out of DOS 6. **DirCmdr Plus** is a menu-driven interface for the DIR command to help you figure out the 17 different switches and all their combinations for one of the most frequently used DOS commands. **FormCmdr** provides a similar, easy-to-use interface for the FORMAT command, and includes automatic drive type detection.

Steenburgh's Stuff, which is included on the disk that comes with this book, is unmatched for batch file power and simplicity.

Order your copy of **Steenburgh's Stuff** by sending $19.95 (plus $5 for shipping outside North America and $0.90 sales tax for Virginia residents) to:

Tay-Jee Software
Post Office Box 835
Lexington, Virginia 24450-0835

Or call **800-378-3966** (**703-261-7023**) to order with your VISA or MasterCard. This offer expires December 31, 1995.

BONUS SAVINGS CERTIFICATE

Steenburgh's Stuff
Version 3

SPECIAL OFFER

For readers of Ronny Richardson's
The Ultimate Batch File Book
Register your copy of

Steenburgh's Stuff

and receive as a FREE BONUS a copy of

6th Sense - DOS Utilities

Offer expires December 31, 1995